Implementing SugarCRM 5.x

Install, configure, and administer a robust Customer Relationship Management system using SugarCRM

Angel Magaña

Michael Whitehead

BIRMINGHAM - MUMBAI

Implementing SugarCRM 5.x

Copyright © 2010 Packt Publishing

All rights reserved. No part of this book may be reproduced, stored in a retrieval system, or transmitted in any form or by any means, without the prior written permission of the publisher, except in the case of brief quotations embedded in critical articles or reviews.

Every effort has been made in the preparation of this book to ensure the accuracy of the information presented. However, the information contained in this book is sold without warranty, either express or implied. Neither the authors nor Packt Publishing, and its dealers and distributors will be held liable for any damages caused or alleged to be caused directly or indirectly by this book.

Packt Publishing has endeavored to provide trademark information about all of the companies and products mentioned in this book by the appropriate use of capitals. However, Packt Publishing cannot guarantee the accuracy of this information.

First published: September 2010

Production Reference: 1080910

Published by Packt Publishing Ltd.
32 Lincoln Road
Olton
Birmingham, B27 6PA, UK.

ISBN 978-1-847198-66-2

www.packtpub.com

Cover Image by Vinayak Chittar (vinayak.chittar@gmail.com)

Credits

Authors
Angel Magaña
Michael Whitehead

Reviewer
Mark Berthelemy

Acquisition Editor
Swapna Verlekar

Development Editor
Swapna Verlekar

Technical Editor
Azharuddin Sheikh

Copy Editor
Neha Shetty

Indexer
Tejal Daruwale

Editorial Team Leader
Mithun Sehgal

Project Team Leader
Ashwin Shetty

Project Coordinator
Joel Goveya

Proofreader
Jacqueline McGhee

Graphics
Geetanjali Sawant

Production Coordinator
Aparna Bhagat

Cover Work
Aparna Bhagat

About the Authors

Angel Magaña based in Los Angeles, California, currently works as a CRM consultant helping businesses of all sizes realize the benefits of SugarCRM. He is a seasoned veteran of the technology world, initially getting his start in the CRM industry back in 1996 with GoldMine Software (now FrontRange Solutions). During his years at GoldMine, he authored numerous technical documents and contributed heavily to development and product management efforts that helped make GoldMine a leading and award winning solution.

His affection for open source software began in 1998 when he started exploring Red Hat Linux, Apache, MySQL, and PHP; now widely known as the LAMP stack. As an advocate of open source technologies, Angel has continually focused on emphasizing their feasibility and viability in relation to CRM and small business needs.

SugarCRM first caught his attention in 2005. Impressed by what he saw, Angel quickly moved to familiarize himself with its capabilities, and shortly thereafter deployed his first instance. Since then, Angel has continuously refined his SugarCRM skills while also sharing his knowledge with others as an active member of the SugarCRM user community. In addition to his numerous contributions on the SugarCRM Forums, his projects on `SugarForge.org` have earned him two "Project of the Month" recognitions. Angel also maintains a blog at `http://cheleguanaco.blogspot.com`, where he shares additional insights on customizing and troubleshooting SugarCRM.

Away from the computer he is an avid soccer fan and regularly writes about the local soccer scene for `LAist.com`. When he is not playing, watching or writing about soccer, he is out running, riding his bike or enjoying the outdoors. He is fluent in English and Spanish, with a little French in between. His two dogs are a constant source of amusement.

First and foremost, I want to thank my loving wife Ana. This book would not be possible without all her support, never ending encouragement and vote of confidence throughout the years. Knowing she was in my corner was the best inspiration any one could ask for. I love you very much.

I also want to express my many thanks to my family and friends for all their support, help and encouragement throughout the years.

Lastly, many thanks to the folks at SugarCRM and the user community at large, past and present. Their willingness to share their knowledge with others, including myself, is invaluable and helped make this book possible.

Michael Whitehead is a leading authority on the design and implementation of Customer Relationship Management (CRM) systems. Michael's experience and expertise spans a thirty year career in software architecture, design and development as well as business management and ownership of multiple technology organizations. Among many other accomplishments Michael is the contributing author of the SugarCRM Open Source User Guide.

Michael has authored this book for entrepreneurs and small/medium business leaders, like himself, to help propel the success of their businesses through the disciplined application of CRM best practices. More than just a practical guide for the implementation of SugarCRM, this book explores and explains the business implications—and benefits—of customer relationship management for the small/medium business.

Michael is currently the founder and President of The Long Reach Corporation (www.thelongreach.com). Long Reach blends real world CRM expertise with commercial open source technologies to develop and deliver cost effective CRM solutions for small/medium business and divisions of large enterprises. Long Reach offers a full range of SugarCRM implementation, customization and training services. Long Reach is also the developer of Info At Hand™, a complete, commercial-grade, customer-centric business management solution built on SugarCRM Open Source.

About the Reviewer

Mark Berthelemy is a Solutions Architect for a large UK-based business process outsourcing company. He has spent his professional life designing and implementing database-backed systems to support key business processes: customer relationship management, content management, and online learning.

He specializes in the following:

- Learning technologies, such as content management systems, learning management systems, content authoring tools, collaboration tools
- Helping senior management understand the potential of such tools
- Understanding the human factors involved in the successful implementation of new IT systems
- Providing configuration services, training, and support
- Acting as the interface between IT, Management, and the Learning & Development team

Table of Contents

Preface	**1**
Chapter 1: Doing Business—Better	**7**
Small and medium-size businesses: The good, the bad, and the ugly	**8**
Typical small business needs	10
The business benefits of CRM technology	12
What is Customer Relationship Management?	**12**
CRM customization	15
What will a CRM do for my business?	17
What are my CRM options?	**19**
Deployment options	20
What is SugarCRM?	**21**
Why choose SugarCRM?	22
How will this book help me tailor SugarCRM to my business?	**24**
Our case study: RayDoc Carpets, Doors, and Windows	**25**
Our hero: Doc	26
What does the future hold for RayDoc?	26
Summary	**27**
Chapter 2: One Size Does Not Fit All—CRM Your Way	**29**
Identifying the CRM needs of your business	**30**
Which business activities will be a part of your CRM?	**31**
Account and contact management	33
Lead and opportunity management	33
Sales Force Automation (SFA)	36
Sales analytics	37
Customer service and contracts	39
Knowledge management	40
Activity management	40
E-mail management	41

Marketing automation	41
Employee directory	42
Interface consolidation	42
Document management	43
Reporting and analytics	43
Business models and their specific requirements	**44**
B2B or B2C?	44
Products or Services?	45
Average transaction value, sales cycle, and the recurring business model	46
Business location	46
Size does matter: Two or two hundred?	48
International needs	49
How do I make shrink-wrapped software suit my business?	**51**
Customer-centric business management	**53**
Planning your installation	53
Your CRM data hub	54
Requirement analysis	**56**
RayDoc CRM requirements	56
Your CRM requirements worksheet	58
Summary	**60**
Chapter 3: CRM Deployment Options	**61**
Deployment alternatives	**62**
Choosing a server operating system	**66**
Specifying your server hardware	68
Web-based application platforms	**72**
Backup and security considerations	**74**
Server security	75
Emergencies and natural disasters	76
Bandwidth capacity and reliability considerations	76
Performing the installation	**79**
Summary	**79**
Chapter 4: SugarCRM Basics	**81**
CRM processes and terminology	**81**
Accessing the SugarCRM system	82
A quick tour of SugarCRM	84
Themes	85
SugarCRM basics: Data relationships	86

SugarCRM navigation: Accounts and contacts	**87**
List and detail view screens	88
Main panel and subpanels	90
Edit view screens	92
Data relationships and searching	94
SugarCRM basics: Security	95
The sales pipeline: Leads and opportunities	**96**
Aggregating opportunities: The sales pipeline	101
The dashboard	103
Calendaring	109
Sales activities	**113**
Creating a note	116
Creating a task	116
Scheduling a call or meeting	117
Managing e-mails	118
E-mail templates	120
Advanced user-interface features	**121**
Printing information	121
Getting help	122
Exporting information	122
Mass operations	123
Input business card	123
Create from vCard	124
Quick new item	125
Summary	**125**
Chapter 5: Extending The Business Role of Your SugarCRM System	**127**
Resetting the database	**127**
Marketing campaigns	**128**
Targets, leads and contacts	129
Creating an e-mail template	134
Adding targets to the campaign	136
The mass e-mailing queue	137
Campaign metrics	**139**
Summary	**140**
Chapter 6: The SugarCRM Ecosystem	**141**
SugarCRM Community Edition	**144**
SugarForge.org and SugarExchange.com	144
Module loader	145

Enhanced search	147
Google connectors	149
Microsoft Outlook connector	151
Microsoft Office integration	157
ZuckerReports	159
Development toolkit and enhanced studio	163
Open quotes and contracts	164
VeryThinClient	164
Security suite	165
SugarCRM Professional/Enterprise Editions	**165**
Product catalog and products module	166
Product catalog	167
Products module	168
Quotes module	168
Forecasting	170
Standard and custom reporting	172
User teams	175
Enhanced role management: Field level access	175
Participating in the SugarCRM online community	**176**
SugarCRM user forums	176
Summary	**177**
Chapter 7: Managing Your CRM Implementation	**179**
Key steps to a successful CRM implementation	**180**
Planning the implementation	181
Some common pitfalls	**183**
It takes a team to win	**184**
Setting project goals and specifications	**186**
Selecting a CRM development partner	**186**
System development	**188**
Data import	189
Pilot testing	190
The CRM training process	**190**
Session 1: Initial management training and product exposure	191
Goals:	191
Attendees:	191
Next steps:	191
Session 2: Management training completion and issue management	192
Goals:	192
Attendees:	192
Next steps:	192

Session 3: Present final system adjustments (optional)	193
Goals:	193
Attendees:	193
Next steps:	193
Session 4: General user training session	193
Goals:	193
Attendees:	194
Next steps:	194
Session 5: Training completion (optional)	194
Goals:	194
Attendees:	194
Next steps:	195
CRM training materials	**195**
Slide 1: What is a CRM system?	196
Slide 2: What are our business goals?	196
Slide 3: What functional areas of CRM will we use the most?	196
Slide 4: What is SugarCRM?	197
Slide 5: CRM basics 1—system access, screen layout, navigation	197
Slide 6: CRM basics 2—accounts and contacts	197
Slide 7: CRM basics 3—opportunities and the sales pipeline, home tab	198
Slide 8: CRM basics 4—calendaring	198
Slide 9: CRM basics 5—activities (calls, meetings, tasks, notes)	198
Slide 10: CRM basics 6—e-mail	198
Slide 11: CRM basics 7—advanced interface features	199
Slide 12: Extending CRM 1—RSS news and external sites	199
Slide 13: Extending CRM 2—marketing campaigns	199
Slide 14: Extending CRM 3—document management	200
Slide 15: Extending CRM 4—project management	200
Slide 16: Extending CRM 5—customer service management	200
Slide 17: Extending CRM 6—always in touch	200
Slide 18: Extending CRM 7—reaching out	201
Going live: Stepwise introduction	**201**
Continuous feedback and enhancement	**202**
Summary	**203**
Chapter 8: Linking Your Customers to Your SugarCRM	**205**
Capturing leads from your website	**206**
Customer self-service portals	**211**
Self-service portal configuration	212
Installing Joomla!	213
Installing the SugarCRM portal component for Joomla!	214

Table of Contents

Creating a new Joomla! user	218
Using your new self-service portal	219
Summary	**223**
Appendix A: Installing SugarCRM on Linux	**225**
Basic CentOS Linux installation	**228**
Configure the CentOS Linux installation	**232**
Configuring PHP	**235**
Installing SugarCRM Community Edition	**236**
Appendix B: Installing SugarCRM on Windows Server	**247**
A word about our installation	**248**
Selecting a version of Windows	**248**
Installing SugarCRM using MySQL and Apache	**249**
Installing Apache web server	250
Installing PHP	251
Installing MySQL	254
Installing SugarCRM Community Edition	256
Installing SugarCRM with Microsoft SQL server	265
Installing SugarCRM on Internet Information Services (IIS)	266
Permissions	**267**
Appendix C: Data Import and Export	**269**
Importing accounts and contacts	**270**
Pre-import analysis	271
Import accounts	272
Import contacts	275
Importing leads and opportunities	276
Updating records	276
Exporting information	**279**
Export contacts from your current contact manager	280
Other options	281
Appendix D: The System Administrator Role	**283**
System administration duties	**284**
Who should be the system administrator?	**285**
Should more than one user be given system admin capability?	**286**
Administration duties at system installation time	**286**
Configuring system settings	287
Defining currencies and rates	289
Defining security roles	289
Configuring system tabs	291

Configuring tab groups	291
Adding system users	291
Password management	292
Using Studio	293
Defining system e-mail	294
Recurring administration duties	**295**
User management	296
Resetting passwords	296
General maintenance	296
Checking for updates to SugarCRM	297
System backups	297
Data backups	298
Checking available storage	299
Using the Upgrade Wizard	300
Using the module loader	301
Appendix E: Customizing SugarCRM	**305**
Making changes to SugarCRM modules	**306**
Non-upgrade safe and upgrade safe	306
Customization Studio	307
Dropdown Editor	311
Logic hooks	314
Model-View-Controller (MVC)	316
Module Builder	318
Integration using SOAP and REST API	319
Appendix F: A Word About SugarCRM 6.0	**321**
What does SugarCRM 6.0 include?	**321**
Should I use SugarCRM 6.0?	**322**
Index	**325**

Preface

SugarCRM is a popular **Customer Relationship Management (CRM)** system. It is available in both free open source and commercial versions, making it an ideal way for small or medium-size businesses to try out a CRM system without committing large sums of money. Although SugarCRM is carefully designed for ease of use, attaining measurable business results requires careful planning and research. This book distills hard won SugarCRM experience into an easy-to-follow guide to implementing the full power of SugarCRM. SugarCRM is an extensive PHP/MySQL based application, but with its rich administration interfaces, no programming is required to get measurable benefits from its use.

What this book covers

Chapter 1, *Doing Business – Better*, discusses the business size classifications and their varying technology needs. We also discuss the benefits of using CRM technology and systems, the definition of a CRM system, available CRM options and deployment models, customization considerations and their importance to a CRM system, an overview of SugarCRM and what makes it an effective CRM solution.

Chapter 2, *One Size Does Not Fit All – CRM Your Way*, goes through the process of analyzing the CRM needs of specific businesses, and uses the RayDoc case study as an example of how to match CRM capabilities to the needs of a business and focus primarily on the business objectives and benefits sought from the implementation of a CRM system. We also address the practical issues of how to get your CRM customized, what sorts of partners to look for to help you in that process, how to document your customization requirements, and how to manage a customization contract.

Preface

Chapter 3, *CRM Deployment Options*, takes a systematic approach to making the right deployment choices for your business. We take a detailed look at the alternatives available for a CRM deployment including On-Demand, Collocation, On-Premise, and a Shared Server hosting option for small organizations. We also discuss some important points to be considered while deploying a CRM system in detail, such as selecting an operating system (Windows Server or Linux), hardware configuration of the server, the required infrastructure, data backup and security concerns, and the Internet bandwidth.

Chapter 4, *SugarCRM Basics,* takes a guided tour of SugarCRM, covers the basic CRM functions, and shows how they are interpreted and performed within SugarCRM. We also discuss the basic CRM concepts, such as common CRM processes and terminology, creating accounts and contacts, relating multiple contacts to a single account, following links between related data to get a full view of a customer, creating and tracking the Sales Pipeline from leads to opportunities to contacts and accounts, creating and monitoring sales activities and accumulating activity history, and scheduling activities with colleagues by referring to their calendars.

Chapter 5, *Extending The Business Role of Your SugarCRM System*, deals with the expansion of the role of your CRM system within your business, beyond that of basic CRM functions. We cover removing the sample data and resetting the database to eliminate the default data and creating and running e-mail marketing campaigns.

Chapter 6, *The SugarCRM Ecosystem*, explores a number of free add-ons for SugarCRM Community Edition that can extend it even further in a myriad of directions. Along the way we will also take a look at the process of using the Module Loader tool and the benefits of upgrading to Professional or Enterprise Edition.

Chapter 7, *Managing Your CRM Implementation*, discusses some of the real-world challenges of introducing a new CRM solution into an organization. The goal of this chapter is to leave you with a good understanding of how to approach and structure your own CRM implementation project. You will discover that one of the keys to a successful CRM implementation is to approach it in a step-wise manner, we therefore focus on some important topics, such as key steps to a successful CRM implementation, the CRM training process, and continuous feedback and enhancement.

Chapter 8, *Linking Your Customers to Your SugarCRM*, discusses important topics, such as capturing customer leads and requests for information from the public website directly within the CRM system, efficiently tracking customer service requests, and related product/service flaws to improve customer satisfaction. We also discuss developing a customer self-service portal in conjunction with the CRM system to allow clients to file or monitor their own service cases.

Appendix A, *Installing SugarCRM on Linux*, discusses the steps required for the installation of SugarCRM on CentOS Linux server. It also discusses the installation of CentOS Linux server and the configuration of PHP and Apache web server.

Appendix B, *Installing SugarCRM on Windows Server*, provides all the necessary steps for installing SugarCRM on a Windows server. It also provides guidelines for installing SugarCRM with Microsoft SQL server and Internet Information Services (IIS).

Appendix C, *Data Import and Export*, provides the guidelines for importing and exporting data from accounts and contacts. It also discusses the insertion and extraction of data from the CRM system through import and export tools when the role of the CRM tool grows within an organization.

Appendix D, *The System Administrator Role*, discusses the functions and responsibilities of a System Administrator for a SugarCRM installation, covering installation time and post installation topics.

Appendix E, *Customizing SugarCRM*, discusses the techniques for customizing SugarCRM using various customization tools, such as the Studio, Module builder, Logic hooks, Dropdown Editor, and Model-View-Controller (MVC).

Appendix F, *A Word About SugarCRM 6.0*, briefly discusses SugarCRM 6.0 and how it is different from SugarCRM 5.x and its benefits.

What you need for this book

You need a basic understanding of computing and database terms. The book also assumes a certain level of proficiency with common computing tasks, such as browsing the file system, downloading files, and so on. More advanced tasks, such as manipulating your firewall, DNS server (if necessary), or adjusting security are not discussed and may require the assistance of a qualified professional.

To follow the examples, you will need access to a server upon which you can install Linux, Windows, and/or other necessary components, such as PHP, Apache, and MySQL.

Who this book is for

If you are a small or medium-sized business owner/manager with reasonable IT skills, a system implementer, or a system administrator who wants to implement SugarCRM for yourself as either a first CRM or as a replacement for existing solutions, this book is for you. Existing SugarCRM users who want to broaden their understanding of the topic will find this book valuable too. No programming knowledge is required to use this book.

Conventions

In this book, you will find a number of styles of text that distinguish between different kinds of information. Here are some examples of these styles, and an explanation of their meaning.

Code words in text are shown as follows: " Unzip the contents of the installation package to the folder named `C:\Program Files\Apache Software Foundation\Apache2.2\htdocs`."

A block of code is set as follows:

```
<?php
$dictionary['Account']['indices'][] = array('name'
                    =>'idx_custom', 'type'=>'index',
                    'fields'=>array('custom_c'));
?>
```

Any command-line input or output is written as follows:

`/echo "0,10,20,30,40,50 * * * * cd /<path-to-sugar>;<path-to-php> ./scheduler.php" | crontab -u apache/`

New terms and **important words** are shown in bold. Words that you see on the screen, in menus or dialog boxes for example, appear in the text like this: "we also see a few buttons just above the main panel—**Edit**, **Duplicate**, **Find Duplicates**, and **Delete**".

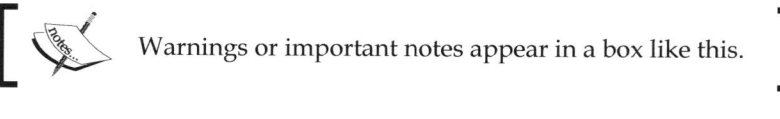
Warnings or important notes appear in a box like this.

Tips and tricks appear like this.

Reader feedback

Feedback from our readers is always welcome. Let us know what you think about this book—what you liked or may have disliked. Reader feedback is important for us to develop titles that you really get the most out of.

To send us general feedback, simply send an e-mail to feedback@packtpub.com, and mention the book title via the subject of your message.

If there is a book that you need and would like to see us publish, please send us a note in the **SUGGEST A TITLE** form on www.packtpub.com or e-mail suggest@packtpub.com.

If there is a topic that you have expertise in and you are interested in either writing or contributing to a book, see our author guide on www.packtpub.com/authors.

Customer support

Now that you are the proud owner of a Packt book, we have a number of things to help you to get the most from your purchase.

Errata

Although we have taken every care to ensure the accuracy of our content, mistakes do happen. If you find a mistake in one of our books—maybe a mistake in the text or the code—we would be grateful if you would report this to us. By doing so, you can save other readers from frustration and help us improve subsequent versions of this book. If you find any errata, please report them by visiting http://www.packtpub.com/support, selecting your book, clicking on the **errata submission form** link, and entering the details of your errata. Once your errata are verified, your submission will be accepted and the errata will be uploaded on our website, or added to any list of existing errata, under the Errata section of that title. Any existing errata can be viewed by selecting your title from http://www.packtpub.com/support.

Piracy

Piracy of copyright material on the Internet is an ongoing problem across all media. At Packt, we take the protection of our copyright and licenses very seriously. If you come across any illegal copies of our works, in any form, on the Internet, please provide us with the location address or website name immediately so that we can pursue a remedy.

Please contact us at copyright@packtpub.com with a link to the suspected pirated material.

We appreciate your help in protecting our authors and our ability to bring you valuable content.

Questions

You can contact us at questions@packtpub.com if you are having a problem with any aspect of the book, and we will do our best to address it.

Doing Business—Better

On the face of it, you have to wonder why we do it. Why we work all the long hours, often making a less than comfortable income and dealing with seemingly endless problems in all different areas of the business. Whether it is about handling internal staffing issues, supplier problems, customer complaints, government paperwork, or technology challenges—some days it never seems to stop!

Of course, we do it because we love it, as being a vital part of a small or medium-size business allows us to accomplish many goals, while simultaneously, influencing the performance of the business significantly. Helping to realize a vision of a business we believe in, gives us so much satisfaction that we are prepared to put up with everything else it entails. However, we are not crazy—if we could find a way to reduce the pressure and workload that comes with being a part of a dynamic small or medium-size business, we would likely embrace it, with all our might. Even more so, if it helps grow the business and makes our customers happier—that would be quite something.

However, while there are many technologies that profess to deliver these benefits, many of the available solutions are often too expensive, complicated, or too poor a match to the specific requirements of our business for them to deliver a significant benefit.

This book is about being a part of a **Small or Medium-Size Business (SMB)** and their unique technology requirements. The principal constituencies within a small or medium-size business addressed by this book include: **Senior Management** (the CEO, owner, executives or partners), the **Information Technology group** (the CTO, an IT manager, specialist, or advisor), the **Sales Department** (Sales Manager or quota-bearing sales executive or representative), as well as the **Administration** (both the managers of finance and administration and the rank and file employees). The objective of this book is to demonstrate and explain how to improve your business processes, business performance, and quality of life using **Customer Relationship Management (CRM)** tools created specifically for managing small and medium-size businesses.

This chapter will discuss the following important points:

- Business size classifications and their varying technology needs
- Benefits of using CRM technology and systems
- The definition of a CRM system
- Available CRM options and deployment models
- Customization considerations and their importance to a CRM system
- An overview of **SugarCRM** and what makes it an effective CRM solution

After reading this chapter, you should have a clear understanding of not only the make up of a CRM system, but also the data and communication sharing challenges they intend to address.

Small and medium-size businesses: The good, the bad, and the ugly

Let us stop a moment to consider and clarify our definition of a small or medium-size business, as it covers a wide range of organizations, so definitions may vary depending on whom you ask. For example, **Gartner Group**, a U.S. based information technology research and advisory firm, has one definition, while their competitors, your local government, or other influential parties may have another. For our purposes, we will define a small or medium-size business as one that falls into one of the following categories:

- **Small office/home office businesses**: The proprietor may or may not work with other people on a regular basis. If others are involved, they may be outsourced contractors, commissioned salespeople or agents, or one or more partners who operate their businesses under similar models. These businesses vary widely and some involve lots of travel, while others very little. This is very relevant, as travel is a frequent cause of poor information flow within an organization and between an organization and its customers. CRM tools are specifically designed to address such issues. These businesses tend to have employee counts in the range of 1 to 20 individuals, with annual sales under US$2 million. According to **SCORE**, a U.S. based small business advisory council, these businesses represent the fastest growing part of the U.S. economy.

- **Small services based businesses**: These would usually have office premises that deal directly with businesses and/or consumers. Some common examples include financial, legal or real estate services, graphic design services, door and window replacement, home renovation, carpet cleaning, and others. They represent a multitude of industries and services. Often, these organizations have mobile staff, visiting customers that would benefit from tools, providing them access to customer and other information stored at the organization's office. These organizations typically employ somewhere between 5 to 50 individuals, with sales between US$0.5 million to 10 million.
- **Small-to-medium size product/services based businesses**: These typically have an established storefront to interact with other businesses and/or consumers. This can include almost any retail sales or service activity with an average sale value high enough to merit tracking customers or clients individually. In terms of employees, these firms usually employ between 10 to 100 individuals, with sales ranging from US$1 million to 20 million.

If your business has more than 100 employees, you are on the verge of becoming — or have already become — a more sophisticated, complex, and wealthier organization with different needs than those of the businesses described previously. If your business falls under the 100 employee level, this book is definitely for you.

It should be noted that while businesses with less than 100 employees are classified as small or medium-size, there is nothing small about the job of administering and managing these organizations! Being your own boss (of the organization, or of a department within it) may mean there is nobody around to tell you what to do. However, it also means that you have to manage and prioritize your own responsibilities, which are often numerous. In a typical small business the owners, managers, and employees usually fill multiple roles. At one moment the owner might be running finance, while at the next moment, sales. All the while, a customer service request also awaits response, a proposal requires input, an issue needs to be addressed with the landlord, and so on.

This is due to the fact that small businesses have limited resources, both human and financial. The latter of the two also forces small businesses to be cautious, creative, and smart with their money.

For many a year, these same financial limitations also prevented small businesses from accessing critical business management tools aimed at helping them grow, such as advanced CRM systems.

That, fortunately, is in the past.

Open source has been a driving force behind this change. The open source movement is a software development philosophy dictating that source code, or recipes, used to create a solution are to be made freely available to anyone who needs them without any restrictions or financial considerations. The ever growing acceptance and maturation of solutions developed under this philosophy has brought many new tools to the masses by eliminating financial barriers.

Today, organizations of even the smallest size can easily access business management tools, that rival in sophistication the expensive systems, once the exclusive domain of large organizations.

Typical small business needs

A glance at the income statements for a typical small business should expose a need to lower administrative costs. If it does not, it usually means the owner's quality of life may be suffering, as they are likely to be doing it all by themselves. It can also indicate that administration is being very poorly managed. Unfortunately, even though administration costs are usually high, the administration resources that exist are typically overworked, and struggle to meet the workload. This usually does not get much better until the 100 employee milestone is passed.

Another key need for those managing smaller businesses is the need to get out of the office more. Reasons will vary, from spending time with the family to winning new customers or servicing existing ones, but in the end, it needs to happen without the business collapsing upon itself. Often, the usual day spent managing a smaller business consists of the following:

- Numerous visits from employees regarding a variety of questions
- Shouting instructions across the office
- Dropping by the various departments for updates
- Several hours dedicated to handling phone calls
- Sending e-mails to contacts
- Working long hours to bring paperwork up-to-date

Getting out of the office often means traveling some distance on business. Such scenarios serve well to highlight another need, that is, access to business information when away from the office, either through laptops or smartphones, and regardless of whether or not an Internet connection is available.

This kind of connectivity and flexibility is what it takes to compete in today's increasingly demanding and cost-conscious business environment. However, most small and medium-size businesses do not have access to systems that provide such connectivity.

Readily available tools that they might have, are usually client-server based meaning that some software are loaded on a shared server and more software are loaded on each user's computer. In addition to technical limitations inherited by such applications, there are also significant financial concerns relating to licensing, and even yearly maintenance fees that one must further consider. These types of tools also tend to lack extensive connection points, making it difficult to access the system when a user is away from their desk, as they no longer have access to the computer with the installed software that normally provides it.

Widespread Internet usage introduced new models for these systems. Soon after Internet and web usage became the norm in the mid-90s, software vendors began to modify their systems to work within a web-based environment, instead of the traditional client-server model of years past.

Web-based systems offered a number of advantages never seen before. They do not require software to be loaded on each user's computer in order to provide access to its information and equally important, access is nearly universal. To access such systems, a user simply uses their web browser of preference, such as Microsoft Internet Explorer, Mozilla Firefox, or Apple Safari, and merely points the browser to a specific web address. The geographic location of the user is irrelevant.

SugarCRM is a web-based system offering all these benefits and more when compared to its competitors. In addition to the availability advantages, SugarCRM is also open source. This latter point means that one is free to install and use the application for as many users as one's infrastructure can handle, without incurring any licensing fees whatsoever. For those who are more technically inclined, this also means one has full access to all the code used to create the application and one is free to modify it; thus, providing an unparalleled level of extensibility and customization.

SugarCRM directly addresses all the aforementioned information accessibility and connectivity needs. It allows you to get out of the office, yet stay in touch. It lets you see your family or win more business without excluding you from the organization's information loop. It reduces administrative load and costs by ensuring that the company and customer information only needs to be keyed in once and is well-organized and easily accessible. SugarCRM is accessible not only by home computers and road-warrior laptops, but also through handheld devices, such as a BlackBerry or iPhone, using the device's built-in web browser.

[ *Chapter 6* explains details of wireless and mobile device access]

The business benefits of CRM technology

The introduction and subsequent mass adoption of personal computers in the business world during the early 1980's, had a deep and profound impact on the workplace that continues to be felt to this day. In a similar manner, CRM technology continues to play a significant role in business since its early beginnings some 20 years ago. The technology has established itself as a necessary tool for efficiently managing any business, including—and perhaps most importantly, the small and medium-sized.

Until recently, smaller businesses typically could not afford management tools of this type. Even when they could, those tools were more oriented towards larger businesses and were often impractical and unwieldy. The maturation of these technologies has addressed these issues and simultaneously helped small and medium-sized businesses better compete against any and all competitors.

Throughout this book, I will endeavor as much as possible to deal with CRM from a business, not a technical, perspective. However, the later chapters do become quite technical in nature as we discuss the architecture of the system and various techniques for customizing it. The information in this book will focus on SugarCRM, the leading open source CRM tool. SugarCRM is an excellent example of a very capable, yet affordable CRM tool, focused on the needs of smaller businesses.

In this book, we will not just discover the specifics of installing and implementing SugarCRM, but also explain the business context and broader business perspective associated with CRM implementations in smaller businesses. Through the course of the various chapters in this book, we will examine what CRM is, what SugarCRM can do for your business, how to implement it effectively, and how it should be customized to maximize the benefits it can afford your business. By the end of the book, you too will be able to leverage SugarCRM to better manage your business.

What is Customer Relationship Management?

Before you implement your CRM system, you should understand what CRM is and is not, as well as how it compares to other tools with which you may already be familiar.

A CRM or Customer Relationship Management system is: *a system that manages information and processes pertaining to the relationship and interactions with your customers*. However, it extends beyond technology. It is also a work philosophy for which the system merely serves as a receptacle.

CRM encompasses not only the sales aspect of a business relationship, but also the ongoing service and support aspects. The system should provide at least basic information about the companies or organizations you interact with and the people you work with at those companies. Typically, these are referred to as **accounts** and **contacts,** respectively. Accounts can be your customers, but they may also be your suppliers, your partners, or your subcontractors.

You may already be familiar with one or more simple contact management systems, such as **Microsoft Outlook**, **ACT!**, or **Maximizer** that touch on some of the related needs for an effective CRM. Among these, Microsoft Outlook tends to be the one that most readers are familiar with, and is worth examining further as a basis for comparison to a true CRM system.

Although it is used mostly as an e-mail client, Outlook is also a contact manager. It keeps track of the people you know—often both personal and business contacts—in one system. Each person stored in Outlook can contain attributes and other pertinent information such as the company they work for, their phone number(s), e-mail address(es), mailing address(es), birthday, and anniversary. Outlook also offers tools that allow you to customize the application to store additional data and others to easily link multiple person entries to a single company.

Unfortunately, some of those tools and features can be rather limiting for many businesses. You must remember that Outlook's strength is in the management of e-mail, not the management of relationships, although for some businesses its capabilities might be adequate.

In contrast, CRM tools, such as SugarCRM are designed from the ground up as tools aimed at helping you to manage your business relationships effectively. Relevant areas of functionality that may seem limiting in Outlook are usually much more *feature-rich* in SugarCRM. For example, SugarCRM provides a built-in customization studio that allows you to easily add custom fields or modify the look and feel of the application. In short, it can be more easily adapted to suit many more varying business needs than Outlook. It is also designed with various features for not only tracking a greater variety of information, such as Opportunities, Customer Service Inquiries, Leads, and others, but also quickly establishing relationships between these various entities and their related accounts or contacts.

Conversely, it is important to note that while SugarCRM will often excel in areas where Outlook may struggle, there are also areas where the scenario is reversed. Perhaps the best example is that of the e-mail capabilities in SugarCRM. Given the fact that Outlook was designed to be an e-mail client first and foremost, it is far more *feature-rich* than the SugarCRM e-mail client. You should not expect the e-mail capabilities of SugarCRM to meet or exceed those of Outlook. *Chapter 6* discusses different methods for effectively addressing this need.

Some may consider the above observation an obvious one, but the example is used to underscore the importance of understanding the point that SugarCRM is a tool designed for a specific task: to improve the management of customer relationships. While highly extensible and customizable, it cannot be everything to any and all businesses. It also has its limitations and not acknowledging them upfront often leads to frustration, or poor user adoption rates, this in turn usually translates to a business never fully realizing the benefits of a CRM system.

From this, you might have already begun to ponder what you should look for in a CRM system. As CRM tools have matured over the years, a core set of features and capabilities have become widely recognized as fundamental components. These core features are partly based on well-known sales methodologies, marketing best-practices, and other popular trends and processes from the business world. A CRM system should include tools that address the following:

- **Sales force automation (SFA)**: The ability to capture lead (potential customers) information separate from actual customers; the promotion of leads to opportunities and sales forecasting tools.
- **Opportunity management**: Tracking of revenue opportunities, including attributes, such as the sales stage and likelihood of winning the business.
- **Sales pipeline tracking**: Graphical representation of the sales pipeline offering drill-down from the bar or segment of the chart, to the data that underlies it.
- **Definition of sales teams and territories**: This helps manage information sharing and tracking sales performance by territory.
- **Marketing automation**: Tools that automate the execution of marketing campaigns, such as bulk e-mail.
- **Lead source analysis of sales and opportunities:** Analytic tools providing insight on the return from differing marketing efforts.
- **Product catalog management**: It also takes care of tracking sales inventory, corporate assets, and client products covered by support contracts.
- **Quoting**: Allows a sales person to generate quotes pertaining to products or services offered by your business.
- **Flexible reporting**: Analyzing CRM data from differing perspectives is critical to track the effectiveness of business practices and sales and marketing efforts, identifying isuses, and other trends within the business.
- **Service case tracking**: Service or support capabilities, such as tracking product defects, managing support contract renewals, and tracking service inquiries from customers.

- **Activity management**: This can be used for arranging meetings, scheduling calls for customer follow-up or setting reminders to perform other tasks.
- **Employee directory**: This simplifies communication among fellow employees.
- **Interface consolidation**: This helps eliminate data silos within your business. Consolidating information and data from disparate systems or sources makes it easier for everyone in the organization to know what is happening with any given customer and in turn, provide a better customer experience.
- **Document management and revision control**: This helps in managing and retaining reference copies of important documents, such as company policies.

A well-conceived CRM must also have a truly outstanding user interface, as the whole purpose of the system is to make the organization's information accessible quickly, easily, and naturally. If users do not utilize the system because it is too complex to access or use, it will be difficult to realize its potential benefit.

Remember, the software on its own will not do anything for your business. Its effectiveness is directly tied to the quality and volume of data that is provided.

CRM customization

Few, if any, CRM systems would be useful without customization capabilities. This is such a critical component that it warrants its own section to provide a more in-depth discussion of the topic.

If you are skimming this book thinking that CRM customization is an advanced topic and not applicable to you, stop right now and listen to some advice for a moment. Customization is a fact of life and indeed, is generally a positive one for most business applications. The negative aspect of customization is that it can sometimes be long and involved and can often be quite expensive. The positive side is that it takes an off-the-shelf, shrink-wrapped software application and adapts it to the way your business actually works.

When evaluating or comparing CRM options, customization capabilities should be near the top of your requirements list. CRM systems are known to need customization more frequently than other business applications. You should refrain from assuming that the customization experience will be similar to that of implementing other systems, such as an accounting solution. After all, the average Sales, Purchase, and General Ledger accounting system works pretty much the same way for any business: set up your structure of initial account codes, and away you go. CRM systems are vastly different. Customization needs for a CRM system will vary greatly from business to business, even within the same or similar industries.

Every business has a set of processes that they use to conduct day-to-day operations, whether it is procedures for handling service inquiries or those related to the qualification process for potential new customers. Sometimes these processes are well known and documented. At other times, formal guidelines may not exist but instead are executed out of habit or comfort. In the end, few, if any of these processes are likely to completely mirror each other across a broad selection of businesses.

Think about how you handle the tracking of potential revenue opportunities or quarterly sales goals for your business. Do you do it in exactly the same way as it is done at the company where a friend or family member works? Chances are that the answer is, "no".

The challenge of customizing a CRM system lies in the clear definition of the business processes that dictate your day-to-day operations and their subsequent translation into functionality within the CRM system. This is the primary reason that CRM customizations can take time to plan and implement.

As you become familiar with some of the capabilities offered by CRM solutions, you will notice that CRM customizations generally fall into the following classes:

- **Cosmetics**: Changing color schemes, adding company logo.
- **User interface**: Suppressing certain features from being seen by all or specific users, rearranging screen layouts, adding and deleting fields from screens, changing field names, and editing the set of options presented in drop-down boxes.
- **Major application changes**: Adding entirely new modules to the application, or making major changes to the business logic and functionality of existing modules.
- **Application integration**: Linking the CRM application with other business applications and processes, to more thoroughly automate and integrate your business operations.

Most advanced products make it easy to change the cosmetic aspects of the system. Earlier, user interface changes were fairly difficult and expensive to perform, but all that has changed.

With the release of the **Customforce** tool by Salesforce.com some years ago, the customization of the user interface of its CRM was greatly simplified. Its introduction raised the bar to a significant degree in this key area. Salesforce.com deserves recognition as an innovator in this field of technology and it has caused nothing short of a revolution in CRM. Today, most CRM manufacturers (including SugarCRM) offer this extremely important and useful capability. However, some up-and-coming solutions (namely Highrise by 37signals) do not offer these capabilities.

Major application changes will always require the services of a software consulting and development firm, unless you happen to have those resources in house. These changes involve tailoring a CRM to manage aspects of a business that are not uniform across the gamut of small businesses.

The vast majority of CRM manufacturers, including SugarCRM, offer methods for programmatically interfacing their respective CRM solutions with other systems.

Like major application changes, application integration requires a certain level of technical expertise and is usually best left to individuals specializing in that type of work.

What will a CRM do for my business?

A CRM system is to some extent a **groupware** application for managing your business. Groupware is a term used to describe computer software designed to help a group of people work together in a collaborative manner. As such, a CRM application helps everyone in the business (especially all those in direct contact with customers) to quickly and easily access the historical and planned activities of the business involving a specific customer. This is clearly very useful and helps avoid miscommunications with the client that are the usual result of a lack of communication within the business. With a CRM system, everyone in the business can record all of their interactions with a client, helping all their colleagues understand the current state of any issues, sales opportunities, and so on.

Equally important, a CRM system records all new business leads and keeps track of promising qualified leads as specific opportunities. These opportunities are recorded with an expected date on which the business will be closed, the current stage of the sales cycle for this opportunity, and a value indicating the likelihood of closing or winning the business.

This information, aggregated across the business, provides a clear view of the organization's sales pipeline. Visual charts of this information are typically *live-linked*, making it easy to drill down to view the individual data items that were aggregated to build the chart. The classification of opportunities by sales person, by lead source, or by expected close date is a simple activity, easily performed and fantastically informative.

A properly implemented CRM solution used by all customer-facing staff will help you track the performance of your business more closely, with much less work. It will also help you get a clearer view of future needs, allowing more effective planning.

Just as the customer is the focus that ties all business activities together, your CRM system can be the business tool that ties together all your business information. Particularly custom integration into other business systems, such as your public website and other technologies that allow customers to leverage self-service websites where they can submit orders, create and review service inquiries, and manage their own information profile.

Another key area in which a CRM can help greatly is in customer communication. After all, a CRM knows who your customers are, is connected to the Internet, holds all your key marketing documents, and can send and receive e-mails. There are very few tools that are as useful as a CRM when it comes to sending out customer newsletters on a monthly or quarterly basis, selecting only those customers who have purchased specific products, or keeping track of any customers who have indicated that they do not want to receive marketing e-mails.

These powerful capabilities add up to make big changes at most businesses where they are adopted.

Some of the benefits you should expect include:

- **Increased sales**: Marketing capabilities help increase lead generation. Tracking of leads and opportunities provides insight into the sales pipeline, win-loss ratios and identifies cross-sale opportunities.
- **Cost reductions**: Single point of entry for customer data increases efficiency. Instantaneous sharing of information within organization helps keep everyone in the loop, about any given customer in an efficient manner.
- **Happier customers**: Customers deal with employees who are informed about their past or upcoming activities and their overall standing.
- **Better managed business**: Sales pipelines are visible and better understood. The most productive lead sources and sales staff are clearly identified. Positive and negative business trends are clearly visible well before they represent a significant risk to the business.

While they are exciting, these benefits are difficult to achieve without some degree of discipline within your business.

As mentioned earlier in this chapter, a CRM system is merely a tool and will not on its own yield any of these benefits. Diligent use, training, proper customization and knowledge of your business processes are also critical components of a successful implementation.

What are my CRM options?

Depending on whom you talk to, CRM started somewhere between the mid 1980's and the early 1990's, with efforts from companies such as **Oracle**, **PeopleSoft**, **Siebel Systems**, and **System Applications and Products (SAP)**. But true CRM, involving not just the accumulation of static customer databases, but also a genuine enhancement of business processes, began only recently, around the turn of the millennium. This evolution of CRM would not have been possible without the increasing influence of the Internet and the development of web services. The Internet has connected multiple business systems together despite being in different locations and implemented using different technologies.

Originally, CRM systems from the big four companies named previously were uniformly expensive, required heavy customization, and were unwieldy for any but the largest firms. In 2001, Siebel Systems had sales worth US$2.1 billion, based on a business model in which each customer spent millions of dollars implementing the software they produced. However, their market share and gross sales slipped in later years as the built-for-the-web generation of medium-size CRM systems came to market from firms such as Salesforce.com, NetSuite and other vendors who have since ceased operations.

Years from now, history is likely to show that the introduction of SugarCRM in 2004, revolutionized the CRM marketplace by eliminating financial barriers, that in turn allowed smaller firms to gain access to the latest CRM technologies.

One easily identifiable trend is that since 2000, the market has been rapidly moving to *web-based* CRM tools as indeed it has in many other business application areas. The advantages are many: ubiquitous access, efficient use of expensive user licenses, and simplified integration with other business systems through web services.

Some of the more highly-regarded CRM solutions available for smaller business today include the following:

- **NetSuite** (http://www.netsuite.com/): This firm offers NetSuite CRM+ and other solutions. One of its main differentiators is its ability to seamlessly integrate CRM with their Financial and E-Commerce solutions.
- **Salesforce.com** (http://www.salesforce.com/): This firm is one of the key champions of the *software-as-a-service* model. While a popular solution, the Salesforce.com CRM is often perceived as one of the more expensive options. Salesforce.com has led the field in innovations, such as end-user customization, and **Application Programming Interfaces (APIs)** for business process integration.

- **Microsoft CRM** (http://www.microsoft.com/crm): In spite of not being one of the most cost-effective solutions, Microsoft CRM offers a rich feature set and easily incorporates itself into the already existing Microsoft based infrastructure such as, Microsoft Small Business Server.
- **SalesLogix** (http://www.saleslogix.com/): Sage Software (formerly Best Software) produces this leading CRM for smaller businesses, as well as ACT!, the leading contact management software. It offers great functionality, but is widely recognized as a costly solution.

Deployment options

In today's CRM market, there is not only a choice of vendors, but also a choice of deployment options. The options are as follows:

- **On-Demand or hosted model**: The On-Demand model (a phrase popularized by IBM advertising), formerly known as the **Application Service Provider** (**ASP**) model is the simplest (and often, the most expensive) way to implement and adopt a CRM solution. The CRM vendor simply hosts the CRM application, and provides the customer with a **URL** (**Universal Resource Locator** or a web address) at which to point their browser. No fuss over software installation, no messy application patching and maintenance, but also, no data on your premises—the vendor keeps it all on their systems, a fact that makes many customers uneasy.
- **On-Premise**: The On-Premise option is the one that the industry has practiced for years. The vendor licenses you its application software, and in turn you install the software on your own server, taking up the responsibility of not only maintaining and securing the server, but also your data. You also take on the responsibility for maintaining the software as it evolves, maintaining and backing up the server and data, and for the maintenance of the network infrastructure to which the server is attached. These are things you are not going to do without access to some fairly knowledgeable computer networking people, either your staff, or whose services are retained on a regular basis.
- **Hosted application pack**: An intermediate version of these two models, that many businesses find attractive, involves licensing the software, but then hiring a hosting firm to provide and maintain the server on which it runs. Of course, the concerns about offsite data remain.
- **Server appliance**: The Server appliance option involves purchasing a server, pre-loaded with licensed software. This reduces concerns about installation problems and the capacity and performance of the server you might use yourself, but does not eliminate the problem of maintaining and updating the server and its software image, as well as backing up your data.

You should be aware that not every vendor supports all deployment options. Some of the best known medium-size vendors only support the On-Demand model, including Salesforce.com, and NetSuite. While all the 'No Software' talk (especially from Salesforce.com) can sound attractive, you may have to balance that against the monthly per-user licensing costs and the thought of having someone else holding on to all your customer data.

That being said, network technicians are not cheap either, and backing up your data regularly is not something every small business is set up to do well. Different models will appeal to different organizations. That is why this range of choice exists!

What is SugarCRM?

Now that we have a better understanding of CRM as a whole, the available options and some of the capabilities, let's discuss how SugarCRM fits into that context. So, what is "SugarCRM?"

SugarCRM is both a company and a full featured mature open source CRM application.

SugarCRM, the company, was created as a commercial open source company in 2004, headquartered in Cupertino, California, U.S.A. minutes away from technology giants, such as **Apple**. Its business model is to not only develop an open source CRM product, but to also develop enhanced versions of the same product as commercial ventures. The organization's financial resources come from a combination of venture capital funding as well as customers using the commercial products.

SugarCRM, the product, is offered in three different flavors: **Community Edition (CE)**, **Professional Edition (PRO)** and **Enterprise Edition (ENT)**. The Professional and Enterprise Editions are two of the aforementioned commercial offerings; thus, CE is the only edition that is free of licensing costs. All three are open source, meaning the source code for all editions is accessible, albeit the source for PRO and ENT is only available to paying customers.

In addition to the licensing costs, another important distinction between CE and the other two, is the *feature set*. If we place each edition on separate tiers, the Enterprise Edition would be the topmost tier. It is the most feature-rich of the three editions and includes all available functionality. Professional Edition would reside in the tier directly below as it contains a subset of the features found in ENT, but still more than those in CE. Lastly, Community Edition would be at the very bottom. The latter contains a subset of features found in PRO. Given the differences, it is important to clarify that this book focuses on the Community Edition.

Another important differentiator between the various editions is the available deployment options. All editions support on-site and on-demand deployment models. However, SugarCRM (the company) does not offer on-demand subscriptions on its data center for CE users. Community Edition users interested in using an on-demand deployment must either host it themselves or find a suitable third-party that can offer the required service to them.

Being open source usually means you can easily download the application from somewhere out in the vastness of the Internet. SugarCRM is no exception. The product's official Internet home is located at http://www.sugarforge.org/, where you can download not only Community Edition, but also community contributed enhancements for it which we will explore later in this book.

It is worth noting that the nature of open source is such that if one day (perish the thought), SugarCRM, the company was no more; SugarCRM, the product would carry on, as the community at large has full access to the source code and would be able to continue to improve it. The two (company and product) are quite separate entities in law. Thus, using SugarCRM should not make you worry about the stability of the vendor.

The project was established on April 23, 2004, and saw its 1.0 release on August 4, 2004. Since that date, SugarCRM has been downloaded hundreds of thousands of times, and both the product and the company have matured dramatically. The current 5.5 release (current as of this writing), was released in December 2009 and bears little resemblance to the original 1.0 product in appearance and functionality.

Why choose SugarCRM?

The large selection of CRM options available today has a tendency to make the process of picking the right one for your business a bit daunting. Given the breadth of options, it is only natural that you would ask yourself, why should I use SugarCRM?

There are many reasons as to why SugarCRM is a great CRM solution for many businesses. Some of those relate to the technical aspects of the application, while others relate to the application's ability to address the needs of small and medium-size businesses. Let us discuss some of these reasons in greater detail as follows:

- **Open standards**: SugarCRM's most obvious differentiator is its *licensing model*. It is an open source licensed application, meaning its source code is freely available to the public at large. On the surface, this may sound like something only the technical crowd would care about, but that is far from the truth. Open source means that there are not any licensing fees to worry about, regardless of how much data you wish to store or how many users you wish to have accessing the system. Your limitations are more directly tied to the ability of your infrastructure to scale and/or to handle your increased needs, as SugarCRM itself will not limit you in any way.

In the SugarCRM world, openness takes on additional significance. SugarCRM is built using other popular open source technologies such as **PHP** and **MySQL**, which means you are free to do what you wish, with not only the code, but the data. Your data is not locked in a proprietary system or to a specific vendor. Perhaps more importantly and to the point, an open source license helps cut expenses.

- **Deployment options:** The architecture of SugarCRM facilitates its deployment on a wide variety of platforms, ranging from the ubiquitous **Microsoft Windows** to more niche players like **Sun Solaris**. SugarCRM is thus able to easily leverage your already existing infrastructure for on-site deployments.

  It can also just as effectively leverage low cost hosting providers or cloud based computing services, such as Amazon's EC2 if you prefer to not take on the responsibilities associated with on-site deployments. The on-demand approach can help your business save money by reducing or eliminating the costs involved in maintaining related infrastructure, for example, electricity charges, IT services, hardware expenses, and in some cases, office space.

  Since SugarCRM is so easily ported from one environment to another, you can also easily switch between on-site and on-demand (or vice-versa) at any time. Many organizations opt to begin with a hosted deployment and later make the transition to an on-premise solution when the needs of the business require it.

- **Customization and extensibility**: Direct access to the source code used to produce SugarCRM means there are virtually endless possibilities for what can be accomplished from a customization standpoint. However, most businesses will never need to make modifications to the source code, as the system provides many other mechanisms for customizing SugarCRM and extending its reach within your business. Combined with its robust Application Programming Interface (API) and open underpinnings, there are few customization or extensibility challenges that SugarCRM cannot overcome.

  While the availability of the source code erases many limitations you might otherwise encounter with other products, it is also important to set specific limits on the extent of customizations you wish to perform. Otherwise, you may quickly find yourself in a scenario where your CRM system is in a constant state of customization, but never actually used in production. It may also lead you down a path where said customizations make future upgrades a difficult or very time consuming task. Later chapters will expand on this topic.

- **Internationalization**: Today, businesses of every size, from the very small to very large multi-national organizations, are all competing on the global marketplace at one level or another. This phenomena has forced software vendors to design applications that are better suited to such conditions and better equipped to handle distributed work forces, even if they don't all speak the same language or use the same currency. SugarCRM includes this functionality out-of-the box. It is designed for the global business environment, even if your business is only now getting into it.

For many businesses, the savings from the elimination of licensing costs alone is a sufficient reason to adopt SugarCRM. However, as you can see, there are a number of other reasons that make it a viable solution for just about any business.

How will this book help me tailor SugarCRM to my business?

This book will guide you through your journey of discovering what Customer Relationship Management is and what it can do for your business. Issues such as, identifying the specific CRM needs of your business, implementing and adopting a CRM, and customizing the CRM to optimize its use within your business, are all dealt with in detail in the chapters that follow.

As much as possible, the chapters of this book have been sequenced to mirror your own time sequence through the installation and adoption of SugarCRM. Some of the extended details of installing SugarCRM and importing your data into it are located in the *appendices*, to keep them from slowing down the plotline as you progress through the book.

This book is titled *Implementing SugarCRM: Introduce the leading Open Source CRM application into your small/medium-size business with this systematic, practical guide*, and SugarCRM is the practical focus of all our CRM examples in the book. However despite that, generic CRM principles and practices are detailed and explained at each stage to help you recognize when and if SugarCRM is ever insufficient for your needs, or requires some customization work to suit your business better.

Throughout this book, we will not only refer to a specific tool—SugarCRM, but also to a specific (and mythical) company whose progress through the installation, adoption, and customization of a CRM shall be explored. Our fictional case study will involve **RayDoc Carpets, Doors, and Windows**, and its owner **Doc Newhart**.

> In actual fact, there are several real world Docs with whom SugarCRM was implemented throughout the writing of this book, to ensure that their real-world problems, issues, experiences, and comments were mirrored accurately in this volume.

As this book progresses through the natural sequence of stages involved in the introduction of a CRM, at each stage, the relationship between CRM theory and the practical experiences of Doc Newhart will be described and explained. The solution of real everyday business problems, gaps between CRM theory and practical benefits, and unexpected drawbacks and bonuses in live CRM implementations will all be dealt with in detail.

Our case study: RayDoc Carpets, Doors, and Windows

RayDoc Carpets, Doors, and Windows is a fairly average small business. It has slightly rundown commercial premises, with office space in the front, and workshops and carpet cleaning bays in the back. It has annual sales of about US$3 million a year and its staff is comprised of Doc, his wife Maureen, Kay, the receptionist, a junior partner Andrew, and a staff of about 22 employees.

The name RayDoc once celebrated the teaming of Ray and Doc to create this business, but Ray is long gone, and Doc now runs things by himself. Well, by himself is not quite true, Maureen actually runs the office and between herself and Kay, takes care of nearly all the paperwork and administration in the company.

Some of the services provided by RayDoc include; carpet and upholstery cleaning at customers' offices or homes, the provision of rotating supplies of clean carpet runners and boot trays for businesses during the winter, deep cleaning of large Indian and Persian rugs in the bays behind the offices, the sale and installation of replacement doors and windows, and general contracting and building services. RayDoc owns several vans and mini-vans that are used by staff to get themselves and their equipment to their jobs and to bring large carpets back to the office.

While some of RayDoc's customers have had only one transaction with RayDoc, much of their business is with existing customers: businesses that have their carpets cleaned on a regular basis, property management firms that always get their doors and windows repaired or replaced by RayDoc, and home owners who have come to count on RayDoc for a broad range of services over the sixteen years it has been in business.

Doing Business – Better

Our hero: Doc

Doc likes to focus on finding new business opportunities and networking with potential and existing customers. He also spends much of his time finding new suppliers of interesting new products, and making sure that the bigger jobs they get are always done to the customer's satisfaction.

A street-smart individual, Doc is somewhat bored by the rather mundane nature of much of his business after all the years he has been running it. Also, he consciously avoids a lot of the everyday administrative work and instead searches for more interesting business opportunities, or just customers to talk to. Doc comes from a fairly rough working class background, as do a lot of young men doing the carpet cleaning for him, who are pretty rough themselves.

Doc prides himself on his business sense and to some degree on his marketing abilities as well. His main advertising expense is running an advert on the local cable TV Guide channel. As a boy, Doc did not care much for academic achievement as he was too impatient to get on with living his life. Skilled with his hands, he has mastered many trades. However, at 45, he knows he is doing a lot of things the hard way at RayDoc, and wants to get the company working smarter. He has hopes of taking more and more of a back seat in the business before too long, and he needs to put more business systems and processes in place before that can happen.

Doc has been hearing about CRM systems from some of his friends and customers for a few years now. Recently, he had a long chat in a local bar with an old friend who owns another small business, who was extolling the virtues of being able to get at all his business information from home, while out of town and even from his fancy smartphone, all because of the new CRM he had purchased. That was it. Doc wasn't going to have his old friend be able to say he knew more about running a business than he did. He needed to find out about this CRM stuff and quickly!

What does the future hold for RayDoc?

RayDoc has been holding its own for several years now, neither growing nor shrinking. Making reasonable, but not exciting incomes for Doc and Maureen and showing just enough promise for Andrew to stick around, hoping for Doc's retirement. Part of a younger generation of well-educated tradesmen, Andrew has often tried to encourage Doc and Maureen to adopt newer business management tools, but this has been difficult, as Doc has resisted change and Andrew's responsibilities have kept him out of the office supervising on-site employees nearly all the time. However, he will be a willing and supportive ally for Doc in his CRM initiative.

An automated system that documents all of RayDoc's customers and their history with RayDoc is just as essential for Andrew's succession plan as it is for Doc's early retirement.

Summary

In this chapter, we introduced the topic of Customer Relationship Management and touched upon a number of important points as follows:

- CRM applications have been evolving rapidly since the late 1990's, and are now delivering on their promise of enhancing business profitability, improving customer satisfaction and levels of service, as well as streamlining business processes.

- CRM applications, once highly priced, are now affordable even for the smallest of businesses.

- Most small businesses employ business systems that are not accessible outside their office, acting as a force that limits business communication with outbound workers, and tends to create communication barriers.

- For smaller businesses, there are many valid CRM choices, namely, NetSuite, Salesforce.com, Microsoft CRM, and SalesLogix. We have chosen SugarCRM Community Edition as our example CRM for this book, as it is free, and contains most of the latest features that make CRM adoption compelling for small and medium-size businesses.

- CRM systems may be deployed as *On-Demand* web-based services, as application software to be installed on your own servers, or as server appliances delivered pre-loaded and ready to run. The choice is yours and involves some tradeoffs between cost and convenience.

- To truly deliver on their promises, CRM systems typically must be customized to suit your business. There are several levels of complexity to this customization and the most recent CRMs help you do quite a bit of it yourself, rather than paying for expensive computer services staff to do it for you.

- CRMs can help you track the sales performance of your business more closely with less work, see the future more clearly, and plan more effectively.

- SugarCRM is a *web-based* open source CRM solution introduced in 2004, available as a free Community Edition or as an enhanced, commercial Professional or Enterprise Edition.

- SugarCRM's web nature helps reduce administrative costs and makes it easy to use, greatly simplifying the methods involved in accessing customer information.
- This book will take you through the entire process of determining your CRM needs, implementing and installing a CRM, getting your data into the CRM, rolling it out to your business and training staff and, customizing the CRM to maximize your business benefits.
- Throughout this book, we will follow the experiences of Doc Newhart, and his fictional business RayDoc. The tales of his experiences here are taken from the real-life experiences of multiple CRM installations within smaller businesses.

In the next chapter, we will use the knowledge that we have gained about CRM systems to analyze our own business, identify its CRM needs, and understand what to look for in a CRM, and its customization and configuration capabilities.

2
One Size Does Not Fit All—CRM Your Way

In the first chapter, you learned about the history of how CRM software developed, how its affordability and accessibility for smaller businesses has been improving in recent years, and how important it is that a CRM be easily customizable to suit your business.

You were also introduced to *RayDoc Carpets, Doors, and Windows* and met Doc, its proprietor. In this chapter, we will begin the process of analyzing the CRM needs of your specific business, and continue using our RayDoc case study as an example of how to match CRM capabilities to the needs of a business.

Throughout this chapter, and indeed throughout this book to the extent possible, we shall focus primarily on the business objectives and benefits sought from the implementation of a CRM system, not simply on the mechanics of installing and using the SugarCRM system.

To help us attain this goal, several extensive sections of this book are devoted to the business analysis process that you will need to go through in order to determine how your business can best benefit from a CRM system. This exercise will enable you to identify the customizations you may need to make to an off-the-shelf CRM product, such as SugarCRM, to tailor it to the manner in which you conduct business. As the book progresses, the business analysis sections will deal with successively more ambitious and advanced business functions, helping you identify your needs in these areas, as well as guiding you through the process of implementing those customizations, introducing the CRM system into your business, and other tasks important to a successful implementation.

One Size Does Not Fit All – CRM Your Way

This chapter contains the first such business analysis section. The goal of this section is to provide a broad overview of the ways in which businesses differ, helping you to position and identify your own business within the multi-dimensional space of all smaller businesses. Do the CRM needs of a three-person firm, in a single office that sells to other businesses through the Internet differ from those of a fifty-person firm, with ten regional offices that sells to consumers by making house calls? They certainly do, and those differences are an example of the type of issues that we will be dealing with shortly.

It is not that difficult to change your business using a CRM system, but first you have to understand the CRM needs of your business and who to involve in identifying them, so that you make the right changes. Involving other stakeholders from your business will help ensure that the new system gains acceptance when it is introduced and is an important part of the identification process.

A CRM solution cannot succeed without user acceptance. One of the most effective ways of obtaining user acceptance is ensuring users are getting value from the CRM system. Without that sense of value, the challenge of user acceptance will be difficult to overcome. This is the primary reason why it is important to include individuals who represent differing facets of your organization when working through the process of identifying the business issues that the system should address. The most successful CRM implementations are those where the culture of the business and the use of its CRM system are seamlessly intertwined with each other.

Once we have studied the varying CRM needs of different businesses, we will see how Doc Newhart needs to apply CRM to improve the way RayDoc operates. We will also use a *CRM Requirements Worksheet* to identify the specific CRM needs of your business.

Lastly, we will address the practical issues of how to get your CRM system customized, what sorts of partners to look for to help you in that process, how to document your customization requirements, and how to manage a customization contract.

Identifying the CRM needs of your business

Some of the high-level characteristics of a business that cause one to have very different CRM requirements from another include the following:

- **The business model**: One location or many? Franchises? Regional Sales Offices? Products or services? High or low unit sales value?
- **The customers**: Where are they? Who are they—businesses or individuals?

- **The scale**: How many employees—2? 25? 50? 100?
- **The culture**: E-mail or personal visits? Are there any data security concerns?
- **The international needs**: Multiple language support? Date format? Currency format?

Compensating and adjusting appropriately for these varying requirements will make the difference between a CRM that suits your needs (and is quickly embraced and adopted) and a CRM system that never feels like a good fit, quickly falling into disuse and abandonment.

To genuinely understand issues a CRM system is meant some measure of customization to become a truly effective tool within an organization, we need to only examine some of the main issues a CRM is meant to address. This list includes the following:

- Differences in the lead capture and promotion process
- Flexible opportunity tracking for products, services, or both
- Varying needs for analyzing data, such as the sales pipeline and leads
- Procedural differences in handling service inquiries, tracking product faults, and service contracts
- Activity management and task delegation for customer and non customer related matters
- Integration with other industry specific, or horizontal data or systems
- Document repositories for different departments

To be an effective tool, a CRM system must be able to adapt to the specific needs of an organization and still meet basic CRM needs, such as providing task delegation capabilities. Over time, this same flexibility will allow the CRM system to adapt to a changing and hopefully, growing business.

Which business activities will be a part of your CRM?

As you approach the process of implementing a CRM within your business, one of the more important decisions you must make is the *application scope* of your CRM. You must make a high-level choice as to your philosophy about your CRM—are you using it uniquely to manage the sales process, or do you see it having a major role in your overall approach to business management?

You need to examine the following lists of capabilities, and decide which of these you will implement in the CRM implementation for your business—at least for the initial implementation phase:

- Sales force automation and lead tracking
- Calendaring and activity management
- Sales pipeline tracking and monitoring
- Tracking of service calls
- Web-to-lead capture
- Document management
- E-mail
- Integration with other systems, such as your accounting solution
- Reporting and analytics

Depending on the nature of your business, some more advanced and useful capabilities to include within your CRM are as follows:

- Project tracking and management
- Marketing automation
- Knowledge management
- Management of e-marketing campaigns
- Advanced report generation
- Definition of sales teams and territories
- Integrated views of financial metrics and performance
- Product catalog management, tracking sales inventory, corporate assets, and client products covered by support contracts
- Creation of client quotations and/or invoices

To help you sort through these topics, and help you make better-informed choices, they are explained here in greater detail with an emphasis on the kinds of choices, customizations, and variations commonly seen in smaller businesses.

Deciding which of the basic application areas to include in your CRM implementation is the first stage of identifying the set of customizations that your CRM installation will require. Later on, in *Appendix E*, we will discuss in detail how to actually perform some customizations to your SugarCRM installation, but for now our task is merely to identify the areas of the application that are most likely to require customization, based on the nature and needs of your business. Let us examine the initial list of standard capabilities.

Account and contact management

Fundamentally, a CRM application is designed to capture information about your accounts and the contacts you deal with at those accounts. By accounts, we mean the complete set of other firms with whom you conduct business. Terminology will vary depending on your type of business, but accounts normally represent partners, suppliers, and other companies or organizations.

While accounts generally represent some form of company or organization, a contact is regarded as an individual with whom you conduct your business. A contact is normally related to an account, but can also exist independently. They typically represent individuals who have purchased a product or service from your business, or perhaps someone with whom you are in regular communication with at an account who has made that purchase.

This much is true of CRM use at most businesses, but even this basic capability needs modification at many firms. Some firms focus much more on contacts as they sell to individuals, a philosophy dubbed **Business-to-Consumer** or **B2C**, for short. Other businesses, however, focus almost exclusively on accounts, as they sell only to other businesses, a model labeled **Business-to-Business** or **B2B**.

Many firms go to the extreme of customizing the navigation system of their CRM so as to only show either accounts or contacts and to clearly represent their model. The good news is that nowadays most quality CRM systems, including SugarCRM, provide this customization capability through out-of-box functionality.

Lead and opportunity management

The next major differentiator between firms and their associated CRM implementations lies in the area of leads and opportunities. Leads are commonly recognized as an individual representing potential revenue, usually having demonstrated some level of interest in your products or services. They differ from contacts, as contacts are individuals who already have an established relationship with your business as a buying customer.

An opportunity is used to track potential financial commitment associated with the sale of a product or service to an account, contact, lead, or combination thereof. In addition to the monetary value they represent, many businesses also keep a record of other pertinent information, such as the date on which the deal is expected to close, the products or services being sold, the staff member responsible for managing the sale, and other equally important information.

If your firm uses prospect or potential customer lists, sometimes obtained at tradeshows or even purchased, then you are likely to have a need to distinguish between a lead and a contact. This separation will help keep your database tidy by not cluttering your customer list with entries of individuals who may never buy one of your products or services.

For some businesses, this differentiation is completely unnecessary and instead, these individuals are stored as contacts. In such scenarios, it is common for an attribute to be assigned to each contact which in turn distinguishes potential from existing customers, or even other categories.

Much like other areas of the system, it would be useful to be able to customize the CRM user interface, so as to remove any menus or navigation associated with leads for firms that don't need them. Most good CRM solutions, including SugarCRM, provide this capability.

If you choose to keep leads and contacts separate from each other, you will find that at some point, you will need to promote a lead to a contact. This promotion usually does not occur until after the lead has been qualified. The qualification process is used not only to confirm basic information about the individual, such as their e-mail address, but also identify potential revenue opportunities they may represent. Once an opportunity has been identified, they can be promoted to a contact, linked to an account, and an opportunity. Graphically, it would look something like the following:

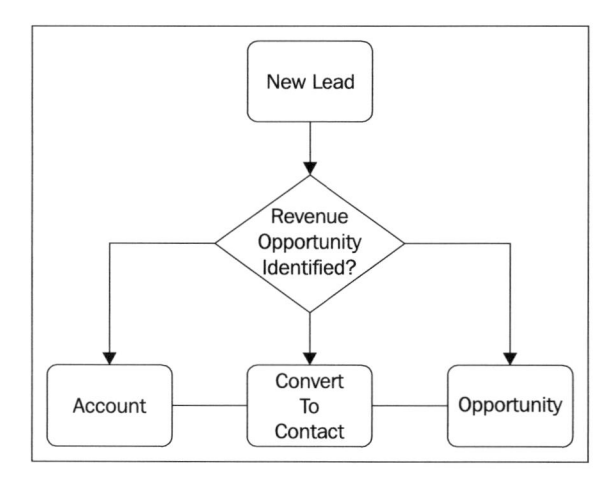

Different firms have many different ways of generating leads, for example, from an Internet site, from advertising, by word of mouth referral, direct mail campaigns, and so on. Regardless of which of these your business uses, it is important to measure the success rate of each campaign. This type of analysis will allow you to determine which marketing techniques will yield the most value to your business. CRM systems, including SugarCRM, allow you to track this information by means of an attribute found on leads, opportunities, accounts, and contacts.

This attribute is called the *lead source*, and a value can be assigned to one of the aforementioned entities by selecting the appropriate lead source value from a predefined list displayed in a drop-down box. The use of a drop-down box in this scenario helps highlight an important point relating to customizations; when planning customizations you should bear in mind the type of data you are collecting.

Some scenarios are better served by a *checkbox*, while others are best served by a drop-down box, as in the case of the *lead source* value. A drop-down box is effective for this scenario because it helps reduce data entry errors that would typically make subsequent metrics worthless. However, its use would be limited if you were not able to define the list with your own values.

Populating drop-down boxes with options that are uniquely relevant to your business is a very common form of CRM customization, and one that is becoming widely supported as a "do-it-yourself" feature by all mainstream CRM systems, including SugarCRM.

Another option that commonly needs customizing is the *sales stage* of an opportunity. While there are relatively standard industry-accepted terms for the different stages of the sales process, they vary quite a bit by the nature of the business involved, its size, its customers, and the length of the typical sales cycle. The list of stages of the sales cycle you intend to track is a customization you will most likely want to make to your CRM.

Related to the sales stage is a percentage representing the likelihood of a sale being won, ranging from 0% to 100%. Some organizations pay little attention to the percentage of likelihood and track opportunities solely based on their sales stage. Other organizations do just the opposite, and rank opportunities by percentage likelihood, paying little attention to the sales stage. Yet others track both. You need to decide which is important to you, and make sure that the list of opportunities and the charts of sales in the pipeline present that information, give you the ability to filter, and focus on opportunities based on that information.

Sales Force Automation (SFA)

One very important productivity tool that a CRM system can provide is often referred to as **Sales Force Automation** or simply **SFA**. While this can include functions such as dashboard, fundamentally, sales force automation is an automated flow of sales leads into the CRM, their conversion into opportunities, and their tracking as a successful or unsuccessful conclusion. This includes features, such as the following:

- Lead capture from a public website, or from partners
- Promotion of a lead to an opportunity or contact after it has been qualified
- Automatic e-mail notifications to sales people when a new lead or opportunity is assigned to them
- Tracking of current and historical account activities against both contact and account profiles
- Association of key documents to accounts and contacts, such as proposals, contracts and agreements, and marketing collateral

A key improvement in productivity comes from automated lead capture into your CRM, from an information capture form on your public website, or from leads sent to you from a supplier or other partners. If you have a current supply of sales leads, you should identify how to automate their entry into your CRM. Many CRM systems, such as SugarCRM, have a **SOAP**-based (**Simple Object Access Protocol**) application programming interface that external systems can use to enter, read, or modify data from the CRM system. If you do not have a current supply of sales leads, you should consider creating an information capture form on your public website and devise a strategy for diverting traffic to your website.

Once a lead has been qualified as a genuine sales opportunity, it needs to be re-classified as an opportunity within the CRM system. Most CRM tools have the ability to convert a lead into an opportunity. You need to decide if this is how you will use your CRM to manage the transition from leads to opportunities.

Your CRM server will most likely be connected to the Internet and have access to an e-mail system. As a result, it has the capability to automatically e-mail salespeople when they are assigned a new lead or opportunity, or for that matter, a number of other types of information. Typically, your CRM will let you enable or disable this automated notification system and you will need to decide if your CRM will use it or not.

Sales analytics

Each opportunity in a CRM system has an expected sales value, a sales stage, and an expected closing date. Adding up this information across all the opportunities in the system produces a prediction of the future sales of the business, known as the **sales pipeline**.

The sales pipeline is a key tool for anyone managing a smaller business. Usually a smaller business has more limited financial resources to buffer it from a downturn in business, making it that much more important to be able to detect a negative sales trend at the earliest possible moment.

It is critically important to remember that the information represented in the sales pipeline is only of value if users are diligently using the CRM system. Outdated or erroneous sales information is of little value and does not help you properly gauge the health of your business.

Like most software designed to summarize financial activity for management personnel (known as **Executive Information Systems — EIS** or **Decision Support software**, or **Business Intelligence software — BI software**), most CRM systems present the sales pipeline in a graphical chart form, frequently with the ability to highlight some portion of the chart and 'drill down' to the source data that underlies that portion of the chart.

A series of charts that support sales and business management functions is often called a **Dashboard** or a **Digital Dashboard** and is a powerful tool for ensuring that sales are on track in the coming months, as well as for diagnosing and uncovering shortcomings in the sales process, product features, pricing, and personnel.

One Size Does Not Fit All – CRM Your Way

SugarCRM includes a variety of dashboards that represent both pending and closed opportunities. In addition to presenting the data from different angles, you are also allowed to select and click on a segment of the dashboard, to drill down and inspect the data that makes up that particular section of the dashboard. A sample of the SugarCRM dashboard screen follows:

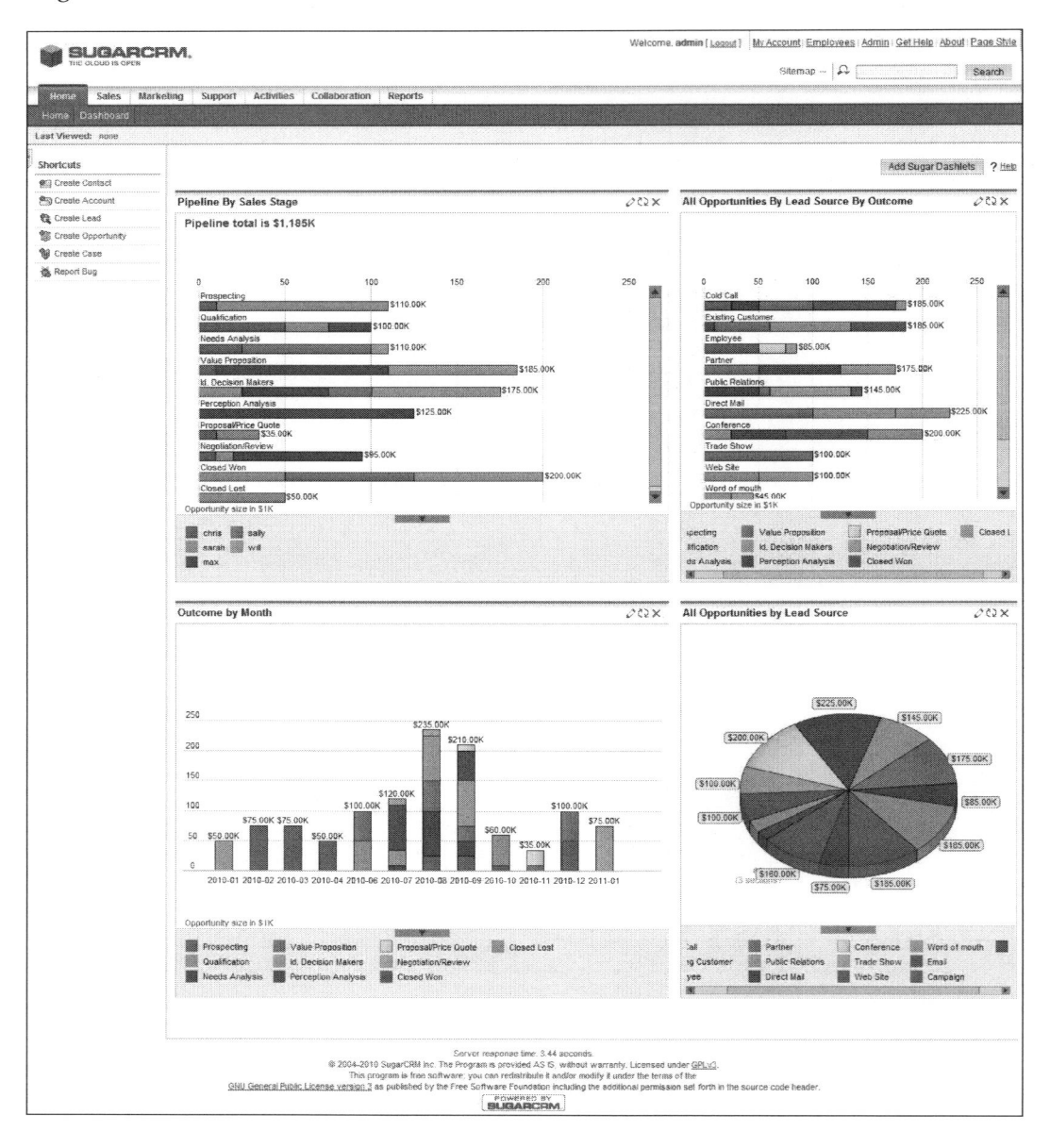

[38]

A fundamental choice that has to be made when presenting the sales pipeline is whether or not to discount the opportunities in the pipeline by the percentage likelihood of their closing. The latter is often referred to as the weighted value. For example, should a US$100,000 opportunity with a 25% probability of closing be counted as US$25,000 or as US$100,000? While the truth is that it will most often result in no income, or US$100,000 of income, the fact that the opportunity is considered only 25% likely to result in a sale may mean that you prefer to count this opportunity as only US$25,000 in the pipeline. Both practices are very common, and only you can decide which behavior is correct for your business.

Customer service and contracts

Every CRM offers at least basic customer service and support features. Some of the capabilities typically offered are as follows:

- **Case management**: A service incident, trouble ticket, or case (different systems and industries use different terminology) can be created with a date stamp, contact information for the customer reporting the issue, and a description of the nature of the problem. If a potentially defective product is involved, the type or model of the product and the serial number of the unit can be tracked.

- **Software bug tracking**: If a service case involves a defect or issue in some customer software system then a *Bug Report* is created and it will note the software involved, along with its revision and the nature of the issue (bug or desired enhancement). It will also track the status of the issue, that is responsible for resolving it and will record the eventual disposition of the issue. If the CRM system provides sufficient customization capabilities, you may be able to retool this feature for the purpose of tracking product defects or other issues.

- **Service contract management**: Service Contracts are typically tracked using the model of a master agreement for each account with any number of subcontracts per master agreement. Each subcontract may be related to any number of assets being supported. Each subcontract and asset in turn will have a service incident history associated with it to track the case history by item of equipment and by subcontract. A mechanism usually exists to remind account managers when service contracts are nearing their renewal dates, so that a proposal for the renewal may be prepared and sent to the customer.

Not every business needs these service and support features. You will need to identify what your business requires in the service and support area and decide if the standard features are a good fit for you, whether or not some need to be hidden as they are not required, or if some extended capabilities need to be custom-built for you.

Knowledge management

The employees at your business represent experience and knowledge. Each possesses differing levels of knowledge pertaining to a wider variety of subjects including; the manner in which certain processes are conducted at your business, the solution to a specific problem or fault with one of your products, and the best techniques for handling a customer service situation.

These are all immensely valuable to an organization. Among other benefits, it helps ensure that rules are being followed and helps improve customer service. The problem, however, is that in many organizations, this information exists only in the minds of the various employees, where its value becomes limited.

CRM vendors have long recognized a need for businesses to have a place where they can store not only customer data, but also these invaluable nuggets of knowledge that help a business function more efficiently.

Knowledge management tools are highly adaptable and can be used to store anything ranging from information related to the most recent product promotions your organization is conducting to scripts that tele-sales staff use when placing calls. Customer service departments or call centers tend to have a natural inclination towards these tools. These tools facilitate the process of tracking problems with their respective solutions, that in turn help propagate knowledge among staff. In addition, they help simplify the process of training new staff members, and ensure that loss of business critical knowledge is kept to a minimum if a staff member leaves your organization.

Activity management

A CRM system is almost certainly the best place for you to enter all your appointments, meetings, scheduled calls, and planned tasks — in short, all the business activities that have a time and date associated with them. Not only does entering this information in the CRM help you to associate the activities with the related accounts and contacts, thereby helping to generate accurate account history, but it also provides a groupware environment for scheduling meetings. This groupware environment is aware of all the scheduled activities for everyone in the company.

Prior to adopting a CRM system, most small and medium businesses used Microsoft Outlook, Outlook Express, or Microsoft Exchange to fulfill their business activity management needs. Other popular solutions include Lotus Notes and many other lesser known groupware products. While Outlook is a reasonable calendaring solution for an individual (and Exchange helps to link together calendars across a business), this solution can never help you to position these activities within the larger CRM context. Tracking of history and getting insight into future or past activities relating to specific accounts or contacts is cumbersome in those environments.

If all this talk of Outlook and Exchange, Lotus Notes, Outlook Express, and so on, is foreign to you—don't worry. They are simply other ways of addressing needs that your CRM will satisfy nicely and more effectively, as they are specifically designed to improve the management of relationships with your customers.

E-mail management

Since its introduction to the masses in the early 1990's, the use of e-mail has skyrocketed. The business world quickly latched on to this new tool as it offered a means for communicating with others that was expedient and inexpensive.

Nowadays, an e-mail address is as common as a phone number, and it is frequently relied upon as a primary tool for businesses to communicate with customers. Over the years, this shift has also been reflected in CRM products.

Modern CRM systems, such as SugarCRM include components that allow you to manage your e-mail communications either through a built-in e-mail client or by connecting to other popular e-mail tools, such as Microsoft Outlook. The value of such functionality is equivalent to that of tracking any other interaction you may have with your customers. E-mail correspondence becomes another item in the customer's history, much like logging a phone call would.

CRM systems provide this functionality to ensure that all communication points are taken into account to produce a more accurate view of any given customer. Without it, your staff is unaware of matters that may have been discussed exclusively through e-mail.

A consolidated view of any and all communications helps improve customer service at your business. You should ensure that your CRM system is capable of managing e-mail effectively, either through built-in tools or through extensions that connect it to your preferred e-mail client.

Marketing automation

One of the most valuable traits of a CRM system is its ability to consolidate data about customers. Such consolidation is helpful for many facets of your business, including your marketing team.

All businesses require some level of marketing in order to generate new business. Sometimes this is in the form of online marketing, other times e-mail and even direct mail. Regardless of which option your business utilizes, your CRM system must be able to facilitate the process of mining your customer data and execute marketing campaigns.

Search features should allow you to segment the database using the criteria of your liking. The CRM system should be able to perform bulk e-mail campaigns, as well as merge form letters through Microsoft Word or other popular word processing solutions.

Equally important, your CRM system must provide tools that assist in tracking the effectiveness of such campaigns. In the case of bulk e-mail campaigns, you would want to make sure that you can track the number of click-throughs and other statistics. Later in the process you will also need the ability to monitor the number of leads and opportunities obtained through those campaigns, and measure the amount of revenue they represent. This type of automation helps your business focus its marketing efforts on those methods that are most beneficial to your business.

Employee directory

If your business has only a handful of employees, then an employee directory is likely unnecessary. You may choose to remove access to it from the user interface of your CRM system in such cases.

However, as a company grows and reaches 25, 50, even 100 employees, it gets harder and harder to remember everyone's extension number, their e-mail address, their position, even their face. Even a smaller business will make good use of an employee directory if the business is spread out across multiple regional offices.

An employee directory is a very handy list of everyone's contact information, and it often includes a thumbnail image of the individual in situations where you just cannot put a name to the face, or a face to the name.

Interface consolidation

Interface consolidation refers to a series of tools and techniques used within a CRM that allow employees to spend much of their day within the CRM system, with few business activities not integrated in some way within the CRM.

Some of the activities and features commonly integrated into a CRM just to reduce the need to jump out of the browser interface to perform miscellaneous business tasks include the following:

- News feeds (RSS, Atom)
- Integrated web-based e-mail
- Integration of external web links and applications
- Views of financial metrics

Clearly, by adding news, e-mail, commonly used external websites and links to financial systems, the CRM becomes an environment that your employees can live in, one that they can log into in the morning and leave up and running all day. You should give some thought to the other types of information you wish to include within your CRM implementation.

Document management

A document that is only stored on the hard drive of the computer of one of your employees is not a company resource. A document that has a copy stored on every hard drive in the company is not standardized or revision-controlled. In between these two situations is the right answer—the document repository within your CRM system.

Typically, your CRM system will allow users to store documents within the system and include a title description, file type, status, and revision number. Some keywords to make it easier to find the document are also normally entered. Unlike storing it on your computer's hard drive, a document repository usually allows the user to update a document with a later revision, while keeping each previous revision intact, in case you ever need to revert to it. A document's status indicates whether it is a draft document, an old archived document, or an approved current version.

Web-based document management provides key benefits for any business, allowing all important business documents—medical claim forms, HR policies and guidelines, employee handbook, designs, specifications, sales collateral, contracts, and so on, to be accessed and downloaded remotely. Document management is a vital capability for any business, and you need to decide which documents your business needs to store in your CRM and how to organize them.

Reporting and analytics

CRM systems excel at their ability to capture and store large volumes of data. Everything from customer phone numbers to the latest revenue opportunities can be and are stored within it.

The true value of a CRM system however, comes from the ability to access this data in different ways, not the ability to store it. When a staff member searches for a contact in order to retrieve their phone number, they are relying on a very basic ability of the CRM system to supply data to a user.

The type of data that needs to be supplied (and the format) will vary based on who the user is and also on the intended purpose. A sales manager, using the same system, may be more interested in seeing a list of all opportunities expected to close in the current quarter. In contrast, a member of the marketing team may be more interested in seeing the number of leads generated by the most recent marketing campaign.

To provide this type of insight, a CRM system must include the ability that allows you to generate *reports* and other *analytic* tools. Here lies another important reason why a CRM system based on open source technologies can be many times more valuable than one based on proprietary technologies. In the case of the former, you are free to use the built-in reporting and analytic tools, or if they do not suit your needs, you can leverage the data through other tools more to your liking. In the case of a proprietary system, the ability to leverage other tools to meet your needs usually means additional expenditures, assuming an option exists.

Business models and their specific requirements

In the previous section, we looked at the different components of the basic CRM applications and identified a number of reasons why those applications might need to be customized for your business. In this section, we look at your business itself and examine it for reasons why your CRM might need to be tuned to suit it perfectly.

Businesses vary widely in their fundamental nature. Who do they sell to and how? What do they sell—a product or a service—and how expensive is it? Where is the business itself located and does it have multiple locations? Let us look at some of these distinguishing characteristics of a business, and see how they affect the CRM needs of a business.

B2B or B2C?

One of the first differentiators in CRM needs pertains to your customers. Are you a B2B (Business-to-Business) or B2C (Business-to-Consumer) business model? Meaning, do you sell to other businesses or individuals?

In a firm with a B2B business model, the typical CRM data model of accounts and contacts is usually a good fit. In extremes, some firms will prefer to remove menu access to contacts and focus on the accounts—leaving contacts only as names associated with accounts. CRM systems, whose design focus gravitates around this concept, are sometimes referred to as **account-centric systems**.

But in a B2C business model, many firms prefer to remove the navigation access to accounts, leaving a focus on the contacts—the individuals with whom the firm does business. CRM systems that focus on individuals are commonly referred to as **contact-centric systems**.

SugarCRM is a bit of a hybrid, in that it offers functionality that favors an account-centric approach, but, with some customization and creative repurposing of functionality, it is also effective for contact-centric needs.

Products or Services?

What is the nature of your business? Do you make or re-sell products, anything ranging from ceramics to washing machines? Do you sell services, such as house painting, landscaping, or window cleaning, or do you do both on a regular basis, like the car mechanic who charges for his labor by the hour, but also sells the replacement parts he uses when making repairs? If you only sell products, does a sale also include product support or warranty services? Does the product regularly wear out or need service on a predictable timeline, representing a recurring revenue opportunity? For instance, a car that needs regular oil changes.

If you have an element of product warranty or support in your business, you will want to be able to track the duration of support on specific products for each customer. If your product needs regular service, such as a car, you may also want to record a good time to contact each of your customers for a service.

In a CRM system, products and services are dealt with rather differently. Products are usually listed in a catalog and are very standardized. When they are sold, they generate a one-time income event.

If your products have significant value and accompanying support services (such as computer equipment—a PC or a printer), your CRM will need to capture the make and model (ideally, the serial number as well) of the product and link it to the customer record to track entitlement to contracted support services. As a result, your CRM will need to understand the concept of an asset and a service contract.

If your business delivers services to its customers, and those services are delivered over a significant period of time, your CRM will need to be able to model a sale that is not a one-time income event, but rather a stream of income (and potentially costs) over time. Kelly Girl, for example, delivers a service—the services of temporary office staff. If a Kelly Girl temporary worker was placed on an assignment for three months from June to August, then the sale should be modeled as an income stream of X USD in June, Y USD in July, and Z USD in August. There will also be a corresponding cost stream over the three months of the actual salary paid by Kelly Girl to the worker involved.

These sorts of sales are often modeled as a project that delivers over time and if your business sells these kinds of services, your CRM will need to be able to track these 'income stream' opportunities, as well as the regular 'income event' opportunities.

Average transaction value, sales cycle, and the recurring business model

If your business has a reasonably high average transaction value—say over US$1,000—then it generally makes financial sense to track your customers and your opportunities to sell to them—especially if you have a sales cycle of a couple of weeks or more in which to track the opportunity. This is the classic CRM application—tracking accounts and contacts and the sales opportunities associated with them, and then rolling it all up into a sales pipeline. This gives you a good feel for how sales will go over the next couple of months.

However, what if your usual sales cycle is less than an hour? Or your average transaction value is closer to US$20 than US$1,000?

If you have a business, such as a CD music store, a video rental store, or a specialty frozen meats store, then you have lots of smaller transactions, each of them bordering on impulse purchases by the customer. In this case, your real reason for implementing a CRM is to enhance your recurring business model. If you typically get these same customers coming back again and again, you will get great benefit from tracking those customers in your CRM for marketing purposes. *Opt-in* e-mail marketing campaigns, membership in a discount club as a loyalty mechanism—these are going to be some of your key activities. You will need a CRM that can provide the kind of e-marketing and loyalty marketing capabilities that will propel your business to success.

In this case, you will still keep track of accounts and contacts, but leads and opportunities have much less significance. Your sales pipeline is also bordering on irrelevance. If yours is this type of business, recognize this fact and understand the type of changes your CRM will need in order to help you and your staff focus on what is important for *your* business—not what would be important in another sort of business.

Business location

Where do you sell? Do you sell from your shop? From your office? At your client's premises? Over the Internet?

Where is your staff? Are they in the office? Out servicing and selling to customers? Do they work from a single central office or are they spread across multiple regional offices?

These are some of the most important variables in your CRM equation. After all, if we are trying to manage customer relationships, we need to know where those relationships are happening! That means, we need to know the whereabouts of your customers and your staff.

If your business only generates sales within a single location—your store or office—then clearly your communication challenges are not as great as a business with a dozen outbound international sales representatives working out of their homes.

One of the key questions you need to answer is: *when you or anyone in your business with a customer-facing role is in contact with customers, are they sitting at their computer and online*? If not, you may need special CRM facilities so that they can access customer history when they need it, so that they can enter updated information as it develops.

Let's study two of the more common scenarios as follows:

- **Multiple regional offices**: The CRM server can be located anywhere in the world, and staff in all the offices can access it by username and password access—securely and with good performance—as long as they have a fast and reliable connection to the Internet. Smaller businesses with multiple regional offices are prime candidates for CRM installations, as they are likely to benefit greatly from the improved communications, plus accurate and up-to-date account information provided by the CRM.
- **Outbound sales people**: No matter how many offices you have, these are the most difficult people to service well. Some of the ways in which they can use the CRM other than through a web browser on their home or office PC include the following:
    - Accessing the CRM system through their laptop on a hotel room's high speed Internet connection overnight, to update the system with the day's activities, and look up information in preparation for tomorrow's calls.
    - Connecting their laptop to the Internet at any time using high speed wireless data services like **EDGE (Enhanced Data rates for GSM Evolution)**, available from most wireless carriers.
    - Using a PDA browser for handheld access to a limited subset of the CRM capabilities.

- Using a PDA that has the appointment and contact data within its native applications, wirelessly synchronized with CRM data.
- Using their notebook with a stand-alone "offline" installation of the CRM. When they return to the office, their private CRM installation can be synchronized to the main installation to update any new data from the trip.

If you recognize that your business has the need to service outbound sales people using one or more of the above techniques, you should ensure that the CRM solution you plan to adopt can meet your requirements.

Size does matter: Two or two hundred?

The size of your business affects how you manage your CRM, the features you need from your CRM, and even the importance of the CRM to your organization.

In a smaller business, employees have broader responsibilities—and these narrow as the organization grows. The need for continuity of business process, communication, and documentation becomes greater as the responsibilities get narrower.

A business with fifty employees also has so many more employee-to-employee information pathways within it, when compared to a business with five employees. As a result of this, a CRM system is of even greater value to a larger firm.

Larger firms must deal with the fact that due to narrower responsibilities, individual employees only know a part of a customer's story. Also staff turnover creates a real risk as sales leads, opportunities, and other information created through work by the business may be lost when an employee leaves. If this information is instead stored in a CRM system, not only does your staff have a broader view of a customer, but, perhaps more importantly, the related information transcends any given employee. The employee may leave, but their data lives on in the CRM system, from where another salesperson, hired to replace them may easily pick up the work.

The larger firm also has other issues not likely found in the smaller firm. With a certain scale of organization, information privacy becomes important. Sales leads will not be entered into the system if sales people are concerned that another sales team or person may steal their leads. In a smaller firm, there is a tendency to have everyone know everything. If a lead is stolen, everyone will know to whom it really belonged. However, after a certain point, an organization becomes more compartmentalized and impersonal. Protecting leads and opportunity data becomes a real and valid concern.

All of this gives rise to a complex requirement for an **Access Control Model**, or a **Permissions Management Infrastructure (PMI)**, as it is sometimes called. In this sort of system, roles are defined and the permission to view certain types of data, or to perform certain actions is assigned to these roles. Then employees are assigned one or more roles and prevented from viewing certain records, deleting data, or accessing certain features altogether.

In a North American sales organization, for example, the management of accounts is commonly split into geographical areas, such as the West Coast, East Coast, Central USA, and Canada. Most sales people would only see leads and opportunities corresponding to the region they manage. However, sales managers would want to see leads, opportunities, and sales pipelines for broader geographies. Roles permit this level of control.

Lastly, the size of a business determines the realistic budget allocated for the acquisition and deployment of a CRM tool. In a firm of five people, a CRM implementation budget might be US$3,000 to US$5,000. In a firm of fifty people, that budget would more likely be US$25,000 to US$50,000. It is also important to note that a smaller firm is less likely to have any internal technical support capability, that factors into the overall costs of using a CRM system. In those environments, running a CRM server in the office may be beyond the financial means of the business.

You should give some thought to your firm's needs for data security and permission management, as well as setting an implementation budget for the CRM implementation. Your budget should factor in licensing costs, if any, as well as ancillary services for customization work and the training of your staff. Finally, do not forget to consider the costs involved in managing your own server versus using an on-demand provider.

International needs

If your employees live and work in multiple countries, odds are that your CRM may need to support more than one language. Language support has many aspects to it, including the language used for any and all of the following:

- Information you enter into your CRM
- The user interface of the CRM application
- The online help system
- The written documentation for the CRM
- Applicable currency for monetary values

You will need to determine the language to be used for data entry into your CRM, making sure that you select one that you feel most users can understand, even if it is not their first language.

Many languages use characters and accents that do not exist in the English language. If this is a common need for your business, your CRM tool will need to accommodate such input by allowing users to enter, display, and print this data without hassles.

You CRM vendor should be able to inform you about the supported languages for the user interface, as well as the application's inline help system and printable documentation. An interface and help system that matches the user's predominant language will help user adoption, even if the data being input is not itself in the same language.

SugarCRM has support for numerous languages at the user interface, but printable documentation and the inline help system currently exists only in English. Another aspect of international support is the format in which dates are displayed. The manner in which such values are stored in the database by your CRM system is far less important than the system providing a mechanism that allows its users to select their preferred display format. Common formats include, 12/23/2006, 23/12/2006, and 2006/12/23. SugarCRM handles all of these formats without difficulty.

In addition to dates, different countries have different formats in which numbers and currency are presented. The decimal separator in North America is a period (.), while the thousands separator is a comma (,). In much of Europe, for example, the decimal separator is a comma (,) and the thousands separator is a period (.). Thus, a value represented as 12,234,678.90 in North America, would instead be represented as 12.345.678,90 in Europe, or even Latin America. If your staff will need to be able to present numbers and currency values in varying formats, you will want to check that your CRM is capable of supporting this feature. SugarCRM allows individual users to define these parameters as a part of their individual preferences.

A related topic concerns numeric values representing monetary entries, for example, the expected revenue of an opportunity. Businesses with staff in various countries and using differing currencies face a unique challenge with regards to the handling of these monetary values. Assuming the values all represent a specific currency has the potential to cause a number of problems. If a salesperson in Brazil enters a value in Reais, but the sales manager in Canada reads it as Canadian Dollars, the value would be incorrect.

An alternate solution would be for the business to standardize on a single currency and for everyone to input data under that assumption. The problem with the said approach is that it relies on users to accurately perform conversions between currencies. In addition, the extra step that the user has to take to perform the calculation before entering the data is an inconvenience to the user, and inconveniences lead to abandonment of the system.

Many CRM systems, including SugarCRM, address this problem by allowing the use of multiple currencies and definition of a base currency. Once configured, users are then able to enter values in the currency they are familiar with, and SugarCRM will handle the calculations when the data is displayed.

How do I make shrink-wrapped software suit my business?

As we saw in *Chapter 1*, CRM customizations fall into several classes. They are as follows:

- Minor cosmetics
- Minor user interface changes
- Major application changes
- Application integration

Minor cosmetic changes will need the skills of someone who uses computer graphics software and likely some simple **HTML (Hyper Text Markup Language)** and **CSS (Cascading Style Sheets)** — the code used to generate and format web pages. If none of your employees possess these skills, you will need the services of a local web development and graphical design organization. If you already have a company logo and accompanying color scheme, the costs to customize the look of your CRM should not be significant, but do expect to pay for additional services if you wish to create a new logo, or modify your existing one or color scheme.

Minor User Interface (UI) changes can often be accomplished by using customization tools built into the CRM package. In SugarCRM, for example, the administrative functions allow system administrators the access to a design studio where they can add new fields to a module, modify screens, rename field labels, and other related actions. Drop-down selection lists may be customized, menu options may be renamed or suppressed, and external websites may be linked into new menu items.

You are free to explore these features and use them to make all the minor UI changes you want. Alternatively, some businesses opt to hire a firm that specializes in the customization of CRM systems to perform this and other, more advanced customization work. Note that even if you hire an outside firm to apply the customizations, you or another appropriate individual from your organization will need to provide input to help steer the customizations.

As a precursor to this work, you should document the changes that you want applied, including the text for labels, type of fields that are required (based on your data input needs), field lengths, and other relevant information. It is best to assume that the person receiving your requirements is completely unfamiliar with the manner in which you conduct your business, even if the contrary is true. Remember, while a person customizing your system is able to provide guidance pertaining to the development of your customization, it is still critically important that your requests be as descriptive as possible, thus leaving little room for misinterpretation.

For the vast majority of organizations, major application changes and application integration work will require the use of professional CRM development and customization firms. This type of work can be expensive and as such, some diligence is required in identifying a well suited provider. Some of the key pointers that will help make your decision include the following:

- A recommendation from the CRM vendor.
- Specialization in CRM implementation and customization work, as opposed to broader development services. You want a partner with more CRM experience and knowledge than you have, not one with less.
- Examination and approval of sample work, similar in complexity and size, performed by the customization firm.
- The firm's response time to your inquiries, comprehension of the pain points afflicting your business, and ability to make recommendations.
- Openness. Firms that behave as though they're hiding something, usually are. This behavior sometimes spills over into their unwillingness to share information pertaining to the manner in which the customizations will be performed, which is often public domain.

You may wish to make your customizations in a step-wise fashion, to ensure that each step is affordable and yields measurable real-world benefits, as well as to test the supplier. Take care not to get into a front-loaded agreement that has you shelling out most of your budget for customization before you see changes that give you some level of comfort with the supplier.

Customer-centric business management

Most of this book deals with the issue of helping you to identify and implement SugarCRM in a manner that makes it suitable for your business. However, SugarCRM and its competitors do not focus exclusively on the defined set of topics that originally constituted a CRM system.

Extending your CRM system into a customer-centric business management tool is gaining increasing recognition as an appropriate, and an effective technique for small and medium medium-size businesses.

> Note that a lot of what follows becomes less relevant for organizations whose size exceeds 200 employees. Larger organizations tend to need integrated solutions based around **Enterprise Resource Planning (ERP)** tools, that can resemble aspects of a CRM system, but are significantly more detailed and simply more appropriate to larger scale organizations.

At its heart, a CRM system is about consistently excellent communication—both inside and outside the business. Later chapters will more closely examine CRM extensions and integration components that relate to external communications, but for now, let's look inside the business.

Planning your installation

Perhaps, the most commonly committed mistake relating to the deployment of a CRM system relates to the planning. Proper planning involves not only an evaluation and selection of features to be deployed, but more importantly, the documenting of your business processes.

On a sheet of paper, map out the various departments within your organization. Next, overlay the typical paths that the information takes between those departments as customer transactions are processed. Think about pre-sales requests for information, quotations, order processing, customer queries about pending shipments, and after-sales support and services. You are, in essence, documenting the workflow and business processes of your organization.

The previous exercise will also help you better understand the extent of customizations that may be necessary. Equally important, it helps you define a goal that clearly marks the point at which a customization can be considered complete or a feature can be considered ready for use. Too often, implementations drag on in an incomplete state because the end result is not clearly understood. Defining and understanding it in advance will help you avoid that pitfall.

Your CRM data hub

Documenting your business processes is your first step. Next, you need to understand the manner in which data is shared throughout your organization in order to accomplish the procedure detailed in your workflow documents.

For each transaction think about where new information originates in your organization, and examine which other parts of the business need that information to perform their jobs properly. Jot down notes to highlight the information considered as key to delivering an outstanding customer experience to your customers, within your industry. Note the points at which the customer first interacts with someone at your company, or is entered into a tracking system (example, Excel spreadsheet, Outlook contact, and so on), as well as where they move within the business.

Now examine the CRM system and check various relevant modules to see if they keep track of all the information that you need in order to deliver excellence to your customers. Verify that the modules model all the transactions that are most important for your customers. Gaps in your CRM implementation should then become apparent. These gaps should be addressed by extending your CRM system to manage the information for those transactions. Also ensure that all appropriate employees always have access to the latest information about those transactions.

From time-to-time you will find that these gaps are not easily filled by the more basic approaches to extending your CRM system. You should document these potentially troublesome areas for later analysis, as later discussions with your staff may reveal that only a subset of the data is critical to delivering the level of service you are looking to obtain; thus, simplifying your customization needs.

It is also important to clearly document the manner in which you wish for such extensions to work. In some scenarios, moving data into SugarCRM will suffice, while in others, it might be necessary for you to extract data from SugarCRM, as well as insert data. Such scenarios bring up other potential issues, such as data conflicts and they also require a measure of planning.

When you have plugged all of the gaps with properly designed and integrated extensions to your CRM tool, you will have created what in essence is a customer-centric business management solution. The most noticeable result will be the elimination of the traditional islands-of-information problem that so many businesses (large and small) suffer from.

In case you are unfamiliar with this problem, (or are lucky enough not to have lived it!) data silos or islands is a term used to describe situations where a business utilizes disjointed systems to handle routine business needs, such as an invoicing system, a customer service database application, accounting software to manage the ledgers, plus contact management or CRM software—all working on separate databases. Customer contact information becomes outdated and out-of-sync between the systems. Data gets re-keyed two or three times—a technique not known for improving its accuracy. The business' competitive advantage, expenses, and overall quality of service, all tend to suffer under those conditions.

By producing your quotes and invoices from within your CRM application and data framework, managing customer support and operations from within the CRM, and by including your product and services catalog, marketing campaigns, and sales records within your CRM, you eliminate the *re-keying* of data. Each application also has direct access to the same (and most current) customer data. The result is also more than the sum of its parts, as now the customer service personnel can look at recent and projected sales history. Marketing campaigns can target those customers who have had a certain product line quoted to them. Many other inter-departmental synergies will also develop as you go along, often referred to as cross-sell opportunities.

However, it is possible to have too much of a good thing. Some of the potential drawbacks of too much customization of your CRM include the following:

- You may spend more time or money than is wise for an organization of your size.
- You may create so much customized software that you overextend your vendor's ability to port those customizations to later revisions of the base system.
- You may create a lot of software that is simply not applicable to other organizations and in doing so, end up being the only company running that software—never a good thing. Wherever possible, your goal should be to identify generic extensions to the CRM that your vendor will want to incorporate as standard—reducing your future porting costs and improving the quality of the software, as more people will be running it and finding any bugs that may be present.

Requirement analysis

In this section, we will analyze RayDoc's business and CRM requirements. The knowledge we obtain from this analysis will be used to create your own CRM requirements worksheet. This exercise will help clarify the theoretical and detailed information we have discussed up to this point. It will also give you a better understanding of the processes involved in planning your customizations.

RayDoc CRM requirements

We begin with the analysis of the RayDoc business and its CRM requirements.

To capture RayDoc's CRM needs, we will use the following CRM worksheet:

RayDoc	Choices	Notes
Customer model	**B2B** or **B2C**	RayDoc sells to both businesses and consumers, so it will want to track both accounts and contacts in its CRM.
Revenue model	**Products** or **Services**	RayDoc sells both products (carpets, doors and windows) and services (installation and general contracting services). For its bigger jobs, invoices will be issued to the customer over a period of several months, so RayDoc would benefit from being able to model an opportunity that generates income as a stream, not as a one-time event.
Support services	Yes or **No**	RayDoc does not sell much in the way of support services. The few warranty claims it gets, it will handle by looking at the supplier invoices.
Transaction value	Smaller or **Larger**	RayDoc does not have many transactions under US$100 and most are over US$1,000. Sales cycles are typically 2 to 4 weeks and more than 60% of the sales go to existing customers (hence, the recurring business model is quite healthy). RayDoc will need to track opportunities to measure the sales pipeline. It will also use its CRM to improve its recurring revenue model by conducting e-marketing campaigns and managing a customer loyalty program.
Sales cycle	Shorter or **Longer**	
Recurring revenue	**Yes** or No	
Business locations	**One or two** or Many **outbound sales**	While RayDoc has only the one location, both sales and service staff travel to customer sites and offices regularly. RayDoc would benefit from high speed wireless data services for laptops, PDA browser access to the CRM, or offline CRM support on staff laptops.

Chapter 2

RayDoc	Choices	Notes
Business size	2-20 or **20-100**	RayDoc has about 22 employees—pretty close to the dividing line between very small firms, and those beginning to gain critical mass. The CRM implementation budget is in the range of US$10,000 to US$25,000, including hardware (the server), software (the CRM tool), customization and the first year's operating expenses. Some basic data security and permission management capabilities may also be part of the work required for the implementation.
Lead tracking	Yes or **No**	Doc operates more on the basis of who he knows than what he knows. When he gets a lead, it is typically a real opportunity and does not require qualification. He intends to only track opportunities and remove lead tracking from the user interface.
Weighted sales pipeline	Yes or **No**	Doc runs RayDoc on minimal financial resources. He needs to be warned of any sales downturn that may present itself. Never one to fool himself, Doc wants his CRM sales pipeline to weigh opportunities by their percentage likelihood, not just add in their gross amount.
Activity management	**Yes** or No	Doc and his junior partner, Andrew, disagreed on this one. Doc has never used Outlook or any other calendaring system. Andrew persuaded him to try out the CRM calendaring system, especially for managing the time of service personnel.
Employee directory	**Yes** or No	Doc chose to implement this feature, so he could keep the cell phone numbers for his service personnel within easy reach.
Interface consolidation	News feeds financial views external links e-mail	Doc was not familiar with the concept of Information Management and even a basic CRM was a big step for him. He decided that at least for the first phase of implementation, he would stick with just the basic sales aspects of his CRM.
Document management	**Yes** or No	Integrated document management will let RayDoc keep quotes and contracts linked to accounts within the CRM—something both Ray and Andrew agree will be extremely useful. They will also keep product brochures, basic HR documents and medical claim forms in the CRM, for all employees to access.
International users	Yes or **No**	RayDoc operates only in the United States and does not have a need for most aspects of international support—but does need the application to allow input in multiple languages to better track data pertaining to his diverse customers.

One Size Does Not Fit All – CRM Your Way

When filling out the CRM requirements worksheet for your own business in the next section, you should expect to see some of the same principles at work as you see in the preceding RayDoc worksheet. Some choices are clear from the nature of your business, while others are special requirements your business may have. Other choices are simply personal decisions based on your opinions and those of your advisors.

Your CRM requirements worksheet

In this section, you have an assignment. In the table that follows, circle the choices that are appropriate for your business. Once finished, you should have a good sense of which components of a CRM systems are going to be most useful in your business and which customizations you would want to make.

Remember to consult with other members of your organization as you work through this exercise. You cannot accurately asses the needs of your business in isolation. Other members of your staff will also have pain points that they need addressed by the CRM system, and they must be accounted for when defining your requirements.

Do not forget, there must be value for all intended users of the CRM system or they will resist its usage.

Your business	Choices	Notes
Customer model	B2B or B2C	B2C businesses may prefer to remove accounts and deal simply with contacts as customers.
Revenue model	Products or Services	If you sell services, you may need to be able to model an opportunity that generates income as a stream, not a one-time event. Some CRM tools model this sort of opportunity as a project, delivered over time.
Support services	Yes or No	Businesses with support services are likely to need an asset register and service contract management capability within their CRM solution.
Transaction value	Smaller or Larger	For businesses with transaction values of over US$1,000 and sales cycles of two weeks or more, it makes sense to utilize leads and opportunities and measure the sales pipeline. If you have a small transaction value and short sales cycle, you may use your CRM primarily to improve your recurring revenue model by conducting e-marketing campaigns and managing a customer loyalty program.
Sales cycle	Shorter or Longer	
Recurring revenue	Yes or No	

Your business	Choices	Notes
Business locations	One or two or Many outbound sales	Multiple office businesses will benefit greatly from a CRM. Outbound salespeople may require high speed wireless data services, PDA browser access to the CRM, or offline CRM support on their laptop.
Business size	2-20 or 20-100	Your organization's size will in part determine your CRM implementation budget and influence your ability to manage an internal CRM server. Larger firms will benefit even more from a CRM than smaller firms, but need more sophisticated data security and permission management.
Lead tracking	Yes or No	Businesses with little pro-active lead generation may wish to only track opportunities and remove lead tracking from the user interface.
Weighted sales pipeline	Yes or No	Do you want your sales pipeline to weigh opportunities by their percentage likelihood, or just to add in their gross amount?
Activity management	Yes or No	A consolidated calendar provides insight into who your staff is communicating with and who is not being contacted.
Employee directory	Yes or No	Only needed above perhaps, 10 employees.
Interface consolidation	News feeds financial views external links e-mail	Choose between a simple CRM and one that integrates a wide range of other information—enhancing the CRM function, promoting CRM adoption, and providing many intranet capabilities as well.
Document management	Yes or No	Integrated document management lets you associate documents to accounts and contacts, as well as keeping reference copies of important company resources under revision control.
International users	Yes or No	If you have international users, you need foreign language support for your CRM application, plus multiple date and number format options selectable by each user.

Summary

In this chapter, we began the business analysis process required to maximize the benefit your business will gain from a CRM implementation. Some of the most important topics we discussed were as follows:

- CRM systems require more customization than most other computer applications. Don't just focus on implementing a CRM—focus on implementing it in a way that suits your business.
- Some of the characteristics that will determine the CRM features and customizations your business really needs are the size of your business, the number of locations at which you do business, the existence or absence of a sales team, the type of customers you serve, the products or services your business offers, the average unit sales value, and the need support for international capabilities.
- You will need to determine the scope of your CRM system. Will its use be limited to only managing the sales pipeline, or will it serve as a broader business management resource and be utilized by everyone in the company?
- Making a list of requirements is a critical part of a CRM deployment. You also filled out your own CRM requirements worksheet, after going through one for RayDoc in detail.
- You learned more about the capabilities of CRM systems in general, and especially about the properties of your business that will dictate the manner in which your CRM will be configured and customized.

In the next chapter, we will have a change of pace. The previous two chapters focused heavily on CRM technology as a whole and the manner in which the needs of various businesses will differ. Now, we are prepared to finally move on to the specifics of getting your CRM package—SugarCRM—up and running.

3
CRM Deployment Options

The first couple of chapters introduced somewhat theoretical elements relating to the use of a CRM system in a smaller business. We also discussed the special requirements you are expected to have depending on the nature of your organization, its business model, and customers. Now, we finally get to work and face the challenge of getting a CRM installed for your business.

In this chapter, we will take a systematic approach in making the right deployment choices for your business. First, we take a detailed look at the alternatives you have for a CRM deployment, including **On-Demand** (no installation at all for you), **Collocation** (someone else hosting and installing on a server that belongs to you), a conventional **On-Premise** installation, where you own and manage your own server and lastly, a **Shared Server** hosting option for small organizations.

Although this chapter touches on the use of collocated and On-Premise deployments, detailed instructions for installing in those environments are not provided in this chapter, but are instead found in, *Appendix A and B*.

Before you investigate that section of this book, it is important to review some of the issues that should be accounted for when deploying your own server. Some of the important items from that list include the following:

- Selecting an operating system: You must weigh the value of using **Windows Server** versus **Linux** (or other operating system) and vice-versa.
- Hardware configuration of the server: It must be capable of handling your expected immediate load, plus allow for at least 18 to 24 months of expected growth.
- Identify existing infrastructure that may be repurposed for the task: Your deployment does not require new hardware; it requires hardware capable of handling the current load with some room for growth.

- Establish a powerful data backup and security plan: The data in your CRM system is arguably the most valuable information your business owns. You must treat it as such, and plan for the worst. You must be able to quickly recover from anything, including theft of hardware and a natural disaster.
- Internet bandwidth: The current Internet connection at your office may be sufficient for today's e-mail and web browsing needs, but may not be adequate for responsive use of your CRM system, especially if you are using an On-Demand provider.

As mentioned previously, this chapter does not specifically cover the process of installing your CRM system; however, it does discuss the aforementioned issues in detail. This information should help you make well-informed decisions for your deployment.

Deployment alternatives

One of the advantages of using SugarCRM as your CRM solution is its *flexibility* in a number of areas. For now, the flexibility we are most concerned with is its ability to be installed in a variety of environments. SugarCRM is rather unique in its breadth of supported deployment options.

The four basic options from which you must choose are as follows:

- **On-Demand**: In this situation, you pay a fee for the right to use the SugarCRM application. Fees are usually based on a per month and per user model, but can vary greatly depending on the provider. The advantage of this deployment is the quick time to deployment and elimination of responsibilities, such as backing up the server and so forth. Some of the reasons why businesses choose not to use this model include the following:
  - The data resides on someone else's server
  - There is a limited access to the data beyond the application
  - There are limits on some of the customizations that can be applied to the system

  The latter point can become a real issue if you intend to integrate your CRM system extensively.

- **Collocation**: The main difference between this option and the previous one is that you are supplying the server that will host your installation, as opposed to paying a fee for the right to use a preconfigured one. As you are responsible for providing the server, you are also responsible for making the appropriate hardware purchases that will provide redundancy and high availability. You must still pay a monthly fee while also assuming the responsibility of configuring and maintaining the hardware, although many collocation providers offer maintenance services at an additional cost that may fit your budget. In addition, you are also responsible for installing and maintaining your SugarCRM installation; although, this level of control over your server and installation also eliminates the various limitations inherited by On-Demand environments. Collocation is also helpful for addressing bandwidth and disaster recovery needs. Collocation service providers are able to provide high bandwidth connections that are likely to be *cost-prohibitive* if you were to try to get the same at your office. Their facilities are also equipped with solid security and backup measures. These measures protect your server and its data, part of which includes their inclusion of systems that handle emergencies, such as fire and power outages.

- **On-Premise**: This option should be fairly self-explanatory — you buy a server (or use the one you already have), then install the required software on it. In this model, you are taking on the responsibility for maintaining the hardware, installing the appropriate software and furthermore, addressing the security measures, such as backups, security, fire prevention, and others. However, the result is a system over which you have a complete control. Since this type of endeavor is sometimes beyond the financial means of many small businesses, there is a temptation to cut costs by eliminating some of the components, especially lesser valued items, such as security. Remember, the data in your CRM system is the lifeblood of your business. It is arguably the single most important asset of your business. Treat it as such.

- **Shared Server**: This is the least expensive, not surprisingly, and also the lowest capacity option. You have your SugarCRM instance hosted on a server whose capabilities you rent on a monthly basis and are shared with other users. Those services include not only server space, but also backup and other security services that were discussed previously. Due to the proliferation of hosting providers, costs for shared hosting services are within the reach of nearly all businesses. However, a vast majority of these service providers are in the business of providing generic hosting platforms that customers tend to use for hosting websites, as opposed to applications, such as SugarCRM. While many are able to provide services that are conducive to a positive experience with SugarCRM, it is not uncommon to run into providers whose services hinder its installation, performance, or overall usage. It is also not unheard of for a hosting provider to make system changes that in turn cause SugarCRM to no longer function. Again, their priority is not that you have a working SugarCRM system, but that their services are able to compete effectively in their market. This also means that the features they offer, such as direct access to the data, will vary by provider. For many businesses, the low cost is reason enough to overlook the potential risks and limitations, but nevertheless, you must be careful in your selection of a service provider if you are choosing this option.

CRM Deployment Options

A deployment option that continues to rapidly grow in popularity is the use of **cloud computing** services such, as **Amazon Elastic Compute Cloud (Amazon EC2)** (http://aws.amazon.com/ec2/). It offers many of the same benefits as the collocation option; however, unlike collocation, you do not need to provide a physical server. You are renting a virtual server at costs as low as approximately US$100 per month (at the time of this writing), allowing you to deploy a very comprehensive solution.

In addition to reduced costs, cloud computing also gives you the flexibility to effortlessly scale by adding additional servers by means of a few mouse clicks. This process allows you to double (triple, quadruple, and so on) your processing capacity in minutes—a process that in past years may have taken days to complete.

The popularity of such services is such that you can even find a virtual server with SugarCRM already installed on it, eliminating the potentially complex setup work and bringing it closer to the turnkey model of the On-Demand option.

Let us look at a comparison chart of the various options which are as follows:

	On-Demand	**Collocation**	**On-Premise**	**Shared Server**
Initial cost	Low	Medium	Medium	Low
Ongoing cost	Medium/High	Medium	Low	Low
Initial setup	Easy	Complex	Complex	Somewhat complex
Your ongoing effort	Low	Medium	Medium	Medium/High
Custom fit	Limited	Excellent	Excellent	Varies
Data security	Excellent	Excellent	Self supplied	Excellent
Performance	Excellent	Excellent	Likely excellent	Varies

A couple of important points can be extrapolated from the previous chart.

First, note that your initial expenses will be higher with either the Collocation or On-Premise option. This makes perfect sense, as both require that you provide a physical server which you may have to purchase—unless you already have a suitable server available. Even then, you may still need to buy a **Server Operating System**. On a related note, you may also incur additional costs to develop and implement a data backup and security solution. It would also be a wise investment to pay an experienced SugarCRM consultant a nominal fee to install your system.

The latter point touches on an unproductive scenario in which too many get trapped. Most entrepreneurs tend to have a "hands-on" mentality, meaning they like to do things for themselves as much as possible. Sometimes, this is out of necessity or shortage of financial resources, while on other occasions different motivators explain the behavior. The danger, however, is that installing a piece of software is sometimes a task best left to someone with more experience.

It is not uncommon for some people to spend 3 to 4 hours (or days) attempting to complete the installation, whereas an experienced SugarCRM consultant should be able to do the same in well under an hour. You should weigh the value of your time against the costs that would be incurred from using a consultant. Unless your time is worth less than US$10/hour, you are likely to find that hiring a consultant to perform the task is a far more cost-effective approach.

A second point of importance that should be highlighted on the chart relates to post-deployment costs. An On-Demand deployment requires little upfront investment, but in the long run, it may prove to be quite expensive. Your subscription is based on a per user, per month fee that usually starts at around US$30/month. Thus, a five user implementation would represent US$150/month or US$1,800/year. Furthermore, some On-Demand service providers require a commitment of at least 12 months or longer. Such arrangements represent not only a financial commitment, but also one to the CRM solution, underscoring the importance of diligently evaluating whether or not the feature set it offers will meet your business needs. The financial part may be a trivial matter for businesses with a small user count, as it removes the burden of maintaining a server, and others. However, if your business has more than 10 users, you should consider an On-Premise deployment, not only for financial reasons, but also to meet a wide variety of customization needs that may not be *feasible* in an On-Demand environment.

If you use SugarCRM as an On-Demand service, you will, in all likelihood not have a whole server dedicated to running SugarCRM for your business. Instead, your service provider will most likely be using a shared server facility—a controlled portion of the resources of a physical server—to support your business' CRM deployment.

If you are planning to use your CRM to house a lot of shared documents for your business, you should check with your On-Demand service provider if any disk space limitations are applicable to your subscription—they are often surprisingly low.

From reviewing the table, you should also notice that the Shared-Server approach is the least cost-prohibitive option for deploying a CRM system. It is cost-effective, but your customization capabilities and ability to handle larger loads of data and users will vary greatly depending upon the service provider. You may quickly run into disk space issues if your service provider offers a limited amount of disk space and you intend to use a lot of files, documents, so on in conjunction with your CRM data. Some service providers also place restrictions on the amount of bandwidth you are allowed to use. Larger data and user loads are likely to cause that limit to be reached rather quickly. Due to the wide range of hosting providers and options available today, it is important to evaluate the various features they offer with great scrutiny. Some of the important factors include: disk space limits, shell access, remote MySQL connections, and bandwidth restrictions. In general, even in the best of scenarios, this option should not be used for more than 10 users.

For most businesses with more than 10 employees, the choice between the deployment options is a trade-off between cost versus complexity, and effort. There is also an issue of comfort. Although On-Demand providers take a number of precautions to ensure system availability and safeguard data and servers (such as the use of surveillance equipment, secure server areas, and so on), the thought of relying on another party for this safety is sometimes beyond the comfort level of some businesses.

Regardless of which option you select for your business, it is beneficial to have at least a basic understanding of the related technology features. Some of these features include bandwidth or connection speeds, performance and scalability, and backup and security procedures. This information will make you a knowledgeable consumer and in turn, assist you in your decision making process.

In the case of On-Premise and Collocated deployments, there are additional topics of importance that must be discussed and evaluated. Although we lightly touched on some of these topics earlier in this section, it is important that we examine them in more detail. The section that follows will lead us through this examination.

Choosing a server operating system

Server and network operating systems have been around for a long time. Many years ago, **Novell Netware**, **Banyan Vines**, and numerous variants of **UNIX** (most notably, **Solaris** from Sun Microsystems) were the major players in this marketplace, but today, the largest players in network/server operating systems for small to medium-sized businesses are **Microsoft Windows** and **Linux**.

Choosing which is best for your needs can be a confusing and sometimes a daunting process. Microsoft Windows, for example, is offered in a variety of flavors, including **Web Edition**, **Standard Edition**, **Datacenter Edition**, and others. In addition to pricing, the various editions also vary in their ability to scale, that is, handle more demanding computing needs.

For example, 64-bit versions of the Web and Standard Editions are limited to 32 GB of RAM and do not support **clustering**—a technology used to provide redundancy and increase scalability. Datacenter Edition, on the other hand, not only supports clustering, but is also capable of supporting up to 2 TB of RAM (1000 GB = 1 TB). As you can see, your decision will vary greatly depending on your anticipated needs. If you expect a large volume of data (over a million accounts or contacts), you will want to ensure that you use a version of Windows that supports at least 8 GB of RAM. Data needs ranging in the area of 100,000 or less (accounts or contacts) are likely to function well with 4 GB of RAM, but you should remember the earlier statement that the hardware that you pick today should be capable of handling today's load, plus that expected within the next 18 to 24 months.

If you have never used Linux before, but are considering it for your CRM server, you should prepare yourself for a vastly different selection process. First and foremost, Linux is available in so many different flavors (commonly referred to as **distributions** or "**distros**") that attempting to list all of them in this book would require us to devote an entire chapter to the matter. The various distributions differ mostly on the structure of the file system (that is, the location of configuration files and tools) and included software. Strong opinions on which distribution is best are equally plentiful, but this discussion is beyond the scope of this book. We will, however, discuss the leading distributions, namely, **Red Hat**, **Fedora Core**, **CentOS**, and **Ubuntu**.

Much like Windows, different iterations of these distributions will support different hardware configurations. However, unlike Windows, the costs incurred in using a more scalable version versus a less capable version do not change because the operating system is *free*.

Red Hat is the exception to this rule. Red Hat's **Enterprise Linux Server** is a subscription based product ranging in price from US$349 to US$2,499 per year, per server. The subscription includes software updates and support.

In contrast, costs for Windows Server 2008 begin at approximately US$470 per server for the Web Edition and can be as high as US$3,000 per processor for the Datacenter Edition. You are also likely to incur additional costs for **Client Access Licenses (CAL)**, a license that allows a computer on your network to legally connect to a server and normally costs approximately US$30 each. These costs are for licenses *only* and do not include support services.

CRM Deployment Options

A business with very limited financial resources may conclude that both—Red Hat Enterprise Linux and Windows Server—are beyond their means. Even if you are not in that situation, it is comforting to know that Fedora Core and CentOS are both widely used zero-cost alternatives, and also happen to be derivatives of Red Hat. CentOS in particular is intended to be a clone of Red Hat Enterprise Linux and it has a large following. If you have not heard of it before and are concerned about its viability, the fact that SugarCRM (the company) utilizes 64-bit versions of CentOS for its On-Demand datacenter (at the time of this writing) should help ease your fears.

The final distribution mentioned was Ubuntu. Ubuntu is quite different, in that it has a long history of focusing on growing the adoption of Linux on the desktop. It has gained popularity primarily due to its ease of use. Server installations of Ubuntu are definitely possible and many users today are successfully using it for their SugarCRM implementations. In general, choosing one distribution versus another usually becomes a matter of personal preference and comfort.

The cost involved in purchasing a server operating system has just been explained and the choice is yours. Clearly, were you to base your decision solely on licensing costs, Linux would be a more cost-effective choice. In practice, either of the operating systems is more than capable of fulfilling your CRM needs and in addition, each requires a certain amount of investment to maintain, and these costs are not readily visible up front. As a result, your selection is usually a choice more directly influenced by licensing and ongoing support costs, more so than licensing costs alone.

The level and type of technical resources you have access to will no doubt have some influence on your choice. You will need someone to be on call in case of emergencies, perhaps to come in and set things up for you in the beginning, and possibly to perform backups each week. There are many independent network and server support people who make their living performing this type of work and it should not be difficult to locate a resource. Prices will vary, but working with one of these individuals might cost you US$5,000 to US$10,000 per year and depending on your circumstances, could be a perfect fit.

Of course, the On-Demand option at US$30/per user/per month remains an option as well.

Specifying your server hardware

At home, most of us use our computers as isolated workstations for work or play. A few of us may also connect several computers at home into a network, much in the same manner they are connected at the office. When several computers are connected in a network, there is often value in attaching one or more special computers to the network that is designed to act as a shared resource for all users. These special, typically more powerful computers are called servers.

Most of us are familiar enough with a home or office Personal Computer or PC. The usual product is a so-called three-box configuration—the system unit, the display, and the keyboard. While a computer server can look quite similar to a PC, it has a number of fundamental differences relating to hardware that affect cost.

Note that there are plenty of low-end servers from the likes of **HP** and **Dell** that use non-parity memory, **Parallel Advanced Technology Attachment (PATA)** or **Serial Advanced Technology Attachment (SATA)** disk drives, and a single power supply. They can be used for small SugarCRM installations fairly effectively (those not exceeding 10 users). You should, however, always aim for the highest capacity and reliability that you can afford. Remember, it must serve your needs today and in the future, for a minimum of 18 to 24 months. A lower cost solution may seem attractive today, but rarely pays off in the long run. It is usually best to invest a little more in higher quality components up front, rather than pay for problems down the road as they will be more costly.

Error Correction Codes (ECC) memory for example, has the ability to detect and correct the most common forms of errors that could be made by semi-conductor memory when it starts to fail. Typical PC memory, by contrast, does not have this capability (due to the lack of a feature called parity) and certainly does not have the ability to correct those errors. The only time a PC checks to see if its memory actually works is at system boot time—when you turn it on. As you intend to leave your server on all the time, that approach clearly will not work.

Similarly, power to a server is typically supplied through two physical power supply units connected to it in a redundant manner. Should one unit fail (not uncommon), the fault is reported, but the system continues to function using the working power supply unit. You would then eliminate immediate impact and be allowed the opportunity to replace the power supply at a scheduled maintenance window of time, as opposed to the time of failure.

A **Redundant Array of Inexpensive Disks (RAID)** hard drive configuration is designed to provide performance and redundancy. These types of configurations require the use of multiple hard drives that work in tandem to split data into smaller chunks that in turn reduce access times. There are varying levels of RAID configurations numbered 0 through 6 (skipping 2). The number of drives required to implement a RAID system will vary depending on the level that you select. It can range from two drives (RAID 0) to as many as four (RAID 6).

Redundancy levels are also directly tied to the level that you choose. RAID 0 should never be used in a server environment as it does not offer any sort of redundancy. You should look at using RAID 5 or 6, as they offer the best performance and redundancy. A hard drive failure in such environments would not represent a loss of data. RAID 5 and 6 systems are specifically designed to tolerate such problems without causing loss of data.

The Central Processing Unit (CPU) or processor used in a server is typically a multi-core processor (at least two cores). Depending on your anticipated load, you might be better off with a quad core chip. The general rule of thumb is that the more cores, the better the performance as computing work would be divided amongst the various cores.

System memory size is perhaps the biggest difference between a server and a PC. Most PC users (other than those doing graphics design and other demanding tasks) work happily with 2 to 4 GB of memory in their PC—usually 2 GB is the norm. In contrast, few servers use less than 2 GB of memory, at least those that perform well. Most use a minimum of 4 GB. With more memory, the work being done for many users can stay in memory simultaneously as it is performed, rather than being sent temporarily out to the hard disk if memory runs out of space. As system memory is at least 100 times faster than the hard disk, anything that involves the hard disk will slow down the system substantially. It is also worth noting that database applications, such as SugarCRM, perform better when more memory is made available to the database server.

Some of these differences are summarized in the table that follows:

	PC	Server
Form factor	Desktop, Tower	Tower, Rack mount
Memory type	Non-parity	ECC (Error Checking and Correcting)
Memory size	2 GB to 4 GB	4 GB to 32 GB
Hard disk technology	PATA / SATA	SATA / RAID
Hard disk speed	5,400 RPM to 10,000 RPM	10,000 RPM to 15,000 RPM
LAN interface	Ethernet 10/100, Wireless	One or more Giga-Ethernet
Power supply	Single 250 W to 450W	Redundant 500W
Processor (CPU	Single Dual Core Chip	One or more Quad Core Chip
Video	Often High Performance for Gaming	Low Performance / Generic
Users	One—Local	Many—Remote

Servers are used for many tasks. A network may have a specific server to act as a database server, for example. That type of server would be optimized for fast and reliable disk storage and high memory capacity. Another server might be an application server—one on which applications are run, with the results being communicated to the users on the PCs using those applications. An application server is typically optimized with lots of memory and CPU power—to get through all that application processing quickly. An example of an application server is a SugarCRM server—the SugarCRM application is actually running on the server—and multiple user PCs are just running web browsers that display web pages. These web pages communicate to the users what is going on in their particular session.

For a business with 10 users or less, a SugarCRM server to be used as a combined database and application server should look something like the following:

- 500 GB of disk space on a RAID 5 configuration
- 4 GB of ECC memory
- Two dual core or one quad core CPU
- A single Gig-Ethernet connection to the network
- An Uninterruptible Power Supply (UPS)
- CentOS Linux or Windows Server Standard Edition (32-bit)

For a business with perhaps 25 users, the following would be better suited:

- 1 TB of disk space on a RAID 5 configuration
- 8 GB of ECC memory
- Two quad core CPUs
- A single Gig-Ethernet connection to the network
- An Uninterruptible Power Supply (UPS)
- CentOS Linux or Windows Server Standard Edition (64-bit)

For a business with 100 users, the server specifications would resemble the following:

- 2 TB of disk space on a RAID 6 configuration
- 32 GB of ECC memory
- Four quad core CPUs
- Dual Gig-Ethernet connections to the network
- An Uninterruptible Power Supply (UPS)
- CentOS Linux (64-bit) or Windows Server Enterprise Edition (32 or 64-bit)

Web-based application platforms

In today's computing world, there are three major web-based application development and delivery platforms. They are as follows:

- Microsoft's proprietary **.NET** platform
- Sun Microsystems's partially open **Java** platform
- The Open Source **LAMP (Linux-Apache-MySQL-PHP)** platform

Each of these environments provides a comprehensive set of tools for developers to build and test web-based applications and for users of the applications to access them. In addition, all have their dedicated followers and advocates.

SugarCRM utilizes the latter of the aforementioned technologies, a stack developed by the open source community that is widely known as LAMP.

LAMP stands for Linux, Apache, MySQL, and PHP (plus Perl and Python—two other popular open source scripting languages beyond the scope of this book).

The LAMP stack looks like the following:

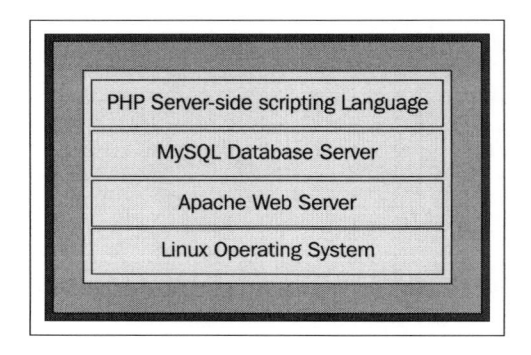

| PHP Server-side scripting Language |
| MySQL Database Server |
| Apache Web Server |
| Linux Operating System |

As you can see, Linux and Apache are the base upon which the LAMP stack is built. They form a formidable system that has helped immensely in the maturation and adoption of not only Linux and Apache, but also a number of open source applications that leverage it, such as SugarCRM.

MySQL, a popular open source database server, was developed by MySQL AB of Sweden, and is known for speed, scalability, and reliability. Although it does not offer all the features of an expensive enterprise level solution, such as **Oracle** or **Informix**, it is still very well suited to the needs of smaller-sized businesses, including SugarCRM users.

One of the strengths of the LAMP concept is that each of its four components can be used independently—and more importantly, can be replaced with other similar technologies. This capability allows administrators to create highly customized stacks and allow applications that leverage the stack to run under a wide range of operating systems.

Other than the use of alternative scripting languages, for example, **Python** or **Perl**, the most common change to LAMP is at the operating system level. It is not uncommon to encounter stacks that use Windows in place of Linux, a combination referred to as a **WAMP** stack, while the other three components remain the same.

The stack has sufficient flexibility that allows more than one component to be modified simultaneously, while still delivering the intended functionality. For example, another common combination is one dubbed **WIMP**, where Microsoft Windows replaces Linux and Microsoft **Internet Information Services (IIS)** replaces Apache web server.

Generally speaking, Windows has a much greater footprint than Linux; thus, a WAMP stack will require more resources that would be required if LAMP were utilized. For an average 25-person business, your CRM server can get away with 4 GB of memory if you use the LAMP stack, but 8 GB is a safer bet if you want to use WAMP. Aside from that cautionary note, a WAMP stack should function just as well as a LAMP stack, while simultaneously offering the advantage of living within an environment that is familiar to many people, simplifying administrative tasks.

It is extremely important not to take the above statements as justification for using underpowered servers for LAMP based deployments. The comments are a vis-à-vis comparison of LAMP versus WAMP performance on the same server. By extension, this also means that in general, LAMP can perform well with fewer resources, but it has its own limits as well. You should treat your LAMP server as you would any other critical business system. Remember, it needs to handle your needs today and for the next 18 to 24 months.

Lastly, a note on WIMP. The WIMP stack has not always been received well, mostly due to past stability issues between IIS and PHP. In recent years however, many of those issues have been resolved and Microsoft has demonstrated a genuine interest in bettering their support for PHP. Today, while still not as popular as LAMP or WAMP deployments, it is successfully used by a number of organizations.

Backup and security considerations

Backup and security are the two things that are most likely to suffer if you take on the responsibility of an On-Premise deployment. If this is the deployment option you are considering, and you have little experience with a server's backup and security issues, then this is an important section for you.

Clearly, once you get your dream CRM up and running, you will want everyone in the organization to be using it and will want to make it a central data hub for your business. The nature and importance of the data that your CRM system will house makes it imperative that you take the necessary precautions to make sure that the system does not fail, which may in turn produce prolonged down times or worse, data loss.

Accordingly, you will need to devise a data backup strategy to protect the data. One solution is to buy a data backup device—which typically will be tape-based, but could also involve network-attached disk storage. Most backup solutions can be a bit expensive, but, adopting a reliable backup plan is completely mandatory. Losing all your data would be a much more expensive venture.

Some inexpensive backup solutions do exist, such as connecting an external USB hard drive to your server and backing up the server hard drive to the external hard drive. In a similar manner, you can also buy a second drive for your server and backup the main drive to the secondary drive. Note that files that are open at backup time will most likely not be backed up by a simple operating-system level file or drive copy—so be *very* careful.

Many server administrators will opt to use an internal tape backup unit with proper tape backup software that performs a daily incremental backup and a weekly full backup. Rotate the tape used in the tape drive each week and keep at least 5 tapes in the rotation. Testing of said backups should occur once a month. This can be easily accomplished by identifying a document that has been recently created and checking whether or not it can be successfully restored from the backup.

Regardless of which option you choose, make sure that you keep a copy of your backup at a safe location, away from your office, such as at a bank safety deposit box, safe at your home or elsewhere.

Server security

Your CRM server is likely to have a permanent link to the Internet to provide remote users with access to its data while away from their office. The data they will be accessing is perhaps the most vital and sensitive information your business owns. Bells should be going off in your head, warning you to make sure that the server is properly secured, as this combination is too tempting for someone with malicious intentions. Cyber attacks, or the attempted theft of your competitive information are two among the many very real threats for which you must plan.

For a start, security specialists will always tell you that nothing is completely secure. There are simply levels of security—each more cumbersome and expensive than the last—and you need to implement a level of security that is sensible and appropriate in your business context.

Some minimal security measures you should consider include the following:

- A UPS (Uninterruptible Power Supply) to save your server from crashing when there is a power outage. Windows and Linux both have utilities that can receive a message from the UPS notifying the server when the UPS has gone over to battery backup, so that the server can be shut down in a controlled manner if the power remains out for too long.
- A locked server room, so only authorized employees can access the server, reducing its chances of being stolen, being damaged, or having its data compromised.
- A surveillance system is an effective deterrent of theft or vandalism. You should consider installing one that has the ability to monitor your server room.
- A **VPN (Virtual Private Network)** to limit the server's exposure to the Internet, while simultaneously allowing remote users uninterrupted access to the system.
- A firewall between the server and the Internet connection, with only limited and specific access to the web server being permitted from the Internet.

If you are installing the SugarCRM server at your own office, you will typically position the server behind your firewall to protect it from the outside world, but will allow external access by opening ports on the firewall to the web server on your SugarCRM server. From a security point of view, it would be even better to actually have separate web and application servers, with security rules between them—but this is not a necessary security measure for smaller firms.

If your SugarCRM server will be collocated, a similar networking configuration should be used, but you must make sure that you talk to your service provider about this matter.

If you are using an On-Demand service, none of this will be vital to you, except insofar as you may wish to ask your service provider about the security architecture currently in use and how it handles the web server and application server issues.

Emergencies and natural disasters

Backups and security measures are intended to protect you from foreseeable mishaps. Unfortunately, there are other situations that may arise that are often overlooked by individuals maintaining their own servers.

Fire and floods are two additional dangers you must be prepared to handle. Should a fire damage your office, you will want to have proper fire fighting equipment handy that will protect your server.

You must also be prepared for water emergencies, such as a flood or a burst water line in your office. To reduce such potential risks, it would be wise to not locate your server in an area that is near water lines. In addition, your server should not be sitting on the floor of the selected area. It should be placed in a server rack where it cannot be stepped on or easily damaged by rising waters.

Lastly, the area where the server is maintained must be kept cool. Sometimes this requires the purchase of additional air conditioning equipment. A closed room with 3 to 4 servers will warm up rather quickly and heat is not well received by servers. In extreme situations, the heat in such environments can cause the server to reboot or even shut down and in turn cause unexpected downtime.

Bandwidth capacity and reliability considerations

We have all had the experience of visiting a useful website, containing a lot of valuable information, and being frustrated by its low speed or responsiveness. You need to make sure that your CRM users never have such an experience.

Bandwidth, or connection speed, is an important link in the chain of good performance for a web-based CRM system, such as SugarCRM.

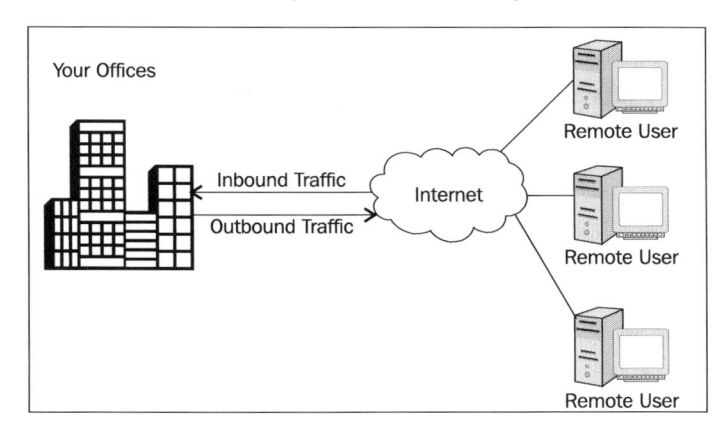

In the previous diagram, the **Outbound Traffic** leaves **Your Offices** for the **Internet** at a speed called the uplink, or upload speed. **Inbound Traffic** arrives at your building through the downlink, or download speed. Notice that for a **Remote User** connecting to the server at your office; it is important that the uplink connection be reliable and fast so as to deliver the data as quickly as possible.

Usually, your employees will complain if the office download speed is slow, as web browsing, or retrieving e-mail from an external e-mail service will be slow.

Employees will also complain (at least the ones who access your CRM system while away from the office) if the office's Internet connection has a slow uplink connection.

So the conclusion we must draw is that if we intend to house our CRM server at the office, we need to make sure that the office has a fast download and upload connection.

Another potential bottleneck for a **Remote User** is the speed of the connection they are using while away from the office. For such users, the speed of inbound traffic will have a direct impact on their experience of using the CRM system. Data travelling from the office to a remote user's computer will travel only as fast as the slowest link between the two. For example, if the server at the office is able to deliver data through its outbound traffic link at a rate of 10 mbps, but the inbound traffic link being used by the remote user is limited to one tenth of that speed, the data from the office to the remote user's computer will be received at 1 mbps and not at 10 mbps.

The last scenario highlights some of the challenges in determining the appropriate speed for your office. In the last example, increasing the speed of the outbound traffic connection at the office would have yielded zero benefits as the bottleneck was at the receiving end.

Another factor to consider is the day-to-day importance of Internet usage within your business. A software development company, for example, will most likely have higher bandwidth requirements than a T-shirt printing firm, or for that matter, RayDoc Carpets.

For an average white collar business (if there is such a thing), 2 mbps of download speed for each of the 25 employees/users will normally suffice. With a CRM server at the office being accessed by remote employees during the day, or at night from home, you will most likely need something like 1 megabit of upload or uplink speed for each of the ten concurrent remote users. Your needs may dictate that you get a dedicated connection to your CRM server in order to eliminate saturation of your connection from other activities.

You should avoid uplink speeds lower than 1 megabit if you intend to access SugarCRM remotely. It will still work on slower connections of course, but you may find that the response time is less than desirable and it may frustrate you.

Many Internet connections tend to be faster in the download direction than the upload direction. These connections are referred to as *Asymmetric*. If your CRM server is located at your office, your business becomes a candidate to have an Internet connection that is closer to being *Symmetric*, or balanced, in its upload and download speeds.

When you use an On-Demand service for your CRM deployment, or have your server collocated, your server benefits from the fact that the Internet connection at the provider's location is much faster in both directions than it is at your office. It is also a more reliable connection. Typically, these providers will utilize multiple suppliers for their Internet connection *pipes*, so that if the connection provided by one supplier fails, those from another supplier will automatically carry on moving traffic.

This redundancy is usually difficult for small businesses to afford. If you intend to use an On-Premise CRM deployment, the lack of this redundancy may be something you will have to accept. Nevertheless, you should investigate pricing for redundant connections in your area, as well as keep yourself informed on the level of guaranteed availability offered by the Internet Service Providers in your area. It also does not hurt to solicit input about them from your business associates.

Lastly, if you choose the On-Demand or Collocated deployment option, be sure you know the amount of bandwidth you are allowed to consume (per user or for your whole server), or you might end up paying for bandwidth surcharges. Some providers do not have any restrictions, or the limits are not practical, but it is important to understand any restrictions in advance so as to avoid any additional charges.

Performing the installation

In order not to interrupt our CRM business analysis context with a lot of procedural instructions, the actual details of installing SugarCRM may be found in *Appendices A and B* that cover the complete process of installing SugarCRM on CentOS Linux and Microsoft Windows network operating system environments.

Summary

In this chapter, we covered the practical considerations of installing and running SugarCRM in your business. The key points included are as follows:

- Comparing the advantages of an On-Demand service versus a Collocated, On-Premise, or Shared Server. We also compared the up front costs of maintaining your own server versus paying monthly fees for an On-Demand service. We also explained the minimal support for customizations available with an On-Demand service or Shared Server.
- If you choose to deploy SugarCRM on your own server, you will need to select the operating system and hardware configuration for your server, and also make decisions regarding server security and Internet connection bandwidth.
- Using Windows or Linux as the server operating system on your SugarCRM server and learned about the LAMP stack. We also examined some popular variations of the LAMP stack including WAMP and WIMP.
- For security, you should consider a UPS (battery backup), a locked server closet, a firewall, VPN, and a surveillance system to protect your server from intrusions, theft or damage.
- Your offices should have an Internet connection of at least 1 megabit for both download and upload speeds. You will need about 2 megabits of download speed for every 25 employees, and about 1 megabit of upload speed for every 10 concurrent remote CRM users.
- *Appendix A and B* include the procedural details of the actual installation of SugarCRM within the Linux and Windows Server environments respectively.

In the next chapter, we assume that you have deployed SugarCRM and venture into using your new CRM in earnest, explaining a lot of the basic CRM terminology and concepts as we go along.

Why is a CRM system so much better than a contact manager? What are the normal navigation techniques for operating a CRM solution? How do I get my data into a CRM application? All these topics and more are coming up next.

4
SugarCRM Basics

Now that we have covered some of the essentials offered in CRM systems, itemized its value to a smaller business, and studied the theoretical aspects of customizing it to properly fit each business that uses them, it is time we made use of the SugarCRM server that we deployed in the previous chapter.

In this chapter, we will take a guided tour of SugarCRM. Our task-oriented, systematic treatment will also relate the specifics of the SugarCRM system and its user interface with the general principles of CRM systems.

This chapter will cover the basic CRM functions and show how they are interpreted and performed within SugarCRM. These basic CRM concepts include the following:

- Common CRM processes and terminology
- Creating accounts and contacts, and relating multiple contacts to a single account
- Following links between related data to get a full view of a customer
- Creating and tracking the Sales Pipeline from leads to opportunities to contacts and accounts
- Creating and monitoring sales activities and accumulating activity history
- Scheduling activities with colleagues by referring to their calendars

CRM processes and terminology

A CRM tool is a system that first needs to be taught all that there is to know in terms of the static information about your accounts and the contacts you have at those accounts. Once the CRM gains that knowledge, it leverages that knowledge by retaining and organizing information about all your daily business activities relating to those accounts and contacts. After a few weeks of regular use, the CRM system will be capable of easily presenting valuable historical information relating to your accounts and contacts, including successful and unsuccessful sales opportunities, interactions with your staff, or their customer service inquiries.

SugarCRM Basics

Let us take a quick look at SugarCRM to get an initial feel of the powerful organizational and managerial boost it will give to your business.

Accessing the SugarCRM system

Before you start using the system, ensure that you have the appropriate software installed and configured on your system. All you will need is the following:

- **A current web browser running on your computer**: SugarCRM has been tested with and supports a variety of browsers. The following browsers are known to work with SugarCRM:
    - Firefox version 2.0 and higher (www.mozilla.org/firefox)
    - Apple Safari version 3.0 and higher (www.apple.com/safari/)
    - Microsoft Internet Explorer version 6 and higher (www.microsoft.com/ie)

    You may encounter problems if you try to access SugarCRM using older web browsers like Internet Explorer 4 or Netscape 4.x. If you are unsure about which web browser version you are using, click on **Help | About**, or similar options on the menu bar in your browser. The version number will be displayed.

- **JavaScript and cookies support enabled in your web browser**: Both JavaScript and cookies support must be enabled in the security settings of your browser and are usually turned on by default.

    If you encounter problems accessing the system, check your browser configuration settings to ensure both JavaScript and cookies support are enabled. (See **Tools | Internet Options | Privacy** and **Security** tabs in Internet Explorer, or **Tools | Options | Privacy** and **Web Features** tabs in Firefox.)

- **Network access to a server that is running the SugarCRM software**: Your system or network administrator will be able to provide you with an Internet address (URL) at which the system can be accessed. If you do not already have an access to an instance of SugarCRM, refer to *Appendix A and B* for instructions on installing of Linux and Windows respectively.

Next, we need to log in to the system and choose a language and a theme (which determines how the application will look). If you do not provide the correct username and password, SugarCRM will not give you an access to the system.

Using the admin area within the system, your System Administrator assigns login credentials—a username and password—to every system user. This admin area is only accessible to users with administrative privileges. If you do not have a username and password combination, contact your system administrator.

To access SugarCRM, type the URL into your web browser's address bar. You should see a screen similar to the one that follows. This is the SugarCRM login screen. If you do not see a login screen, verify that you have entered the URL correctly. If you did not make a typing mistake, contact your system administrator to verify that you have the correct URL.

Clicking on **Options** will allow you to select your desired **Language**, assuming languages other than English (US) have been installed. A **Theme** can also be selected from within the **Options** section. The choices you make are specific to your username and will not affect other users who also access the system.

The language selection directly impacts your ability to interact with the system by providing an interface written in a language with which you are comfortable. Themes are used to make visual changes, such as colors and graphics, and are more a matter of personal taste. Note that if you are connecting to your SugarCRM system through a low bandwidth connection, you will be better off using a theme that utilizes fewer graphics. The following screenshot shows a SugarCRM login screen:

Once the SugarCRM login screen appears, follow the following steps to log in:

1. Type your username in the **User Name** box
2. Type your password in the **Password** box
3. Select the **Language** and **Theme** that you want to use (if applicable)
4. Click on the **Login** button

SugarCRM Basics

A quick tour of SugarCRM

After you have successfully logged into the system, the **Home** tab is displayed, as shown in the following screenshot. Note that this overview assumes that you have logged into the system using an account that has administrator level privileges. Various key elements of the screen layout are highlighted as follows:

1. **Navigation tabs**: By default, they are organized into functional groups. Clicking the main header allows you to choose a module, such as **Contacts** or **Accounts**.

2. **System links**: **My Account, Employees, Logout**, and **About**. The **Admin** link is only available to users who are assigned administrative privileges.

3. **Search box**: It helps to search for a text string within key data held by SugarCRM.

4. **Last viewed**: It is a useful trail of recent records you have viewed.

— [84] —

5. **Navigation shortcuts box**: These are specific shortcuts that are useful within each module.
6. **Quick new item box**: It is a quick data-entry box to create a new item for the current module.
7. **Main screen body**: On the **Home** tab, this includes **Cases**, **Opportunities**, **Appointments**, **Leads**, **Tasks**, and the sales pipeline graph. Additional items can also be added by using the **Add Sugar Dashlets** button.

The screen layout in the **Home** tab uses the same layout for all the other tabs. As you move between the tabs, the shortcuts available in the shortcuts list change according to a specific tab. The main screen body displays the information indicated by the *tab name*. The **Quick New Item** box changes to offer quick access for creating new items based on the tab, for example, **New Contact**, **New Account**, **New Opportunity**, and so on.

Themes

Earlier we mentioned that you can choose an alternative theme to change cosmetic aspects relating to your SugarCRM usage. Let us take a quick look at that before we move on. In the **System Links** area of the screen (top right), click on the **Page Styles** link and change the theme value to **Links**. Changing the theme value will cause SugarCRM to automatically apply the new settings.

Notice that many aspects of the SugarCRM screen will vary by changing the theme. The navigation tabs are no longer tabs, instead they are converted into a side menu system. Essentially, the shortcuts have switched positions with the tabs. In addition, the color scheme and graphics are very different.

Regardless of which theme you use, the same CRM information is displayed. It is just laid out differently. Pick the theme that you prefer, or change it now and then to keep some fun in your use of the CRM system. If you are interested in customizing an existing theme or perhaps creating your own to match your company's branding, you will find the necessary information in *Chapter 5*.

> For the rest of this chapter, we will assume that when you installed SugarCRM, you also opted to install the sample data. (Refer to a section about *Database Configuration within the appendices on installing SugarCRM* for further information.) Later on, we will quickly re-do the installation to remove the demo data and then import your own organization's data.

SugarCRM basics: Data relationships

Before we get too deep into specific functional areas of the application, it is important to understand certain aspects of the system's internal relationships and hierarchy.

Throughout this book we have referred to *Accounts*, *Contacts*, *Opportunities*, and other data entities that make up a CRM system. We have also discussed that some of the main objectives of a CRM system are to store this type of information and also easily demonstrate relationships among them. It is this philosophy that allows a CRM system to not only provide you with information about the sales that are pending, but also the clients they relate to. In order to accomplish this, rules dictating the manner in which data entities are interrelated, or can be connected, must exist within the CRM system. To better understand SugarCRM, we must first examine these rules that help build its hierarchy.

Within the world of SugarCRM, an Account is the top level entity. All other data items, including Contacts, Opportunities, Cases, and so on can all be easily linked to an Account by default. You are also permitted to link as many of those items as you like to any given Account. This functionality allows multiple contacts to be linked to a single account and is commonly referred to as a one-to-many relationship.

The following illustration depicts the hierarchy:

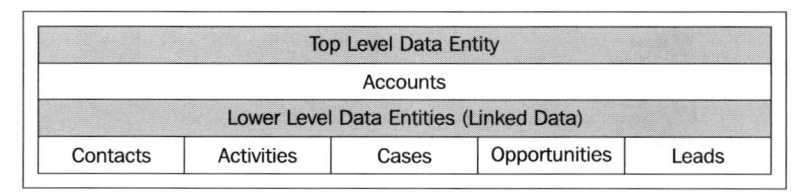

Top Level Data Entity				
Accounts				
Lower Level Data Entities (Linked Data)				
Contacts	Activities	Cases	Opportunities	Leads

While lower level data entities are easily linked to Accounts, they are limited in the manner in which they can be linked to each other. A Case, for example, expects to be linked to an Account by default. It can be associated with a Contact only after it is first linked to an Account. This example highlights an area that may require customization depending on whether your business uses a B2B or B2C model.

In addition, there are some relationships that can only be established in a single manner. A good example is that of a Task and an E-mail. It is possible to establish a relationship between the two, but in order to do so; you must access the e-mail in question and establish the relationship there because attempting to do the reverse is not allowed. Were you to try it by accessing the Task, you would be left with the impression that it was not possible to establish the relationship.

Chapter 4

A final important point concerning relationships between the lower level items is that they often represent one-to-one relationships. The Task and E-mail example that was just explained highlights this quite well, as only one Task can be linked to any given E-mail.

SugarCRM navigation: Accounts and contacts

So—here we are—SugarCRM!

Let us get a little more familiar with using the system. First, (and I will assume that you have switched back to the normal Sugar Theme from now on) try accessing a few of the modules, by first placing your mouse over the group header tab and then selecting one of the displayed module names. For example, hover over **Marketing**, and then choose **Accounts** to access the accounts module as shown in the following screenshot:

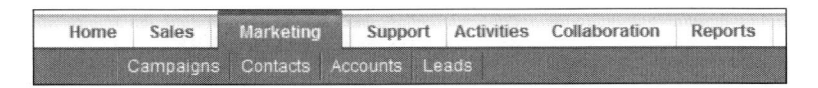

Different sets of information are organized within different modules, and each module has a tab that you click on in order to access and use it.

The modules in SugarCRM Community Edition 5.5 are grouped in the following manner:

Group header tab name	Modules
Home	Home, Dashboard
Sales	Accounts, Opportunities, Leads
Marketing	Campaigns, Contacts, Accounts, Leads
Support	Cases, Accounts, Contacts
Activities	Activities, Calendar, E-mails, Calls, Meetings, Tasks, Notes
Collaboration	E-mails, Documents
Reports	Dashboard

The Professional and Enterprise Editions of SugarCRM expand on this list and some of the additional items provide modules for products, quotes, forecasts and reports, as well as team sales and workflow features.

[87]

SugarCRM Basics

The system administrator can control which modules are accessible to specific users, and in some cases, users can also hide or rearrange tabs. Users can also choose not to use groupings and instead use tabs that represent each module, depending on their navigation preference. If you are not using the group tabs approach, you will find that SugarCRM can only display 12 tabs across the navigation area. Additional modules are accessible through an overflow area available to the very right of the last tab that is visible. Using a theme that lists the modules on the left side like a menu system (such as **Links** or **Pipeline**) eliminates the need for the overflow area as all the modules accessible to the user are automatically displayed.

List and detail view screens

Proceed to hover over **Sales** and click on the **Accounts** tab. This shows you a list of all accounts in the system. Screens that show a list in SugarCRM are called **list views**. This screen is the **Accounts list** view. If you have the demo data installed, your screen should look something like the following:

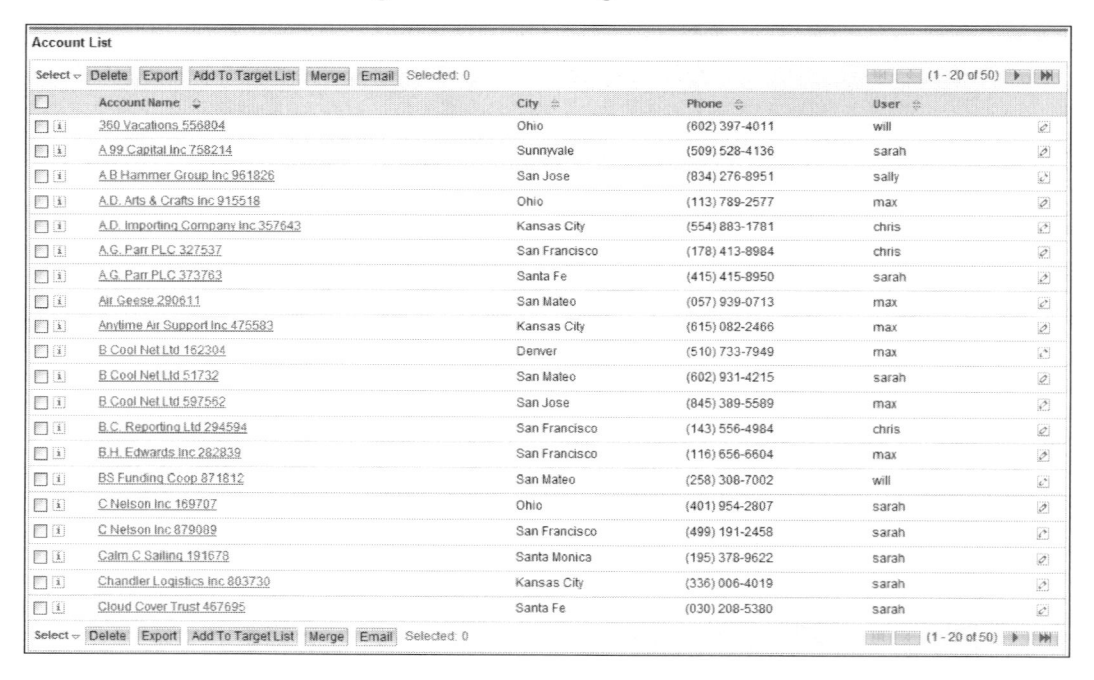

Account Name	City	Phone	User
360 Vacations 556804	Ohio	(602) 397-4011	will
A 99 Capital Inc 758214	Sunnyvale	(509) 528-4136	sarah
A B Hammer Group Inc 961826	San Jose	(834) 276-8951	sally
A.D. Arts & Crafts Inc 915518	Ohio	(113) 789-2577	max
A.D. Importing Company Inc 357643	Kansas City	(554) 883-1781	chris
A.G. Parr PLC 327537	San Francisco	(178) 413-8984	chris
A.G. Parr PLC 373763	Santa Fe	(415) 415-8950	sarah
Air Geese 290611	San Mateo	(057) 939-0713	max
Anytime Air Support Inc 475583	Kansas City	(615) 082-2466	max
B Cool Net Ltd 162304	Denver	(510) 733-7949	max
B Cool Net Ltd 51732	San Mateo	(602) 931-4215	sarah
B Cool Net Ltd 597562	San Jose	(845) 389-5589	max
B.C. Reporting Ltd 294594	San Francisco	(143) 556-4984	chris
B.H. Edwards Inc 282839	San Francisco	(116) 656-6604	max
BS Funding Coop 871812	San Mateo	(258) 308-7002	will
C Nelson Inc 169707	Ohio	(401) 954-2807	sarah
C Nelson Inc 879089	San Francisco	(499) 191-2458	sarah
Calm C Sailing 191678	Santa Monica	(195) 378-9622	sarah
Chandler Logistics Inc 803730	Kansas City	(336) 006-4019	sarah
Cloud Cover Trust 467695	Santa Fe	(030) 208-5380	sarah

Let's imagine that we are looking at a list of RayDoc's accounts—a sample set of accounts, contacts, leads, opportunities, and so on for the RayDoc organization. Clearly, the names of the companies are made up as we cannot expose information about real companies here, but the sample data here has been created to demonstrate all the key capabilities of the system that are needed to make your CRM deployment a real success.

At the top right of the list of accounts, you can see some controls and information that indicate that there are actually 50 accounts in the system, and that you are currently looking at accounts 1 through 20. **Next** and **Previous** controls are provided to step through sections of the full list of accounts, as well as to go to the overall start or end of the list.

You can also see an **Account Search** panel at the top of the screen, which is useful in searching for a specific account by its name, or by other fields, such as the city or phone number as shown in the following screenshot:

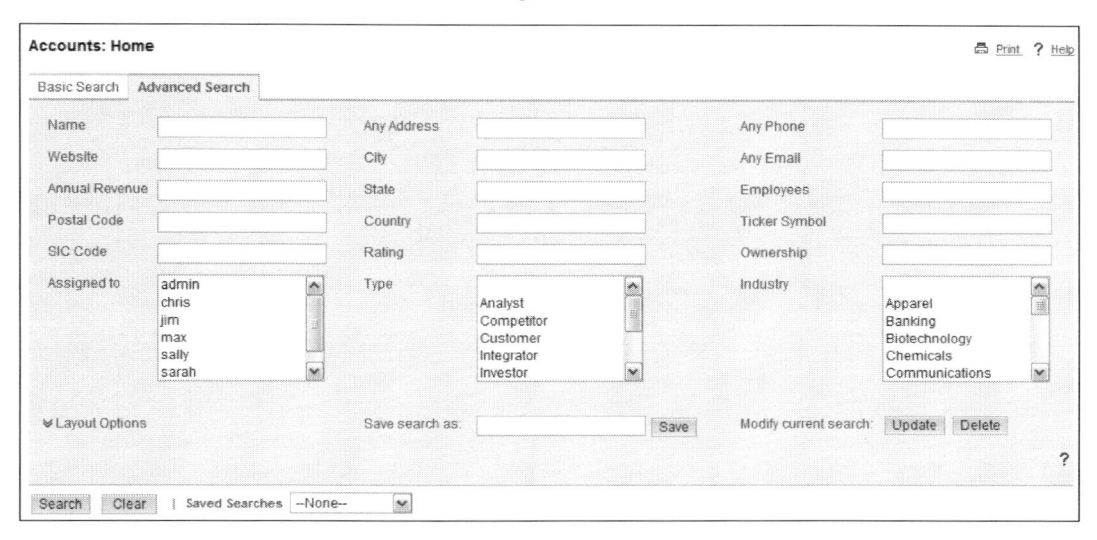

It is important to understand that this search panel is really a filter panel—only accounts that match the filter criteria will be listed. More than one limiting criterion may be applied. You can look for all accounts that start with *a*, and that are in *New York City* and all accounts that satisfy **ALL** of these constraints (filter conditions) will be listed. To go back to view the entire list of accounts, simply click on the **Clear** control in the search panel to remove all filter conditions. To access a more comprehensive set of filter conditions, click on the **Advanced Search** tab.

It is important to understand that the **Accounts List** shown to you by default is the entire set of accounts in the system. Sales people using the system may wish to focus exclusively on their own accounts. This may be done by selecting the **Only My Items** checkbox in the search panel. This feature is another area of functionality that relies on the previously mentioned **Assigned To** value.

As you move your mouse pointer around your browser window, you can see that each account name has a link on it. If you click on the name of an account, you will go to the detailed view for that account. Let's do that now, and click on **NW Capital Corp 582183**.

Main panel and subpanels

Examining the **Accounts Detail** screen reveals a block of general information about the account at the top and a series of blocks of information below containing related information, such as **Activities**, **History**, **Contacts**, **Opportunities**, **Leads**, **Cases**, and so on.

The block of general information at the top is referred to as the main panel and is shown in the following screenshot:

The blocks of related information below the main panel are called subpanels. So we see a subpanel for **Activities**, one for **History**, another for **Contacts**, and so on as shown in the following figure:

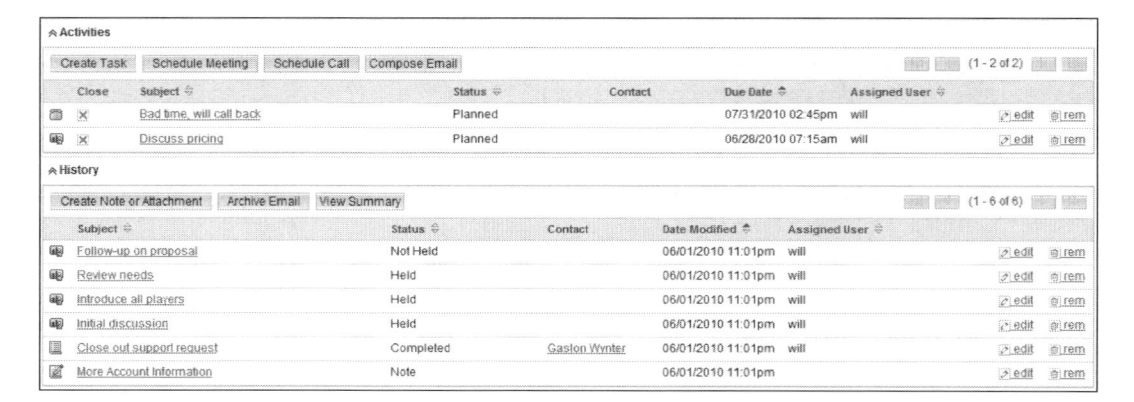

We also see a few buttons just above the main panel—**Edit**, **Duplicate**, **Find Duplicates**, and **Delete**. These buttons act on this specific account record, allowing us to edit, duplicate, or delete it.

Clicking on **Find Duplicates** allows you to search the database for records that are potential duplicates of the current entry. If any are found, you are allowed to merge the records to create a single surviving, master record. This functionality helps keep your database as clean as possible.

Just above each subpanel, we also see a number of buttons. Let's take a look at the **Activities** subpanel as a specific example. This subpanel offers buttons for **Create Tasks**, **Schedule Meeting**, **Schedule Call**, and **Compose Email**. While we will discuss these different activities in more detail shortly, for now it is enough to understand that these buttons allow you to add new activities into this detail view screen, which are automatically linked to or associated with the current account.

You will further notice that there are links on the **Subject**, **Contact**, and **Related to** fields within each open activity in the **Activities** subpanel. Clicking on these links will take us to the detail view of the activity, the related contact, or the related item. This is your first glimpse of the enormous power of the links within a CRM system that speed up the navigation between related information.

Still within the **Activities** subpanel, to the right of each activity listed, notice the links **edit** and **rem**. These are provided to allow you to quickly edit or unlink the activities from the account.

Similar principles apply to the remaining subpanels—buttons and links are provided to create new items, edit or remove existing items, or to go to the full detail view of those related items' information.

The detail view screen layout also includes the following additional handy controls:

- **Hide controls for each subpanel**: Enables the user to limit vertical screen scrolling to focus on the data that is important to them specifically, and to reduce the bandwidth requirements of each screen. The latter is helpful for environments with limited bandwidth or resources. Each hidden subpanel may be restored by clicking on the **Show** link, which appears on collapsed or hidden subpanels. Hiding a subpanel is a *sticky* action—the subpanel will stay hidden indefinitely until you click on the **Show** link.
- **VCR controls**: On each detail screen, there are **Next** and **Previous** links at the top (also known as nudge controls) that enable the user to step through the detail view of records in a module, without having to return to the list view to select a record. **Start** and **End** Controls are provided to go directly to the first and last records in a module.

SugarCRM Basics

- **Return to List**: This link at the top of each detail view may be used to return to the list view for that module.
- **View Change Log**: Each module's *change log* feature tracks changes made to specific fields on a record-by-record basis. A change log entry is automatically created each time an audited field is changed. The entry notes which field was changed, the old and new values, the user that made the change, and the date of the change.

Edit view screens

If you look on the left-hand side of your screen, you will see the navigation shortcuts box. From this menu (assuming again that you are using the standard Sugar theme), click on the **Create Account** shortcut. You will see the **Account Edit** view screen, of which a section is displayed in the following screenshot:

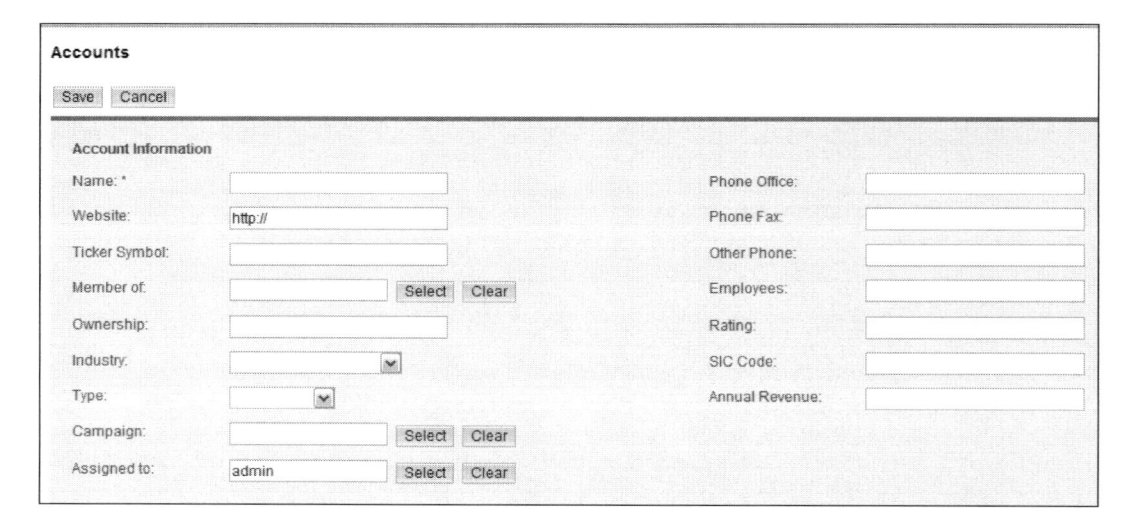

To gain some first-hand experience we are going to create an account for RayDoc. Enter the data for the RayDoc business using the following information and then click on the **Save** button.

```
Account Name: RayDoc

Phone Office: (310) 555-1212

Website: www.raydoc.com
```

Chapter 4

One important thing to note at this point is that you have now saved some data within SugarCRM for the first time. In a browser-based system like SugarCRM, data is not saved until you click on the **Save** button. Were you to close the browser before clicking on **Save**, the data would have been lost. Another important point to note is that data is not saved to your PC or notebook, instead it is saved directly to the SugarCRM server. As a result, the data is immediately accessible to any other user of the system, assuming security settings do not restrict their access to it.

The beauty of this approach versus the older generation of systems is that it allows the data to be accessed from anywhere, so long as the user's PC is connected to the Internet with a browser running on it. Your view of the data will be exactly the same whether you are 100 feet or 100 miles away from the server.

Returning to our data entry example, now that you are on the RayDoc account detail view, we will proceed to add a linked contact. Click on the **Create** button in the **Contacts** subpanel and you should see the following:

Fill in the new contact record form with the data below:

```
First Name: Doc
```

```
Last Name: Newhart
```

Note that only a limited number of fields are displayed. If you wish to populate additional fields that are not displayed, click on the **Full Form** button. Once you are done entering the data, click on the **Save** button. Another important point to highlight is that the system automatically inherits the phone number from the related account record. The same will be true for other coinciding fields, but you are free to change the data for either the account or contact independently. The copy behavior only applies when creating a new entry.

Now that the record has been saved, the detail view for the **RayDoc** account should contain the **Doc Newhart** entry within the Contacts subpanel, as demonstrated in the following screenshot:

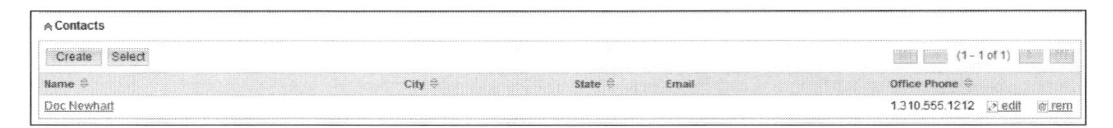

Name	City	State	Email	Office Phone
Doc Newhart				1.310.555.1212

To reinforce the ability to link back and forth, up and down, and sideways within SugarCRM (and any good CRM system)—click on the contact name of **Doc Newhart** to view his Contact Detail view screen. From that screen, click on the account name link to return to the Account Detail view screen for RayDoc. Notice that the **Last Viewed** links area on the upper left, just below the navigation tabs, is accumulating a list of recently accessed records to simplify the process of returning to them.

Now add another contact to the RayDoc account entry, repeating the process that we just described. However, do not enter any other data than your name. You should now see two contacts listed in the **Contacts** subpanel of the Raydoc account detail view screen. This is another important point. We have re-used all the basic account information in the main panel of the RayDoc account for the second contact. We did not have to type it in again. In addition, if any of the RayDoc account information changes, we will only have to edit the RayDoc account record, not the information that we have about our contacts there. This is one of the key advantages of a CRM system over a contact manager like Microsoft Outlook 2003. It understands that accounts and contacts are two separate types of information that are linked together, not crammed together into one unsatisfactory amalgam.

Data relationships and searching

Again, to reinforce the speed and power of navigation in SugarCRM, browse to your own contact record. Now go back to the RayDoc account detail view and then on to Doc's contact record. A contact can lead to an account, which can lead to other contacts at that account—all rather quickly. Moreover, it is very relevant to your everyday work needs.

Go ahead now and explore the contact list view on your own by hovering over the **Marketing** tab and clicking on **Contacts**. Notice that you can search for a specific contact in the **Contact Search** panel above the list of contacts. Clicking on **Advanced Search** displays a more comprehensive list of fields to search, as displayed in the following image:

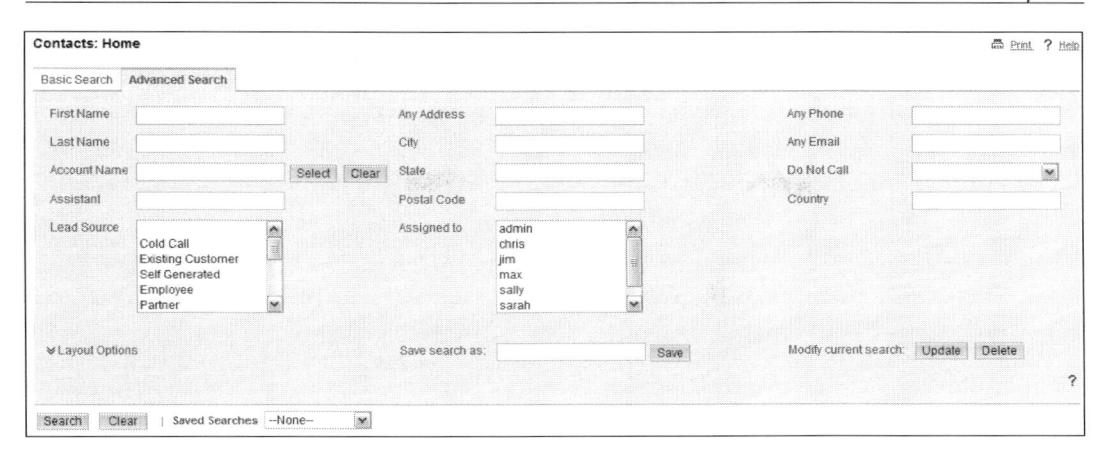

One helpful feature inherent to the search capabilities is the idea of being able to search for an individual based on their first or last name independently. As your database grows, the value of this feature will become more apparent as there will be many cases where you might not remember an individual's full name, but do remember their first or last name.

Along these same lines, it allows you to search for portions of a value by means of a wildcard character. For example, to search for contacts whose last name contains the letters *son*, as in *Gunderson*, you could type *%son* in the **Last Name** field and SugarCRM would yield the matching results.

SugarCRM basics: Security

Now that you have some familiarity with the process of entering data, searching, and establishing relationships among different entries, it is time to discuss the important topic of security and access control. Other than the earlier mentioned username and password, you may have a need to control the records that are accessible to the various users who will be accessing your SugarCRM installation.

This is an important topic to discuss with your stakeholders and project leaders. By its very nature, CRM systems are designed to allow all users access to all data by default. This makes perfect sense, as the core philosophy of the system is to facilitate communication among a group of users. Over time, however, you will want to make adjustments to the security settings to control which users can view, edit, or delete certain data.

For now, the most obvious component of security that you will note is the use of an **Assigned to** field on all data entries. As you work with SugarCRM, you will notice that every record in the database, regardless of whether it is an Account, Contact, Opportunity, or other, contains this field. By default, SugarCRM will automatically populate this field with the name of the user that initially entered the record into the system, but allows users to select a different assignee.

Note that by default, it is only possible to assign a record to a single user. The ability to assign data to multiple users, referred to as a **Team**, is out-of-box functionality that is meant only for Professional and Enterprise Edition subscribers.

This mechanism is integral to the security underpinnings of SugarCRM. While it may be of little significance if you are a single user, tampering with the field can cause problems, such as not being able to access certain records and other oddities.

More advanced security features, discussed in *Chapter 5* of this book, all rely on this field, hence it is important.

The sales pipeline: Leads and opportunities

Now that you have practiced putting accounts and contacts into the system and linked contacts to accounts, let us go on to learn about a few more data types your CRM system can organize for you.

Most modern CRM systems are designed to incorporate the concept of *leads* and *opportunities* as independent data entities. They are kept as separate items of information, even though they may sound very similar to each other. The generally accepted distinction between them is that a lead is information pertaining to an individual that has come to you in such a way where you cannot be certain that they are interested in your products and services. They need to be qualified. On the other hand, an opportunity is what a lead becomes once you have been in touch with the person and confirmed that they do have a genuine and qualified interest in what your company has to offer (they have a real business problem, the money to fix it and you're talking to someone who has purchasing power).

In CRM terms, the process of selling goods and services to your customers comes down to a series of steps that look something like the following:

1. Acquiring and tracking leads
2. Qualifying them as real opportunities

3. Quantifying these opportunities and setting an expected closing date for them
4. Aggregating all opportunities together into a sales pipeline to see the big picture
5. Closing the opportunities as sales

The intended benefits to your business from such a design are as follows:

- You can forecast your expected sales over the next couple of months in a more tangible and quantifiable way than ever before. The sales pipeline is your distant early warning system, as it shows you when your business levels are falling off, or growing faster than anticipated. In a smaller business, it is your best friend when it comes to business planning, giving you a more detailed and distant view into the future, helping you to make appropriate staffing and expenditure decisions.

- All your sales leads, opportunities, and account history are now formally recorded in a central system that the business owns. Your vulnerability to threats and blackmail from sales personnel, or to the sudden defection of sales personnel, is reduced. If a sales person leaves the organization, you still have all the leads and opportunities the business paid to develop, along with the account history needed to help a new sales person take over the account quickly and effectively.

- The sales person on an account is not the only person in the organization with access to details of activity history. Other personnel with direct customer contact now have information that empowers them to make more educated decisions about issues relating to any of your customers.

How did all of this impact Doc after the initial roll out of the system? Our initial task was to find all his leads. Most of them were fairly dormant in the inboxes of the sales staff—something to do on a slow day if they felt like it.

So Doc had to round up all the sales people and *harvest* all these leads. On an ongoing basis, most leads came to the company, from suppliers that RayDoc partners with, and not directly to the individual sales people, and so could be entered in the system by Kay, in her spare time. They would then be simultaneously assigned to a sales person, ensuring someone would be responsible for tracking them. Leads that came directly to a sales person would have to be entered by that sales person—and this would be used as matter for training in the near future.

SugarCRM Basics

Once all the historical leads were gathered together, Kay typed them into SugarCRM. Now, let us enter one ourselves to get familiar with the process. Hover over the **Marketing** tab, and then select **Leads**. Click on the **Create New Lead** shortcut on the left-hand side of the screen and you should see the following screen:

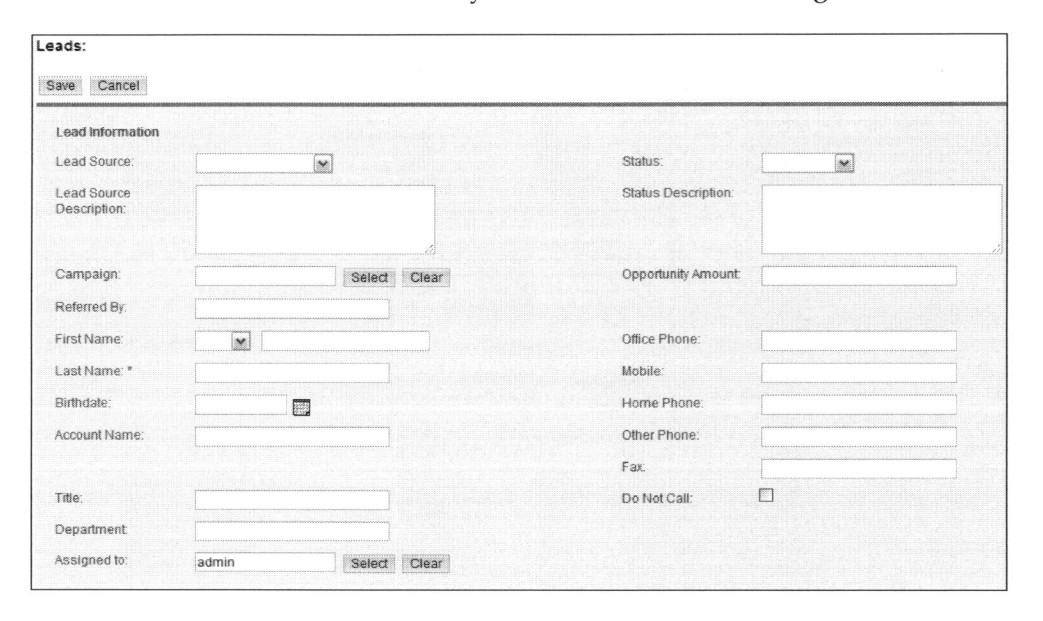

Using the following information, enter the new Lead record and click on the **Save** button. You should now see the Lead detail view screen, with its main panel and subpanels for **Open Activities** and **History**. These subpanels will let you track the day-to-day activities your sales people are conducting with the leads that you pass on to them.

```
Lead Source: Word of Mouth

First Name: Mr. Fred

Last Name: Namath

Account Name: SPAR Aerospace

Office Phone: (562) 555-1313
```

One key field for each lead is the **Status** field. It is automatically set to **New** when a lead is first entered and should be set to **Assigned** when the lead is assigned to a particular sales person. It automatically becomes **Converted** if the lead is converted into an opportunity. Diligent use of this field allows you to effectively measure the number of new leads your business is obtaining, as well as gauging the number that have been converted into potential sales or opportunities.

Another key field is the **Lead Source**. When combined with the status field, it becomes easier to measure the proportion of leads you are generating per lead source, usually representative of a specific of marketing campaign. Such information is considered a key business enabler, as it allows you to quickly see where your marketing dollars are best invested, and which yield the most actual revenue.

To continue our example demonstrating the lifecycle of a lead, let us imagine that Doc, or one of his sales people calls up the lead, **Mr. Namath.** After talking with him for a bit, the sales person determines that **SPAR Aerospace** is a genuine potential new account for RayDoc. As a result the **Fred Namath** lead should be converted to an opportunity to record and track this activity. At the top of the Lead detail view screen is a **Convert Lead** button. Click on it now and you should see a screen like the following:

SugarCRM Basics

As you can see, converting the lead basically turns the lead into a contact and optionally allows you to simultaneously create an account, an opportunity, or even an appointment. If you wish, you may also create a note or attachment (an uploaded file, such as a Microsoft Word or Excel file) to be linked to the **Account** record.

Based on Doc's conversation with Fred, we have chosen to click on the **Create Opportunity** box to enter data corresponding with the potential sale of replacement windows. Note that you must provide an amount and expected close date for the opportunity. When you are done, click on the **Save** button to save all the new information records at once. You will then see a screen like the following, which confirms the successful lead conversion:

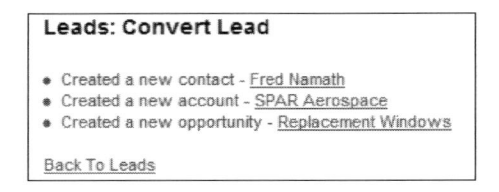

Leads: Convert Lead

- Created a new contact - Fred Namath
- Created a new account - SPAR Aerospace
- Created a new opportunity - Replacement Windows

Back To Leads

Now hover on **Sales** and click on **Accounts**. Use the search panel to find the account record for **SPAR Aerospace**. Click on that record to view the detail screen of the account entered through the *lead conversion* process. (Note that main and subpanels have been split into two images although they should appear on the same page on your screen):

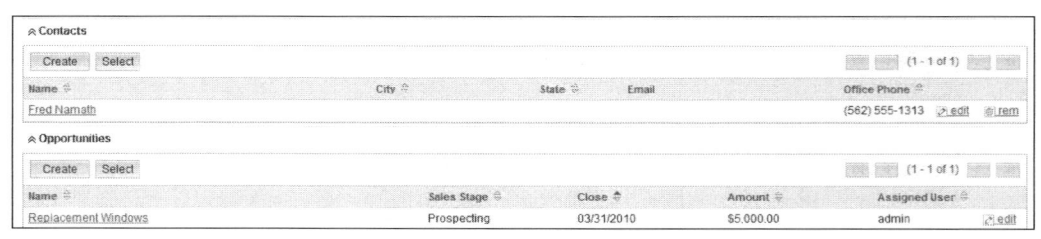

[100]

Notice that in addition to the original lead, we now have an account, plus a contact and an opportunity linked to that account. Again, practice your navigation skills a bit. Click on the opportunity and make sure that the resulting screen shows the related contact. Click on the contact. That screen should show you the account it is linked to. Click on the account. We are back where we started. This is the joy of CRM—everything is connected. You can link volumes of account history, contact history, related contacts, related opportunities, leads and other data, then go back and quickly navigate through all the relationships.

Aggregating opportunities: The sales pipeline

Now that we have worked through the process of creating accounts, contacts, and leads, as well as converting leads into contacts, opportunities, and accounts, we can start assembling a sales pipeline. Hover on **Sales** then click on **Opportunities** to see a list of all the opportunities in our demonstration RayDoc set of data. You should see a screen like the following:

Name	Account Name	Sales Stage	Amount	Close	User
Kitty Kat Inc 452275 - 1000 units	Kitty Kat Inc 452275	Value Proposition	$50,000.00	06/13/2010	max
WEST ARKANSAS 384702 - 1000 units	WEST ARKANSAS 384702	Value Proposition	$50,000.00	04/01/2011	chris
A 99 Capital Inc 758214 - 1000 units	A 99 Capital Inc 758214	Prospecting	$50,000.00	12/10/2010	sarah
SEA REGION S A 720941 - 1000 units	SEA REGION S A 720941	Id. Decision Makers	$10,000.00	02/14/2011	sally
A.D. Importing Company Inc 357643 - 1000 units	A.D. Importing Company Inc 357643	Negotiation/Review	$10,000.00	07/13/2010	chris
C Nelson Inc 879089 - 1000 units	C Nelson Inc 879089	Negotiation/Review	$10,000.00	04/13/2011	sarah
Kitty Kat Inc 680761 - 1000 units	Kitty Kat Inc 680761	Qualification	$25,000.00	10/01/2010	sarah
K Kringle Inc K.A. Tower & Co 633432 - 1000 units	K Kringle Inc K.A. Tower & Co 633432	Needs Analysis	$50,000.00	05/03/2011	chris
Income Free Investing LP 892941 - 1000 units	Income Free Investing LP 892941	Perception Analysis	$50,000.00	09/04/2010	max
White Cross Co 446002 - 1000 units	White Cross Co 446002	Id. Decision Makers	$25,000.00	09/19/2010	sarah
360 Vacations 556804 - 1000 units	360 Vacations 556804	Value Proposition	$50,000.00	08/12/2010	will
Anytime Air Support Inc 475583 - 1000 units	Anytime Air Support Inc 475583	Qualification	$25,000.00	10/15/2010	max
Chandler Logistics Inc 803730 - 1000 units	Chandler Logistics Inc 803730	Proposal/Price Quote	$25,000.00	11/06/2010	sarah
Kaos Theory Ltd 235674 - 1000 units	Kaos Theory Ltd 235674	Qualification	$25,000.00	03/06/2011	will
C Nelson Inc 169707 - 1000 units	C Nelson Inc 169707	Closed Lost	$50,000.00	10/10/2009	sarah
B.H. Edwards Inc 282839 - 1000 units	B.H. Edwards Inc 282839	Value Proposition	$50,000.00	12/16/2010	max
NW Capital Corp 582183 - 1000 units	NW Capital Corp 582183	Value Proposition	$25,000.00	03/13/2011	will
SEA REGION S A 117635 - 1000 units	SEA REGION S A 117635	Negotiation/Review	$25,000.00	02/16/2011	sally
B Cool Net Ltd 51732 - 1000 units	B Cool Net Ltd 51732	Closed Lost	$10,000.00	09/30/2009	sarah
B.C. Reporting Ltd 294594 - 1000 units	B.C. Reporting Ltd 294594	Needs Analysis	$25,000.00	09/05/2010	chris

SugarCRM Basics

Clearly, being able to see all the opportunities we have identified for future business is very useful. However, there are drawbacks. By default, we can only see 20 of the 51 opportunities in the system, thus limiting our immediate view of the pipeline. We have to page back and forth to see the remainder of the entries or adjust our system settings to accommodate more entries per page.

The list also shows an estimated value and close date for each opportunity along with the sales stage to indicate where we are in the sales process for each opportunity. However, we do not see the percentage indicating the probability of closing the sale, nor do we see an automatic totaling of the opportunities. We might also like to see a total of the opportunities weighted by the percentage probability of closing them—to gain a more realistic expectation of future sales.

First let us take a detailed look at an opportunity to understand what information an opportunity record holds. We generated an opportunity in the last section, but did so without actually using the Opportunity edit view screen. To access the edit view, click on the first opportunity listed and then click on the **Edit** button. You should see a screen similar to the following:

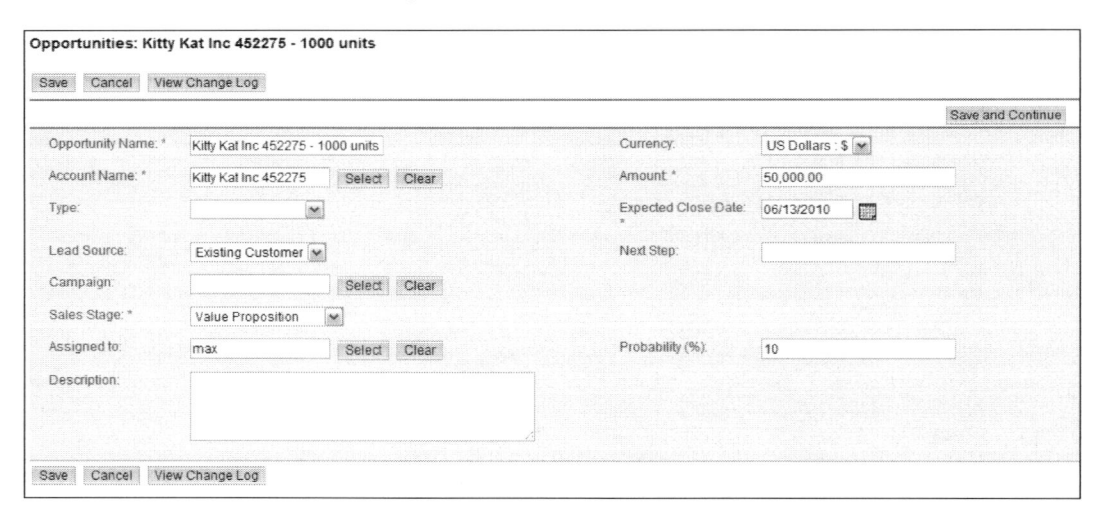

[102]

One key attribute of an opportunity is the **Sales Stage**. In the preceding screenshot you can see the drop-down box for sales stage with the various available options. (These options can be customized if they do not match with the way your business works.)

Other important information contained in an opportunity is the **Expected Close Date** for the business. The percentage **Probability** of closing the business, the **Lead Source** for this opportunity, and the **Type** of business (new or existing) involved are the variables that give further information about an opportunity. Now that we have reviewed the various bits of data an opportunity contains, proceed to click on the **Cancel** button to exit the screen.

The opportunities list view screen is very useful; however, there are clearly a number of views and questions that it does not address. Some of those include the following:

- What is our best lead source?
- What is our total sales pipeline?
- How does the sales pipeline break down by month for estimated close dates?
- At which stage of the selling process do most of our opportunities come in?
- Who are the most successful sales people at the moment?

The dashboard

To answer the aforementioned questions, high quality CRM systems provide graphical dashboards with visual breakdowns of opportunity data, totaling them overall, and sub-totaling by key indicators, such as sales stage, lead source, and account representative.

SugarCRM Basics

You may have already seen one such graphical chart on the **Home** tab screen, but to see the complete set of charts, hover on **Home** and then click on the **Dashboard** link. You will see a screen like the following:

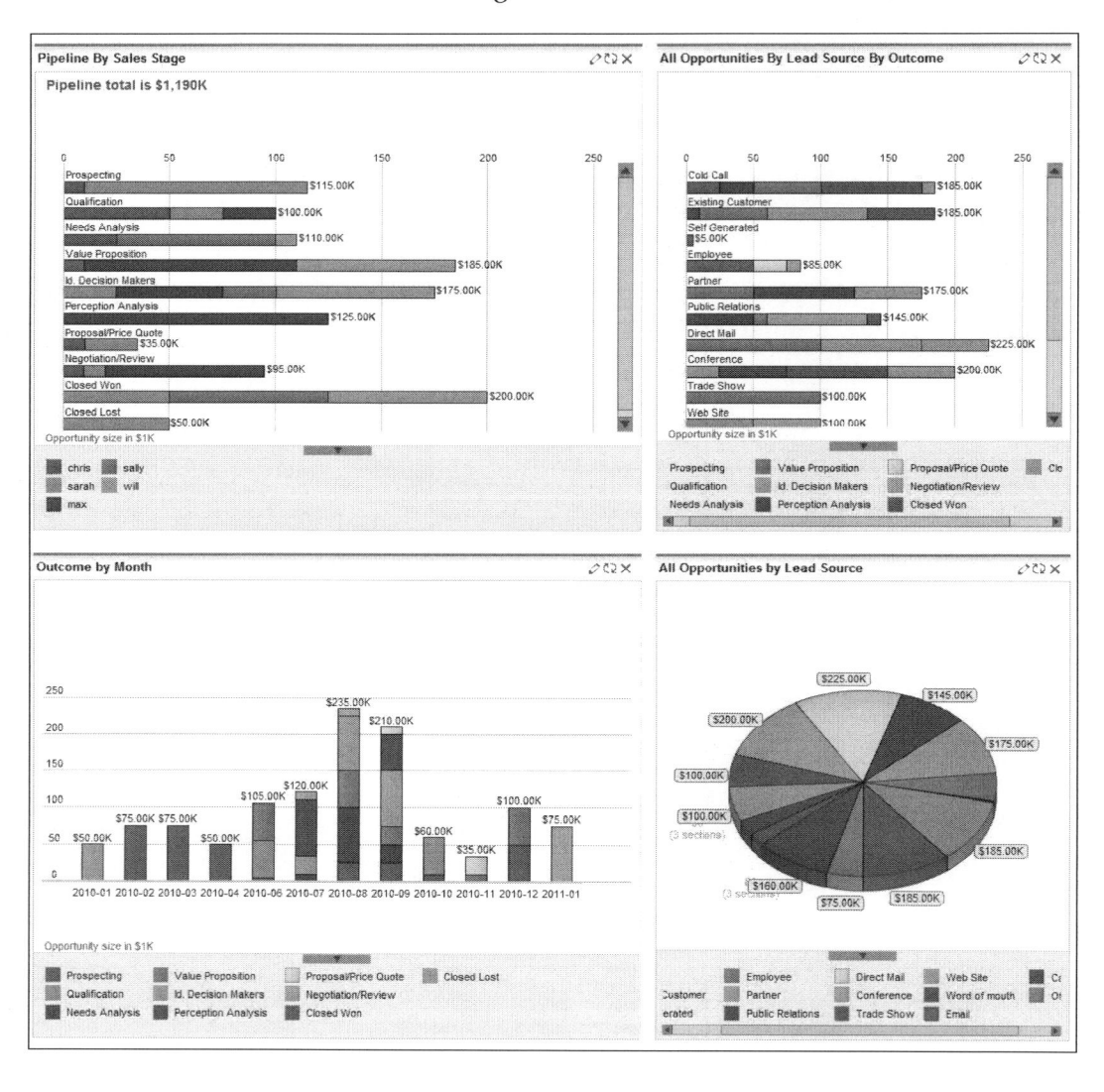

Chapter 4

The four charts displayed are explained as follows:

1. **Pipeline by sales stage chart**: This chart is also available on the **Home** tab, except that the one on your **Home** tab shows only data for opportunities specifically assigned to you, not the entire organization's data. This chart is usually used by the owner of a small business, or the sales manager, as it provides an overall sense of the maturity of the sales pipeline. He or she can answer the question—"Is there enough future business to meet sales targets?" In addition, the stacked bar chart presentation gives a visual indication of which sales people have the greatest dollar value of opportunities and which one of them has an undue proportion of their opportunities in the early stages. In Doc's case, he uses this chart to watch out for any sales person who may be bluffing about how much business he or she has coming in, as this normally shows up by a lot of opportunities, most of which are in the early sales stages. Following is the same chart:

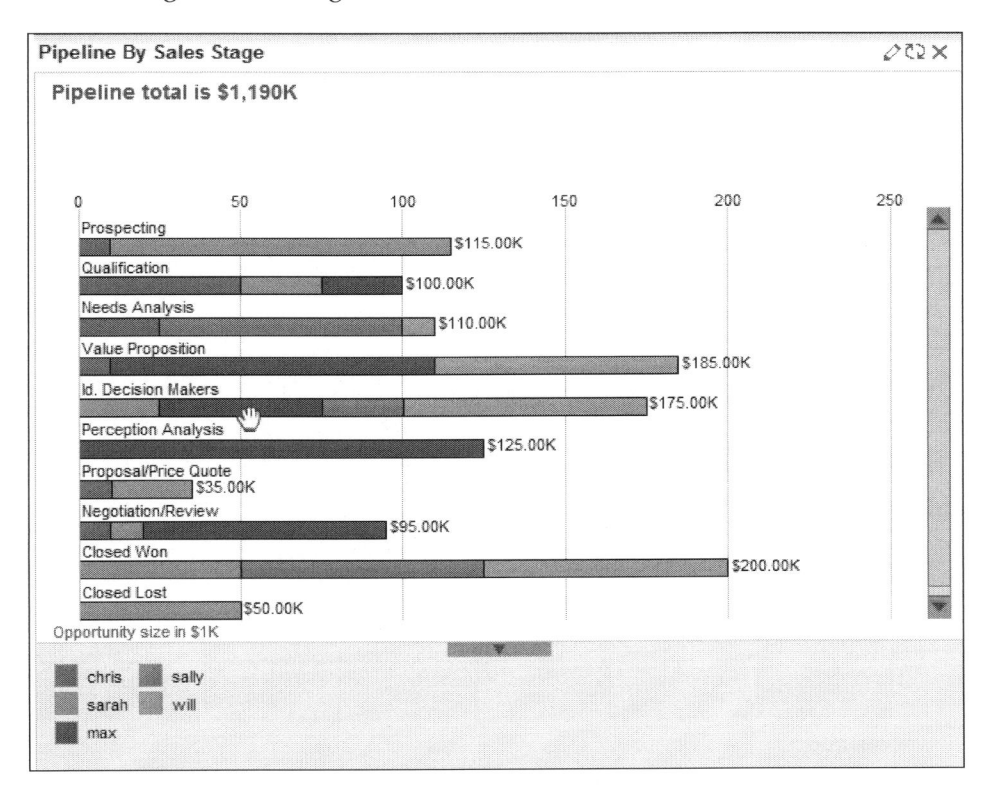

2. **Opportunities by lead source by outcome chart**: This chart is handy for giving you a quick visual indicator of which lead sources are producing the greatest value of opportunities. The color-coded, stacked bars help demonstrate which lead sources are especially good, or bad, at being converted into sales. It shows Doc whether his money is better invested in advertising replacement doors and windows in a home improvement magazine, or on the TV Guide channel in his local market.

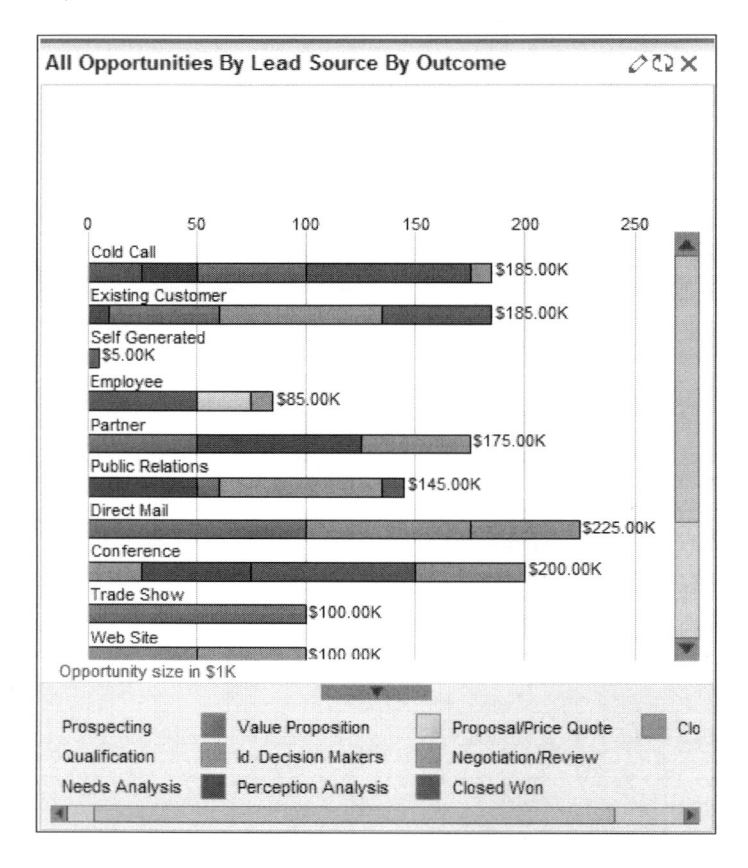

3. **The outcome by month chart**: This chart shows projected and closed sales on a per-month basis. The stacked bars break down the opportunities depending on whether their sales stage is closed won, closed lost, or anything else (meaning the opportunity has its expected close date in the month shown, but it has yet to close in favor of our business, or a competitor).

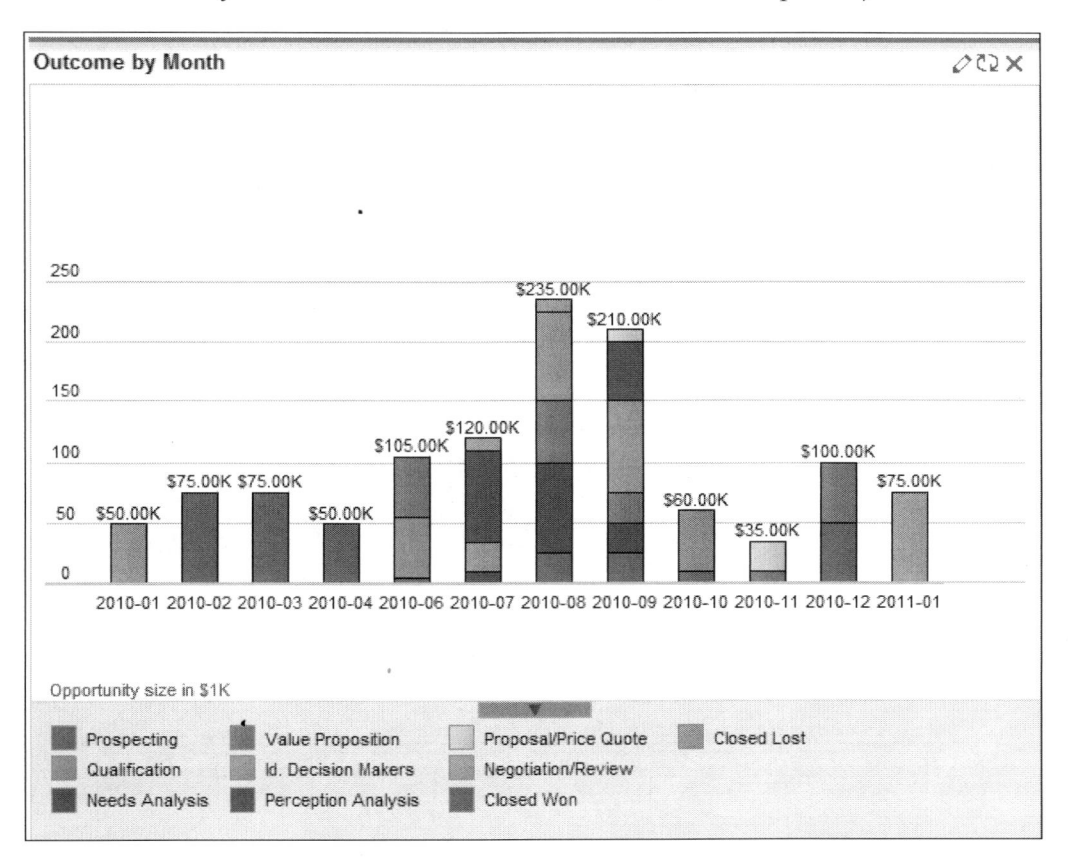

SugarCRM Basics

4. **The all opportunities by lead source chart**: This chart provides a useful pie-chart visualization of all opportunities, segmented by their respective lead source value.

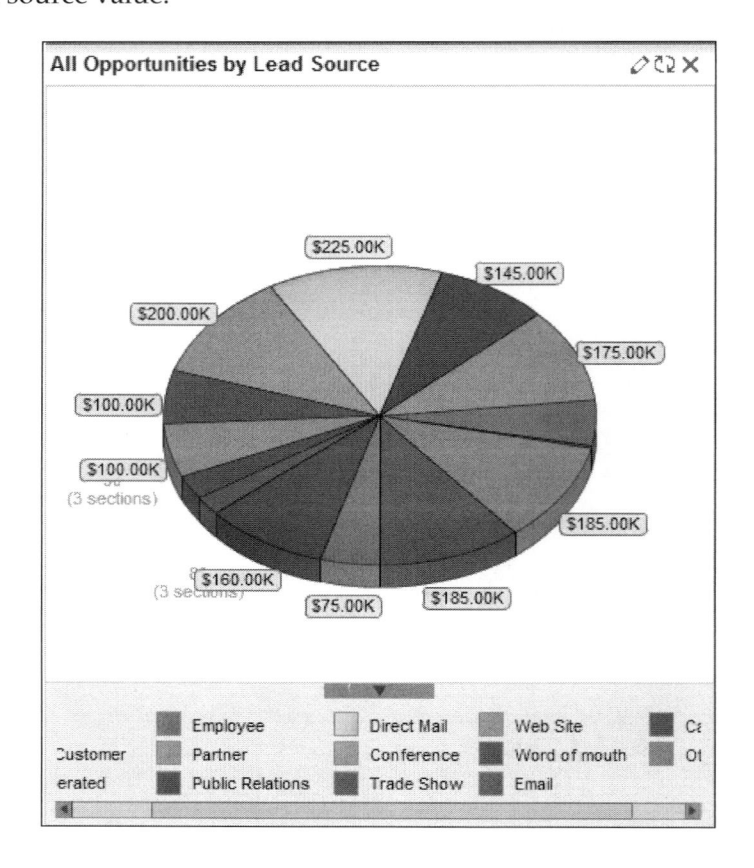

![All Opportunities by Lead Source pie chart showing segments labeled $225.00K, $145.00K, $200.00K, $175.00K, $100.00K, $100.00K (3 sections), $185.00K, $160.00K (3 sections), $75.00K, $185.00K. Legend: Customer Generated, Employee, Partner, Public Relations, Direct Mail, Conference, Trade Show, Web Site, Word of mouth, Email.]

Each of these charts has an edit control at the top right that allows you to set a few filters on the data driving the chart. Opportunities shown on the charts can be limited to those from specific sales people, those due to close in specific time frames, those with specific sales stages, or from specific lead sources.

Each chart also provides you with the ability to mouse over areas of interest to see more information. If, on the first chart, you roll your cursor over the leads in the prospecting stage, the area under the chart will show the number of opportunities set to that stage and their total value.

[108]

Lastly, each chart offers a facility known as **drilldown**. To see the functionality in action, roll your mouse cursor over the opportunities at the prospecting stage within the first chart. Next, click on the bar in the chart that represents those opportunities. The system will bring up the **Opportunities List** screen automatically filtered to show only those opportunities that are behind the chart's graphical representation of the data. This handy feature allows users who prefer visual presentations of data to quickly see the information they need, while simultaneously offering the same information for those who are more comfortable with simple text and numbers.

Combined, these capabilities of the dashboard should significantly improve your ability to forecast your sales for the next few months, understand which lead generation strategies are working most effectively for you, and to root out problems with sales people who may habitually overstate the value or probability of their sales pipeline, or repeatedly fail to close business by forecast dates.

For the sales people themselves, this tool can act as a motivator to generate new opportunities, or to close business that is visibly lagging against its forecast dates, as well as being an organization tool.

Calendaring

In any business there are series of small events—meetings, telephone calls, notes, e-mails, or reminders to revisit an issue in a few months. A very important aspect of any CRM is the ability to schedule these activities and to associate them with the respective accounts and contacts they involve.

SugarCRM includes a full group calendaring system permitting users to easily manage these activities or delegate them to other users. The system includes both a graphical calendar and a list-based calendar. Let us take a moment now to examine the first option.

SugarCRM Basics

To access the graphical calendar, hover over **Activities** then click on **Calendar**. You should see a screen like the following:

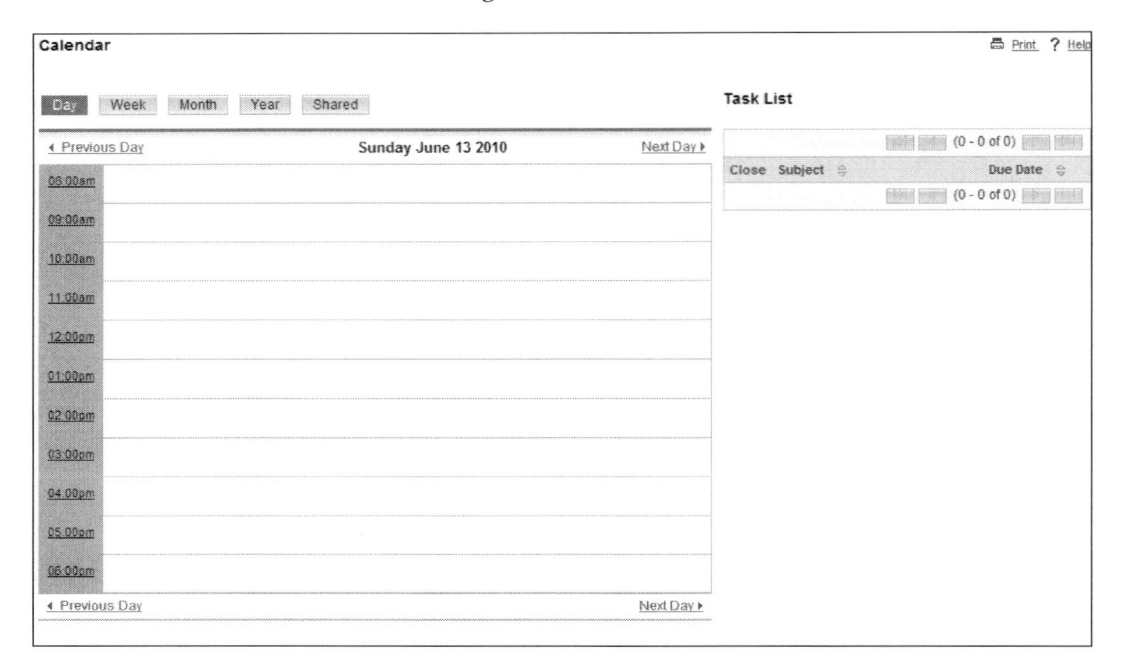

This is the *default* view for the **Calendar** tab—the day view for current date. As you can see, there are buttons that allow you to change the view to the current week, month, or even year. In addition, within each of these views, there are nudge controls to go to the previous or next day, week, month, or year.

There is an additional view, accessed by clicking on the **Shared** button. This is helpful for keeping tabs on the activities of other users. Clicking it will allow you to display the scheduled activities of multiple users within the same calendar, saving you the trouble of checking each user's activities independently and simplifying the scheduling of activities involving multiple users.

Take a moment right now to click on the **Week**, **Month**, **Year**, and **Shared** buttons to get familiar with the display layouts and the navigation buttons offered by the application. Notice that on each of these views, you can click on the figure of any day to *zoom* to the day view for that date.

The day view, unlike the other views, also shows a list of current tasks down the right-hand side of the screen. These tasks are specific to the currently logged in user, as are the activities shown on the calendar (except for the shared view).

To see how the calendar works, let us take a moment to schedule an appointment for tomorrow at `11 AM` with `Rachel Wason` of `Kitty Kat Inc 452275` to discuss their plans for renovations. From the current screen, click on the **Next Day** link. When you see the activities for that date, click on the **11:00 AM** link on the left-hand side of the calendar display. A small pop-up box that lets you quickly schedule a call or meeting should appear at that point. Choose the radio button for **Meeting**, enter **Discuss Renovation Plans** for the subject and then click on **Save**.

You should now see the detail screen for the meeting, which should resemble the following:

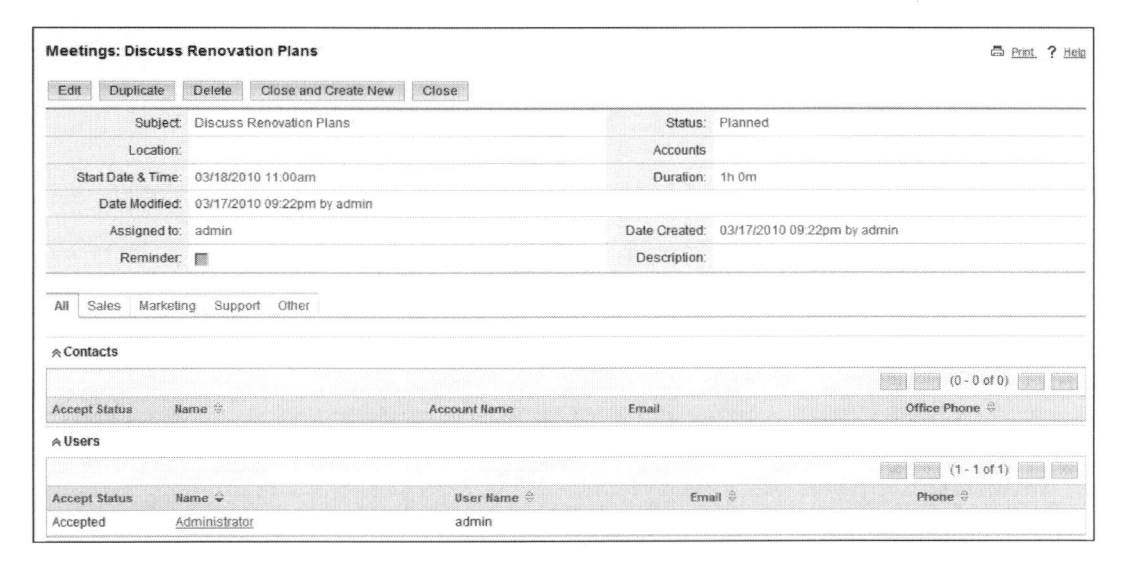

Meetings: Discuss Renovation Plans			Print ? Help
Subject: Discuss Renovation Plans		Status: Planned	
Location:		Accounts	
Start Date & Time: 03/18/2010 11:00am		Duration: 1h 0m	
Date Modified: 03/17/2010 09:22pm by admin			
Assigned to: admin		Date Created: 03/17/2010 09:22pm by admin	
Reminder:		Description:	

All | Sales | Marketing | Support | Other

Contacts

Accept Status	Name	Account Name	Email	Office Phone

(0 - 0 of 0)

Users

Accept Status	Name	User Name	Email	Phone
Accepted	Administrator	admin		

(1 - 1 of 1)

To invite other participants—either employees from your company (defined as *users* within the CRM system) or customers (from contact data within the CRM database)—click on the **Edit** button and scroll down to the **Add Invitees** area at the bottom of the screen. In this case, type Rachel into the first name box, and click on the **Search** button. Your screen should look like the following:

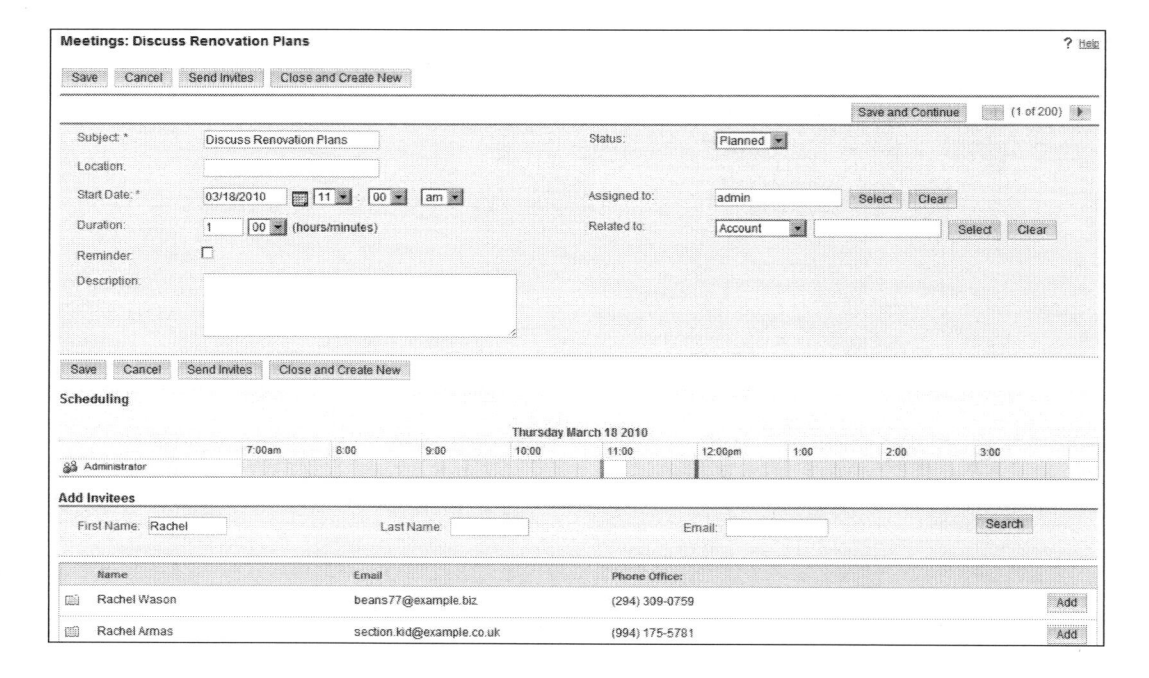

Now just click on the **Add** button to the right of Rachel Wason's name to add her to the list of invitees for the meeting.

Note that a small icon to the left of both **Rachel Wason** and **Rachel Armas** tells you that they are contacts. Users would instead show an icon like the one shown for the administrator in the **Scheduling** section of the screen.

From the meeting's edit view you can add more details to the record of the meeting that were not available on the little pop-up box when you first created it. You can specify an account related to the meeting, adjust the duration of the meeting (it is set to an hour by default), enter a location for the meeting, and add or delete attendees from the list of invitees.

To illustrate some of these capabilities, let us set the meeting duration to 30 minutes, and let's invite **Jorge Grounds** from **Kitty Kat Inc 452275**, while also linking the meeting to the **Kitty Kat Inc 452275** account. When you are done, your Meeting detail view should look like the following:

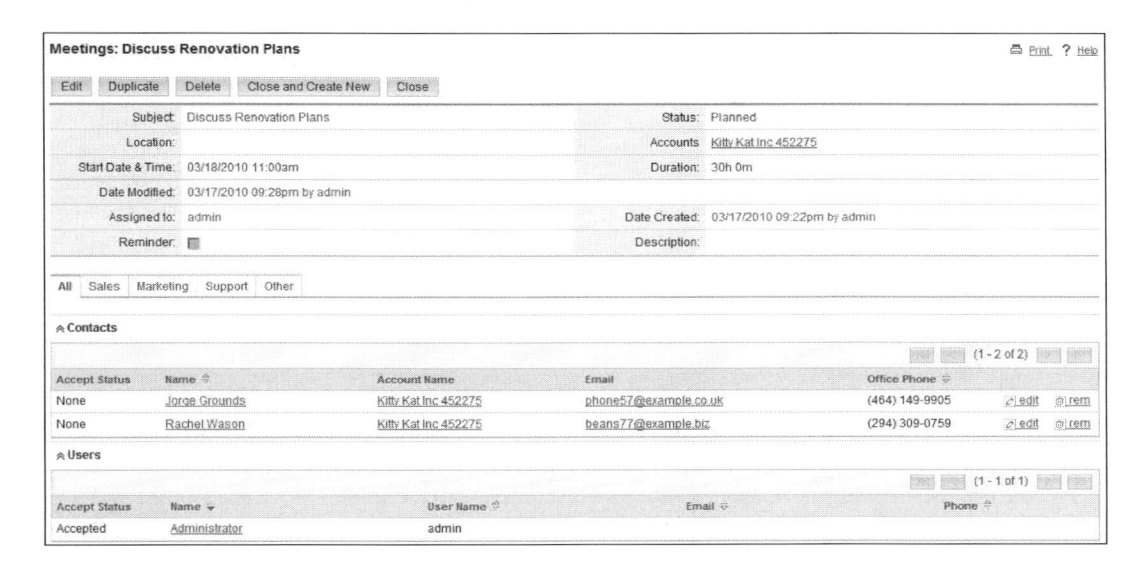

Meetings: Discuss Renovation Plans				Print ? Help
Edit Duplicate Delete Close and Create New Close				
Subject:	Discuss Renovation Plans	Status:	Planned	
Location:		Accounts	Kitty Kat Inc 452275	
Start Date & Time:	03/18/2010 11:00am	Duration:	30h 0m	
Date Modified:	03/17/2010 09:28pm by admin			
Assigned to:	admin	Date Created:	03/17/2010 09:22pm by admin	
Reminder:	☐	Description:		

All Sales Marketing Support Other

▲ Contacts

(1 - 2 of 2)

Accept Status	Name	Account Name	Email	Office Phone		
None	Jorge Grounds	Kitty Kat Inc 452275	phone57@example.co.uk	(464) 149-9905	edit	rem
None	Rachel Wason	Kitty Kat Inc 452275	beans77@example.biz	(294) 309-0759	edit	rem

▲ Users

(1 - 1 of 1)

Accept Status	Name	User Name	Email	Phone
Accepted	Administrator	admin		

Again, the ability of a CRM system to connect all your customer information comes into play here. Click on the link **Kitty Kat Inc 452275** and you will see the detail screen for that account, with a number of open activities including the meeting you have just added. On that activity it shows **Rachel Wason** as a contact. Click on the link to her detail view and you will see the new meeting listed among her open activities. Now click on the subject of that meeting and you are back to the detail view for the meeting.

This gives you an initial overview of the calendaring capabilities within SugarCRM. In the next section we will learn more about the calendar in general, as well as the various activities that users of the system can create and track.

Sales activities

The previous section taught us some of the basics involved in using the calendar. We also learned the process of adding a meeting, but meetings are only one of the five types of activities you track within SugarCRM. The five different types of activities are **Meetings**, **Calls**, **Tasks**, **Notes**, and **E-mails**. Let us now look at these activities in more detail.

SugarCRM Basics

All five types may be created and viewed within the **Activities** tab of the SugarCRM system. Click on the **Activities** tab and take a look at the list of shortcuts available within this module. There are shortcuts to go to the list view for each of the five kinds of activities, or to create an activity of any kind except an e-mail (for which you must go to the **Emails** tab). Note that the calls list view is the default screen you see when you enter the **Activities** tab.

The e-mail activities are something of a special case within SugarCRM, as they have their own tab in addition to their presence within the activities tab. You will notice that when you click on any of the e-mail-related shortcuts, the **Emails** tab lights up to show that you are in the **Emails** module.

In a somewhat similar fashion, you will notice that if you click on any of the call-related or meeting-related shortcuts, the **Calendar** tab lights up to indicate that you are now within the **Calendar** module. So in effect, only tasks and notes are contained completely within the activities module.

Activities are important within a CRM system for two different reasons. Firstly, they help everyone maintain their schedule of activities and issue reminders for them. The **Home** tab makes a point of highlighting **My Upcoming Appointments** and **My Open Tasks**, to further underscore this point.

Secondly, it is very important that each user's activities be scheduled within the CRM system (as opposed to Outlook or others). This will ensure that everyone in the organization is aware of the upcoming and past activities relating to your potential and current customers. This activity history is vital to assist sales managers and general managers, as well as any sales personnel who inherit accounts from a previous sales person. It will help them quickly gain a comprehensive understanding of the status of any account.

Let us look at the activities for **Kitty Kat Inc 452275** in greater detail. Click on the last viewed entry for this account to get you there quickly—or click on the **Account** tab and then look them up. The top part of the screen should resemble the following:

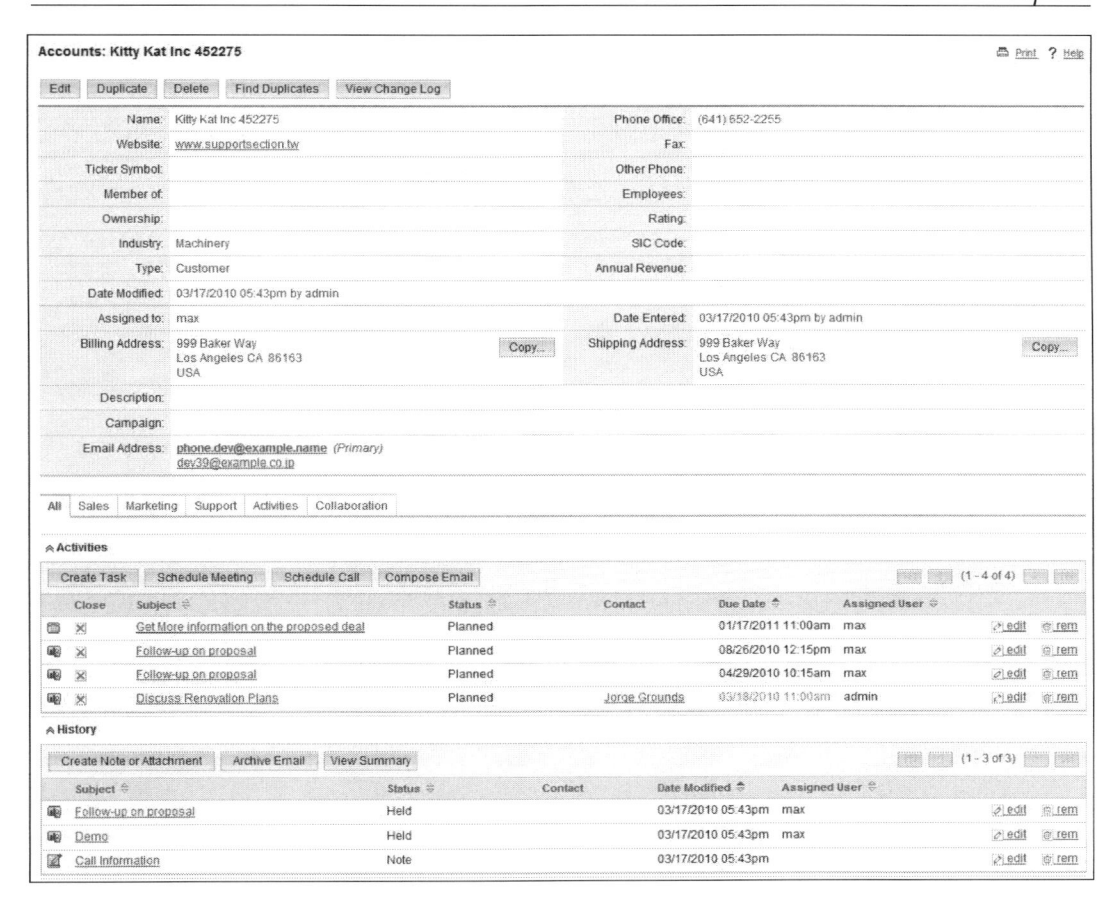

Accounts: Kitty Kat Inc 452275				Print ? Help
Edit Duplicate Delete Find Duplicates View Change Log				
Name:	Kitty Kat Inc 452275	Phone Office:	(641) 652-2255	
Website:	www.supportsection.tw	Fax:		
Ticker Symbol:		Other Phone:		
Member of:		Employees:		
Ownership:		Rating:		
Industry:	Machinery	SIC Code:		
Type:	Customer	Annual Revenue:		
Date Modified:	03/17/2010 05:43pm by admin			
Assigned to:	max	Date Entered:	03/17/2010 05:43pm by admin	
Billing Address:	999 Baker Way Los Angeles CA 86163 USA	Copy... Shipping Address:	999 Baker Way Los Angeles CA 86163 USA	Copy...
Description:				
Campaign:				
Email Address:	phone.dev@example.name (Primary) dev39@example.co.jp			

All | Sales | Marketing | Support | Activities | Collaboration

Activities

Create Task | Schedule Meeting | Schedule Call | Compose Email   (1 - 4 of 4)

Close	Subject	Status	Contact	Due Date	Assigned User	
X	Get More information on the proposed deal	Planned		01/17/2011 11:00am	max	edit rem
X	Follow-up on proposal	Planned		08/26/2010 12:15pm	max	edit rem
X	Follow-up on proposal	Planned		04/29/2010 10:15am	max	edit rem
X	Discuss Renovation Plans	Planned	Jorge Grounds	03/18/2010 11:00am	admin	edit rem

History

Create Note or Attachment | Archive Email | View Summary   (1 - 3 of 3)

Subject	Status	Contact	Date Modified	Assigned User	
Follow-up on proposal	Held		03/17/2010 05:43pm	max	edit rem
Demo	Held		03/17/2010 05:43pm	max	edit rem
Call Information	Note		03/17/2010 05:43pm		edit rem

Each activity has a small icon to the left showing whether it is a meeting, call, note, e-mail, or task. In the **Activities** subpanel, you will only see meetings, calls, and tasks. The **Activities** section represents items that are pending or yet to be performed. E-mails and notes, as well as closed meetings, calls, and tasks, are all listed under the **History** subpanel. They represent items that have already occurred.

The meeting we scheduled earlier is listed as a pending activity with **Rachel Wason** linked to it and a status of **Planned**. To illustrate how account history works, let us pretend that we have held that meeting.

To denote this, you would click on the close box for that meeting—shown as an **X**. Doing so allows you to edit the meeting where you can add notes pertaining to the meeting and adjust other values, such as the duration, if necessary. Once you are done, click on **Save**. Now the meeting is shown under the **History** subpanel, with a **Held Status**. A diligent use of this functionality will allow you to quickly build intelligence about your potential and current customers, all within an easy to access system.

SugarCRM Basics

Creating a note

Let us explore some more types of activities, starting with notes. Imagine that when we met with Kitty Kat Inc 452275 they discussed a significant renovation of their premises, including new doors, windows, and carpets. Rachel Wason actually went through a PowerPoint presentation of the renovations that had artist drawings of the resulting building, a breakdown of the numbers, sizes of new doors and windows, and square footage of the new carpets needed. To make sure that anyone who is in contact with this account has access to this detailed information, let us make a note on the detail view of this account. We will also attach the PowerPoint file.

In the **History** subpanel, click on the **Create Note or Attachment** button. Notice the **Account Name** is pre-filled. Select the appropriate contact; enter a subject for the note and some descriptive text in the **Note** field. To attach the PowerPoint file, click on the **Browse** button and select the appropriate file. Once you have selected a file, click on the **Save** button. The file will be uploaded, and the note will be saved for all to access through the **History** subpanel on the **Kitty Kat Inc 452275** account detail view screen.

Creating a task

Now that we have had a meeting, and added notes to the account history, we need to create a reminder for ourselves to prepare a quote for Rachel at Kitty Kat Inc 452275. From the Account Detail screen, go to the **Activities** subpanel and click on the **Create Task** button. You will see the Task Edit view, that will look like the following screenshot:

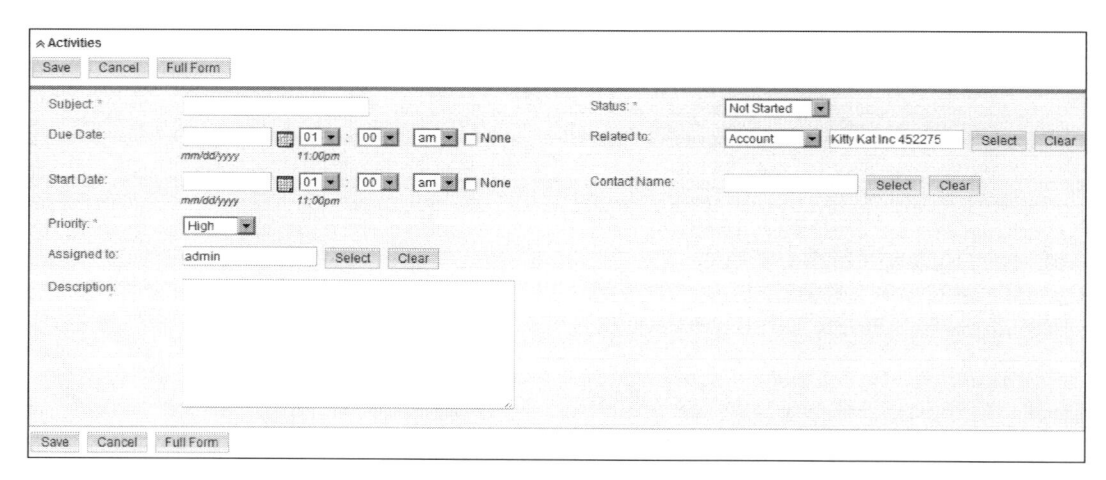

[116]

Type in a **Subject**, then select a **Due Date** and **Time** by clicking off the **None** checkbox at the end of the due date and then selecting a date using the calendar pop-up. You can also set the **Priority** of the task, assign it a **Status** (**Not Started, In Progress, Completed, Pending Input**, or **Deferred**), and enter a **Description** for the task.

Click on the **Save** button once you are done to return to the Account detail view for **Kitty Kat Inc 452275**, with a new task in the **Activities** subpanel. Now click on the **Home** tab and you should see this task listed in your **My Open Tasks** area. You will also notice that if you go to the **Activities** tab and click on **Tasks** in the shortcut bar, you should see all your tasks listed, including this one.

Scheduling a call or meeting

After few days, Doc completes his proposal for Rachel before the due date that he had set for himself. He then marks the task as "completed" and wants to e-mail the proposal to Rachel, and then call her a few days later to follow up. He e-mails the proposal to Rachel (see the section on managing e-mails coming up next), asking her when would be a good time for a call. She replies with an e-mail mentioning the time and date, and Ray needs to book that call into his calendar. He clicks the **Activities** tab, then the **Schedule Call** shortcut. He is presented with a screen like the following:

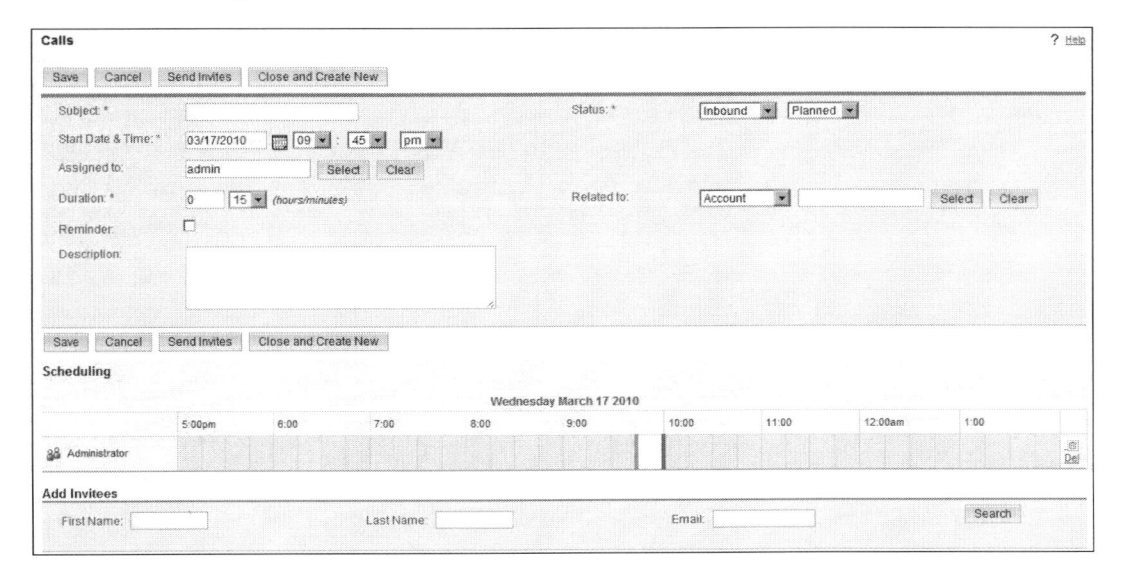

SugarCRM Basics

He starts entering details for the call by typing in a **Subject**, setting a **Date** (using the calendar pop-up) and **Time**, and selecting an **Account**. As he browses the bottom section of the screen, he realizes that he has a problem. The start and stop time for his phone call are marked on the timeline of his day with a dark colored block. Unfortunately, there is a blue segment of his day marking a pre-existing commitment and the proposed time for the new call conflicts with this. This example highlights the manner in which the calendaring system not only helps you manage your activities by providing a way to easily track them, but also by alerting you of potential conflicts in scheduling to avoid double-booking specific time slots. In this case, it provides sufficient warning to prompt Doc to contact Rachel about a new time.

Your CRM system also allows you to book calls and meetings that involve multiple employees and customer contacts. This is accomplished by adding additional individuals as **Invitees** at the bottom of the edit screen for the corresponding activity. To search for and add additional invitees, enter their first or last name to search, then click the **Add** button next to the entry you wish to include. To avoid scheduling conflicts, the free/busy status of any employee entry is displayed in the same way Doc's was displayed.

You may be asking yourself what is the point of adding customers as invitees if you cannot see their calendar of commitments? Doing so will allow you to send them invites through an e-mail by clicking the **Send Invites** button at the top of the edit view. The invite will not only alert the recipient about an activity, but also provide pertinent details, such as the scheduled date and time.

If the recipient happens to have access to the SugarCRM system that sent it, they would also be able to log into the system and accept, tentatively accept, or decline the activity from their respective **Home** tab. Accepting it would automatically put the activity on that user's calendar, while declining it would mark it as declined and not add it to the user's calendar.

Managing e-mails

In the last section, when Doc needed to e-mail Rachel with the proposal, he did so from within SugarCRM. This is because SugarCRM includes its own e-mail client that allows you to send and receive e-mails and automatically links those e-mails to their respective accounts or contacts.

Let us review the process that Doc would have used to send his e-mail. First of all, if it is still visible, click on the **Last Viewed** link for **Rachel Wason** to access its detail view, or look up the contact from within the **Contacts** module.

Within the **Activities** subpanel for that account, locate the **Compose Email** button and click on it. You will see the **Compose Email** screen, that would have looked something like the following in Doc's scenario:

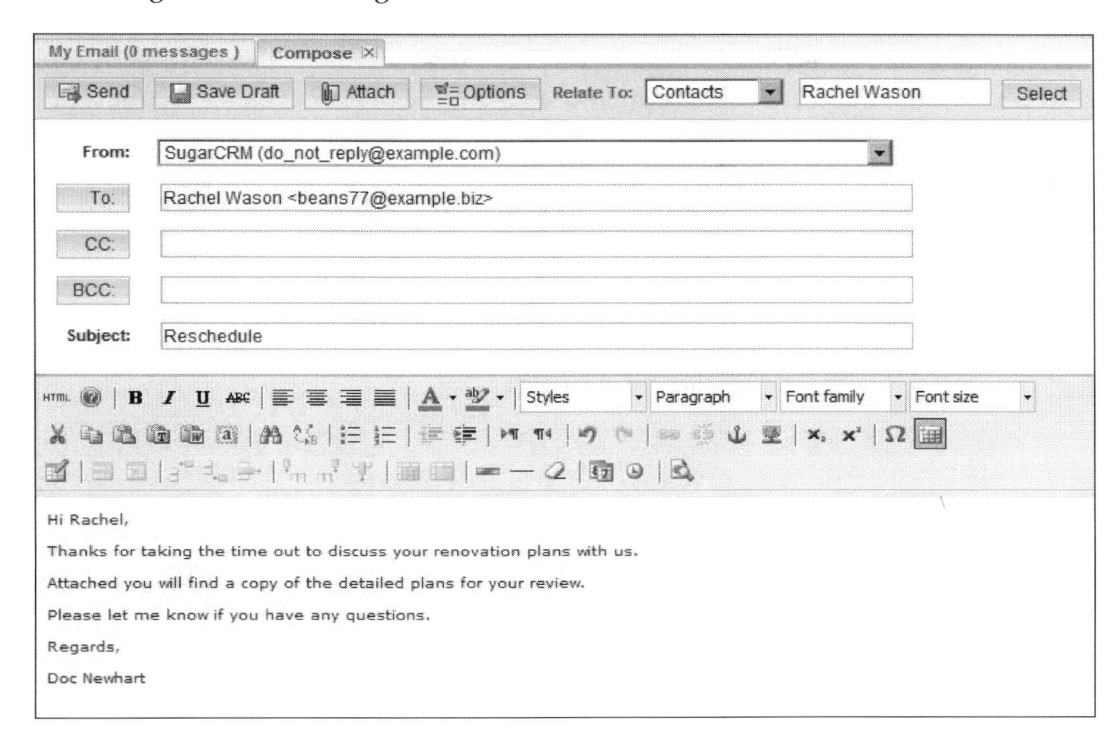

![Compose Email screen showing an email to Rachel Wason with subject "Reschedule" and body text from Doc Newhart regarding renovation plans]

Notice that Doc has used the **Browse** button to attach the proposal to the e-mail. When Doc clicks on the **Send** button to send this e-mail to Rachel, he will get a confirmation that the e-mail has been sent. He can then click back to the **Rachel Wason** contact detail record to see that the sent e-mail is now included in the **History** subpanel, allowing anyone else at RayDoc to see the latest communications.

Let us learn a little more about the e-mail capabilities of SugarCRM. Hover on the **Collaboration** tab and click on the **Emails** link to access the e-mail client.

The e-mail client requires some configuration before it can be used to send or receive e-mails. Email settings can be defined by hovering over the **Activities** tab, selecting **Emails**, and then clicking on the **Settings** button. You will need to know your e-mail server connection information in order to complete the process.

E-mail templates

Email templates can be referenced when composing an e-mail (notice the **Use Templates** field on the **Compose Email** screen in the previous screenshot). When you create an e-mail template, you can insert variable placeholders for information, such as **First Name**, **Last Name**, **Address**, or **Email**. The saved template can then be applied and the variable placeholders are then filled with real data extracted from the linked account or contact record. This is especially helpful in scenarios where the e-mail is intended for one or more individuals, or sent through an e-mailing campaign for bulk marketing (discussed later in this book), as it personalizes each message so the recipient is left with the impression that the conversation is only with them and not just a part of a mass e-mail. The following image demonstrates an e-mail template with some variable placeholders already inserted. Notice its resemblance to the compose e-mail window.

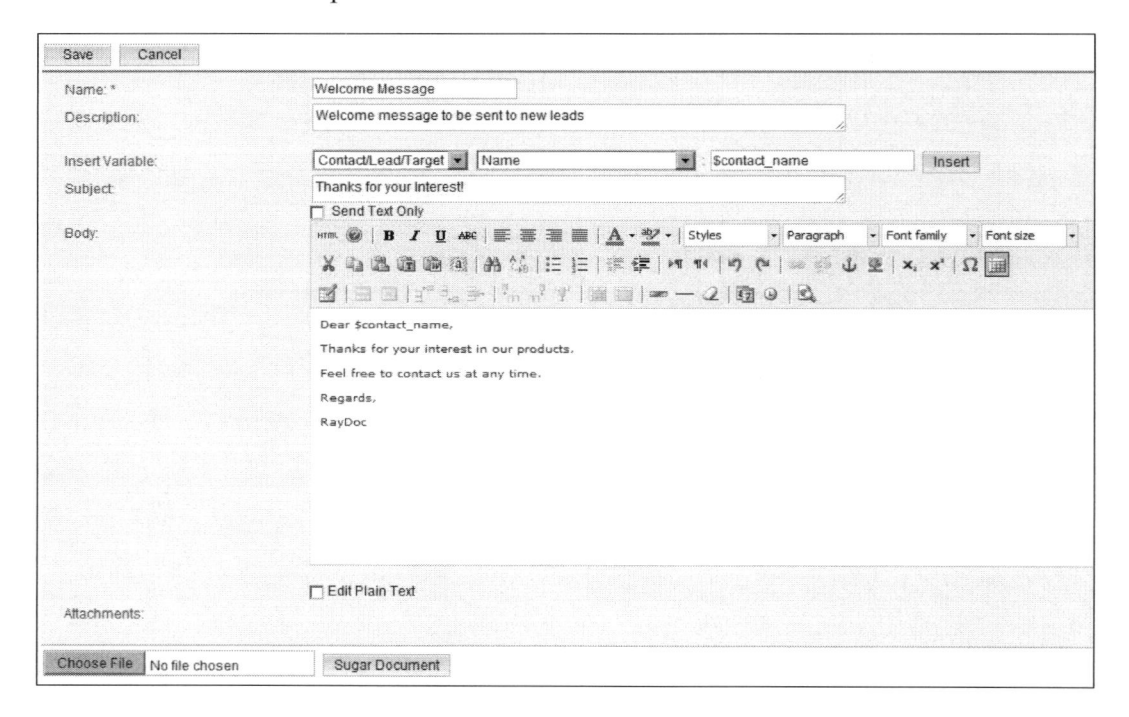

Advanced user-interface features

Before we leave this introductory chapter, we need to address some important SugarCRM user-interface features which include the following:

Printing information

Most of the list and detail view screens in SugarCRM have a **Print** icon at the top right of the main body of the screen. Clicking on this icon changes the screen content to a more printer-friendly version of the same information that you can then print by using your browser's **Print** button. The following image shows an **Account List** view screen transformed for printing:

Account Name	City	Phone	User
RayDoc		(310) 555-1212	admin
SPAR Aerospace		(562) 555-1313	admin
MMM Mortuary Corp 527118	Kansas City	(488) 317-8179	chris
BS Funding Coop 907660	Kansas City	(120) 905-7588	chris
NW Bridge Construction 23984	Los Angeles	(239) 740-1196	chris
A.G. Parr PLC 327537	San Francisco	(178) 413-8984	chris
Powder Puff Suppliers 191582	St. Petersburg	(665) 780-5793	chris
X-SELL HOLDINGS 774114	Cupertino	(176) 316-0894	chris
K Kringle IncK.A. Tower & Co 389028	San Mateo	(891) 224-7866	chris
3rd Round Funding 293847	Salt Lake City	(174) 175-8694	chris
TJ O'Rourke Inc 219021	Santa Monica	(583) 087-0023	chris
Kitty Kat Inc 452275	Los Angeles	(641) 652-2255	max
B.C. Investing International 504338	Alabama	(698) 003-3680	max
Grow-Fast Inc 662443	Salt Lake City	(885) 407-2250	max
A.B Hammer Group Inc 132186	San Jose	(954) 280-7273	max
CUMBERLAND TRAILS 626770	Santa Fe	(477) 740-2844	max
2 Tall Stores 889459	Sunnyvale	(777) 938-4849	max
CONS TRUST (AZ) 817814	San Francisco	(149) 916-3250	max
Itty-Bitty Conglomerate Inc 548773	Santa Monica	(389) 558-9509	max
First National S/B 909917	Alabama	(613) 361-5997	max

Getting help

As with the **Print** icon, most SugarCRM list and detail view screens contain a **Help** icon at the top right of the main screen body. Clicking on the **Help** icon will cause the system to display context-sensitive help, similar to the following:

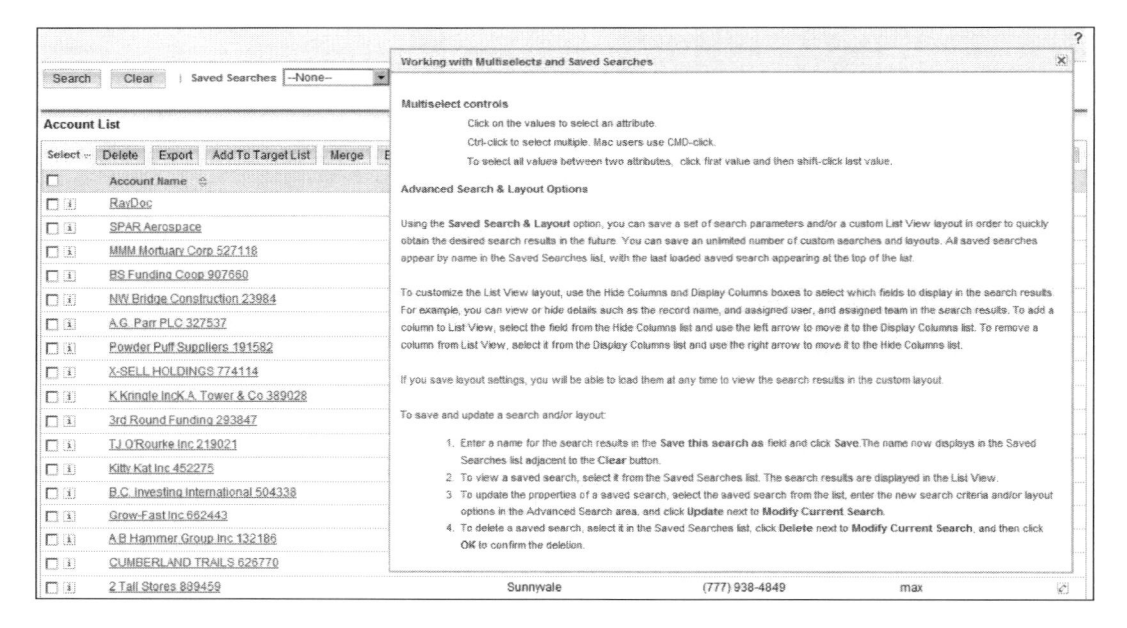

It is not intended as a tutor, but does provide useful information pertaining to the current area of the system in which you are working.

Exporting information

Essentially, all list view screens within SugarCRM have a highlighted **Export** link at the top left and bottom left corners of the list of entries. This feature allows you to export records from the current list by simply selecting them. To select them, either check the box immediately to the left of the line item or choose one of the options under **Select**.

Once you have made your selections, click on the **Export** link and your information will be output to a **Comma Separated Values (CSV)** format file (that may be easily read by Microsoft Excel). Try it, and open the exported file from your desktop using Excel to see what it contains. Here is a sample result that will look the following screen:

[A spreadsheet table showing exported account data with columns: id, name, date_entered, date_modified, modified_user_id, created_by, description, deleted, assigned_user_id, account_type]

Mass operations

The ability to select records from the list as described in the **Export** example, allows further actions to be performed on the selected items. For example, you can use the **Update** and **Delete** buttons at the bottom of the screen to make mass changes to the records or delete them respectively:

- If we use the **Account List** view screen as an example for an **Update**, multiple accounts could be reassigned to another user, or assigned a new industry classification or type. Simply select the appropriate records in the list, then choose a new account type, such as **Customer**, and lastly, click on the **Update** button. You may change the value on multiple fields simultaneously by simply defining the appropriate values in their corresponding field in the **Mass Update** section of the screen.

- The **Delete** button works under the similar principle, it requires you to select the records you wish to delete before you click on the **Delete** button.

- Note that SugarCRM does not include an undo feature, so you must be careful when you use these features.

Input business card

One of the best-kept secrets in SugarCRM is the **Enter Business Card** shortcut. It is available on the **Home** page and on the **Contacts** module. This feature allows users to enter a new contact, but as seen in the image that follows, it also provides the option to create a new account, opportunity, and follow-up meeting all in the same screen.

SugarCRM Basics

This feature not only reduces the keystrokes required to enter data, but also facilitates the follow-up process. With one simple screen, you are able to enter the individual's information, as well as those of the place they work, and set yourself a reminder to call them to discuss their needs, or chat with them about how you can be of service to them. The business card is shown in the following screenshot:

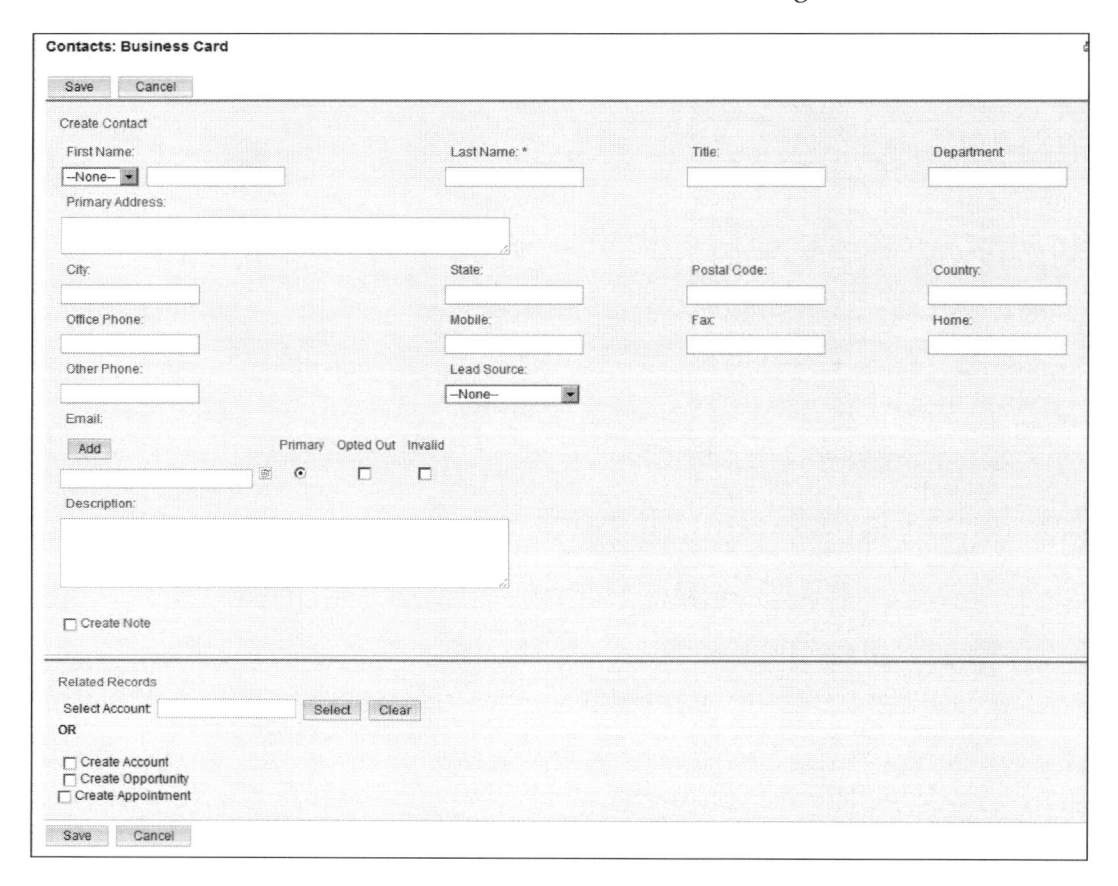

Create from vCard

On the **Contacts** tab there is a shortcut called **Create from vCard**. This feature lets you create a contact quickly if you already have a vCard file available from your contact. Many people these days tend to attach a vCard with their e-mails, so this can be a really quick and handy form of data entry for new contacts.

If you have the vCard for a new contact on your desktop, for example, just click on the **Create from vCard** shortcut and you will see the screen as shown in the following screenshot. Then click on the **Browse** button, and use the dialog box that appears to find the vCard that you want and select it. Lastly, click on the **Import vCard** button and you are done.

Quick new item

Almost every module in SugarCRM has a **Quick New Item** box on the lower left side of the list view screen. This box will vary according to the module or tab you are in, and will allow you to create a new item corresponding to the currently selected module. For example, clicking on **Contacts** would present the contacts list view and the **Quick New Item** box for creating a new contact entry.

It does not contain all the fields that it is possible to include for the new item, but it does have all the mandatory fields, allowing you to quickly add a new entry.

Summary

In this chapter, we covered the basics of using a CRM system, such as entering information into the system, and navigating quickly through the links between related items of information. Some of the key topics we covered include the following:

- How to access the CRM system. How to use different themes to brighten up the user interface and the major components of the screen layout.
- How to navigate through the CRM system, use the different module tabs and discuss the list, detail, and edit view screens for each module.
- How to enter accounts and contacts, and the links between them.
- What the structure of a main panel and related subpanels of information on each detail view screen looks like.
- How Leads become Opportunities and how Opportunities are aggregated to form the sales pipeline.

- How Dashboard helps you visually interpret your sales pipeline, breaks it down by month and by sales person, and provides a distant early warning system for business upturns and downturns.

- How to use the SugarCRM calendar to plan your business days, check for schedule conflicts and discuss your colleague's calendars.

- How to enter business activities within SugarCRM and the value of accumulating activity history for all your accounts and contacts.

- How a number of special user-interface features increase the speed of the data entry process and ease the execution of several common tasks.

In the next chapter, we will complete the exploration of how SugarCRM delivers on comprehensive CRM functionalities by dealing with the more advanced CRM topics, such as *Interface Consolidation, Project Management, Document Management, Customer Service Management*, and other topics. We will also erase the sample data from the CRM, import your own data, and then explore more advanced ways in which CRM systems can assume a broader role within your business.

5
Extending The Business Role of Your SugarCRM System

In the last chapter, we introduced the CRM basics of accounts, contacts, leads, opportunities, the sales pipeline, as well as the use of a consolidated calendar.

In this chapter, we deal with the expansion of the role of your CRM system within your business, beyond that of basic CRM functions. We will cover a number of other related applications that are most commonly found in modern CRM systems. These applications are frequently added to a CRM system to take advantage of the fact that the CRM system is used by most people at a company and already contains all the information about the customers, partners, and suppliers of the business.

These advanced CRM topics include the following:

- Removing sample data: Resetting the database to eliminate the default data
- Marketing campaigns: Creating and running e-mail marketing campaigns

Resetting the database

To start off this chapter, let's first get rid of the sample data in your SugarCRM installation so that it can receive your data. This exercise will help you get familiar with the process of importing data that you are likely to find quite helpful in the future as your use of SugarCRM grows.

The quickest way to clear out the sample data is to re-install SugarCRM. Note that this step is only necessary for the purposes of completely purging all the sample data. It is *not* a requirement for a successful import. Our main goal is to reset the database to a state where it no longer has any data.

Our first step will be to re-enable the SugarCRM installer, which in turn will allow us to easily eliminate the sample data. To re-enable the installer, navigate to the SugarCRM installation folder and edit the `config.php` file using your text editor of choice. Locate the line that reads as follows:

```
'installer_locked' => true,
```

change it to:

```
'installer_locked' => false,
```

Save the changes, open up your web browser. Assuming you followed the instruction in Appendix A or Appendix B to initially install SugarCRM, you should be able to once again launch the installer by browsing `http://<ip address of server>/sugarcrm/install.php`.

Proceed through the installation wizard as normal, but take care when you reach the page prompting you for the database information. Make sure you enter the *same* database name that you used while installing the sample data for the **Database Name** field. Before clicking on **Next**, enter any additional values you may need to connect to your database server, such as **Database Administrator Username**, and then verify that **Populate Database with Demo Data?** is set to **No**. Click **I Accept** to confirm that you wish to overwrite the database and continue with the remainder of the installation process until you have finished. The next time you access this installation of SugarCRM, it should be free of any sample data.

Now read through *Appendix C* and import your account and contact data into the SugarCRM system. The *Appendix* also gives you instructions for exporting your account and contact data from your current contact manager (using Microsoft Outlook as an example), should you need assistance. If you like, you can also import leads and opportunities into SugarCRM from Salesforce.com, or from a custom comma or tab-delimited file. Once you have imported your own account and contact data, feel free to start adding opportunities as well, so that the dashboard begins to reflect the true state of your business.

Marketing campaigns

So far, we have seen how a CRM system, such as SugarCRM, can be used for managing customer-related information and history, as well as tracking opportunities, and a sales pipeline. Now, let's begin to explore some marketing automation aspects and other functionality that make CRM systems a data hub for many businesses. Let's start with e-mail marketing.

A particularly powerful and potentially profitable aspect of a CRM system is the ability to conduct e-mail marketing campaigns. CRM systems contain all the necessary tools for creating effective e-mail marketing campaigns; they track your leads and contacts, and include e-mail sending capabilities within their feature set. Let us study an e-mail marketing campaign in detail.

To illustrate how a marketing campaign is developed, managed, performed, and then tracked for success, we will develop a sample marketing campaign for RayDoc. You may wish to develop one for your own business in parallel, while you follow the example in this book.

Targets, leads and contacts

To start, we will need to discuss some related terminology. A new type of information is involved in creating a marketing campaign—the **Target**. Following are some of the important points relating to targets and their relationship with leads and contacts:

- Targets feed into a marketing campaign. Targets can come from rented lists, web registration forms, trade shows, your leads, or your contacts. You may or may not have an existing business relationship with the person. For our example, we will assume that you have created an e-mail campaign called *My July E-mail Campaign* whose recipient list sums up to 12,000 targets, made up of 10,000 e-mail addresses you purchased, and a subset of your contact list, totaling 2,000 entries.

- Leads are the result of a campaign. They are people who respond to a campaign, but are not necessarily people who have bought your products yet. A campaign can be an *ongoing* inbound campaign like your standard website registration form. Alternatively, the campaign could be an outbound e-mail campaign. Let's say you get 200 people who followed the link to the special website registration form for your *My July E-mail Campaign*, completed, and submitted the form. These 200 people are now leads inside of SugarCRM. They should be tagged with a lead source value of *My July E-mail Campaign*, to properly track your campaign's effectiveness at generating leads.

- Now you start a lead qualification process by analyzing the information you collected about these leads. You find that 50 of these leads fit your target qualification criteria. You now assign these 50 leads to the appropriate sales people.

- The sales people then attempt to contact the leads and initiate a selling process. Let us say Doc speaks to one of these leads and the lead expresses an interest in knowing more about the product. Doc will now convert this lead into a contact and create an opportunity.

Extending The Business Role of Your SugarCRM System

To summarize, targets feed into campaigns, leads are the results of campaigns and contacts are the qualified leads who are interested in buying or have bought your products. Future campaigns can in turn leverage those same records to generate additional contacts, leads, and identify further up-sell or cross-sell opportunities.

Now that you understand the theory, let us get some practice. Hover over the **Marketing** tab and click on **Campaigns** to access the Campaigns module.

In SugarCRM, you create a marketing campaign to manage the sending of bulk e-mails and its recipients, or targets. You can add targets to the target list for a campaign either by selecting them from contacts or leads, or by importing them in bulk from either *Comma Separated Values* (CSV) or *Tab Separated Values* (TSV) files. We will look at this part of the process a bit later in this chapter. Let us start by creating a campaign for RayDoc.

Doc has just started to get a supply of a new type of laminate wood flooring called Superflor that he is excited about. It has an excellent look and manufacturing quality to it, comes from one of his key suppliers, and he gets it at a very competitive price. He wants to get word out on it and get some early sales to show to his supplier.

You must define your e-mail settings before attempting to define a campaign; otherwise you will find that the process of creating a campaign cannot be completed. To define your e-mail settings, click on **Admin | Inbound Email | New Bounce Handling Account** and you see a screen similar to the following:

Enter **Marketing** for the **Name**, and then provide the settings corresponding with the e-mail account you wish to use in the remaining fields and proceed to click **Save**.

Once you have finished defining your e-mail account settings, you can create the Superflor marketing campaign. To create it, hover on the **Marketing** tab and click on **Campaigns**. Next, click on the **Campaign Wizard** shortcut. You will notice that you have three choices, namely, **Newsletter**, **Email**, and **Non-email based Campaign**, as illustrated in the following image:

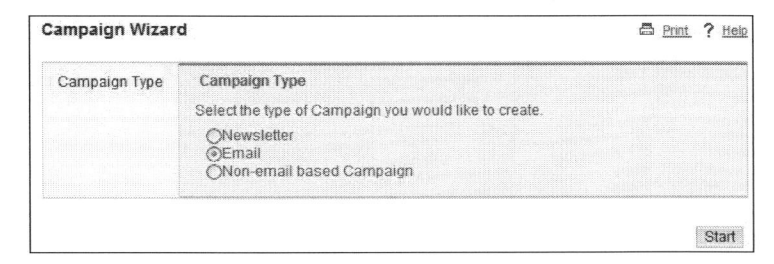

Note that from the three options, SugarCRM has the ability to automatically track metrics only for the **Newsletter** and **Email** options. The **Non-email based Campaign** option relies entirely on manual input in order to measure the effectiveness.

In addition, there is a subtle difference between Newsletter and Email campaigns. The former is intended for periodic messaging. For example, when a company gives updates to their customers monthly. The latter is intended for bulk e-mail marketing campaigns, such as a quarterly promotion.

Lastly, they differ from each other in the way they handle unsubscribe requests. A recipient that unsubscribes from a Newsletter is removed as a recipient of the specific Newsletter campaign that included them as a recipient. However, a recipient that unsubscribes from an Email campaign is instead marked as having opted-out from *all* bulk e-mail activities. For our example, choose **Email** and click **Start**. You are now presented with the following screen:

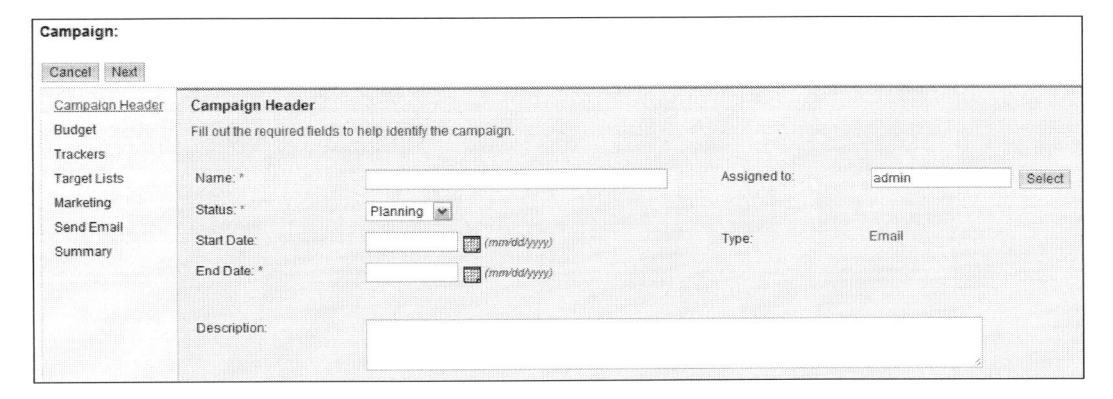

[131]

Extending The Business Role of Your SugarCRM System

Enter the following information to define the Campaign:

Name: Superflor

Status: Active

Start Date: Today's date

End Date: A month from today

Click on **Next** once you have entered the given values. You should now be presented with the following screen, where you can enter financial information relating to the campaign:

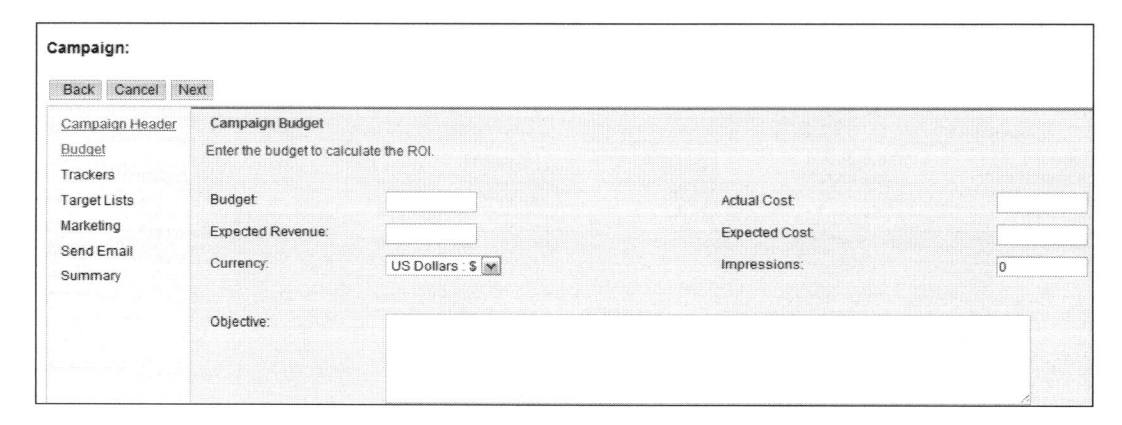

This is helpful for your later metrics, as it will allow you to properly gauge the cost of each lead that you obtain from the campaign. Once you have entered the information, click on **Next** to access the **Campaign Tracker URLs** screen, similar to the following:

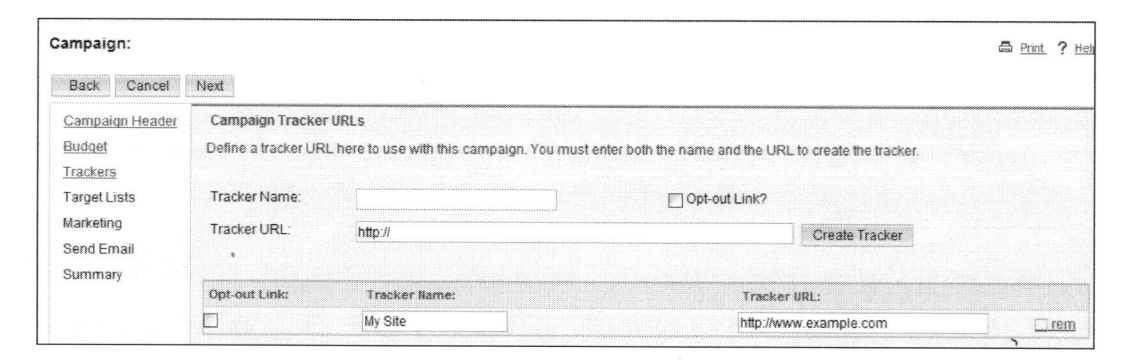

Tracker URLs are used to measure your click-throughs, or the number of times a recipient visits a page on your web site. It is an effective tool that monitors the number of recipients who visit specific pages on your website.

A Tracker URL is composed of two parts: the first is a descriptor of your choice and the second part is the website address. The address represents a page on your website where a recipient of the e-mail sent through the campaign can obtain more information about a specific product or service that you are promoting. The name is derived from the fact that SugarCRM automatically tracks the number of times the page is visited by means of a click-through on the e-mail that contained it.

Our campaign will include one Tracker URL entry with the following information:

- **Tracker Name:** `My Site`
- **Tracker URL:** `http://(your company's website address)`

Click on the **Create Tracker** button once you have entered the given information. You must have noticed the **Opt-out Link?** check box to the right of the **Tracker Name** field. Checking it would allow you to define the link as an unsubscribe link. If a recipient clicks on it, the recipient's e-mail address is automatically marked as having opted out from all e-mail communications.

Click on **Next** to proceed, and you will be asked to provide a target list containing the intended recipients of an e-mail as shown in the following screenshot:

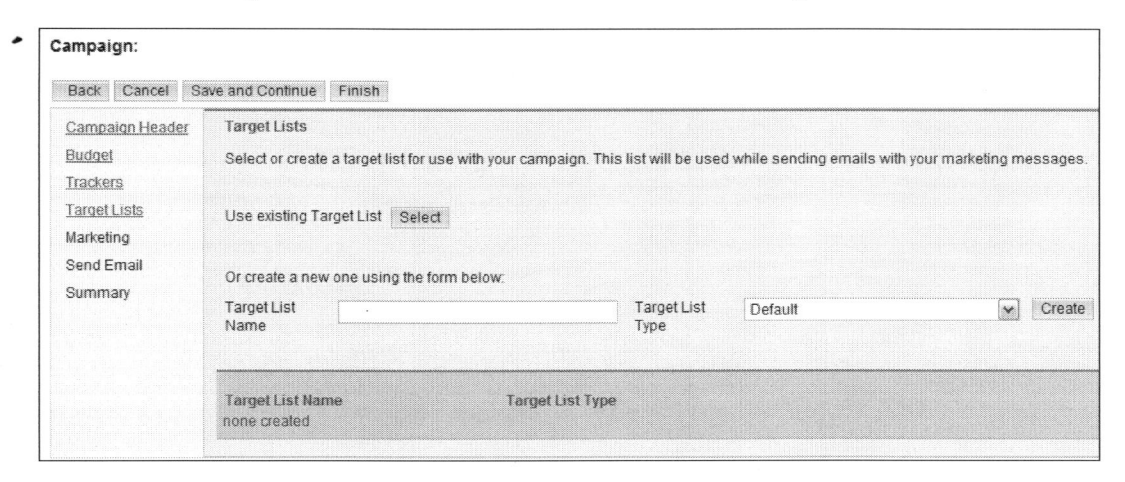

As we have not yet created a target list, we will define an empty one. Enter `Superflor Target` for the **Target List Name** and click on **Create**. Instructions on populating the target list with recipients will be provided shortly within this chapter.

Click on **Save and Continue** to access the **Marketing Email** definition screen. Enter `Superflor Intro` in the **Name** field, and define the rest of the values as illustrated in the following screenshot:

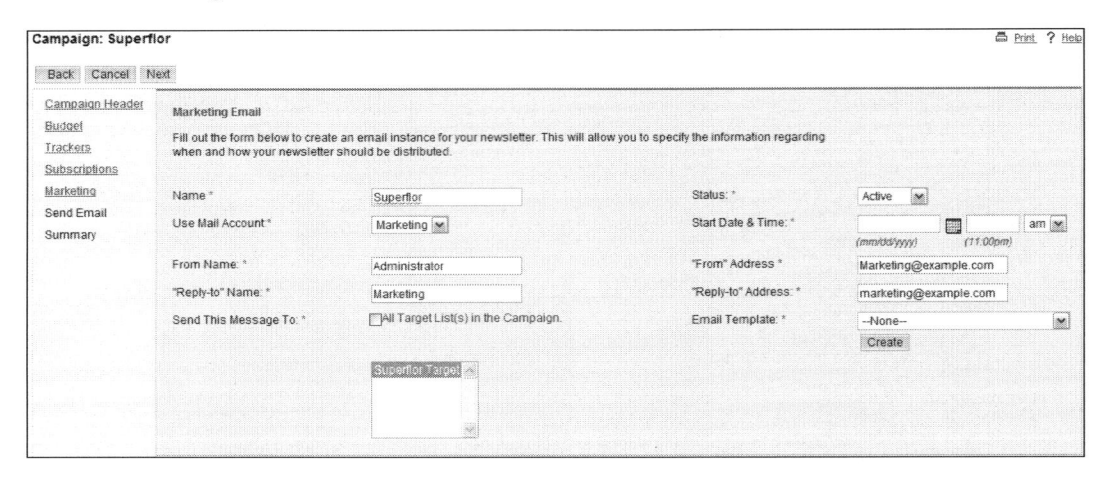

Assuming that you have defined your e-mail account as described earlier in this section, you should be able to select **Marketing** for the **User Mail Account** setting. Select it, set **Status** to **Active**, and enter the current date and time for **Start Date & Time**.

Notice that **Email Template** is not yet defined and the drop-down only demonstrates the options for system defined templates. The following section will cover the process of creating an e-mail template for use within our campaign.

Creating an e-mail template

To execute an e-mail marketing campaign, Doc will need an e-mail template. To create it while defining the campaign, click on the **Create** button on the **Marketing Email** screen. Alternatively, if you wish to create a template at any other time, you can do so by hovering over the **Collaboration** tab, clicking on **Emails**, and then selecting the **Create Email Template** shortcut. The following screen then appears:

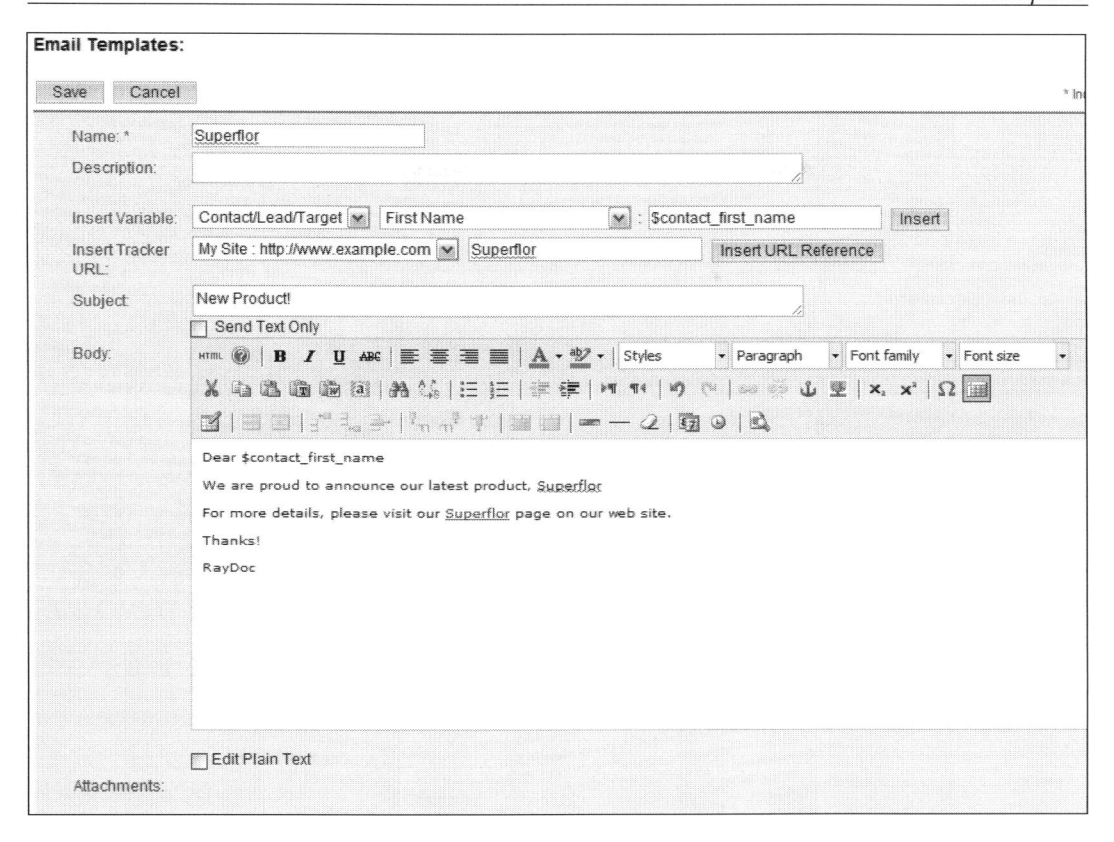

Proceed to enter some text into the body of the message. If you wish to embed fields from SugarCRM, use the **Insert Variable** options to embed it at the cursor's current location, as demonstrated in the preceding screenshot—immediately following **Dear** within the body of the message. The **Insert Tracker URL** option allows you to add the tracker links that are in turn used to measure your click-throughs. To insert it, select the desired Tracker URL from the drop-down menu and enter the desired text for the link. In this example, the text **Superflor** has been used. Clicking on **Insert URL Reference** will then insert a link with the provided text at the cursor's current location.

Click on **Save** once you are satisfied with your message, and click on **Next** to proceed to the next stage of the campaign definition. You will be prompted to send the e-mail or simply finish. Click on the **Finish** button.

Adding targets to the campaign

Now we need to add some targets to this e-mail marketing campaign. We will be adding them to the test target list that we defined earlier in the chapter. While on the detail view for the campaign, click on the **Superflor Target** in the **Target Lists** section of the campaign summary screen as shown in the following screenshot:

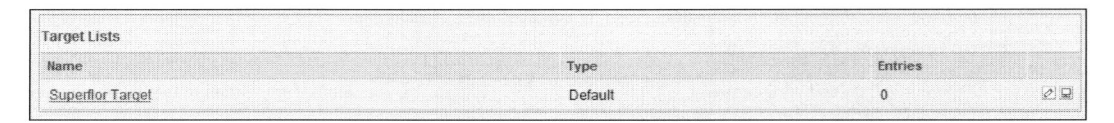

Target Lists		
Name	Type	Entries
Superflor Target	Default	0

Next, you need to select some targets to the **Superflor Targets** list. To add them, click on the **Select** button for **Targets**, **Contacts**, **Leads**, or **Users** to choose the appropriate entries. Once you have finished making your selections, your **Superflor Target** list should resemble the following image:

[136]

Now that we have selected some targets (in practice, of course, you would select many more) we can send our e-mails. For example, hover on the **Marketing** tab and click on **Campaigns** to choose the **Superflor**, and then click on the **Send Emails** button at the top. You will be prompted to select a target list of recipients. Only those target lists that are associated with the campaign will be displayed. Check the box next to the **Superflor** entry and click on **Send** to send the e-mail as shown in the following screenshot. If your future campaigns include multiple target lists, you can choose as many of them as you like when you send the e-mails.

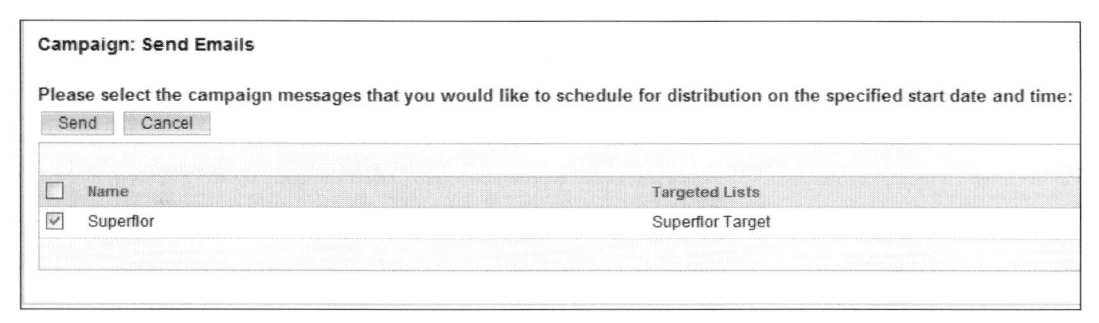

Campaign: Send Emails

Please select the campaign messages that you would like to schedule for distribution on the specified start date and time:

Send   Cancel

Name	Targeted Lists
Superflor	Superflor Target

The labeling on the **Send** button can be a bit misleading. In reality, the e-mails are being placed in a queue instead of being immediately delivered. The queue must be processed by SugarCRM in order for the e-mails to be delivered. The following section discusses the e-mail queue in greater detail.

The mass e-mailing queue

Now that we have successfully configured the various components that comprise an e-mail marketing campaign and placed them into the queue, the question that arises is, how do we actually deliver these e-mails?

Assuming that your SugarCRM *Scheduler* is configured and running, the system will automatically process the queue when the day and time that is defined within the e-mail marketing campaign is reached. If you have administrative access to the system, look in the **Mass Email Manager** section within the **Admin** control panel and you will see the various e-mails in the queue.

Another method for checking your e-mail queue is to click on the **View Status** button on the detail view screen of a given campaign. The relevant section is illustrated in the following image:

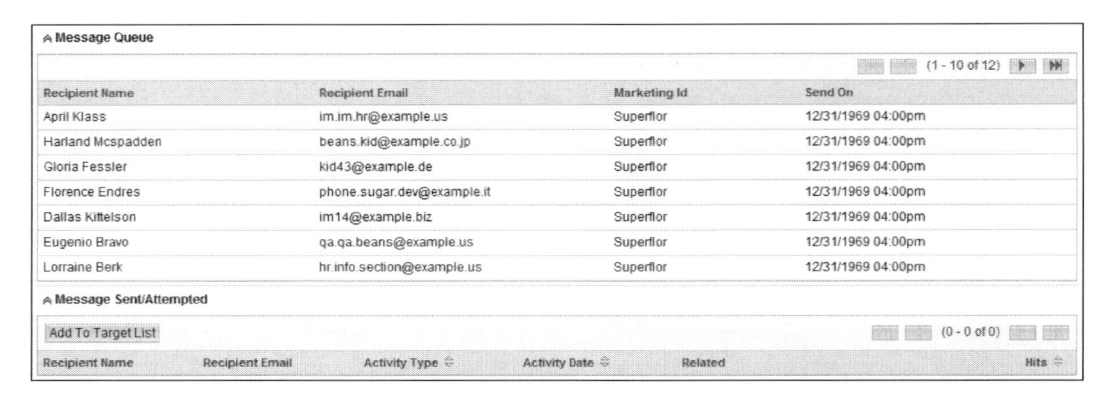

Recipient Name	Recipient Email	Marketing Id	Send On
April Klass	im.im.hr@example.us	Superflor	12/31/1969 04:00pm
Harland Mcspadden	beans.kid@example.co.jp	Superflor	12/31/1969 04:00pm
Gloria Fessler	kid43@example.de	Superflor	12/31/1969 04:00pm
Florence Endres	phone.sugar.dev@example.it	Superflor	12/31/1969 04:00pm
Dallas Kittelson	im14@example.biz	Superflor	12/31/1969 04:00pm
Eugenio Bravo	qa.qa.beans@example.us	Superflor	12/31/1969 04:00pm
Lorraine Berk	hr.info.section@example.us	Superflor	12/31/1969 04:00pm

Message Sent/Attempted

Add To Target List

Recipient Name	Recipient Email	Activity Type	Activity Date	Related	Hits

A closer look at the image reveals that there are two important sections, namely, the **Message Queue** and **Messages Sent/Attempted**. The **Message Queue** displays the messages that are to be sent. More importantly, the latter sections shows the messages that have been sent.

Of course, this assumes that the previously configured e-mail settings are operating correctly. Examining the **Messages Sent/Attempted** section will reveal potential issues that are related to the send process. If you notice any entry within this section that is marked as **Failed**, verify your system e-mail server settings by clicking on **Admin | Email Settings**.

Some common reasons for such problems include the following:

- Incorrect **Simple Mail Transfer Protocol (SMTP)** mail server address
- Mistyped SMTP username or password
- Missing PHP libraries, such as **Internet Message Access Protocol (IMAP)** or **Secure Socket Layer (SSL)**

If you are using a hosted version of SugarCRM, you may have a limited set of tools at your disposal for troubleshooting. However, one good way of testing the process is to use the **telnet** tool to manually connect to your mail server from your SugarCRM server, and manually issue the relevant SMTP commands for sending a message. If the manual process fails, SugarCRM will also fail.

Detailed steps on mimicking the behavior through telnet will vary depending on your setup, however, information about performing these steps is easily available on the internet.

Campaign metrics

After the e-mails have been sent, you can monitor the effectiveness of the campaign by accessing the campaign's detail view screen and again clicking on the **View Status** button. In addition to seeing the number of e-mails still in the queue, you will also see the number of recipients who have read your e-mail, the number of click-throughs (and which URL they visited), the number of recipients who have opted-out, and other details as shown in the following screenshot:

Although not shown in the preceding image, the status screen also tracks the number of accounts, leads, and opportunities generated by your campaign. This measurement is based on the Campaign value of said records matching the currently examined campaign.

Lastly, if you click on the **View ROI** button on the campaign's detail view screen, you will be able to see the financial information relating to the campaign, as shown in the following screenshot:

Name:	Superflor	Assigned to:	admin
Status:	Active		
Start Date:	06/27/2010	Last Modified:	06/27/2010 05:50pm by admin
End Date:	07/27/2010	Date Created:	06/27/2010 05:50pm by admin
Type:	Email		
Budget: (USD $)		Impressions:	0
Expected Cost: (USD $)		Opportunities Won:	0
Actual Cost: (USD $)		Cost Per Impression: (USD $)	$0.00
Expected Revenue: (USD $)		Cost Per Click Through: (USD $)	$0.00

Among other information, you will also be able to see the cost of every click-through and impression. These tools allow you to better gauge the campaigns that are most cost-effective.

Summary

In this chapter, we covered advanced marketing automation aspects of SugarCRM that extend the role of your CRM system beyond the narrow confines of pure CRM functions into a somewhat broader tool for attracting new customers. Some of the key topics discussed in this chapter include the following:

- Getting rid of the sample data we experimented with at first and importing your live data
- Marketing Campaigns: How to create e-mail templates that enable each target to get a personalized e-mail, how to assemble lists of targets for e-mail marketing programs, how to control the mass e-mail queue within SugarCRM, and how to track the *click-through* rate of success of an e-mail campaign automatically

In *Chapter 6*, we will complete our exploration of the capabilities of the SugarCRM software by working through a number of business scenarios using additional features, customization tools and techniques, as well as features of other SugarCRM commercial and open source add-on modules.

We will see more examples of various CRM system capabilities that facilitate business needs, such as customer service, project management, and other business needs. After exploring the additional CRM modules available in the commercial Sugar Professional product or elsewhere, you will know that there are few limits to the business management abilities that can be or have been integrated into the SugarCRM framework.

6
The SugarCRM Ecosystem

In the previous two chapters, you have read about the basic CRM functions provided by the SugarCRM system. We have also seen a number of extended capabilities the standard system can perform that take it beyond pure CRM, into a broader business management role.

SugarCRM is supported not only by SugarCRM, the company, but also by a large community of fellow users throughout the world. Many of these individuals are also contributors, as they offer solutions to problems that others may be encountering. This may be in the form of an answer to a technical query or in other cases, they are corrections or enhancements to the system.

While many of these community members offer open source or free editions of the add-ons that they have developed, some are only available for a fee. SugarCRM, the company, provides two places for you to easily locate these contributions. The first, SugarForge.org, contains a wide assortment of enhancements and add-ons of which the vast majority are either free to use and/or open source. A complementary site, SugarExchange.com, is primarily used to maintain a catalog of commercial add-ons and enhancements.

In this chapter, we will explore a number of free add-ons for SugarCRM Community Edition that can extend it even further in a myriad of directions. Along the way we will also take a look at the process of using the **Module Loader** tool. These add-ons can be categorized as follows:

- **SugarCRM Community Edition**
    - **Enhanced search**: Earlier in this book, we discussed the search capabilities available in SugarCRM. Although useful, the default capabilities can be rather limiting. This enhancement expands the default capabilities to permit searching on date range, OR conditions, and other possibilities.

- **Google contacts/calendar connectors**: Google offers a long list of quality web-based services aimed at helping both individuals and businesses of all sizes. Both Google Calendar and Google Contacts are attractive options for smaller-sized businesses because they are easy to use and ubiquitous. The latter also makes it a perfect extension for CRM systems, and these connectors aim at allowing you to extend your CRM data to these Google services.

- **Microsoft Outlook connector**: Integration with Microsoft Outlook is critical to many organizations. These utilities allow you to synchronize data between Outlook and your SugarCRM deployment. If you prefer to use Outlook as your primary e-mail client, you will want to give this a look.

- **Microsoft Office integration**: The prior chapter showed you some of the e-mail marketing capabilities that are a part of SugarCRM. However, many organizations do not exclusively use e-mails for their marketing activities. Direct mail campaigns are another popular form of marketing products and services, usually leveraging Microsoft Office to produce the piece. Office integration components allow you to create form letters in Microsoft Word and execute mail merge leveraging your customer information in SugarCRM.

- **ZuckerReports**: This is a *must* for all Community Edition users. Given that Community Edition does not include a reporting module, you would only be able to generate reports using other tools, such as Crystal Reports, MS-SQL Reporting Services, and others. However, none of those tools are ready for SugarCRM and require intimate knowledge of the database. ZuckerReports offers a streamlined solution to reporting needs and is tightly integrated into SugarCRM.

- **Development toolkit & enhanced studio**: Not all enhancements are specifically targeted at addressing end user needs or day-to-day requirements. Some of them are geared towards admin level tasks or simplifying the customization process. These tools are great examples of this, as they provide simple methods that make the process of applying more advanced customization features far easier.

- **Open quotes and contracts**: This is an important functionality that is not included in SugarCRM Community Edition, but is critical to many sales organizations. This enhancement brings this much needed functionality to Community Edition users.
- **VeryThinClient**: Provides access to SugarCRM data through wireless devices, such as smartphones or connected PDAs.
- **Security suite**: This enhances the security model in SugarCRM to permit the assignment of data to multiple users, or teams, providing greater flexibility over data access.

Additionally, we will examine important aspects of the Professional and Enterprise Editions of SugarCRM that differentiate them from the Community Edition. This comparison should help you make a more informed decision regarding the more appropriate edition for your organization.

- **SugarCRM Professional/Enterprise Edition**
    - **Product catalog and products module**: These two modules within Sugar Pro provide a product catalog defining the products handled by your business, and a products module that lists the physical products in your inventory, on order, or the ones that are sold to clients.
    - **Quotes module**: This Sugar Pro module uses data from the product catalog module to prepare customer quotations.
    - **Forecasting**: This module within Sugar Pro provides the ability to generate individual and roll-up sales forecasts.
    - **Standard and custom reporting**: Reporting is likely to be the single most important feature that differentiates Sugar Pro from the Open Source version. The reporting module in Sugar Pro gets better with each release, and is now a very capable system.
    - **Sales teams**: This is a key feature of Sugar Pro. Sales Teams provides you with the ability to create teams of users who can share data between themselves that other users may not access. Combined with the Access Control Lists from release 4.0, they provide a good solution to data security.

At the end of this chapter, we also have a section about the SugarCRM online forums where users can interact and exchange ideas with other SugarCRM users and administrators.

Let us dive right in to these many and varied extensions to the SugarCRM Community Edition product. By the time we are done, you will be surprised and impressed at the range and capability of the features available to you, to enhance your SugarCRM Community Edition system that will help meet your evolving business needs.

Configuration management, or the tracking and documenting of modifications applied to the system becomes an important practice at this point. Since the enhancements that we will be exploring will be modifying your SugarCRM installation, it is vital to highlight the importance of documenting the changes that have been made as a general best practice. This will help pinpoint the source of any problems, or unintended changes in functionality that may arise through the installation or use of modules or other modifications.

As we go through the various add-ons, we will see how they relate to a small business, such as RayDoc, and discuss the real business value that they offer.

SugarCRM Community Edition

SugarCRM has gained a lot of popularity because of the fact that it is a very cost-effective solution for many small or medium-size businesses. Its value has been greatly enhanced by the large community of users who have followed SugarCRM's lead and have also provided a number of product enhancements and add-ons for free. However, where exactly do you find them?

SugarForge.org and SugarExchange.com

Open your web browser and navigate to `http://www.sugarforge.org`. On this website you will find dozens of projects that can be freely downloaded and installed onto your SugarCRM system. Take a moment to browse around and familiarize yourself with the various projects that are available. Be sure to bookmark the website for your future reference. You might notice that the various projects highlighted in the previous section of this chapter are all freely available for download on SugarForge.

Make a note of the details pertaining to the various projects. For example, the versions of SugarCRM that they support and other details. Some projects, while popular, do not support more current versions of SugarCRM. Overlooking this detail might cause you some frustration and aggravation when attempting to install it, hence you should be quite diligent in your selection.

Another website is SugarExchange.com that can be accessed by using the URL http://www.sugarexchange.com. It contains a variety of other enhancements and add-ons, or in some cases, more feature-rich versions of projects that are already available on SugarForge.org. It follows a model similar to the one that SugarCRM (the company) employs for its offerings. The main difference between the two websites is that SugarExchange.com is intended to be a catalog of commercial add-ons and enhancements for SugarCRM. Take a look at some of the items in the catalog and you will notice that they require purchase, unlike the items in SugarForge.org. Furthermore, you will notice that many of the projects are also not intended for use with SugarCRM Community Edition, as they are only used with the Professional and/or Enterprise Edition.

We will assume that the installation files corresponding with the various enhancements and modules to be examined have already been downloaded. As we progress through the rest of this chapter, we will learn how these installation files are used through the **Module Loader** tool, and then examine the enhancements in greater detail.

Module loader

Before we dive into the functionality provided by the various modules and enhancements, we need to familiarize ourselves with the typical installation process.

Locate the **Enhanced Search** project on SugarForge.org and download the most current installation files. Save them onto a convenient location as we will use them in the following exercise to highlight the usage of the Module Loader tool.

You may have noticed that the installation files are contained in a ZIP archive. Do not unzip these files unless the documentation for the projects specifically instructs you to do so.

Our first step in the installation process will be to access the **Module Loader** tool found within the Admin control panel in SugarCRM. To access it, login to SugarCRM as an admin level user and then click on **Admin | Module Loader**.

A screen resembling the following should now appear:

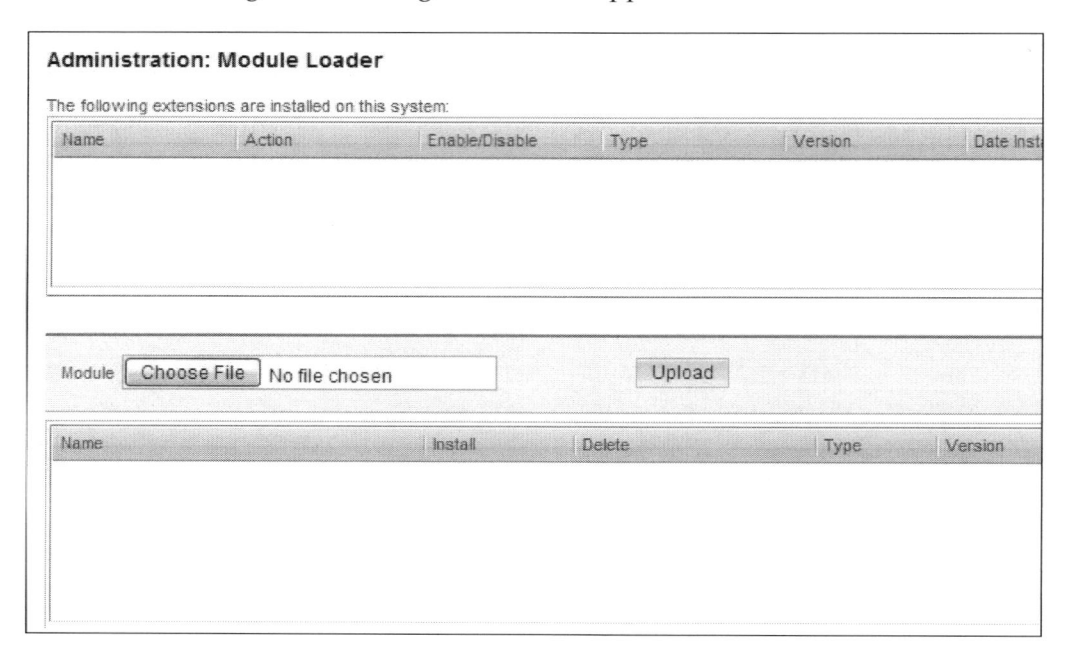

Administration: Module Loader

The following extensions are installed on this system:

Name	Action	Enable/Disable	Type	Version	Date Inst

Module [Choose File] No file chosen   [Upload]

Name	Install	Delete	Type	Version

Next, we need to click on the **Choose File** button. This will allow you to select the installation files corresponding to the module that we wish to install. Navigate to the location of the zip file downloaded earlier and select it. Proceed to click on the **Upload** button.

Clicking on the **Upload** button will copy the zip file to the SugarCRM server and will prepare it for installation. Upon doing so, you will notice that the module is added to the bottom section of the Module Loader tool. To finalize the installation, click on the **Install** button next to the corresponding entry. You will then need to accept the license and proceed through the rest of the Installation Wizard to complete the process.

After successfully installing the module, click on the **Back to Module Loader** button. Notice that the entry for the module has been moved from the bottom list to the top, where all the installed modules and enhancements are displayed. If you decide to disable or uninstall one of the modules at a later time, simply click on the **Disable** or **Uninstall** button next to its entry in the listing.

As we have the Enhanced Search module installed, let us take a closer look at its capabilities.

Enhanced search

All of the tools that we have examined so far have one thing in common; they provide new functionality to SugarCRM. However, none of the previous tools modify the behavior of existing features. The Enhanced Search functionality will be our first trek into this territory.

As stated earlier in this book, the available search features in SugarCRM provide a very helpful way of locating data within the system, but at the same time are rather limited in their capabilities. A common problem that users encounter is that search behavior cannot be changed from the default *AND* connector to *OR*. The inability to do so presents a number of challenges that are magnified if your search criterion requires the searching of more than one field.

For example, if you wish to search for contacts whose office numbers begin with the digits 310 or their State field is set to California, you would find that the default search feature will only return records that have an office number that begin with 310 **and** are also in California; this is not the set of records you are looking for. Enhanced Search modifies this existing functionality to remove this limitation and in general, provide a richer search experience in many different ways.

Installation is performed through the Module Loader and when the installation completes its functionality, it immediately becomes available to all SugarCRM users. Once installed, the **Advanced Search** panel on your list view screens should resemble the following:

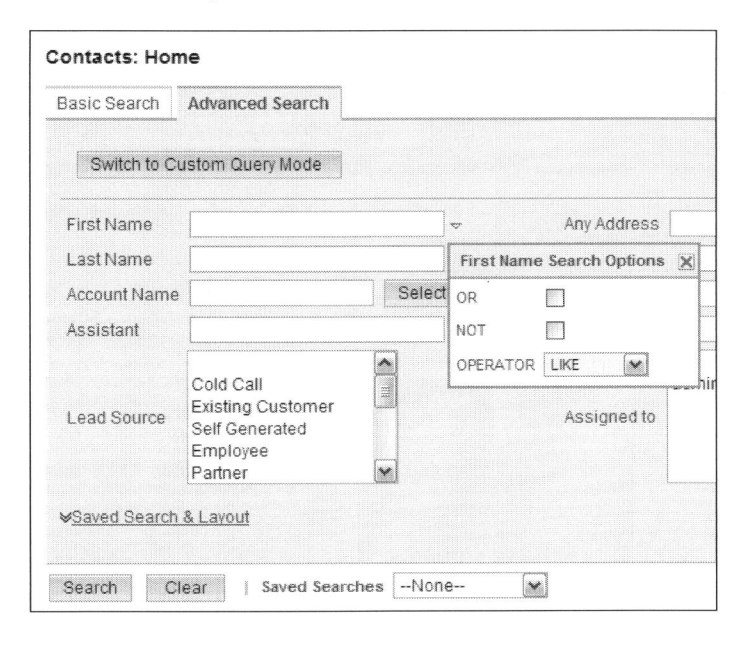

The SugarCRM Ecosystem

Notice the downward facing icon immediately following the displayed fields. Clicking on the icon allows you to select a variety of options relating to your search, including the following:

- **OR**
- **AND**
- **Operator (LIKE, RLIKE, EQUALS, IN, and BETWEEN)**

These options allow you to manipulate the behavior of the search features by changing the default connector of **AND** to **OR** in order to perform a search where the desired results meet the specified criteria on one of various fields being searched for and not on all the fields. The **LIKE** and **RLIKE** operators permit you to search for portions of a value in situations where you don't know the exact value that you want. For example, if you wish to get a list of all contacts whose street address contains **Main Street**, regardless of the number, using **LIKE** with the following search value would give you those results: **%Main Street%**.

This scenario allows us to understand the use of the **RLIKE** option as well. Similar to the **LIKE** option, it is also used to search for portions of a value, but it permits you to seek one from multiple values within the same field. For example, we could use this option to search for contacts whose address is either on **Main Street** or **Broadway Avenue** by using **RLIKE** and the following search value: **Main Street | Broadway Avenue**.

Similar to the **RLIKE** operator is the **IN** operator that allows you to search for multiple values within the same field by specifying the values in the following manner: `'value 1'`, `'value 2'`, `'value 3'`. The difference is that using **IN** causes SugarCRM to search for records that have an exact match to any of the specified values within the specified field, whereas **RLIKE** only requires the field that contains the value without giving importance to any other information within the field.

Lastly, using the **BETWEEN** option permits you to search date fields by defining date ranges. This is a common search request that is not available by default within SugarCRM.

For average users, such as those at RayDoc, the ability to search for data using a variety of methods is extremely powerful and a must.

Google connectors

Freely available on SugarForge.org, these tools will allow you to synchronize data from your SugarCRM system to Google calendar and/or Google contacts (depending on which connector you choose to install).

The principal business need this enhancement addresses is to extend or expose CRM data to non-SugarCRM users or systems. By means of these connectors, you would be able to check activities originally scheduled in SugarCRM within Google calendar. Once in Google calendar, you may use those activities much like any other, including sharing it with others, or synchronize it to your mobile device using Google Sync.

In a similar manner, the connector for contacts allows you to populate your Google contacts list with information from SugarCRM. This again leads to another method in which SugarCRM data can be extended and like the Google calendar scenario, Google Sync can be leveraged to synchronize data down to your mobile device.

Even an organization the size of RayDoc can benefit from such functionality. Synchronizing SugarCRM data to Google calendar, for example, would allow them to share their calendar with clients, allowing them to look for convenient appointment times without first having to contact RayDoc. RayDoc's service personnel would also be able to maintain a list of client names on their BlackBerry devices by using Google Sync in conjunction with the Google contacts connector. This would allow them to see valuable contact information even if they do not have Internet access or if they happen to be in an area where wireless service is not feasible. Of course, if you are using Android powered smartphones, the process is even more seamless as its synchronization between your phone and Google is built-in and does not require the Google Sync component.

Once installed, you need to configure the connector to link it to a specific Google account. You may use a personal Google account or one associated with a corporate account. If you do not already have a Google account, you will need to sign up for one before you can proceed.

The SugarCRM Ecosystem

With your Google account information in hand, and assuming you have already installed one of the connectors, click on the **My Account** link within SugarCRM and then click **Google Account** on the shortcuts menu on the left-hand side. The following screen should appear:

Users: Administrator (admin)

[Edit]

Google account settings

Google email address:

Meetings, Calls, and Tasks

Create and update meetings in Google Calendar:	☐
Create and update call in Google Calendar:	☐
Create and update tasks in Google Calendar:	☐
Add notifications times in Google Calendar:	☐
Upload calls, tasks, meetings only "after date ..." to Google Calendar:	Click here to upload
Only insert calls with "status = planned":	☐
Enter Google Calendar Address:	

Users settings

Allow users to change account settings	☑
Create logs	☑

Adjust the settings by clicking on **Edit** and then **Save**. Note that the settings are specific to each SugarCRM user. This permits users from RayDoc to benefit from the functionality to enable it, while those who do not wish to use it can simply ignore it, all without affecting any other users.

Once configured, data will automatically be synchronized between SugarCRM and Google.

Microsoft Outlook connector

This section of the book, as well as the one that follows (discussing Microsoft Office integration) are intended for Microsoft Windows users only. You may wish to skip this section if you are not using Windows on the workstation that you will be using to access your SugarCRM installation.

SugarCRM's built-in e-mail client is suitable for a number of organizations, but is limited in capabilities when compared to full fledged e-mail client applications, such as Microsoft Outlook. For some organizations, the differences in features are too great and they would be better served by continuing to use Outlook.

The challenge, however, is that doing so means that e-mail communications between you and your customers, or lead, will not be automatically linked to their corresponding record in SugarCRM, nor would it be available to other users for latter reference.

To address this problem, several connectors between SugarCRM and Outlook have been developed. All provide similar functionality; they provide features within Microsoft Outlook that allow an Outlook user to synchronize calendar items, contacts, and e-mails with SugarCRM.

We will be taking a closer look at the **GrinMark** Microsoft Office add-in for SugarCRM solution, given that it also contains functionality that allows us to integrate SugarCRM with Microsoft Word. We will be examining this in greater detail in the following section. However, feel free to explore the other options available on SugarForge.org, for example, **KINAMU** Outlook Connector, as they offer similar functionality.

To begin our examination of the GrinMark add-in, let us first quickly examine its installation process, as it does not leverage the SugarCRM Module Loader functionality. The installation process is initiated by double-clicking the GrinMark add-in installer file (`GrinMarkOfficeSetup.msi`) as you would do for other Windows based programs.

The SugarCRM Ecosystem

You will notice that the installation process utilizes a wizard driven approach common to most Windows applications. The Setup Wizard screen is shown in the following screenshot:

After successfully installing the GrinMark add-in, you will notice that some new options within Outlook are accessible through a GrinMark toolbar. Before you can use them, you must first provide your SugarCRM URL, username, and password. The easiest way to provide this information is to access the **SugarCRM Connection and License Settings** screen. You can access this screen by selecting **Start | Programs | GrinMark | SendTo SugarCRM Config** and then clicking on the **SugarCRM Connection and License Settings** button.

A screen similar to the following should appear:

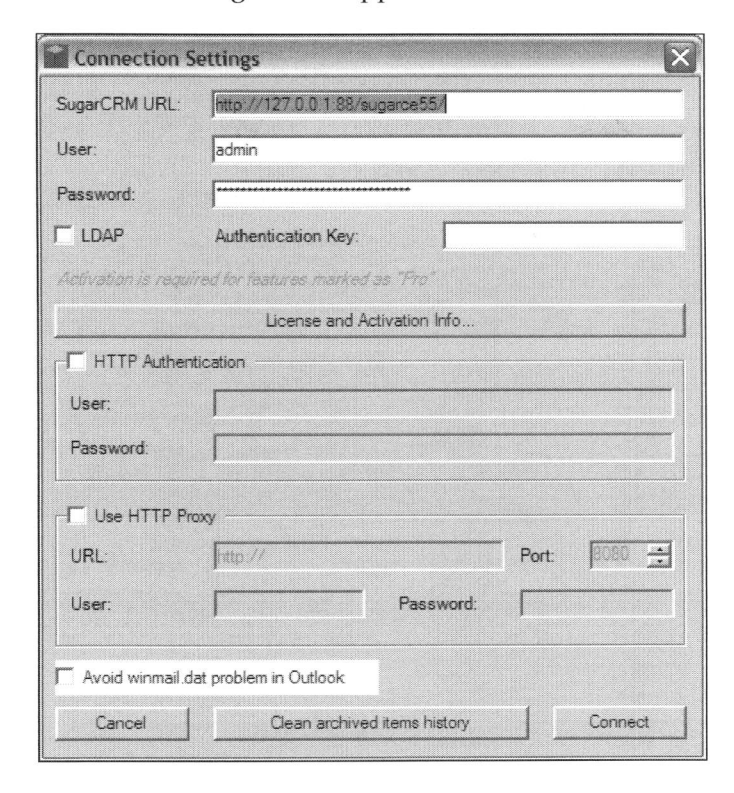

[Screenshot of Connection Settings dialog with fields for SugarCRM URL (http://127.0.0.1:88/sugarce55/), User (admin), Password, LDAP checkbox, Authentication Key, License and Activation Info button, HTTP Authentication section, Use HTTP Proxy section, Avoid winmail.dat problem in Outlook checkbox, and Cancel/Clean archived items history/Connect buttons.]

Once you have finished entering your SugarCRM connection details, click on **Connect** and then click on the **OK** button to close the screen. Now return to Outlook and we will take a look at the various features that the connector offers.

Perhaps the most important feature that the connector offers is the ability to archive e-mails from Outlook to SugarCRM. The process of synchronizing e-mails is quite simple. To archive a message to SugarCRM select it from within Outlook and then click on the GrinMark toolbar.

The SugarCRM Ecosystem

If the **TO** or **FROM** e-mail address of the selected message is already recorded in SugarCRM, the message will automatically be copied and linked to the related contact. In situations where it does not exist, you will be prompted to search for the corresponding record within SugarCRM.

The search screen should resemble the following:

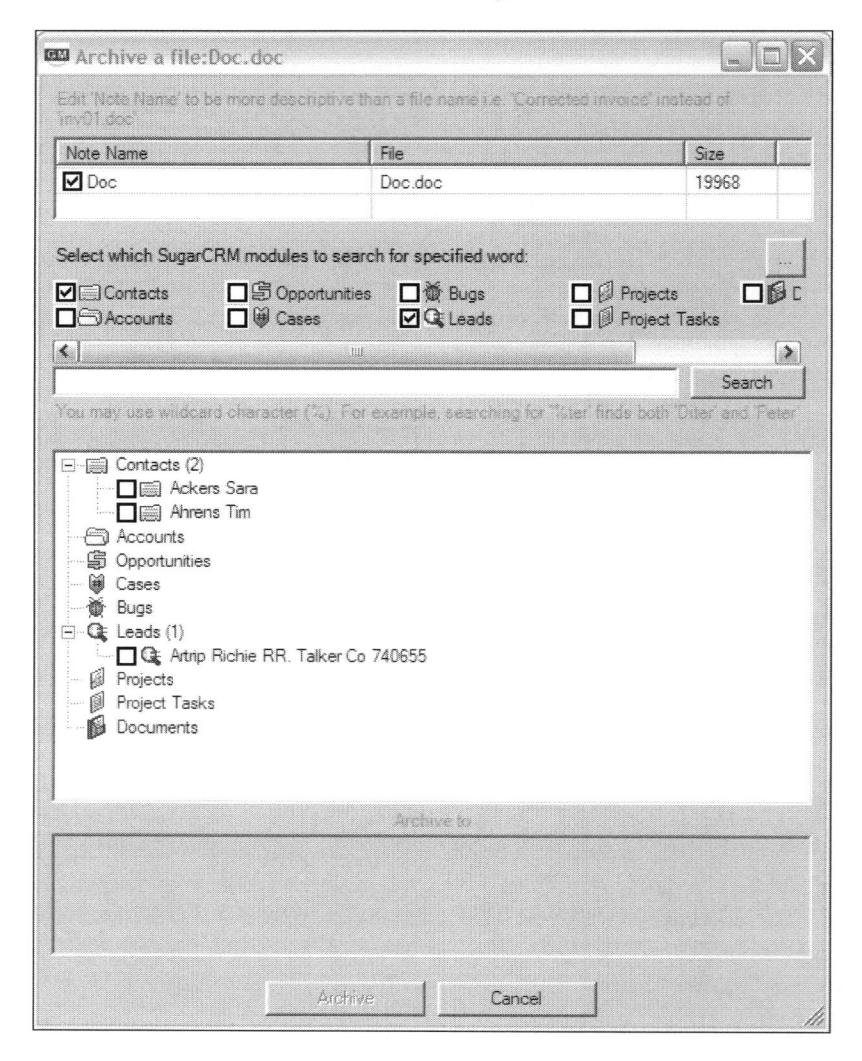

Notice that it allows you to search the various modules from SugarCRM. To search for a record, enter a value in the search field and click on the **Search** button as shown in the following screenshot: Matching results will be displayed in the bottom section of the screen. Once you have identified the appropriate record, select it and then click on the **GrinMark** button.

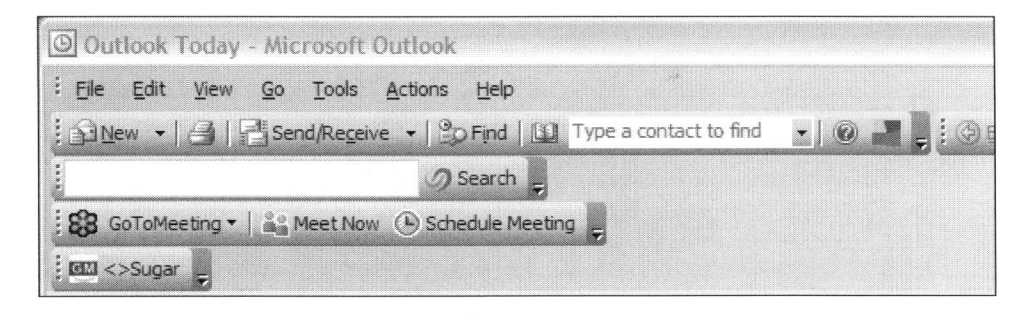

You may notice that the search screen makes it possible to link it to an opportunity, project, case, and other entities. This capability allows you to more accurately track e-mail communications by allowing you to also track the particular entity to which it relates.

The Outlook connector offers further capabilities beyond the archiving of e-mails. Another popular feature is the ability to synchronize activities between Outlook and SugarCRM. An important difference between this functionality and that associated with the archiving of e-mails, is that the synchronization of activities is bi-directional; items entered in SugarCRM can synchronize to Outlook and vice versa. In addition, changes made to them in either application will synchronize to the other. Lastly, you will need a licensed copy of GrinMark in order to utilize this functionality.

Synchronizing activities is similar to the process of archiving e-mails; select an item, and then click on the GrinMark toolbar. Similarly to the e-mail archive process, you are also able to select a related opportunity, project, case, and so on.

The SugarCRM Ecosystem

GrinMark also provides a method to automate the synchronization process between Outlook and SugarCRM through the Contact Synchronizer tool accessed by selecting **Start | Programs | GrinMark | Contact Synchronizer** and the following screen is displayed:

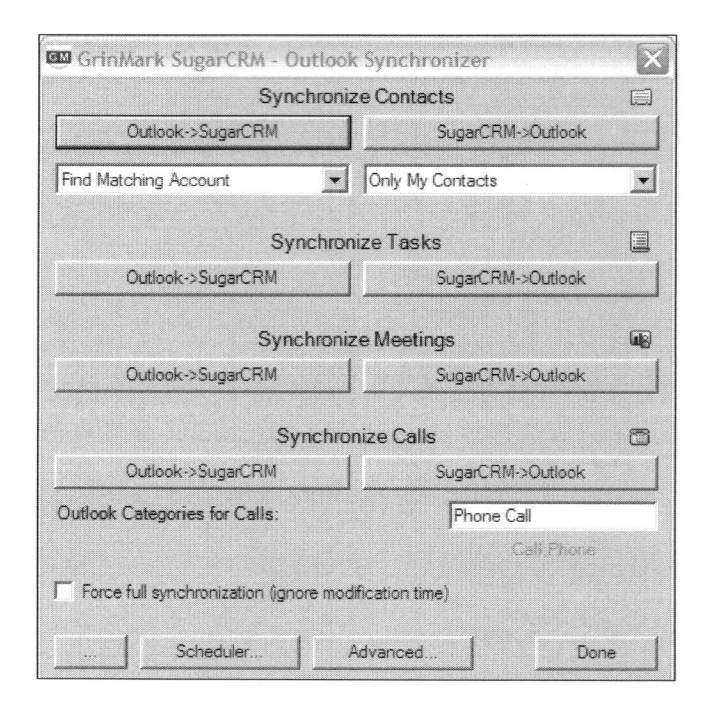

As illustrated in the preceding image, you can quickly synchronize data between the two applications by clicking on the appropriate synchronization button. Notice that you can choose the direction of the synchronization, in addition to the data that it applies to.

Lastly, clicking on the **Scheduler** button allows you to define the frequency at which activities or contacts are synchronized. Further, more detailed information on using GrinMark is provided in the GrinMark **Getting Started Guide** available for download at SugarForge.org.

For the staff members at RayDoc, the connector is an ideal solution to their main concern pertaining to their use of SugarCRM. Over the years, they have developed a number of folders, rules, and other techniques within Outlook to effectively manage their e-mails. They immediately became concerned that they would lose this functionality by being limited to the SugarCRM e-mail client.

The Outlook connector helps eliminate this hurdle by allowing users to continue to use an e-mail system that they are already accustomed to and not requiring them to learn a new one. Remember, users must feel that they are getting value from using the system, or they will find reasons to not use it.

Microsoft Office integration

Ever since the introduction of computers into the workplace, many speculated that it would usher in the era of the paperless office. However, things have not quite worked out that way and the use of paper based communications continues to have a place in today's business world.

Perhaps the most common utilization is for direct mail campaigns, for the purpose of printing a form letter, envelopes, or even mailing labels. While SugarCRM on its own does not have the ability to print these items, it does contain the relevant data, such as names and addresses.

Conversely, Microsoft Word has the ability to easily generate form letters, envelopes, or mailing labels, but it does not contain the data you would want to print on said items. Several solutions on SugarForge.org aim at addressing this specific problem by giving Microsoft Word the ability to read data from the SugarCRM database. The end result is a powerful combination of technologies that allows you to easily and quickly generate form letters, envelopes, or even mailing labels based on your CRM data.

While getting two distinct software packages to talk to each other to produce such results may sound complex, it is actually a rather simple process. As we go through the steps required to make it happen, you may notice that these steps are quite similar to those involved in executing an e-mail marketing campaign. Briefly, the manner in which the integration functions is as follows:

- Create a template in Microsoft Word with embedded fields (similar to an e-mail template)
- Save the letter as a Document within SugarCRM
- Use the GrinMark utility to perform the mail merge

The process of creating the template is rather simple. Begin by writing a letter in Microsoft Word as you would any other letter. Whenever you reach a point in your letter where you would want to insert a piece of data from SugarCRM, type in the appropriate code for the module and field, as such: `$contact_first_name` for the contact's first name or `$account_name` for a contact's related account name.

The SugarCRM Ecosystem

Once you are satisfied with your letter, save it and proceed to add it to the **Documents** module in SugarCRM as a new entry, making sure to enable the **Template?** checkbox along the way. If necessary, please refer to the previous chapter of this book for details on adding new documents.

The final step is to open the GrinMark Document Templates tool and print or e-mail your merged letter. The GrinMark Document Templates can be accessed by selecting **Start | Programs | GrinMark | Document Templates**. You will be presented with a list of all your document entries from SugarCRM, but you will want to limit your focus to only those that have been defined as templates. Select your template from the list and then click on **Proceed**. Following is a sample of the screen that should appear after clicking on **Proceed**:

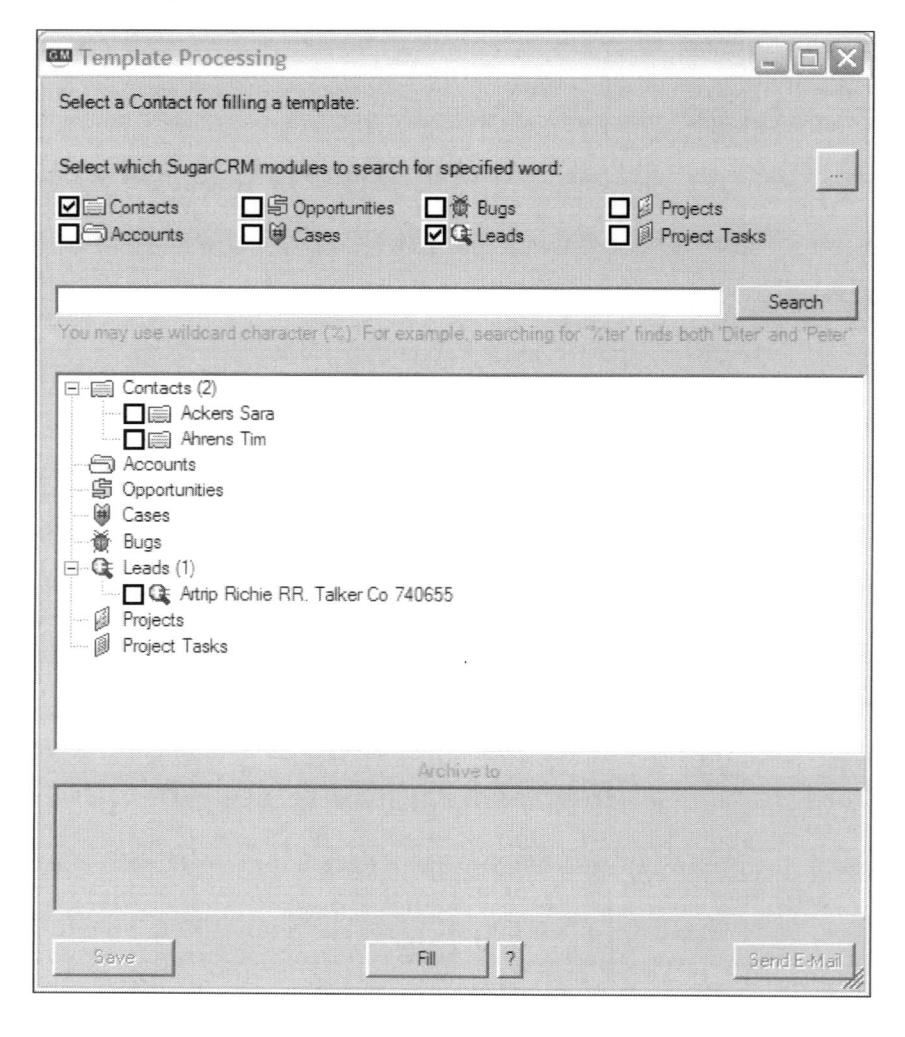

Notice that it allows you to search your SugarCRM system for records that should be included in the merge.

The selection process itself is quite simple in that all you need to do is enable the check box next to the entry you wish to include. Once you have done that, click on the **Fill** button at the bottom of the screen and a copy of the Word document you created earlier should appear, only now, the fields you embedded will be replaced with actual data from the selected contacts. You can now proceed to print, save, or e-mail the merged document.

Note that the SugarCRM Professional and Enterprise Editions both include an add-in for Microsoft Outlook, Word, and Excel as a part of the subscription price. While the principles are generally the same between this and add-ins, such as GrinMark's, the mechanics involved in generating a mail merge are significantly more streamlined. Additionally, the process is more tightly integrated with the mail merge capabilities built into the various modules in SugarCRM, including contacts, leads, accounts, and campaigns.

For RayDoc, the ability to print personalized service contracts or letters leveraging their SugarCRM data makes this enhancement very worthwhile. RayDoc is also planning on using this functionality to create collateral that they will send out to new leads as they enter the system.

If the volume increases, they will consider upgrading to Professional Edition to take advantage of the more streamlined, SugarCRM provided, Word add-in.

ZuckerReports

Diligent use of your CRM system yields many important benefits, but obtaining the insights that it can offer your business requires the ability to generate reports or other metrics. SugarCRM Community Edition, however, does not include a reporting solution and its metrics are limited to the dashboards that we discussed earlier in the book.

ZuckerReports addresses this very important need quite effectively, making it one of the most popular modules available on SugarForge.org.

The SugarCRM Ecosystem

Installation can sometimes be a challenge due to its size in comparison to other modules, but those issues are usually resolved by adjusting one or more of the following `PHP.INI` settings:

- `upload_max_filesize`
- `post_max_size`
- `max_execution_time`

Values of `50M`, `50M`, and `300` respectively, should suffice. Remember, if you need to adjust your settings, do not forget to restart your web service to apply the modifications. Once installed, ZuckerReports offers many powerful capabilities.

First and foremost, it offers a tool that allows you to create a variety of reports based on any of the modules—default or custom—included in your SugarCRM system. This is accomplished through a simple interface that most SugarCRM users will easily adapt to.

Reports are created by first producing a template that defines parameters, such as the target module, fields, filters, and other report parameters. To get a feel for the process, let us create a report that lists all of the opportunities in SugarCRM.

Our first step will be to access the ZuckerReports module. You can access it by selecting the **ZuckerReports** tab from the main navigation area within SugarCRM. Clicking on it should display a screen similar to the following:

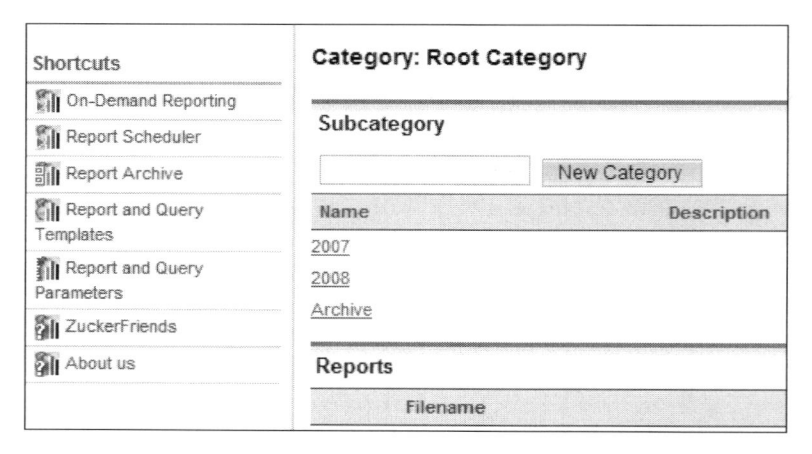

Shortcuts	Category: Root Category	
On-Demand Reporting		
Report Scheduler	**Subcategory**	
Report Archive		New Category
Report and Query Templates	**Name**	**Description**
Report and Query Parameters	2007	
	2008	
ZuckerFriends	Archive	
About us	**Reports**	
	Filename	

Chapter 6

Next, click on **Report and Query Templates** and then **New Listing Template**. Fill in the fields to match the following:

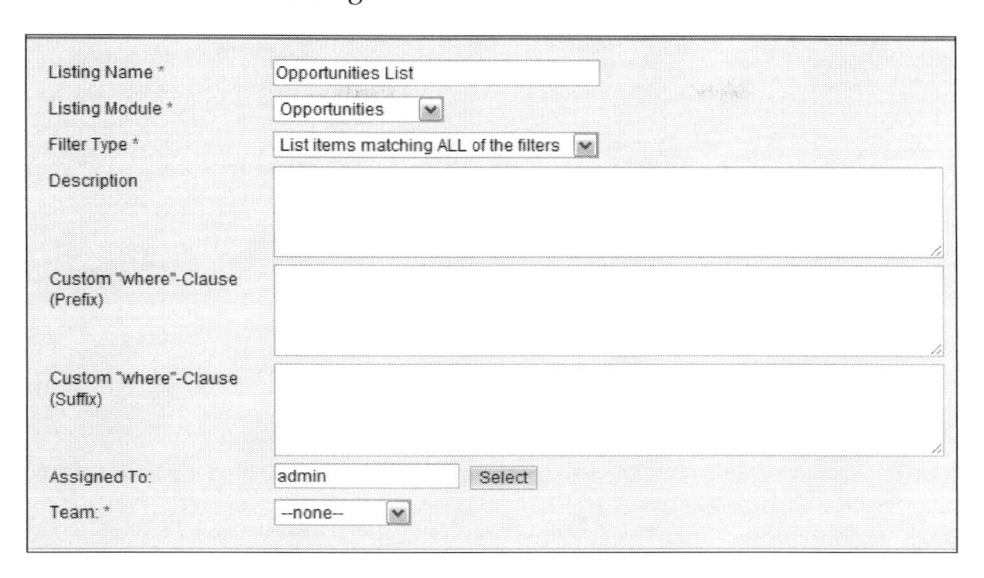

Listing Name *	Opportunities List
Listing Module *	Opportunities
Filter Type *	List items matching ALL of the filters
Description	
Custom "where"-Clause (Prefix)	
Custom "where"-Clause (Suffix)	
Assigned To:	admin [Select]
Team: *	--none--

Click on **Save**. The **New Filter** and **New Order Criteria** sections on the detail view screen allow you to apply filters and sorting orders, respectively. For our example, we will apply a filter to the report that limits the output to only those opportunities that have a value of over US$5,000, as shown in the following screenshot:

New Filter

Add Filter

Field	Amount		Select Filter Value	
Comparator	greater		from Parameter	--None--
			or enter	5000

To apply this filter, enter the values as illustrated in the preceding screenshot and then click on the **Add Filter** button. Additional filters can be applied by repeating the process that has just been described.

[161]

Now that you have defined a basic report template, you can generate the output. Click on the **Run Report** button and you will be presented with the following screenshot:

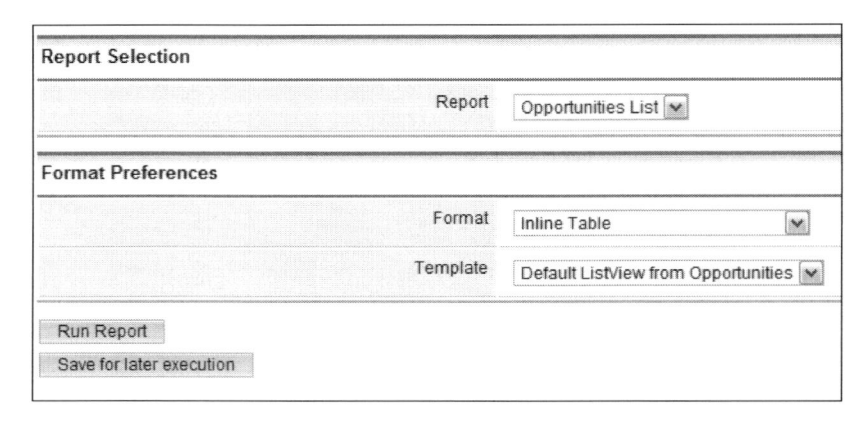

The **Format Preferences** section allows you to modify some of the output features, but for now, leave it to the default settings and click on **Run Report**. The report should now be displayed on screen. This example, while basic, demonstrates some of the features of ZuckerReports. However, its capabilities stretch far beyond those that we just saw.

If necessary, you can also generate more advanced reports by simply supplying the appropriate SQL query, through a **Query Template**. However, perhaps the most powerful feature is its ability to integrate itself with JasperReports, Microsoft Office, and other related tools.

JasperReports is a full fledged reporting and business intelligence solution offering numerous features ranging from the basic summation reports to more advanced ones including drill downs and charts.

Report templates can also be created within Microsoft Word or Excel. This functionality simplifies the report creation process while also providing another option for performing mail merges.

If you are familiar with **iReport**, a complementary tool for JasperReports, you can also use it to generate report templates.

As you can see, ZuckerReports offers a very comprehensive solution to various reporting needs. For an organization such as RayDoc, ZuckerReports can generate and provide the insights that the management needs to monitor the state of the business, for example, tracking the pipeline, lead conversion rates, and many other statistics.

For more information on using ZuckerReports or JasperReports, visit the project's page on SugarForge.org at the following URL:

http://www.sugarforge.org/projects/zuckerreports/ or
http://www.zuckerfriends.com/

Development toolkit and enhanced studio

While the ability to apply customizations manually is a very powerful capability, it is not the most efficient approach, especially if you need to apply a large number of customizations.

The *development toolkit and enhanced studio* modules greatly reduce the amount of work that is required to make numerous customizations. Some common uses include the following:

- Conditional drop-downs
- Calculated fields
- Code fields

Conditional drop-downs are a common need of users. It refers to a data entry technique where values displayed in a drop-down list are dynamic and are dependent on each other. Thus, if a user is entering a record and selects value A for drop-down list 1, the values in drop-down list 2 would reflect values relevant to the selection in drop-down list 1. If a user instead selects value B for drop-down list 1, drop-down list 2 displays a different list of values.

Obviously, this would streamline the data entry process for RayDoc staff and will make it a more user-friendly experience. This will eventually increase the adoption rate of SugarCRM.

> The respective SugarForge.org project pages contain examples and further information on their usage and capabilities at the following websites:
>
> http://www.sugarforge.org/projects/devtoolkit/
>
> http://www.sugarforge.org/projects/enhancedstudio/

The SugarCRM Ecosystem

Open quotes and contracts

Most sales organizations rely on the use of quotes to close deals or opportunities and once they are closed, the said deals may involve service contracts or similar ongoing contracts that an organization may need to track.

SugarCRM Community Edition, however, does not include a functionality that can allow you to easily generate quotes for your leads, nor does it include functionality to track related contracts. This functionality is only available in the Professional and Enterprise Editions.

As a Community Edition user, one of the best solutions available to address these limitations is to use the *open quotes and contracts* module. It is a very comprehensive solution that also includes a product catalog to simplify the quoting process.

Some of the highlights of this module include the following:

- Ability to print PDF versions of contracts or quotes
- Automated versioning of contracts
- Hierarchical product catalog
- Contract expiration e-mail notifications

As you can see from the aforementioned highlights, it is a full-featured solution. If you need a quoting solution that is integrated into your SugarCRM system, this module is definitely worth a look. More information on this is available at the following URL:

```
http://www.sugarforge.org/projects/openqc/
```

VeryThinClient

Wireless access to important business data, such as that stored in SugarCRM has grown tremendously in popularity over the years. Today, remote staff or road warriors—especially those accustomed to using web enabled mobile devices—expect to be able to have access to such information anywhere their mobile device can obtain a signal.

Although SugarCRM is a web-based application, the native mobile client is only available to Professional and Enterprise Edition users. While possible, attempting to use Community Edition as-is through your mobile device's web browser will prove to be rather cumbersome. Fortunately, a solution to the problem does exist and helps bring this functionality to Community Edition users.

VeryThinClient provides a method for providing mobile access. Via this tool, road warriors can easily access SugarCRM data directly from your server and within an interface that is suited for their device.

More information on this tool can be found at the following URL:

http://www.sugarforge.org/projects/verythinclient/

Security suite

A common limitation that SugarCRM Community Edition users encounter is the inability to assign a record to more than one user. The Professional and Enterprise Editions address this inability through the teams functionality—explained later in this chapter.

Security suite aims at bringing similar functionality to Community Edition users. With Security suite, you can define teams, or groupings of one or more SugarCRM users. In turn, records within SugarCRM can be assigned to one or more of those predefined teams. Much like the "Assigned To" field can control which user has access a record, so can Security suite.

While security restrictions may not be an immediate need for your SugarCRM installation, they usually do become important over time. Security suite is a must for security needs. Detailed information on its functionality is available at the following URL:

http://www.sugarforge.org/projects/securitysuite/

SugarCRM Professional/Enterprise Editions

SugarCRM has been a pioneer of sorts in the business software marketplace. Its most notable difference to its competitors and other vendors in that space is that it is an open source product where most others are closed-source, proprietary systems. Like any other company, they must model their business in such a way that allows them to make some money, or they would cease to exist.

This presents a unique challenge for a company whose flagship product is an open source solution, as the solution is freely available to one and all. SugarCRM has tackled this challenge quite effectively by offering different editions of SugarCRM, as we have discussed earlier in this book.

In this section, we will explore some of the more important differences between the commercial offerings and Community Edition. This information will help you better assess whether or not an upgrade to either Professional or Enterprise Edition is a more appropriate choice for your needs.

Product catalog and products module

CRM systems like SugarCRM and other vendors are all referred to as **front-office** applications. The front of the business is the customer-facing part of the business and it is where these applications are frequently used.

The **back-office** applications are those that interface with internal operations and suppliers, and prepare financial statements and results.

Integrating front and back-office operations into one application is the goal of expensive **ERP (Enterprise Resource Planning)** systems for large enterprises (such as SAP). These solutions typically cost millions of dollars. Arguably, NetSuite (the name of the company and also the name of its premium product) is the best of the systems targeted at smaller businesses in terms of being able to integrate front and back-office activities into a single system. However, it is also quite expensive and only available as an on-demand solution.

In practice, many smaller businesses can gain most of the benefits of an integrated system by simply adding the most frequently and broadly used aspects of the back-end activities into the front-end application—having it also cover what we might perhaps call the middle. That would include the preparation of customer quotations, invoices, sales orders, and potentially even order processing. If your CRM system can help you do this, then the *wide* parts of your company—the customer-facing and customer-affecting parts, have been made much more efficient.

If you have such an extended CRM system (now covering front and middle), and link the resulting invoice or sales order data to your accounting system (by data export, or by web service linkages to online systems), you can create a very effective solution at a bargain price.

You can also create a situation where only a limited number of user licenses are required for the accounting software. Only the real accounting people who are posting transactions to ledgers need licenses—which is not the case with an integrated system. This approach also relegates the accounting function truly to the back-office—minimizing that part of the business which has no direct involvement with the customer or profit creation.

SugarCRM Community Edition does not have any of these back-office (or perhaps, middle-office) capabilities, but SugarCRM Professional and Enterprise do include modules that support this approach.

The initial two modules of this type are the **product catalog** and the **products module**. The product catalog is in the *administrator* area of the system and keeps track of the products you have available for sale, the quantity in stock, and other attributes. The products module then keeps track of the movements of those products—any units that have been quoted, ordered, or shipped to customers. Let us examine these components in greater depth.

Product catalog

There are four product catalog administration functions that are to be used when defining items in the product catalog. These are used for maintaining the items in the product catalog, as well as the product categories, product types, and manufacturers.

The product catalog administration option displays a list view of all current items in the product catalog. You can choose to click on the name of an item in the list to see the detail view for that item, and potentially edit it. You may also use the shortcuts menu in order to create a new item in the product catalog, or switch to viewing manufacturers, product categories, or product types. An import facility further simplifies the process of building the catalog.

Note that product type is a high-level classification of items within the product catalog, while product category is a lower-level classification. One might have a product type for the broad area of software, and a product category for a more narrow area, such as spreadsheet, word processor, or CRM Software. This categorization technique makes for a much more detailed breakdown of products in the catalog.

When creating a new catalog item, or editing an existing item, enter the data including the item name, associated URL, tax class, availability, the supplier, category and type, the cost, list and purchase prices, and the related currency. There is also a default pricing formula, which may be set to fixed price, profit margin, markup over cost, discount from list, or same as list:

- The product types administration option allows you to maintain the product types that are available for the classification of items in the product catalog. Each product type consists of a name and a description, as well as the order in which the entry is to appear in the drop-down list.

- The product categories administration option allows you to maintain the product categories that are available for the classification of items in the product catalog. Each product category consists of a category name, the name of the parent category, a description, as well as the order in which the entry is to appear in the drop-down list (largely irrelevant now with the category tree).
- The manufacturers administration option lets you maintain the manufacturers that are available as selections within the products module. Each manufacturer entry consists of a name and a status (**Active** or **Inactive**, where inactive it will remove it from the drop-down list for manufacturer), as well as the order in which the entry is to appear in the drop-down list.

Products module

The products module keeps track of products that have been quoted, ordered, or shipped.

Take care not to confuse the products module with the product catalog functions within the *administration* area. The latter is merely used to define the products that are available to be sold, while the former is used to monitor the volume ordered, the related customer, and cost to them.

A product may be created from an item in the product catalog, or may be custom-created by simply entering any name desired as the product name. The product list view is shown in the following image:

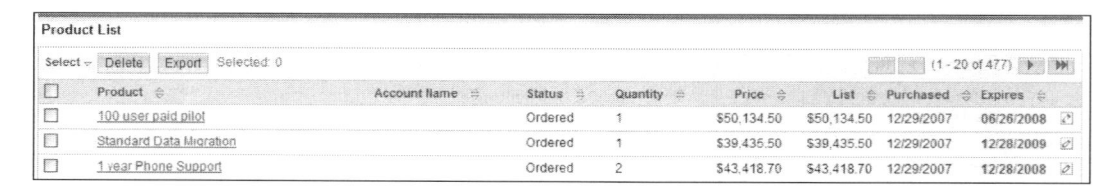

Product	Account Name	Status	Quantity	Price	List	Purchased	Expires
100 user paid pilot		Ordered	1	$50,134.50	$50,134.50	12/29/2007	06/26/2008
Standard Data Migration		Ordered	1	$39,435.50	$39,435.50	12/29/2007	12/28/2009
1 year Phone Support		Ordered	2	$43,418.70	$43,418.70	12/29/2007	12/28/2008

By checking the list of products, employees can determine the activity for products—what quotes, orders, and shipments have been taking place.

Quotes module

The **Quotes** module is another feature that broadens the reach of the CRM system towards back-office type capability. This module uses data from the product catalog module—described previously in this chapter, to prepare customer quotations. The quote list view is shown in the following image:

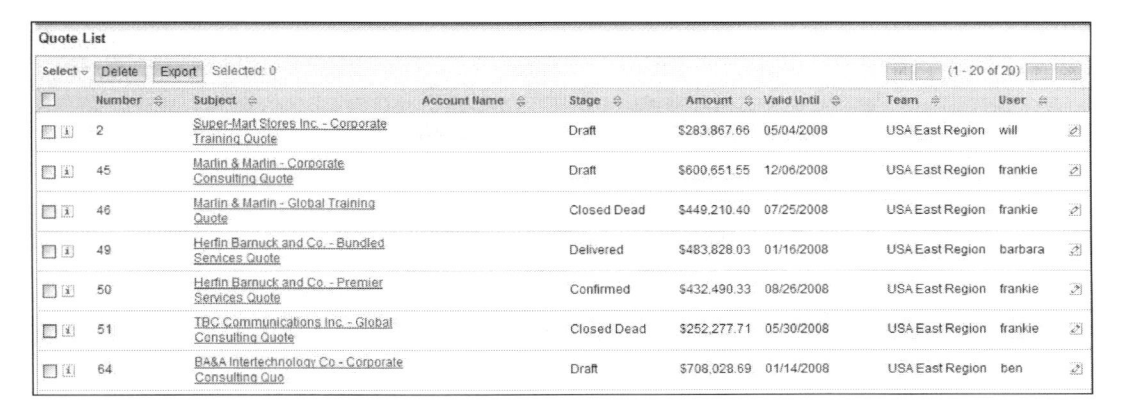

Quote List								
Number	Subject	Account Name	Stage	Amount	Valid Until	Team	User	
2	Super-Mart Stores Inc. - Corporate Training Quote		Draft	$283,867.66	05/04/2008	USA East Region	will	
45	Marlin & Marlin - Corporate Consulting Quote		Draft	$600,651.55	12/06/2008	USA East Region	frankie	
46	Marlin & Marlin - Global Training Quote		Closed Dead	$449,210.40	07/25/2008	USA East Region	frankie	
49	Herfin Barnuck and Co. - Bundled Services Quote		Delivered	$483,828.03	01/16/2008	USA East Region	barbara	
50	Herfin Barnuck and Co. - Premier Services Quote		Confirmed	$432,490.33	08/26/2008	USA East Region	frankie	
51	TBC Communications Inc. - Global Consulting Quote		Closed Dead	$252,277.71	05/30/2008	USA East Region	frankie	
64	BA&A Intertechnology Co - Corporate Consulting Quo		Draft	$708,028.69	01/14/2008	USA East Region	ben	

Upon entering the **Quotes** module, you see the **Quote List** view screen—showing all quotes currently in the system. You can click on a quote to see the details of the quote, and further click on the detail view to edit the quote.

Preparing a quote is simple. Click on the **Create Quote** shortcut, and on the screen that comes up, enter a subject for the quote, the date up to which the quote is valid, and select the **Bill to** and **Ship to** accounts (with a handy button to copy one to the other if they are the same).

Next, click on the **Add Group** button to define the initial product grouping on the quote, and then click on the **Add Row** button to add items to that group. On each row, use the **Select** button to select a product from the catalog then set the quantity, and if you need to, edit the unit price from the default price as shown in the following screenshot:

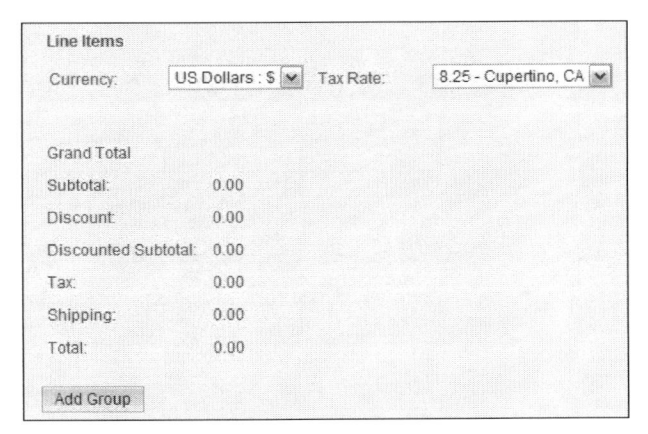

Line Items			
Currency:	US Dollars : $	Tax Rate:	8.25 - Cupertino, CA
Grand Total			
Subtotal:	0.00		
Discount:	0.00		
Discounted Subtotal:	0.00		
Tax:	0.00		
Shipping:	0.00		
Total:	0.00		

Add Group

You can create additional groups to organize sections of your quotation because they address different needs, are to be delivered on different schedules, or for a variety of other reasons.

The SugarCRM Ecosystem

When you are done, simply click on **Save**. The quote may now be used to create an opportunity (if the request for a quote came out of the blue), or a PDF may be generated from the quote—presented either as a proposal or as an invoice. Standard PDF templates are provided with Sugar Pro, which may be edited to include your company logo and address details. A sample is shown in the following figure:

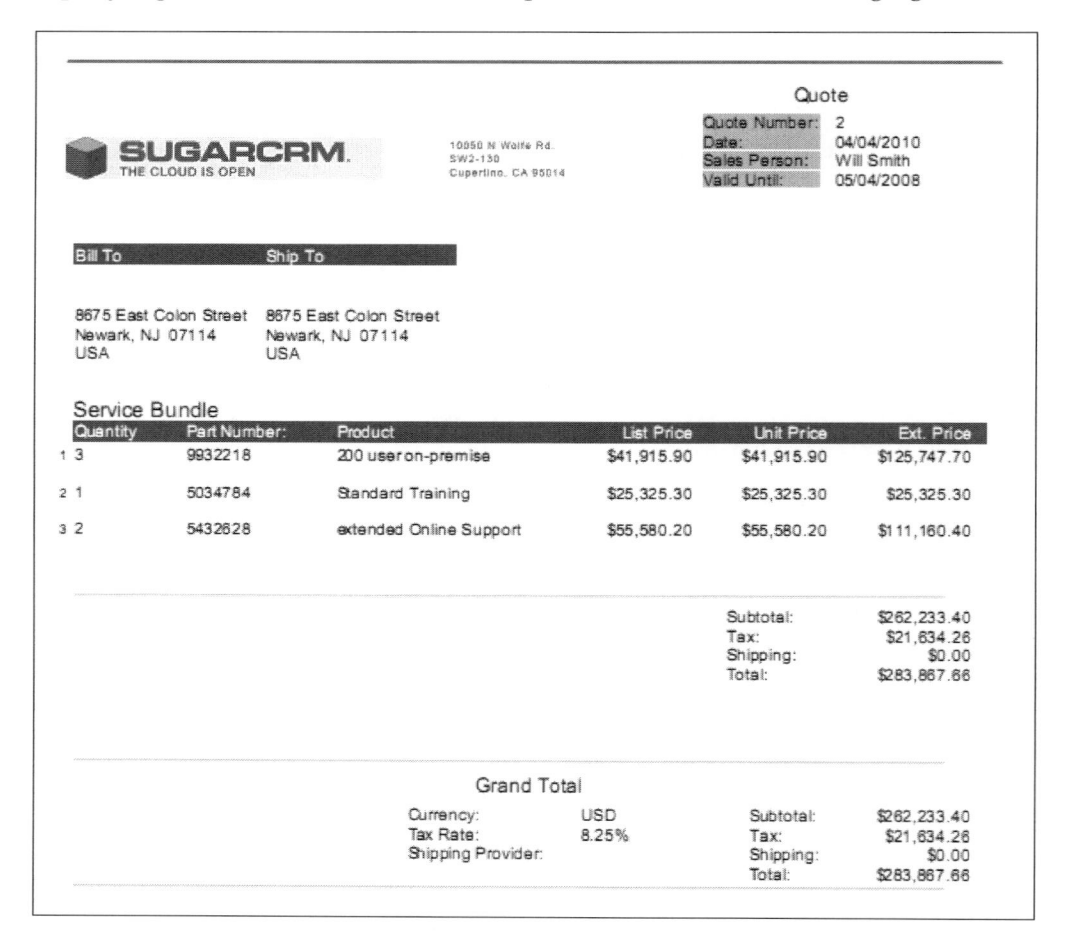

			Quote	
			Quote Number:	2
SUGARCRM.	10050 N Wolfe Rd.		Date:	04/04/2010
THE CLOUD IS OPEN	SW2-130		Sales Person:	Will Smith
	Cupertino, CA 95014		Valid Until:	05/04/2008

Bill To	Ship To
8675 East Colon Street	8675 East Colon Street
Newark, NJ 07114	Newark, NJ 07114
USA	USA

Service Bundle

	Quantity	Part Number:	Product	List Price	Unit Price	Ext. Price
1	3	9932218	200 user on-premise	$41,915.90	$41,915.90	$125,747.70
2	1	5034784	Standard Training	$25,325.30	$25,325.30	$25,325.30
3	2	5432628	extended Online Support	$55,580.20	$55,580.20	$111,160.40

Subtotal:	$262,233.40
Tax:	$21,634.26
Shipping:	$0.00
Total:	$283,867.66

Grand Total

Currency:	USD		Subtotal:	$262,233.40
Tax Rate:	8.25%		Tax:	$21,634.26
Shipping Provider:			Shipping:	$0.00
			Total:	$283,867.66

Forecasting

Sales people (account executives, account managers, sales representatives, whatever the preferred title of the day may be) who work in organizations with a substantial sales team that is overseen by a sales manager or VP of Sales, are generally all too familiar with the phrase—"What is your commit number?" Missing your commit number is getting a little too close to being a shooting offense!

SugarCRM Professional and Enterprise Editions include a mechanism that allows the sales manager to formalize the commit number for each sales person and roll them up to the regional or organizational level. These commit numbers are known by their polite name—the forecast.

The forecasting process begins with the definition of the forecasting periods—typically, financial quarters, or months. This is done in the **Administrator** area of the system.

Once the forecasting periods have been defined, each sales person can set their forecast commitments by using the **Forecasts** tab. Upon entry, this module shows the forecast history. This displays a list of the time periods available to the user, and all historical commitments that the user has made for those time periods. An example is shown in the following image:

Date Committed	Opportunities	Weighted Amount	Best Case	Worst Case	Likely Case
01/04/2008 10:38	18	$ 302,000	$ 241,600	$ 193,280	$ 144,960
01/04/2008 10:38	6	$ 57,500	$ 46,000	$ 36,800	$ 27,600
01/04/2008 10:38	16	$ 276,000	$ 220,800	$ 176,640	$ 132,480
01/04/2008 10:38	15	$ 84,000	$ 67,200	$ 53,760	$ 40,320

From the preceding screen, for example, we can note that one of the users once had a forecast for Q4 for only **US$53,760**—but that it is now **US$40,320**—on the basis of 15 opportunities whose weighted values total **US$84,000**. The following screenshot shows another example of a forcast worksheet:

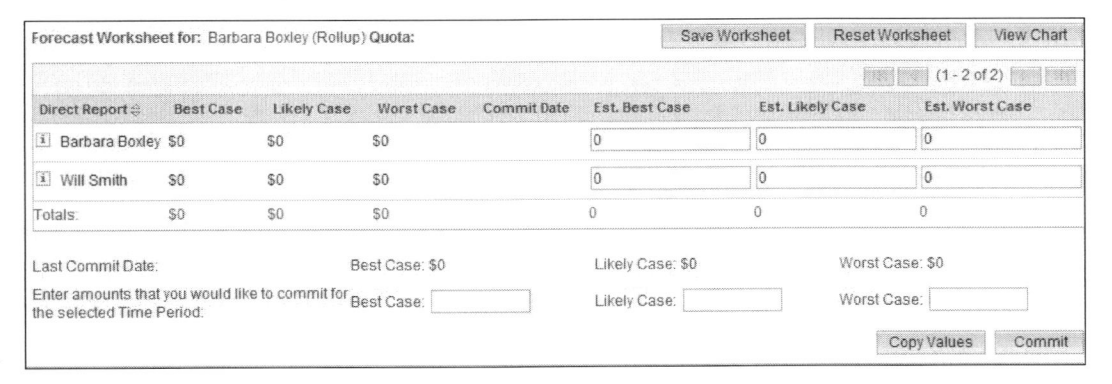

That forecast was entered on a forecast worksheet (as shown in the preceding screenshot), accessed from the **Forecast History** shortcut. On it, the user selects the time period to be forecast, and all opportunities for that period are automatically displayed, with their weighted value. The **Commit** button is used to enter a new commitment for the forecast time period. Note that a history of prior commitments for that time period is also displayed.

If the user supervises any other sales people (each user's profile has a setting for **Reports To**, that defines their supervisor) then they see a variant of the preceding screen that allows them to see a forecast roll-up of their own forecast plus that of all their direct reports. The radio button at the top allows the user to select between **My Forecasts** (which shows a screen like the previous figure), or **My Team's Forecasts**.

This system provides a good hard commitment record for sales forecasting, and a solid, undeniable audit trail! Also, the roll-up system provides a practical and quick way to scale sales forecasting to even large organizations.

Standard and custom reporting

Unlike Community Edition, reporting tools are built-in into the Professional and Enterprise Editions of SugarCRM. Typically, reporting capabilities within business systems fall into two categories: standard reports and custom reporting. Standard reports are just as they sound — a series of pre-defined reports that the creators of the system are certain will be relevant to you — at least from time-to-time.

Custom reporting systems are more difficult to create and they provide the ability for the user to define their own reports. In the case of SugarCRM Community or Professional Edition, the user would want at minimum the ability to specify the module from which reporting information is to be drawn, the columns of data to be presented, and if any columns are numeric and need totaling.

When you first click on the **Reports** module in SugarCRM, you see a list view of all the reports available within the system by default. Feel free to explore them and view their output. If you cannot find one that meets your needs, you can choose to clone one of the default reports and adjust it to fit your needs or create a new one from scratch. Usually, the clone approach is preferred as it saves you the hassle of having to redefine every aspect of the report, although, it does require an existing report that is relatively close to your desired result which may or may not exist. The list view of the reports is shown in the following image:

Report Name	Module	Report Type	Date Created	Team	User	Schedule Report
FY07 Forecast w /GRAPH	Opportunities	Summation with details	01/04/2008 10:35	Global	admin	-- none --
FY07 Forecast	Opportunities	Rows and Columns	01/04/2008 10:35	Global	admin	-- none --
Marketing - Leads by Campaign	Leads	Summation with details	01/04/2008 10:35	Global	admin	-- none --
Open Cases By Priority By User	Cases	Summation with details	01/04/2008 10:32	Global	admin	-- none --
Opportunities By Lead Source	Opportunities	Summation with details	01/04/2008 10:32	Global	admin	-- none --
Partner Account List	Accounts	Rows and Columns	01/04/2008 10:32	Global	admin	-- none --

Chapter 6

To get a feel of this process, let's see what it is like to build a custom report.

For our sample report, we will build a very useful report that lists all the accounts in the system that are classified as customers, and then within each of those accounts, lists the name and contact information for each contact at that account.

So to build this report, first we click on the **Create Custom Report** button and you see the following screen:

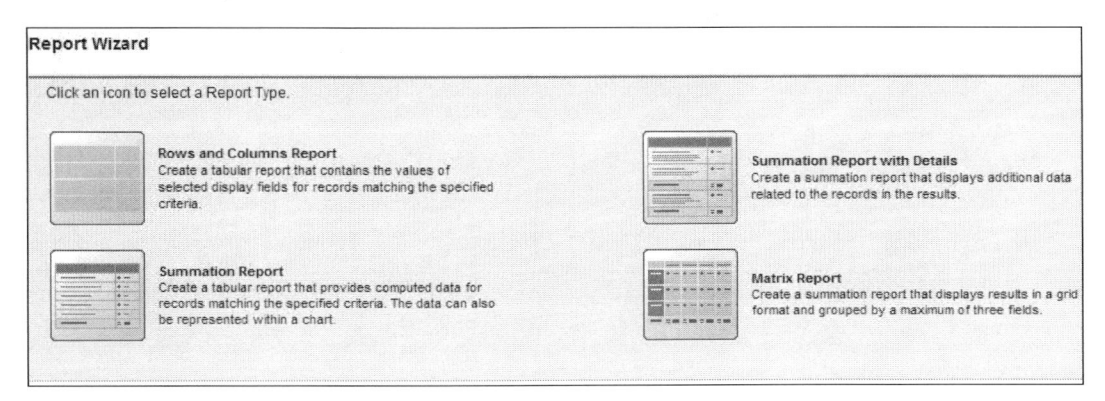

Report Wizard

Click an icon to select a Report Type.

Rows and Columns Report
Create a tabular report that contains the values of selected display fields for records matching the specified criteria.

Summation Report with Details
Create a summation report that displays additional data related to the records in the results.

Summation Report
Create a tabular report that provides computed data for records matching the specified criteria. The data can also be represented within a chart.

Matrix Report
Create a summation report that displays results in a grid format and grouped by a maximum of three fields.

The first step in the process is to select the type of report we wish to create. Click on **Rows and Columns Report**. You will now need to select the module from which the data will be extracted. Click on **Accounts**.

To apply our filter, select the **Type** field on the available fields section on the left-hand side of the screen. After doing so, the screen should resemble the following:

Define Filters

Select Operator: AND   Add Filter Group

Accounts > Type   Is   Analyst   Run-time

Notice that part of the filter definition allows you to select a value for the selected field. Given that we want to focus on accounts whose **Type** field is set to **Customers**, change the drop-down list value to match and then click on **Next** to proceed through the **Reports Wizard**.

On the **Choose Display Columns** tab, we actually assemble the real information of the report. This screen allows us to insert fields from the accounts module as well as any related modules by simply selecting them from the **Available Fields** section.

The SugarCRM Ecosystem

First, insert the account name by selecting the **Name** field from the **Available Fields** section. Now comes the slightly tricky part. If you take a look at the tree structure above the **Available Fields** section, you will see that the currently selected folder pertains to **Accounts**. This selection works in conjunction with the fields list. If you wish to insert fields from a related module, such as **Contacts**, select the **Contacts** folder within the **Accounts** folder. Doing so will update the **Available Fields** section to reflect the **Contacts** module fields, and you can now select it for the report. Proceed to enter the contact's phone number fields as well. The end result should resemble the following:

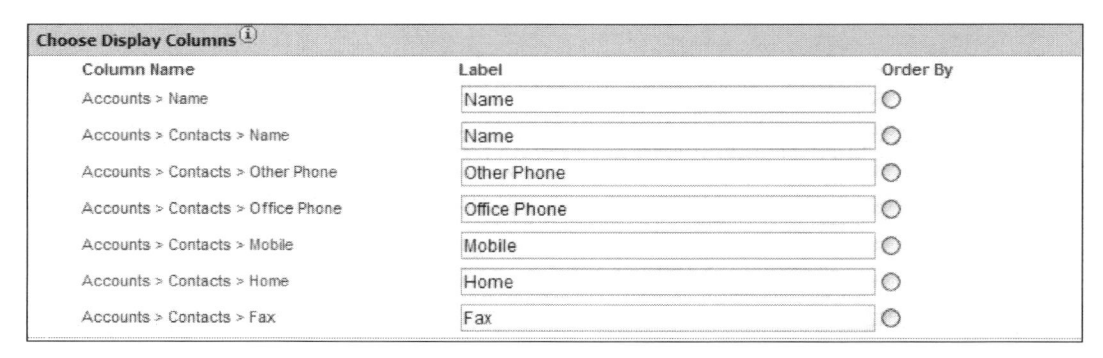

Column Name	Label	Order By
Accounts > Name	Name	○
Accounts > Contacts > Name	Name	○
Accounts > Contacts > Other Phone	Other Phone	○
Accounts > Contacts > Office Phone	Office Phone	○
Accounts > Contacts > Mobile	Mobile	○
Accounts > Contacts > Home	Home	○
Accounts > Contacts > Fax	Fax	○

Click on **Next** to provide a name for your report. Proceed to click on **Save and Run Report** to generate the report. It should look like the following:

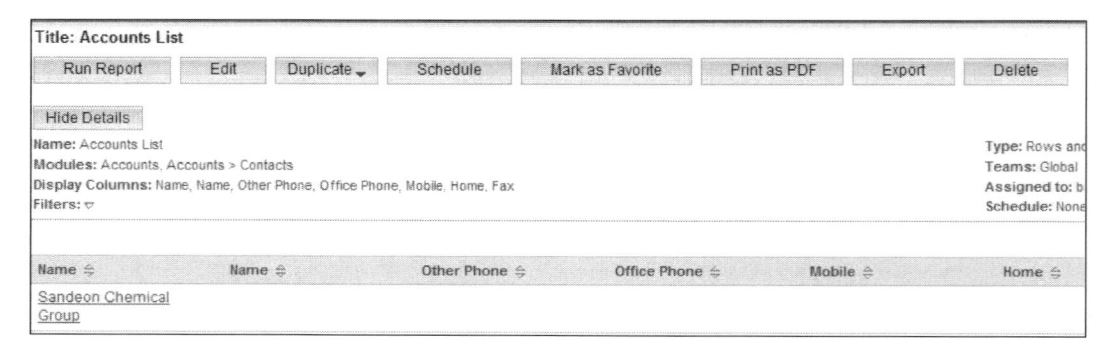

Title: Accounts List

[Run Report] [Edit] [Duplicate] [Schedule] [Mark as Favorite] [Print as PDF] [Export] [Delete]

Name: Accounts List
Modules: Accounts, Accounts > Contacts
Display Columns: Name, Name, Other Phone, Office Phone, Mobile, Home, Fax
Filters:

Type: Rows and
Teams: Global
Assigned to: b
Schedule: None

Name	Name	Other Phone	Office Phone	Mobile	Home
Sandeon Chemical Group					

Notice the option that says **Print as PDF** (to print the report in a PDF format), as well as the **Export** button. They can be used to output the data for use in other tools.

If the user now clicks on the shortcut for **All Reports** and searches for reports with a module value of **Accounts**, the system should show the newly defined report along with others specifically designed for the **Accounts** module as shown in the following image:

[174]

Report Name	Module	Report Type	Date Created	Team	User	Schedule Re
Accounts By Type By Industry	Accounts	Summation	01/04/2008 10:32	Global	admin	-- none --
Accounts List	Accounts	Rows and Columns	04/05/2010 01:45	Global	barbara	-- none --
Customer Account List	Accounts	Rows and Columns	01/04/2008 10:32	Global	admin	-- none --
Partner Account List	Accounts	Rows and Columns	01/04/2008 10:32	Global	admin	-- none --

User teams

SugarCRM Community Edition has a significant weakness in the areas of permission management and data security as its records may only be assigned to a single user. To address this weakness, the Professional and Enterprise Editions allow you to assign data to one or more teams. A team is defined as a collection of one or more SugarCRM users.

Users may be assigned to one or more teams, giving them the ability (say as a Sales Manager) to see sales opportunities and customer information from perhaps the Western, Central, and Eastern regions, if there were a team defined for each region.

The rules for data access are very simple—you can see data if you are in the team to which that data is assigned. If data is assigned to a team to which all employees belong then everyone in the team can see that information. As you can assign more than one team to any given record in the system, the security model becomes rather flexible and is capable of addressing a wide variety of security needs.

Enhanced role management: Field level access

Role management within SugarCRM Community Edition allows you to control a variety of functions that a user can perform within the system. This includes controlling the records that a user can see, edit, delete, export, and so on. Professional and Enterprise Editions expand on this concept by also integrating a *field level control*.

Field level control makes roles a much more detailed security tool. With this capability, users can be prevented from viewing or editing certain fields on a record, although they may have full access to the record as a whole.

The SugarCRM Ecosystem

To define field level controls, simply edit a security role through the **Role Management** tool in the admin control panel, and click on the desired module on the left-hand column.

Clicking on the module will present a list of all the fields it contains, and you can then proceed to choose the level of privileges that the users, who are part of the role, will have to the given field. Once you have finished making your modifications, proceed to save your changes as normal.

Participating in the SugarCRM online community

One of the best places to find SugarCRM information, tips, and technical assistance is on the SugarCRM forums. You can access the forums by pointing your web browser to http://www.sugarcrm.com/forums/. It is not necessary for you to register as a user to read or search the forums, but you will need to register if you wish to post a message.

Another website of importance is the developer's website. There you will find a variety of documents, examples, and other detailed information pertaining to the use of the SugarCRM API, as well as more advanced customization techniques. You can visit the developer website at http://developer.sugarcrm.com/.

SugarCRM user forums

The SugarCRM forums are frequented by both experienced and technically knowledgeable users, as well as those who are new and bewildered. Within the forums, there are major sections dealing with the following:

- Announcements
- General discussion
- Feature requests
- Developers
- Installation & upgrade help
- Translators
- Downloads
- Classifieds
- Help

There are also specific forums for business-oriented discussions on a range of topics and in foreign languages for different users.

New users typically frequent the *general discussion*, *help*, and *installation forums*. Once you get a little better grounded, the *feature requests* and *downloads* areas become very useful and interesting. The *developers* and *translators* areas are rather specialized as indicated by their names. The *classifieds* area is one way to look for a CRM partner—although typically it is frequented by people in the technology business looking for SugarCRM-skilled subcontractors.

While you may read forum posts without registering as a member, to make posts of your own you must register. You can provide a minimum of personal information, or add a photo, signature file, and other personal data to help other people know who they are interacting with.

As a final note on this topic, the general nature of these forums is to foster a sense of community. However, it is important to bear in mind that most other participants are users like yourself and are not obligated to participate in any way. Many choose to volunteer their time and experience to help others for the benefit of the community as a whole, out of kindness or the simple desire to help. From this, it is easy to understand why courtesy and patience are valued traits among forum members.

Summary

In this chapter we have looked at a number of popular add-ons for SugarCRM Community Edition. Each of them extends the system in a direction that enhances the value of the SugarCRM system to your business by adapting it to your growing needs, simplifying user adoption, and system customization.

- SugarForge.org is the primary source of free enhancements and modules, while SugarExchange.com is the primary source of commercial enhancements or modules.

- The Google calendar and contact connectors extend your SugarCRM data to Google services and non-SugarCRM users. It also offers an easy-to-use mechanism for synchronizing data with mobile devices for offline access.

- Microsoft Outlook integration improves user adoption by allowing users to continue using their e-mail client of preference.

- Integration with Microsoft Office can be easily leveraged to generate personalized letters or direct mail pieces for your marketing efforts.

- The enhanced search module adds important capabilities to the advanced search module, such as the ability to toggle between connectors or change the default operand.

- Although Community Edition lacks a reporting solution, ZuckerReports is a full featured reporting solution and is tightly integrated with SugarCRM.

- Some enhancements, like enhanced studio and development toolkit are geared towards simplifying the process of developing and applying various types of customizations.

- Quoting and contract management needs can be easily addressed by the open quoting and contracts module.

- Data assignment capabilities in Community Edition restrict your ability to assign a record to a single user. Security suite enhances those capabilities by providing tools that allow data to be assigned to multiple users by the use of teams.

- Professional and Enterprise Editions of SugarCRM include a variety of features which are not included in the Community Edition, such as teams, product catalog, quotes, forecasting, and other features.

We also introduced various SugarCRM websites—a great place to keep up with the Sugar online community and get more free SugarCRM add-ons—and learned how to use the User forums. The forums can help you find others with similar customization and extension needs with whom to compare notes, and even free open source solutions developed by other users.

In the following chapter, we shall look at the critical issue of introducing your new CRM system to its users, and making sure that the system is received as an easy-to-use, capable, and valuable addition to your business management process. For any CRM system to improve your business efficiency, people have to use it and there are a number of techniques available to ensure that they do.

7
Managing Your CRM Implementation

So far, this book has dealt with the topics of introducing CRM concepts, understanding why CRM requirements differ from one organization to the next, and then studying CRM in detail by installing and using SugarCRM Community Edition (and an array of add-ons) as a candidate CRM solution for your small or medium-size business.

Now that you have a good background in CRM terminology and capabilities, we will study some of the real-world challenges of introducing a new CRM solution into an organization. The goal of this chapter is to leave you with a good understanding of how to approach and structure your own CRM implementation project, with a focus on the following important topics:

- The key steps to a successful CRM implementation
- The CRM training process—awareness, familiarity, and buy-in
- Going live: Stepwise introduction—evolution, not revolution
- Continuous feedback and enhancement

As you will discover, one of the keys to a successful CRM implementation is to approach it in a step-wise manner. A great way to get the CRM ball rolling is a first phase implementation that minimizes disruption and training requirements, while simultaneously maximizing perceived benefits for all key stakeholders.

Key steps to a successful CRM implementation

Before we get too deep into the specifics, you should understand that there is one overriding attribute to any successful CRM implementation: open and frequent communication and collaboration.

The typical groups that are going to be significantly affected by a new CRM system, and therefore, should be involved in its selection, development, and delivery, are the following:

- Executive sponsor
- Project manager
- Implementation team
- Lead trainer
- Internal or external network administration and IT staff
- Finance management
- Sales management
- Sales general staff
- Administration management
- Administration general staff

This group will be your CRM implementation team.

Successful CRM implementations share another important factor. The implementation team should manage the project relatively conservatively—set realistic goals, phase the implementation in modest steps, and view the entire process as one of continual improvement and not as a one-time event. To quote Clint Oram (a co-founder of SugarCRM), "Think big, start small, and move quickly."

Another critical factor of any successful CRM implementation relates to the perceived value it provides. All users must feel that they are receiving some value from the system. This in turn facilitates them to make an effort to support its development and use once it is implemented. For example, sales general staff may be motivated if the system calculates commission reports and will be receptive to the argument that the numbers will only be correct if all opportunities and closed sales are in the system. Perceived value is critical to its success. If users do not feel there is value derived from using the system, they will quickly find reasons to not use it. This is a dangerous position as this type of resistance is a common reason for failed CRM projects.

Planning the implementation

Now that we have these very important principles in your mind, let's plan your implementation.

First, you need to look at the previous list, and translate it into the right people, and the right number of people in your organization. Clearly, the size of the group and the planning effort should be commensurate with the size of the business. For a ten-person organization, it is likely that 3 to 4 people would be required in the implementation process. For a company the size of RayDoc—about 25 people, probably 6 or so will have a role to play. This quickly tapers off, and in a 200-person business you will need no more than 10 to 12 people to be involved in the CRM implementation process.

Your two most important players are the *Executive Sponsor* and the *Project Manager*. Your Project Manager will provide the drive to ensure that the project is executed successfully and your sponsor will provide the encouragement and resources to all other participants to play their part as well. The latter also plays a critical role in establishing CRM as part of the company culture.

Commonly, the executive sponsor may be the President, owner, the finance chief, or sometimes the sales manager. If you have an in-house IT group, the sponsor should not be someone from that group. You need the business and people part of this equation to work out properly.

Although the technical component is also important, it is not the biggest risk. You need to be sure that the CRM implementation is being undertaken because of some perceived business process shortcomings and that the chosen solution will be selected because it best addresses them. The executive sponsor should not only be able to properly convey the shortcomings, but also the business improvements that they seek to obtain from using a CRM system. In short, your project should not be driven by a technology push, but by a business pull.

Your Project Manager should be someone from your organization, not someone contracted for the job. They can work closely with their opposite number on a vendor's implementation team, but they should be someone who all the stakeholders know and trust. Your Project Manager should also be a person known for being very competent and detail-oriented and someone who is also known for communicating openly, taking suggestions, and not being overly political. If the people participating in the CRM implementation team feel that they are just window dressing and not really involved in the process, they will quickly turn negative. If the staff feel that the solution is *imposed*, they will react with cynicism, resistance, and at worst, low commitment.

Managing Your CRM Implementation

Your Project Manager needs to be your champion—someone with the people skills to make employees throughout the organization excited about the new CRM system. As the implementation will increasingly require more work from your Project Manager, you need to address their normal workload to make room for the CRM-related work.

Like any initiative, it is best to work from something other than a blank sheet of paper. While you do not want to present the CRM implementation team with an unmalleable plan at the first meeting, you also don't want to simply ask them "What do you think should be done? What are the goals? What are the potential technology solutions?"

In order to focus and manage the process of agreeing upon a specific set of goals, a specific technology solution, and a particular vendor for customization, it would be advisable for the project manager and executive sponsor to prepare an initial briefing note for the first meeting. This communication should state some of the perceived key shortcomings within the current business processes, potential solutions, the make-up of the CRM implementation team, the proposed timeline, and candidates for the technology to be used.

In terms of the potential solutions being examined, it is best if the short list of candidate systems have demonstrated versions available for members of the team to try out. Clearly, SugarCRM Community Edition is a very good, cost-effective candidate for that list, but it is essential that other opinions on the subject be heard.

A combination of regular meetings of the CRM implementation team, as well as offline investigation and preparation in between meetings, should quickly yield a set of business goals, an agreed-upon technology base, and specifications for customizations. These specifications can be as simple as printed copies of screen layouts with changes marked on them or a more detailed requirements document. Either way, always bear in mind that the person applying the customizations should not be left to assume your desired goal, especially if that person is someone from outside your company.

Remember, that person will use your documentation as a blueprint for your customizations. If your desired goals are left to their interpretation, the end result may not be what your CRM implementation team had in mind.

As a checklist, your planning should aim at achieving the following objectives:

- Identifying Executive Sponsor
- Identifying Project Manager
- Selecting members of the CRM implementation team
- Generating initial briefing note for the first team meeting
- Conducting your first meeting

- Assigning responsibilities and tasks for investigation and team briefing on key topics, such as the following:
    - Identifying and documenting business processes that require improvement
    - Documenting suggested improvements
    - Identifying the top three goals for the implementation
    - Discussing the base technology to be used
    - Showcasing candidates for vendor to perform implementation and customization
    - Discussing phased implementation schedule
    - Discussing the suggested goals for phase one of the implementation
    - Discussing the approach to data migration
    - Discussing the approach to training
    - Discussing the approach to stepwise introduction within the organization
- Delivering briefings at later meetings and key decisions made on the aforementioned topics

Clearly, a larger organization will perform a more comprehensive and slower version of the process just explained, while a smaller one will have a more abbreviated and faster process.

Some common pitfalls

To underscore the points made in the preceding section, and to highlight the importance of planning and communication to the CRM implementation process, the following is a list of some of the classic mistakes typically encountered:

- Failing to get someone to take ownership of the process from start to finish.
- Failing to involve your stakeholders, especially the end users, right from the requirements gathering stage.
- Not having a focus on the current business process, the intended business process improvements, or the specifications for a system that will effect that change.
- The inability to communicate or clearly document current business processes or goals. Do not leave goals open to interpretation as the chances of someone else's interpretation matching your desired goal is rather slim.

- Thinking that implementing a CRM means buying CRM software, installing it on a server, and then telling the intended users about it.
- Not making a particular and continuing effort throughout the project to communicate the benefits specific to each user and stakeholder to ensure their buy-in.
- Biting off too big an initial project phase, or simply proceeding as if phases are a sign of weakness or deficiency. This will load too much expenditure up front, delay implementation, and make the gap in time between initial good will and early project successes too great to bridge.
- Pursuing a very rigid development process. CRM systems are more about people than about technology. A process such as **Agile Programming** is the sort of approach that you should use. In this approach, early prototypes are used to generate feedback. Successive iterations of the user interface ensures that users feel involved, empowered, and happy. Few business users can picture every critical detail of a system or screen at the outset. Likewise, few system architects know exactly what users want. Get fairly close, try it out, and then make the adjustments. Repeat if necessary.
- Not training your trainer early enough, not giving them enough resources to train all users thoroughly, and not planning the roll-out to allow for sufficient training time.
- Failing to define what a successful implementation should look like at the beginning of the project.
- Failing to institute a periodic review of the CRM system and continuing phases of development to further improve business processes and user satisfaction.

It takes a team to win

As we saw earlier in the chapter, a CRM implementation needs the involvement of an entire team of participants. Yes, the executive sponsor and the project manager are of particular importance, but each person or group representing the team is important, and must be continually involved in the process from the beginning till the end.

This continual involvement, coupled with the ongoing effective and frequent communications between all team members, is the one thing that all successful CRM implementations have in common.

Like the introduction of any new business initiative, people know when they are truly involved, or just being invited to meetings guided by an elite few in an attempt to win their cooperation.

The team members who are in management positions should typically be involved in the odd *pre-meeting* meeting to ensure that they are familiar with a specific CRM system, or a solution to a business problem, in advance. They can then back it up in front of the whole group, or help make a change before it goes to the whole group.

One of the most common errors seen during CRM implementations is not paying enough attention in the team collaboration process to get inputs from general sales, operations, and administrative staff. The benefits to be gained from the use of a CRM system are dependent on the analysis and use of the data that these people will enter into the system. For this and two other very important reasons, it is important that these people be onboard from early on in the project's life.

The first reason is the functional aspect. These users are best suited to providing input on constructing an efficient data entry process as they are the ones who will be responsible for entering it on a day-to-day basis. In addition, they can provide insights on the best course of action for screen and view customizations, as well as reports that are needed for everyday use.

The second reason is the human element. The implementation of CRM needs to win these people over and everyone should react more positively if they are involved and have their input heeded, as opposed to a solution imposed on them.

Some of the techniques you may wish to use in managing the CRM implementation team (depending on the size of your business) will include the following:

- Define e-mail groups to keep the entire team up-to-date—psychologically it makes everyone in the team a peer.
- Have the team meet physically once a week throughout the requirements definition process, and have the entire team physically sign off on the requirements.
- During development, the team can meet once every two weeks to review progress against the schedule and to review any escalated issues.
- Once the first pass of development has been completed, the team should again meet once each week. Continue this until the entire organization has been deployed.
- Assuming there are no critical issues, have the team meet again a month after deployment has been completed to review initial feedback and make or plan adjustments.
- Meet again, three months and six months after initial deployment, to perform further reviews.

Setting project goals and specifications

In the initial briefing note presented at the first meeting of the CRM implementation team, you should include suggested project goals, presented in terms of current business processes and talk about the manner in which they should be improved. If required, you should also suggest timelines and phases for the implementation process.

After some initial discussion, and depending on the scale of your business and the CRM implementation, one or more team members should be given the task of documenting the suggested project goals in detail. These can be presented and agreed upon at later meetings.

It will help to first simply agree upon the manner in which each business process can be improved, and not focus on any specific CRM technology.

This approach enables the team to first address the business requirements and then assign one or more members to identify a suggested shortlist of candidates for the core CRM technology to be used for the project.

Once complete, the shortlist of candidates should then be presented to the entire team and a winning candidate should be agreed upon based on its ability to satisfy the agreed upon business requirements and credible references.

Then the team can generate and choose some sketches and specifications of suggested screen layouts for list, detail, and edit view screens. These may only be minor variants of the existing CRM screens, or they may require heavy customization. The overall project timeline and phases foreseen to complete it should also be discussed and agreed upon at this stage.

Once the team has developed and agreed on a set of detailed project business goals, identified the desired project timeline and phases, agreed upon a core CRM technology, and developed detailed drawings and specifications, it is time to look for the CRM development partner. They will help you put your CRM system together and will in effect join the (previously internal members only) CRM implementation team.

Selecting a CRM development partner

If you think you can do this without external help—think again. Ask yourself the following questions:

- Have I worked through dozens of CRM implementations and gained insights into what can go wrong and why?
- Do I have experience in data import and massaging techniques gained from years of CRM implementations?

- Am I comfortable with my ability to interpret a business process into software workflow and screen designs?
- Will I inspire the confidence internally that an external domain expert can?

Your first task in the process of finding the right partner is to assemble a shortlist of candidate firms. A good starting point for your list is the SugarCRM partner directory available at: `http://www.sugarcrm.com/crm/partners/partnerfinder.html`. Make sure that you find a partner who is focused not just on selling or hosting the software, but also on the development of custom enhancements to the standard software—as you will need some without doubt.

You will notice that the directory is organized by major geographical regions, such as North America and Europe. The fact that the firm may not be in your immediate geographic region should not be the reason for eliminating them from your list as there are many reputable organizations based throughout the world.

Other good sources of information are your entrepreneurial peers. It does not hurt to ask your professional colleagues if they have any positive recommendations of firms focused on this type of work.

A final suggestion for building your shortlist of candidates to become your CRM development partner is to simply search for the name of the CRM you intend to use through any search engine of your preference and then look at the advertisements on the right, as well as the links on the left.

Once a member of the team has the shortlist of candidate firms assembled (about three to four is the most you want), then they should bring the list back to the CRM implementation team so that it can be approved and assigned the evaluation work. Do not split up the evaluations—the same one or two people should speak to all candidate firms, and come up with a report and a recommendation to the team.

Emphasis should be placed on personal compatibility with the internal Project Manager, demonstrated competence and knowledge, high quality reference implementations, a credible and acceptable proposed project timeline, and acceptable pricing with perceived high value for the budget.

Before you make your final selection of a partner, the team should make a tentative selection, based on the initial specifications and the candidate firm's estimated development budget. You should then work together to jointly develop a final agreement with a very detailed specification and a fixed development cost. If you can do that successfully, you have your CRM development partner.

Once you make the final selection of your CRM development partner, you will likely have to make a substantial initial deposit against the development work to be undertaken and then you are up and running.

Inevitably, somewhere in this process, the following question is likely to be raised:

- Why not just hire a generic programmer to address our needs, for example, a PHP expert?

The question is usually raised in response to concerns about costs and financial investments that might be required to accomplish your desired goals. The idea being that such a person would demand a lower fee than one who is providing a specialized skill.

While it is certainly possible to meet your needs in this manner, this somewhat mirrors the discussion relating to On-Premise versus On-Demand deployments explained in the earlier chapters of this book. Contracting a programmer without expertise of your selected CRM solution places the burden on you to teach them the important aspects of the CRM system that are relevant to your customization needs.

Given that the programmer is also unlikely to be familiar with the best techniques for customizing the system, you are also risking that the end work may be created using techniques that would not be recommended. For example, using non upgrade safe approaches that in the future can cause other problems.

So while the idea may sound financially attractive at first, you should be cautious of the additional burdens you are placing on yourself. For most organizations, the extra responsibilities and risks outweigh the perceived savings.

System development

The typical CRM development process, even within a single phase of an overall CRM implementation program for your business, is broken down into a number of major areas. These include enhancements to be made to the accounts model, to contacts, to projects, as well as the custom reports and charts you may need.

While some of these alterations may interact with each other, many of them will not. It should be pretty easy to identify clusters of functionality that are fairly independent of each other.

Usually, the best practice is to have the partner develop these offsite, and then introduce each new function cluster to you for evaluation one at a time (typically through a development website that is exposed just to you). Unless you have spent the time and money to develop a remarkably detailed specification, there will always be issues, such as, "I thought that control would be a drop-down, not a radio button", or "I wanted the tab order to go like this ...", or "When you select a value in that field—this other field is meant to be pre-populated."

Performing initial acceptance testing on each function cluster one at a time allows the internal CRM implementation team to focus on it clearly and helps ensure that they get implemented in a manner that meets your specific business needs and requirements. The CRM implementation team can then proceed through the various function-clusters one-by-one, until a full first pass of the application has been implemented and accepted.

Now full acceptance testing on the integrated CRM application should be performed by your team and a formal sign-off should be performed against a specific revision of the software on the evaluation website.

Once that has been done, the CRM application is either hosted by a hosting supplier (which may be your CRM development partner again), or the custom CRM application software is delivered to you for installation on your own server hardware. If the latter, then you will need a further brief acceptance test of the application as installed on your own server.

Data import

While the acceptance testing is going on, any past CRM or contact manager data that you wish to import into your CRM solution should be getting prepared, converted, and imported. Data import, checking, and cleanup can itself easily take weeks to perform (when there is lots of data, and it comes from an awkward and complex source format)—so make sure you allow sufficient time.

Do not think that the big job is to get the data into the CRM, and that you can clean it up afterwards. The big job is to get the data cleaned up. Ask yourself—are there any transformations that should be performed on the data while it is outside a CRM—the assignment of accounts to users, for example—by postal code perhaps? Will you design and run a scan for duplicates?

Another important factor that should not be overlooked is the preparation of the CRM system in relation to your data import. Chances are that the source system does not directly line up with the modules in your CRM system. You may need to add fields or modules specifically aimed at housing the data from your import file that does not already have a natural destination in your CRM system.

Managing Your CRM Implementation

You should also consider the format of your source data. CSV (comma separated values) and other text based file formats tend to be rather popular but are also the most problem-prone. Unfortunately, the built-in import tools of many CRM systems, including SugarCRM, tend to prefer the use of these files, thus presenting a problem. However, these challenges can be overcome by using third party data migration tools that are specifically designed to read data from varied sources and import it into numerous systems, including a variety of CRM solutions.

Many of these data migration and manipulation tools are also open source and freely available on the internet. Some of those tools include **Talend Open Studio**, **Apatar**, **Jitterbit**, and **SnapLogic**. While helpful, effective use of these tools requires some technical savviness.

When you have approved the software customization and development process, and your imported data looks just right, you are ready to start introducing your new CRM to the most important people in the process—its users.

Pilot testing

Pilot testing of the CRM system is a critical step in the deployment process. Each section of the CRM system should be tested by at least one of the users who are most dependent on that section working optimally. For example, the sales management team should test the pipeline charts, the sales staff and finance should test the commission reports for sales and service, and the admin general staff should test the usability of account, contact, opportunity, lead, and case screens. Administrators should evaluate management reports, and so on.

Consider the following, a year after your implementation, no one will remember clearly if it was on time, or on budget. All they will remember is if you produced a system that is now a critical part of the organization's business processes. They will remember if they liked the system, if they felt like a part of its introduction and whether or not they gained some benefit from its use.

Project Managers should not be afraid to send the system back for re-work if the initial pilot testing indicates significant dissatisfaction with the usability of the system, or the accuracy with which it adheres to the desired business processes.

The CRM training process

CRM training has two goals. One is to make the users familiar with the system and teach them how to use it. The other goal is to generate positive momentum and enthusiasm for the implementation.

To accomplish this latter goal, you need to make sure that people like what they see, especially the general sales staff and to some degree the general administrative staff—as these are the two most likely sources of resistance and negative reactions.

Therefore your approach should be as follows:

Session 1: Initial management training and product exposure

Goals:

In the first session, the following points are included under goals:

- To create an awareness in Senior management, to stimulate questions, and to discover any shortcomings early within a controlled group that consists of those individuals most likely to be supportive of the CRM implementation and its goals.
- To finalize and clarify all system access details with IT.

Attendees:

The list includes the following:

- Lead trainer
- Project manager
- Executive sponsor
- Internal or external network administration and IT
- Finance management
- Sales management
- Administration management

After the first session, all the attendees should be encouraged to go and use the system, enter live data, and make note of any problems, questions, or dislikes.

Next steps:

Your next step would be as follows:

- A week later, this same group should re-assemble for session 2

Session 2: Management training completion and issue management

Goals:

The following points are covered:

- To complete the management training, so that Senior management has a good understanding of the system's capabilities, and how to operate the system.
- To make management enthusiastic about the system.
- To ensure management's full support of the broad introduction of the CRM system.
- To allow management to answer questions about the system knowledgeably, and to correct any misinformation later on from the staff.
- To address any management concerns about the system functionality and clarify any misunderstandings. Also, identify any last-minute system shortcomings that must be addressed prior to general introduction of the system.

Attendees:

This is same as session 1 except for IT which is optional.

Next steps:

During session 2, the following points are covered as your next steps:

- Any mandatory fixes must be identified, documented, summarized and agreed upon by the CRM implementation team, and then developed and applied.
- If any fixes were required, this same group should re-assemble for session 3 to review the fixes.

Session 3: Present final system adjustments (optional)

Goals:
During your third session, the following should be considered as your goals:

- To reinforce the perception that the system will evolve over time, and will genuinely be guided by the needs of its users.
- To ensure management's full support of the broad introduction of the CRM system.

Attendees:
This is same as as session 1.

Next steps:
Schedule session 4 a week later.

Session 4: General user training session

Goals:
The following are covered as your goals during session 4:

- Note that there may be multiple classes scheduled for session 4. No class should have more than 6 users in it. Separating users by department is a good idea—Sales staff will have questions on different topics than those in Administration.
- To present the CRM system capabilities and method of operation in a comprehensive and logical manner.
- To stimulate class participation and questions.
- To record user feedback and allow users to pose questions.
- To define initial goals for scope of use (departmental management participation is mandatory for this).

Attendees:

The list includes the following:

- Lead trainer
- Project manager (not all sessions if there are many)
- Sales management
- Sales general staff
- Administration management
- Administration general staff
- All other general staff that will use the system

Next steps:

Optional follow-up session 5, two weeks later.

Session 5: Training completion (optional)

Goals:

Session 5 will show you how:

- To close off any open questions
- To address any questions that have arisen in the last two weeks
- To represent training sections where users seem uncertain
- To ensure a positive attitude on the part of all users
- To record any outstanding concerns or issues

Attendees:

The following is a list of attendees who participate during session 5:

- Lead trainer
- Project manager
- All staff who wish to participate

Next steps:

Your next step would be the following:

- Presentation of training results to CRM implementation team, including any outstanding issues identified.

CRM training materials

The most important prerequisites for the CRM training sessions are as follows:

- A good trainer who can understand the business context, as well as relate to the users at their level.
- A quiet training room with an overhead projector connected to the laptop/PC of the trainer, a meeting table, and plenty of room for all attendees.
- A group of not more than six attendees, to create a constructive learning environment, and also to prevent disagreement during the feedback session.
- All the users should be pre-configured in the system prior to the session, so that they can see themselves already set up as users. So they can use the CRM system during the session to complete exercises and afterwards to continue to familiarize themselves with it.
- Handouts highlighting the key topics discussed in training that users can use to follow along and take notes, and use as a reference point after the session.

It is also important that you take care of your timing utilized for user training. If your CRM implementation team has not yet identified the business processes to be improved, or established the goals of the CRM system, you will find that differing opinions on what should or should not be part of the scope and how it should be addressed in the CRM system will quickly surface and hinder the training process.

Expect each training session to be 75 to 90 minutes long. Any longer, and attendees will want to avoid them—attention spans will only stretch so far.

While the various sessions that we outlined earlier have different goals and attendees, the material to be presented at the main sessions (1 and 4), as well as used for backup material at the reinforcement sessions (2 and 5), is largely common.

The remainder of this section contains suggested content to be used to make up a set of overhead slides and handouts to be used as training material for these sessions.

If you present the material in slides, it is a useful technique to switch back and forth between the slideshow software and the web browser (with a live session on the go) to illustrate general points with specifics from the live software.

Managing Your CRM Implementation

Always be prepared to stop the presentation to answer questions—the users must always feel that the company is listening to them.

Slide 1: What is a CRM system?

This slide defines a CRM system as follows:

- A system that manages the information and processes surrounding your organization's relationship with its customers
- Principal goals are to improve customer satisfaction and retention, sales efficiency, and performance
- Consolidates all communications between your staff and your customers
- Contains sales and marketing automation tools along with service/support tools
- Not a contact manager—it is typically based on the distinction between an Account and a Contact
- Includes opportunity tracking and sales pipeline, lead source analysis, corporate calendar and e-mails

Slide 2: What are our business goals?

This slide discusses the following:

- It asks you to fill in the goals identified by your CRM implementation team
- On your list you may want to include the following:
  - Improvement of customer satisfaction and retention
  - Improvement of sales efficiency and performance

Slide 3: What functional areas of CRM will we use the most?

Slide 3 answers the following:

- Again, you need to fill in the key areas of focus for your organization
- Will you simply use the core basic CRM capabilities, or broaden its use to include Marketing Campaigns, Project Management, Document Management, and so on?

Slide 4: What is SugarCRM?

This slide defines SugarCRM and includes the following:

- A leading CRM implementation from a commercial open source vendor in California
- Delivers CRM capabilities (and more) through a web browser
- Where do users go for support— internally and externally?
- Other resources: manuals, SugarCRM.com, and so on

Slide 5: CRM basics 1—system access, screen layout, navigation

Slide 5 discusses the following:

- Logging in—username, password, selecting language, and theme
- Principal screen layout elements
- Navigating SugarCRM—tab or side panel navigation, shortcuts
- List, detail, and edit views
- Performing searches
- Main panel and subpanels
- Logging out

Slide 6: CRM basics 2—accounts and contacts

This includes the following:

- Account information content
- Contact information content
- Information on relating contacts to accounts
- Permissions and security—who sees my information?

Slide 7: CRM basics 3—opportunities and the sales pipeline, home tab

The following points are covered under slide 7:

- Opportunity information content
- Home tab—my pipeline, my top opportunities
- Dashboard charts

Slide 8: CRM basics 4—calendaring

Slide 8 explains about calendaring including the following:

- Home tab calendar
- Calendar module—day, week, month, year views
- Shared calendar

Slide 9: CRM basics 5—activities (calls, meetings, tasks, notes)

The following activities are covered:

- Creating a task
- Scheduling a call
- Scheduling a meeting
- Making a note—file attachments
- My upcoming: appointments, calls, meetings
- My open tasks

Slide 10: CRM basics 6—e-mail

Slide 10 discusses the following:

- Entering your e-mail settings
- Receiving e-mail
- Sending a single e-mail
- System e-mail notifications
- E-mail templates

Slide 11: CRM basics 7—advanced interface features

The following topics are explained under slide 11:

- Printing
- Getting help
- Data import and export
- Mass update
- Quick new item box
- Input business card
- Create from vCard

Slide 12: Extending CRM 1—RSS news and external sites

Slide 12 includes the following:

- Interface consolidation concepts
- RSS news feeds
- External websites

Slide 13: Extending CRM 2—marketing campaigns

The following points are covered on slide 13:

- Targets versus leads and contacts
- Target lists
- Marketing campaigns
- E-mail marketing program
- Mass e-mailing queue

Slide 14: Extending CRM 3—document management

The following points are discussed in slide 14:

- Document information content
- Document revisions
- Document upload
- Document download

Slide 15: Extending CRM 4—project management

It covers the following:

- Project information content
- Project tasks
- Monitoring project status

Slide 16: Extending CRM 5—customer service management

Slide 16 discusses the following:

- Service cases
- Bug tracker
- Case and bug history

Slide 17: Extending CRM 6—always in touch

Slide 17 explains the following points:

- Pros and cons of various remote access techniques
- VeryThinClient—wireless access
- Google connectors

Slide 18: Extending CRM 7—reaching out

Slide 18 discusses the following:

- Website lead collection
- Customer self-service portals

Wherever possible, provide users with short exercises that they can perform on their respective computers. This will help retain their attention and more importantly, help reinforce concepts being discussed.

You should also consider video recording the session and making the recording available to users. Doing so would allow users to review the material at their leisure or when they need a refresher.

Lastly, the most effective method of learning will vary by individual. Some people prefer visuals, while others are indifferent to them. Make sure to include annotated screenshots and other visual components to highlight or reinforce important points in your presentation.

Going live: Stepwise introduction

Once employees have been introduced to the new CRM system and fully trained, it is time to go live.

A common technique is to conduct general user training in segments, usually by department, and to take each department live after they have been trained. If you adopt this approach, be sure to allow enough time after each department is trained. This will allow them to come to terms with the system, and get any questions that they have answered by the support staff, before the next group goes through. This will help control the workload of the support staff and allow them to be more responsive, as they will not be overwhelmed.

This is a common approach used by a variety of CRM consultants. Throughout this process, it is important that you make absolutely sure that you have an accurate reading on user acceptance in all departments and roles of the organization (from acceptance testing to pilot testing). Once you have taken one group live, negative feedback from another group could indicate that you have a serious problem.

Continuous feedback and enhancement

Just as a business does, every CRM system needs continuous evaluation and enhancement. As your business changes, so must your CRM system. Some of these changes may be the result of changes in your business environment. In response, your CRM must evolve and improve to maintain and advance your competitive standing in your industry.

Until the CRM system achieves a high-level of internal user satisfaction, it should be reviewed at least once every business quarter for usability improvements, in addition to any potential opportunities to automate additional business processes.

Once the system is popular internally, it should be reviewed at least once every six months for potential improvements and enhancements. In particular, opportunities should be sought for more advanced methods (typically involving external connectivity) of improving your customer relationships and satisfaction, such as the following:

- Customer self-service portals
- Automated website lead collection
- Automated client e-mails
- Advising of product shipments and problem resolutions
- E-mail marketing campaigns

Summary

In this chapter, we analyzed the process of managing and delivering a CRM implementation. Some of the key topics that we studied include the following:

- The makeup of a CRM implementation team
- The key steps to a successful CRM implementation
- How to plan your CRM implementation
- Some common pitfalls to avoid in your CRM implementation
- The importance of genuine team involvement
- How to set CRM implementation project goals and specifications
- How to select a CRM development partner
- Managing your data import process
- The CRM training process, for both management and staff
- CRM training materials—suggested content for a CRM training slideshow was provided
- Stepwise introduction of your CRM system as a key to a successful initial CRM implementation and overall long-term CRM program
- Continuous user and customer feedback resulting in improvement of the CRM system as key to keeping your business operating at its competitive best

In the following chapter, we will go on to study more advanced CRM topics that increasingly link your CRM to all your key business processes, as well as to your existing customers and future prospects. Typically, an organization will address these capabilities after the initial phase of the CRM implementation is complete, as a part of its ongoing program of continuous improvement. We will be discussing some fairly complex but important CRM issues, such as integrating your CRM system with your public website and with a customer self-service portal. These are not typical goals of the first phase of a CRM introduction. As such, you may choose to regard the topics that follow this chapter as an overview to those business processes that you may address with future phases of your CRM implementation program.

8
Linking Your Customers to Your SugarCRM

Surely, the most important goal of any CRM system is to make your customers feel positive about your company and to make them feel that exciting things are happening at your company, such as the following:

- That the employees they are in contact with are caring and well-informed
- That new and better information systems are coming into place
- That your company is responsive to product and service issues, and cares about its customers

Limiting CRM system access to only the employees of a business will certainly affect the first of the aforementioned items positively, but not necessarily the other items. To really improve a customer's perception of your organization, one of the biggest improvements you can make is to allow customers to interact almost directly with your CRM system. Some of the activities that make this possible are as follows:

- Capturing customer leads and requests for information from the public website directly within the CRM system.
- Efficiently tracking customer service requests and related product/service flaws to help improve your offerings and customer satisfaction.
- Developing a customer self-service portal in conjunction with the CRM system to allow clients to file their own service cases, check on the latest status of a case, and to update their own customer profile.

Most of us in our own lives can forgive or understand if a family member, friend, or supplier lets us down a bit, or makes a mistake—as long as they communicate with us honestly and effectively. In addition, with early detection of any errors, corrective action can always be put in place more quickly. Integrating your CRM system more directly with your customer is no more complicated than this—promoting more effective, more accurate, and timely communications with your customers. The net effect of such actions is that your customers feel informed, valued, and empowered.

Capturing leads from your website

Capturing leads from your company's website directly into your CRM is one of the greatest early initiatives you can implement in terms of streamlining business processes to save time and effort. This section will guide you through the manner in which this can be accomplished with SugarCRM.

In the past, setting up a process similar to the one just described would have required the expertise and assistance of a programmer and your webmaster. Coordinating everyone's efforts to accomplish the goal would sometimes become a task in and of itself. Days may have elapsed before your lead capture form finally made it up to your website. Fortunately, those days are behind us.

SugarCRM includes a tool that allows you to quickly and easily create a form that you can use to capture leads from your website. Through this tool, you will be able to select the fields corresponding to the data you wish to capture and also create a ready-to-use web form. Let us set up a web lead capture form through SugarCRM's tool.

> The lead capture tool is specifically designed to import data into the Leads module only. Should you choose not to use the Leads module, or you wish to use a similar technique to capture data within a different module, you should use SugarCRM's **SOAP API** to accomplish the task. See *Appendix E* for additional information on the SOAP API.

To begin the setup process, hover over the **Marketing** tab and select **Campaigns**. On the shortcuts menu on the left-hand side, click on **Create Lead Form**, as highlighted in the following image:

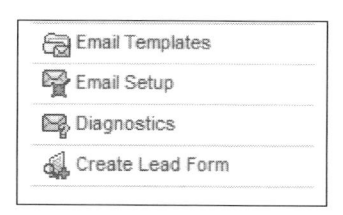

- Email Templates
- Email Setup
- Diagnostics
- Create Lead Form

After clicking on it, you will see a screen that permits you to select the fields you wish to capture through your form, as illustrated in the following screenshot:

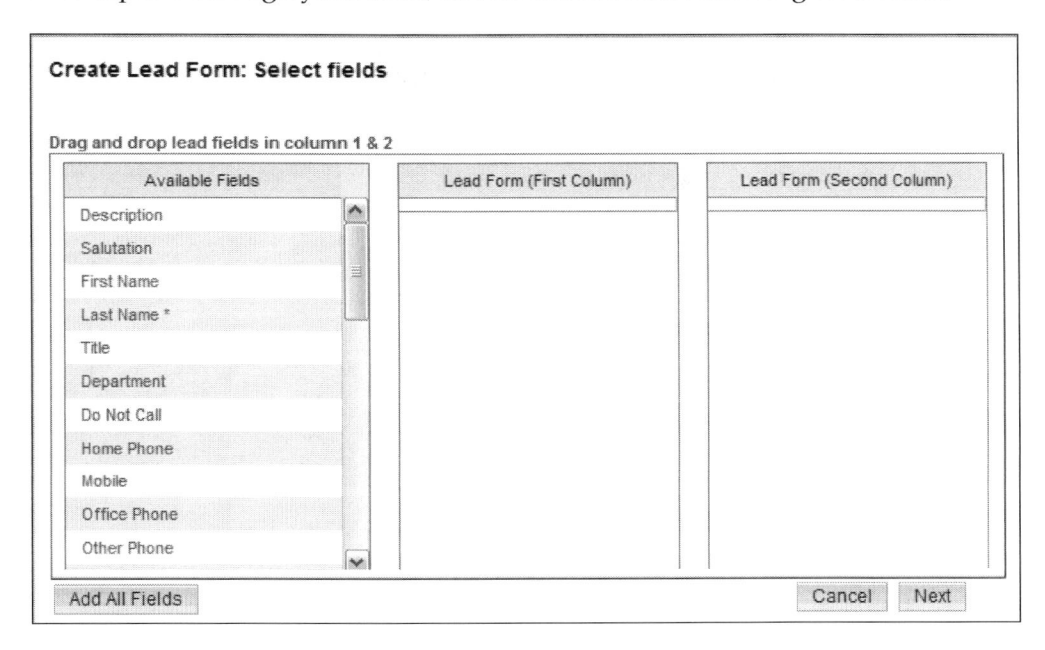

Create Lead Form: Select fields

Drag and drop lead fields in column 1 & 2

Available Fields	Lead Form (First Column)	Lead Form (Second Column)
Description		
Salutation		
First Name		
Last Name *		
Title		
Department		
Do Not Call		
Home Phone		
Mobile		
Office Phone		
Other Phone		

Add All Fields Cancel Next

The field selection process is quite simple. On the leftmost column of the three that are presented, you will see a list of all the fields corresponding to the Leads module (including custom fields).

To select a field for your form, simply drag-and-drop it from the field listing on the left onto one of the two rightmost columns.

Linking Your Customers to Your SugarCRM

It is best to visualize the layout of the form that will be produced as one similar to the edit or detail view layouts. Fields can appear next to each other, horizontally or vertically, but only within one of two columns. Most organizations prefer the vertical approach, which is the technique we will apply. However, feel free to experiment.

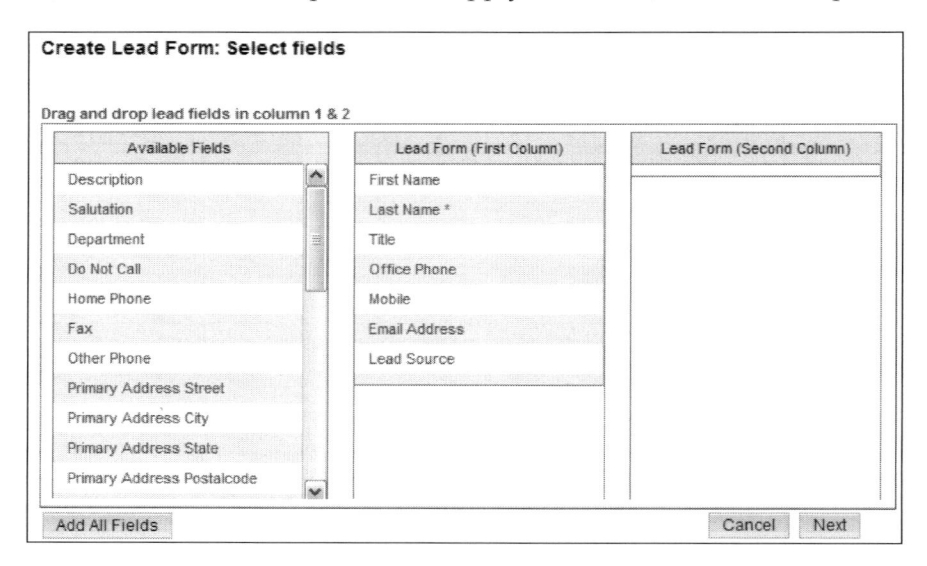

Create Lead Form: Select fields

Drag and drop lead fields in column 1 & 2

Available Fields	Lead Form (First Column)	Lead Form (Second Column)
Description	First Name	
Salutation	Last Name *	
Department	Title	
Do Not Call	Office Phone	
Home Phone	Mobile	
Fax	Email Address	
Other Phone	Lead Source	
Primary Address Street		
Primary Address City		
Primary Address State		
Primary Address Postalcode		

Add All Fields   Cancel   Next

Proceed to select the fields to match the preceding image, plus any other fields you may wish to include. Note that required fields are marked with an asterisk, as they are within the Edit view screen. You must make sure to include all your required fields to ensure that the process will work as expected.

In addition, you will notice that we have selected the **Lead Source** field. Doing so will allow website visitors to make the appropriate selection corresponding to what drove them to your site. Click on **Next** once you are satisfied with your field selection.

Now you need to set some final parameters, as illustrated in the following image:

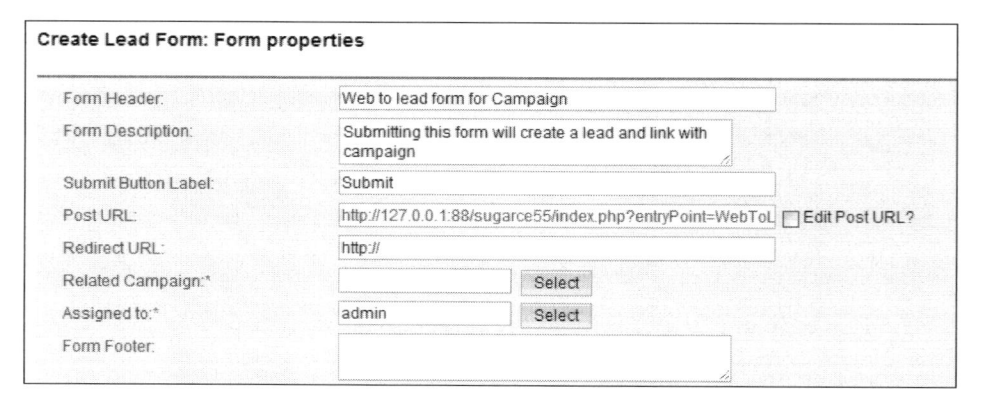

Create Lead Form: Form properties

Form Header:	Web to lead form for Campaign
Form Description:	Submitting this form will create a lead and link with campaign
Submit Button Label:	Submit
Post URL:	http://127.0.0.1:88/sugarce55/index.php?entryPoint=WebToL ☐ Edit Post URL?
Redirect URL:	http://
Related Campaign:*	[ ] Select
Assigned to:*	admin Select
Form Footer:	

[208]

You will undoubtedly want to modify the **Form Header**. This value corresponds to the title of the page that website visitors will see in their browser, so you will want to tailor it to reflect something a bit friendlier than the generic text.

The form we are building is no different than any other web form you may have encountered in your day-to-day web browsing. As such, it too will include a button for visitors to click and send the data they typed in. If you prefer the label of the button to read as something other than the default label of **Submit**, change the **Submit Button Label** accordingly.

The **Redirect URL** and **Related Campaign** fields are also quite important. The former is used to specify a URL that a visitor will be sent to after clicking on the **Submit** button on your lead capture form, while the latter is used to associate a particular marketing campaign to the form. Establishing this relationship is critical as it will help you properly measure the effectiveness of your marketing efforts.

Lastly, the **Assigned To** option allows you to define a user to whom the Leads will be assigned upon being entered into SugarCRM. You may want to consider creating a specific user, such as **WebCapture**, and assigning the Leads to that user. Doing so will permit you to quickly identify records that entered your system through the web lead capture tool versus other means.

Click on **Generate Form** after you have applied your edits and you should see something similar to the following:

Linking Your Customers to Your SugarCRM

The default form should now be presented within SugarCRM's HTML editor. This is a handy capability as it allows you to manipulate the look and feel of the form to make it conform to the already existing look and feel of your website. However, you may wish to ignore that, as additional options allow you to more easily integrate it into your website. To access those features and save the form, click on the **Save Web To Lead Form** button.

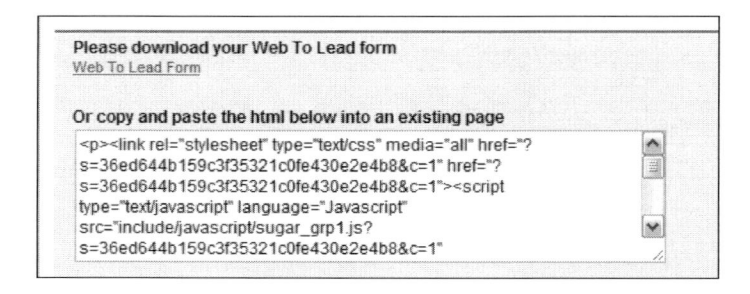

```
Please download your Web To Lead form
Web To Lead Form

Or copy and paste the html below into an existing page
<p><link rel="stylesheet" type="text/css" media="all" href="?
s=36ed644b159c3f35321c0fe430e2e4b8&c=1" href="?
s=36ed644b159c3f35321c0fe430e2e4b8&c=1"><script
type="text/javascript" language="Javascript"
src="include/javascript/sugar_grp1.js?
s=36ed644b159c3f35321c0fe430e2e4b8&c=1"
```

SugarCRM provides the convenience of a fully formatted, ready-to-use web form which can be downloaded by clicking on the **Web To Lead Form** link. However, if you prefer, you may copy the code displayed in the box and then embed it into one of your already existing pages. The second approach would save you the hassle of having to modify the cosmetic aspects of the default page to match your site.

To start receiving data into your SugarCRM system, simply place the form on your web server, fill out the fields and submit the form. Make sure that the server on which it is placed is able to access your SugarCRM system or it will not function.

You can test it by opening the form in your web browser and submitting data, as shown in the following image:

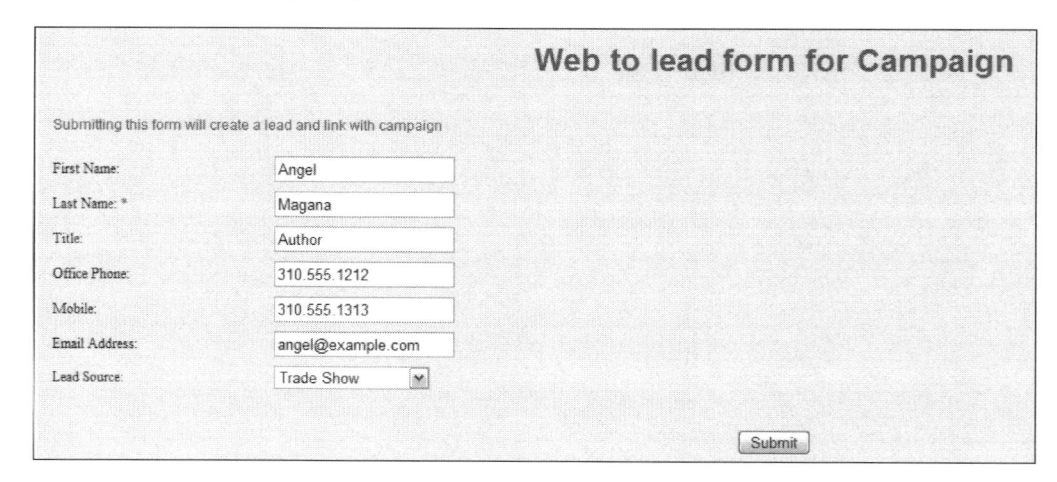

Web to lead form for Campaign

Submitting this form will create a lead and link with campaign

First Name:	Angel
Last Name: *	Magana
Title:	Author
Office Phone:	310.555.1212
Mobile:	310.555.1313
Email Address:	angel@example.com
Lead Source:	Trade Show

Submit

Assuming everything is working as expected, the records will automatically appear within the leads module of your SugarCRM system without any intervention on your part or that of other users. In addition, e-mail notifications of new records will automatically be sent to the defined assigned user to inform them of the new entry so they may act upon it. Through the use of add-on modules, like **SierraCRM's Process Manager**, further actions, like the scheduling of follow up calls, can also be automated. Remember, all of this can happen automatically and herein we begin to see the real benefits of a CRM system.

There are few things quite as satisfying as driving along in the car, and receiving an e-mail on your BlackBerry telling you that a new lead has been received. Especially, when you know that it all happened automatically!

From a process perspective, the concept of having every new lead automatically entered into the CRM system makes it quick and easy to convert that lead into a contact, enter details of new sales opportunities, or include them in e-mail marketing campaigns—all without any data transcription errors, or lost leads, due to human errors.

> One note of caution: most lead capture sites capture as much as 50% bad data. Some visitors to your site will enter anything they fancy in the form; potentially polluting your database. This highlights another reason why it is beneficial to enter them by utilizing a username such as **WebCapture**. Doing so would allow you to easily filter leads to only show those created by **WebCapture** and in turn allow you to cleanse them, either by deleting them or performing other data integrity checks.

Customer self-service portals

After automating the lead capture process, the most common step that follows in linking your customers into your CRM system is the self-service portal.

Just as it sounds, this is a software system that enables your customers to exchange information with your organization in a completely autonomous manner. In this initial implementation, we will show you how to implement a system that allows customers to submit and manage service cases directly within your CRM system.

Most of us have had the experience of needing to contact a call center to address a customer service issue or other matters. Usually, that process involves staying on hold for some time time. If you are lucky, the time that you stay on hold is not long, but at the same time, spending 30 to 45 minutes on hold or being transferred around is not unheard of. To make matters worse, you usually need to make these calls during normal business hours, meaning you are not able to tend to your normal work while you are burning time on hold.

Linking Your Customers to Your SugarCRM

The fundamental capability that the self-service portal provides is empowering customers by allowing them to contact you at a time that is most convenient to them. Customers are no longer bound to specific business hours, nor must they wait in a call queue or navigate a maze of phone options. If they need your company's help to resolve an issue, they simply go to your website and submit their issue.

Likewise, customers do not need to contact you directly to check in on their previously submitted cases. They simply visit your website again and they will be able to review their cases.

This functionality works hand-in-hand with the Cases module that is built into SugarCRM. Typically, users would leverage this module to track service calls that they receive from customers. Through this functionality, all members of the organization are kept up-to-date on any issues that a customer may be experiencing at any given time.

The Bug Tracker module complements the Cases module quite well by providing a central repository where all known product flaws can be tracked. In turn, all cases resulting from any of these flaws can be related to a given bug, allowing you to measure the impact it is having on your customers. Together, they can be used as very effective tools for not only providing customer service, but also prioritizing product development needs and improving customer satisfaction.

However, that process can be inefficient, as it relies on a user to enter the data to produce a case in the first place. Empowering the customer in such a way that allows them to directly interact with the Cases module not only makes it easier for you to get feedback and become aware of problems, but it also gives customers the feeling that you care to hear what they have to say about their problems. That is the goal that the self-service portal hopes to accomplish.

Self-service portal configuration

Before we get too deep into the specifics of configuring and using the self-service portal, you must first understand some important boundaries.

First, although this is a built-in feature of the Enterprise Edition of SugarCRM, it is not a feature of Community Edition. To obtain this functionality, we must use the combination of a SugarCRM add-on available on SugarExchange.com, plus an open source **CMS (Content Management System)** named **Joomla!** If you are already using another CMS package or cannot use Joomla! for other reasons, you may want to skip ahead to the next chapter as you will not be able to utilize the functionality described in this exercise.

The second and last important note is that, at the time of this writing, the add-on did not support versions of SugarCRM Community Edition higher than 5.2.

Now that we have a clear understanding of some important limitations, let us begin the process of deploying this feature.

Installing Joomla!

Assuming you have already installed SugarCRM Community Edition on the target server, you have already established the perfect environment for installing the Joomla! CMS package. Like SugarCRM, it too leverages the LAMP or WAMP system software platforms. Just like SugarCRM, it is also an open source application.

You can download Joomla! from the project's site, located at `http://www.joomla.org`.

> Our exercise will use version 1.5 of Joomla! (Full Package). It is assumed that you have already successfully downloaded and installed it onto your server. If you require help with the process, visit the Joomla! website to review its documentation and obtain further assistance.

Assuming Joomla! is operational, proceed to access the administrator page. It should resemble the following:

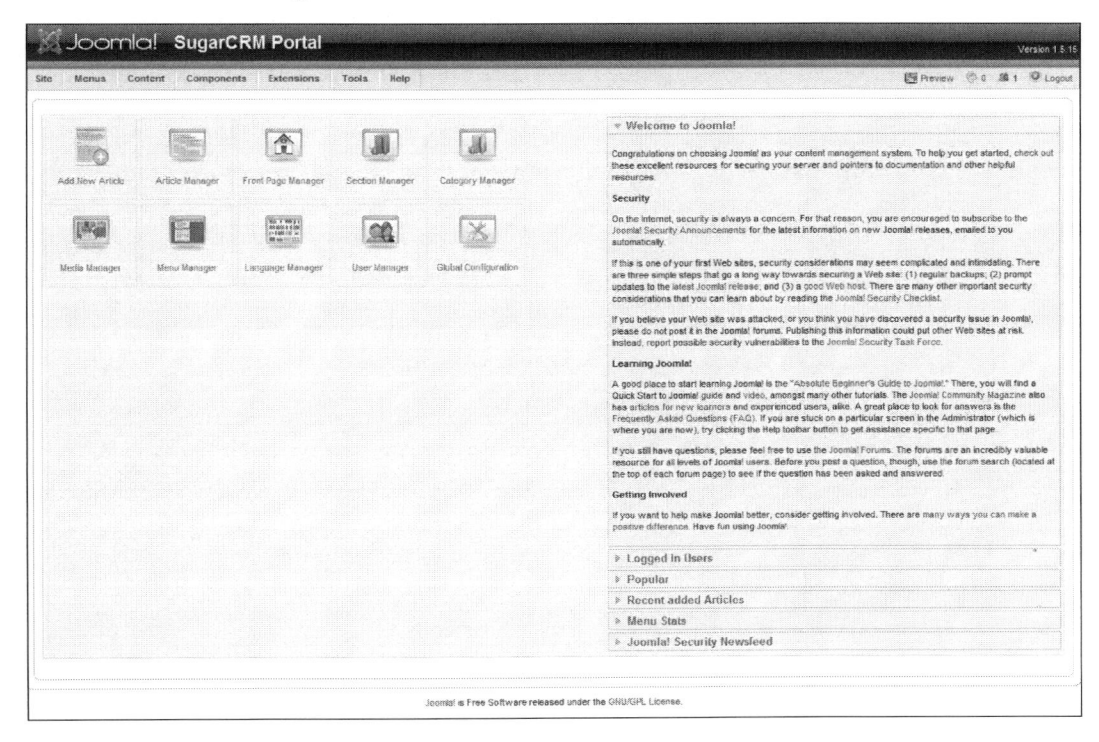

Let us leave it at the admin page for now.

Installing the SugarCRM portal component for Joomla!

Our next step will be to download and install the **Sugar Portal for Joomla** add-on. This add-on will act as a bridge between Joomla! and SugarCRM to provide the functionality that we are seeking.

You can download it from the Sugar Portal for Joomla project page located at the following URL:

`http://www.sugarexchange.com/product_details.php?product=474`

The Sugar Portal for Joomla consists of two Joomla! components, to extend its functionality as follows:

- **com_sugarbugs**: This links the Joomla! portal to SugarCRM using Sugar's SOAP communications facility to provide searching, creating, and editing of software bug reports.
- **com_sugarcases**: This links the Joomla! portal to SugarCRM using Sugar's SOAP communications facility to provide searching, creating, and editing of services cases.

Our example will focus on the cases component.

In order to install and use these objects within Joomla!, you will first need to define a portal user within SugarCRM. This will represent the set of SugarCRM credentials that Joomla! will use to communicate with the CRM system.

Within the admin area of SugarCRM, create a new user—typically with the username **Portal**, and the **Portal Only User** checkbox selected. This user will be used exclusively for this purpose and will not be a valid login for SugarCRM as a normal user. This is shown in the following screenshot:

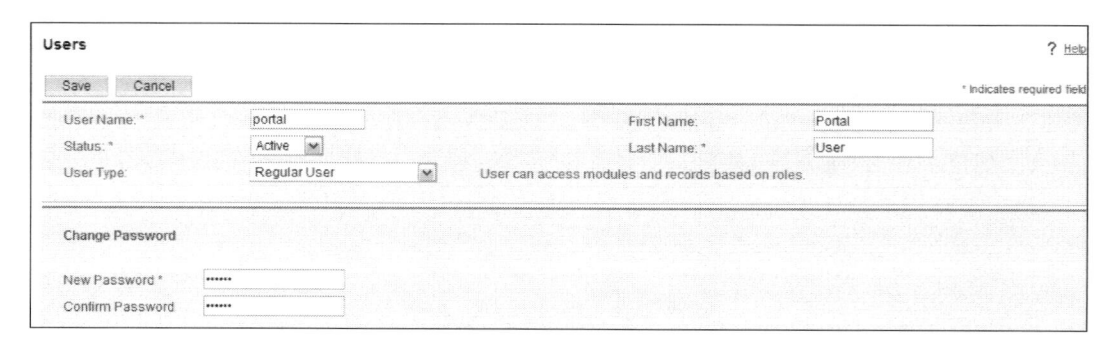

> IMPORTANT: You must download and read the installation instructions (`install.txt`) on the Sugar Portal for Joomla project page BEFORE proceeding. The document contains important information pertaining to configuration changes that must be manually applied to SugarCRM in order to enable the portal functionality.

Next, you must use the administration area within Joomla! to install the various components needed by Joomla! to link to SugarCRM. You should first install `com_sugarcases` and then `com_sugarbugs`. Assistance on installing Joomla! components can be found at `http://www.joomla.org`.

Once the components are successfully installed within Joomla! we need to configure them so that they communicate with your instance of SugarCRM. Let us take a look at the process of configuring the SugarCRM cases component.

In Joomla!, select **Components | Sugar Cases | Configuration**. Update the **Password**, **Sugar Soap Location**, and **Username** fields to reflect the portal user and password combination created earlier in SugarCRM.

You will also need to enter the URL that corresponds with your installation. The URL can be easily obtained by looking at the address field on your web browser while working within SugarCRM. For example, your test installation may indicate a URL of `http://127.0.0.1:88/sugarce52/` or `http://sugarcrm.example.com/` (as shown in the following screenshot). In either case, you will want to append the text `soap.php` at the end of it, so it reads as `http://127.0.0.1:88/sugarce52/soap.php` and `http://sugarcrm.example.com/soap.php` respectively. Save your changes when done.

GLOBAL	Password	Enter new: •••••• Confirm: ••••••
GLOBAL	Row Color	#dfe9ff
GLOBAL	Sugar Soap Location	http://127.0.0.1:88/sugarce52/soap.php
GLOBAL	Use Sessions	✓
GLOBAL	Username	portal

Linking Your Customers to Your SugarCRM

You will then be given the opportunity to select the SugarCRM case record fields that you wish to display within Joomla! Leave it set to the default settings for now, as shown in the following image. You can always modify it later should the need arise.

Lastly, you will need to add SugarCRM cases to the Joomla! menu system so that website visitors are able to access it.

To add the menu option, select **Menus | User Menu** and click on **New**. Select **Sugar Cases** and enter **Support Cases** for the **Title**. Set the **Access Level** to **Registered** and verify that **Show the Title Page** is set to **Yes** under the **Parameters (System)** section. Click on **Save** when done. The following screenshot shows how menu options are added:

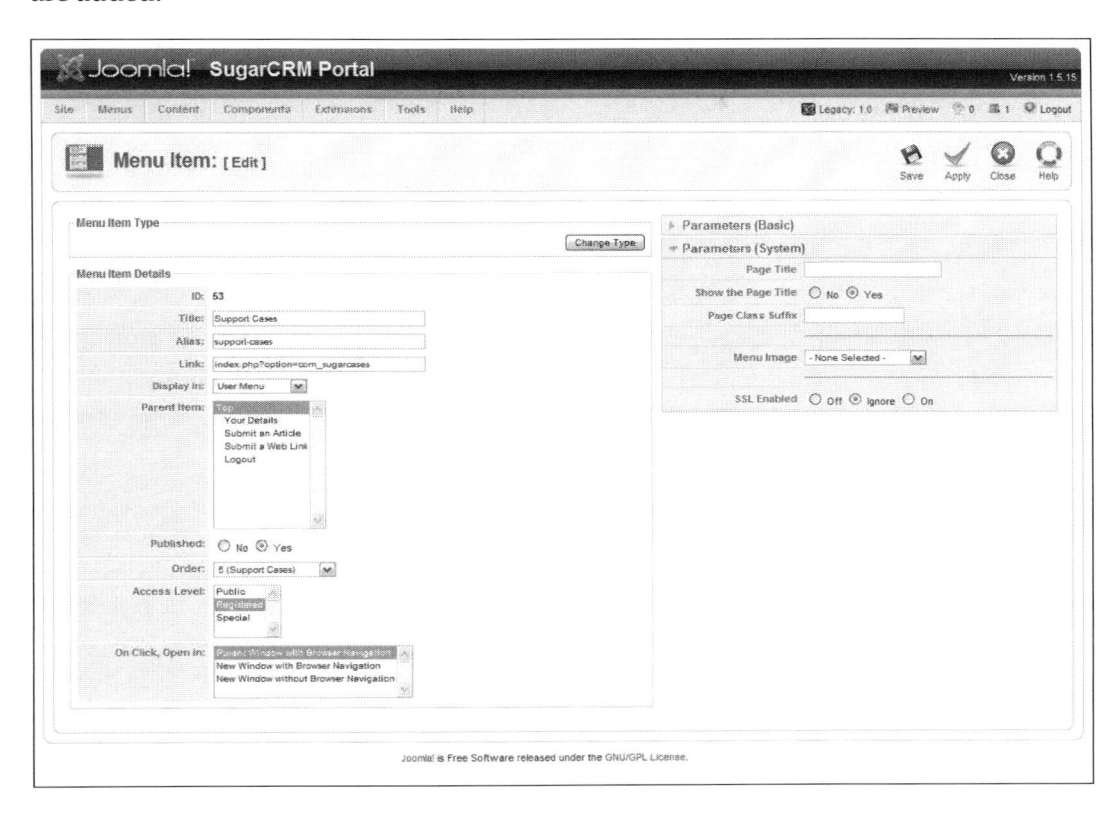

That should do it for the Joomla! side, but how do we tie the data in SugarCRM to a specific Joomla! user?

This is accomplished by means of the portal fields on a contact record. Switch to SugarCRM and access the contacts module. Select a random contact and access its edit view screen. At the very bottom of the screen you should find the following:

The **Portal Active** checkbox enables/disables portal access for the current contact record. The value specified in the **Portal Name** field is of greater importance as it is used to establish the relationship between a Joomla! user and a SugarCRM contact (this is displayed in the following figure). In turn, that allows Joomla! the ability to display and manage cases related to the specified contact.

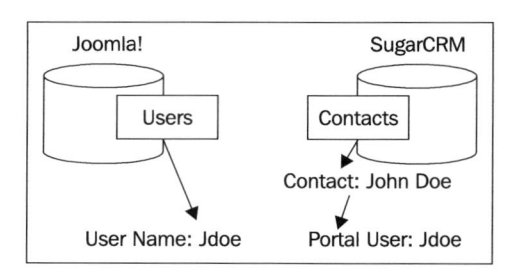

```
    Joomla!                    SugarCRM
   ┌──────┐                   ┌──────┐
   │ Users│                   │Contacts│
   └──────┘                   └──────┘
                          Contact: John Doe
   User Name: Jdoe         Portal User: Jdoe
```

Enter a value in the **Portal Name** field and enable the **Portal Active** checkbox on the record, and save the record. Take note of the value you specified in the **Portal Name** field as you will need to create a Joomla! user with the same name as described in the next section.

Creating a new Joomla! user

Use the Joomla! administration menu to navigate to **Site | User Manager**, and then click on the **New** icon to create a new user. Once you have entered the user information (note that you need to set **Group** to **Registered**), click on the **Save** icon. Make sure that the user that you have created matches the value from the **Portal Name** field from SugarCRM.

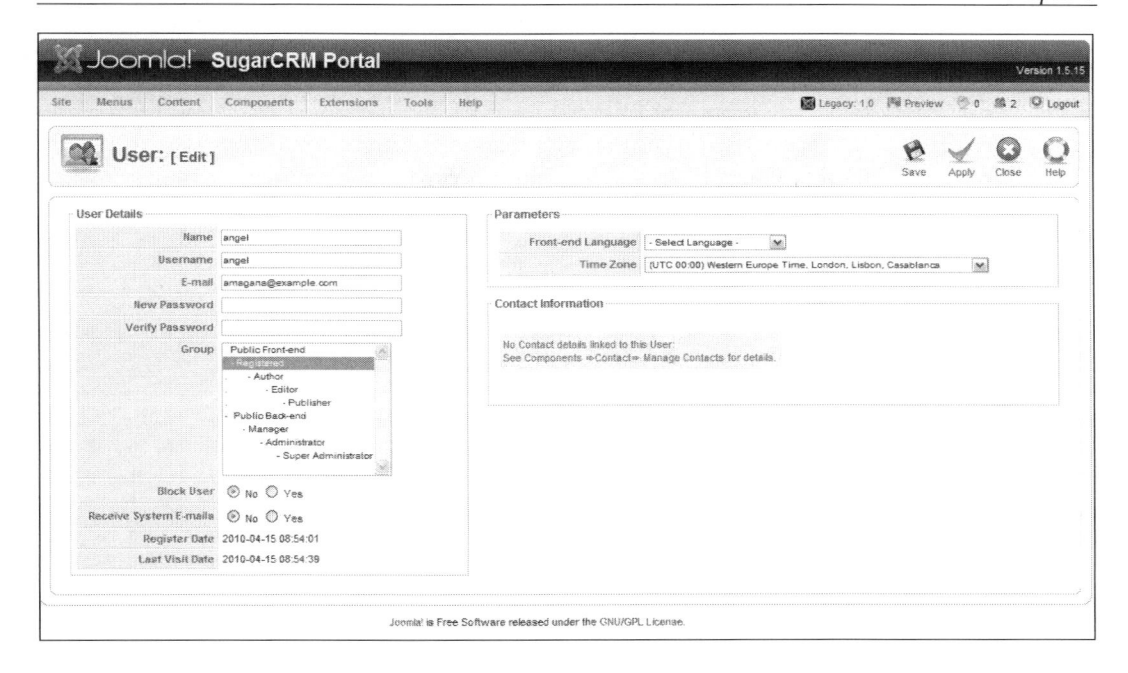

Using your new self-service portal

You should now be able to use your self-service portal. Log out of Joomla!, and log in to the regular Joomla! website as the new Joomla! user that you just created by navigating to `http://localhost/joomla`.

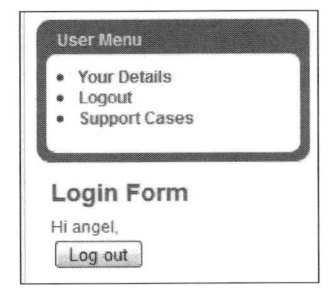

Click on the link for **Support Cases**. From here, you have choices for **Home** (which lists all cases that relate to your user), **New** (to create a new case), and **Search** (to look for a specific case). Note that the following image demonstrates a default Joomla! page. You will most likely want to modify it to match the branding of the rest of your website or general corporate imagery and style guidelines. Rest assured that such modifications can be made through standard CSS modifications and Joomla! customization techniques.

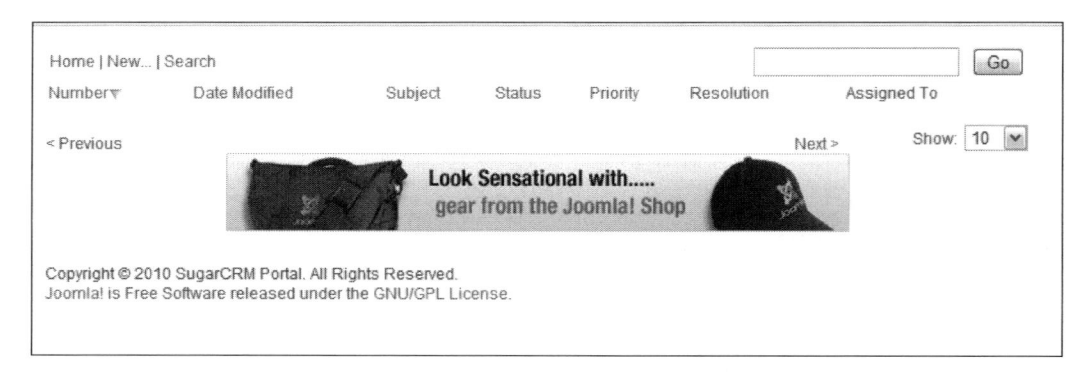

Click on **New** to create a new case. Enter a name for the case, and a description, as shown in the following image:

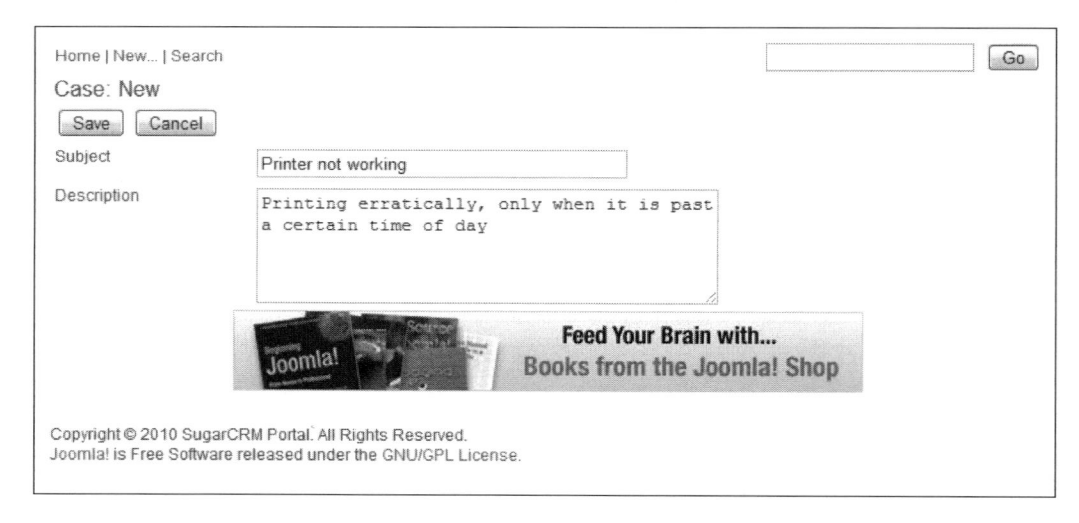

[220]

Upon clicking on **Save**, the case is submitted and entered into SugarCRM. Within the portal, you should see the following:

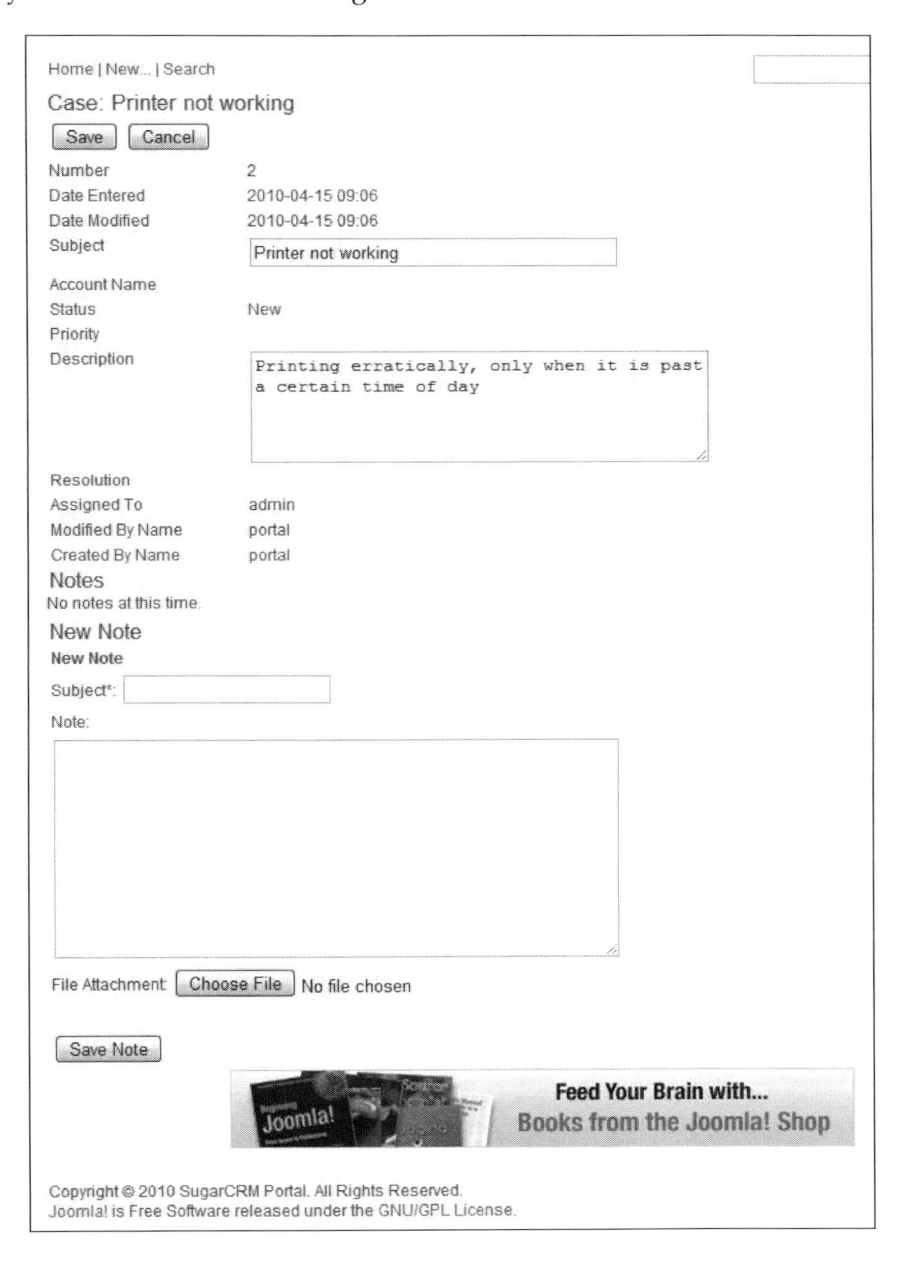

Now, switch to SugarCRM and take a look at the Detail view screen of the contact associated with the Joomla! user who has just submitted the case. This is depicted in the following image:

As you can see, the case was not only entered into SugarCRM, but it was also automatically linked to the corresponding contact.

While we have only illustrated self-service case management capabilities here, it does serve the purpose of highlighting possibilities rather well. This component uses the standard SOAP interface for SugarCRM and by investing some development time to further the related Joomla! components, you could create all sorts of customer self-service applications, such as document sharing portals, project tracking portals, and so on.

This sort of technology use is only going to grow faster and faster in the coming years. Now that you have seen what it can do for a business, do you really want to compete without these tools against companies that are using them to their full potential?

Summary

In this chapter, we have covered two key techniques for linking your CRM to the outside world, and more specifically to your current and potential customers.

Lead-capture applications are simple to set up, and have immediate impact on the bottom line in terms of both creating revenue, and cutting administration costs.

Developing customer self-service portals is a key technique to maximize the return from your CRM investment. They keep your customers better informed and happier, while improving efficiency and reducing costs in the customer service and support areas.

From here, the sky is the limit. The future will hold many new developments in the CRM field. One widely anticipated trend is that CRM systems act as their own portal—offering carefully controlled and regulated direct access to the CRM for customers and suppliers. This will allow them to see only that information and navigation capability that the system is set up to allow them.

At the current speed of evolution and development in the CRM field (especially in the red-hot field of CRMs for smaller businesses), we can expect this type of development, and many others, within the next year or so. I look forward to updating this book to describe them.

A
Installing SugarCRM on Linux

One of the first challenges that you will encounter with regards to the installation of SugarCRM on a Linux powered server is deciding on a well-suited distribution of Linux.

Earlier in this book, we touched on the fact that numerous options exist, which in turn makes the selection process a bit daunting. Fortunately, there are some parameters that we can use to help us make a choice. More specifically, you want to make sure that you select a distribution that contains versions of the required software (Apache, PHP, and MySQL) that meet the SugarCRM system requirements.

You can familiarize yourself with the supported versions by visiting the official system requirements web page on the SugarCRM website, located at the following URL:

`http://www.sugarcrm.com/crm/products/supported-platforms.html`

Take a look at the web page now and you will notice that, by default, it shows you information pertaining to the most recent version of SugarCRM. At the time of writing this book, that was Version 5.5.1.

Installing SugarCRM on Linux

If you are in the process of installing an older version, such as Version 5.2 or even 4.5.1, the shortcuts on the left-hand side of the web page can be used to display that version's system requirements.

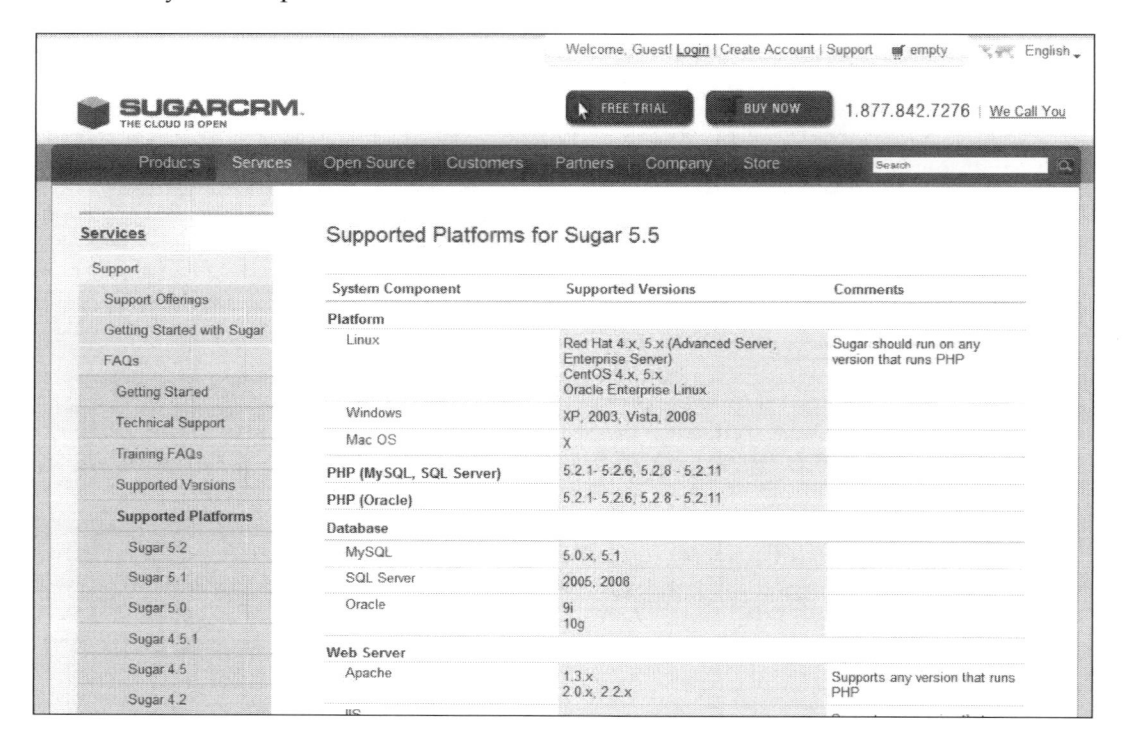

Now back to the topic of selecting an appropriate distribution.

A quick search on the internet for information on which distribution is best will surely yield a long list of results. There are many differing opinions on the qualities that make one distribution better than others, so much so that it becomes less than helpful.

We are going to sidestep that discussion. Our example will utilize the CentOS distribution, Version 5.4, for a couple of important reasons.

First, CentOS is based on the Red Hat Enterprise Linux distribution, arguably the most popular distribution in use today. The importance of this point is not that one should follow the crowd, but that a large user community represents widespread support.

Appendix A

On a related note, it also means that the system has been exposed to a larger variety of environments (for example, differing hardware configurations, varied user loads, and others) when compared to other distributions. Normally this type of exposure would result in more thoroughly tested, stable, and fault tolerant software. Coincidentally, this approach is a basic tenet of open source development, to allow a maximum number of individuals access to the code so that they may improve it or identify problems in a timely manner.

The final reason for selecting CentOS is far simpler: SugarCRM's data center uses it. It is hard to argue against its use given the fact that SugarCRM (the company) uses it to provide the SugarCRM On Demand service. CentOS has proven itself in an environment specifically designed for SugarCRM and for a large number of users. It should be able to handle your SugarCRM needs just as well.

You now need to get your hands on CentOS and install it. To get a copy of CentOS, visit http://www.centos.org and click on the download link. Notice that there are links for i386 (32 bit) and x86_64 (64 bit) Versions. SugarCRM is rather neutral in this regard and either of the two versions will work. However, in case you are wondering about the feasibility of the 64 bit Version, it is the same as that used at the SugarCRM data center.

The remainder of this section will assume that you have already downloaded the necessary software and created the necessary discs, or are able to read the ISO files. Detailed information on creating the discs can be found at the following URL:

http://www.centos.org/docs/5/html/CD_burning_howto.html

> While visiting www.centos.org, you might have noticed that Version 5.4 of CentOS includes Version 5.1.6 of PHP. If you are installing a version of SugarCRM newer than 5.2, you will need to update the version of PHP to the one listed on the Supported Platforms web page you visited earlier. Step-by-step instructions on installing the updates are available at the following URL:
>
> http://wiki.centos.org/HowTos/PHP_5.1_To_5.2

Installing SugarCRM on Linux

Basic CentOS Linux installation

To install CentOS Linux Server carry out the following steps:

- Insert the CentOS installation CD, disc 1 (or DVD if you downloaded the DVD image) into the target system and reboot. You should be able to see a screen similar to the following:

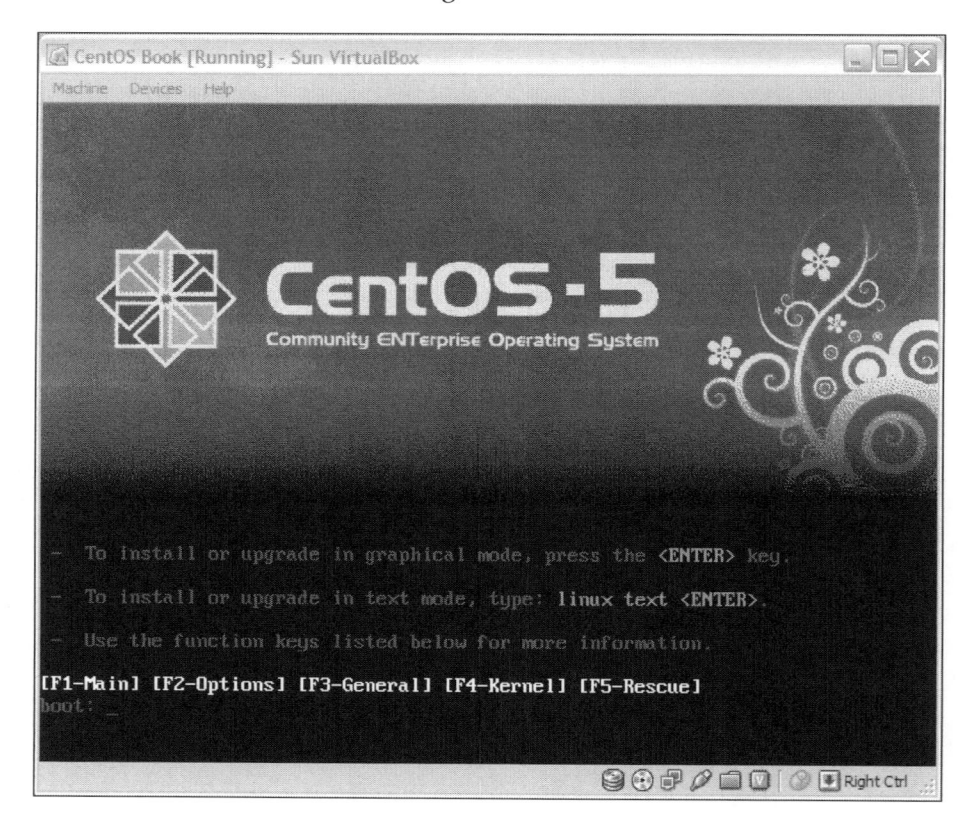

- Hit the **Enter** key to start the installation process.
- Choose **Skip** when prompted to test the CD images. You should see the following screen:

Appendix A

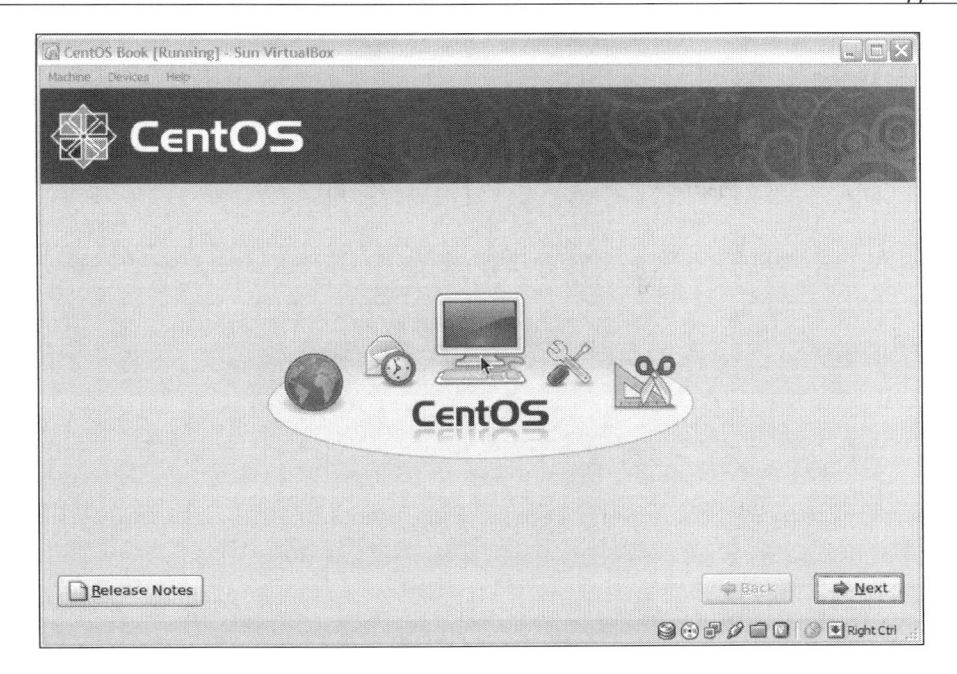

- Proceed through the installation wizard choosing your desired language, keyboard layout, and other parameters. Continue the installation process until you get to the following screen:

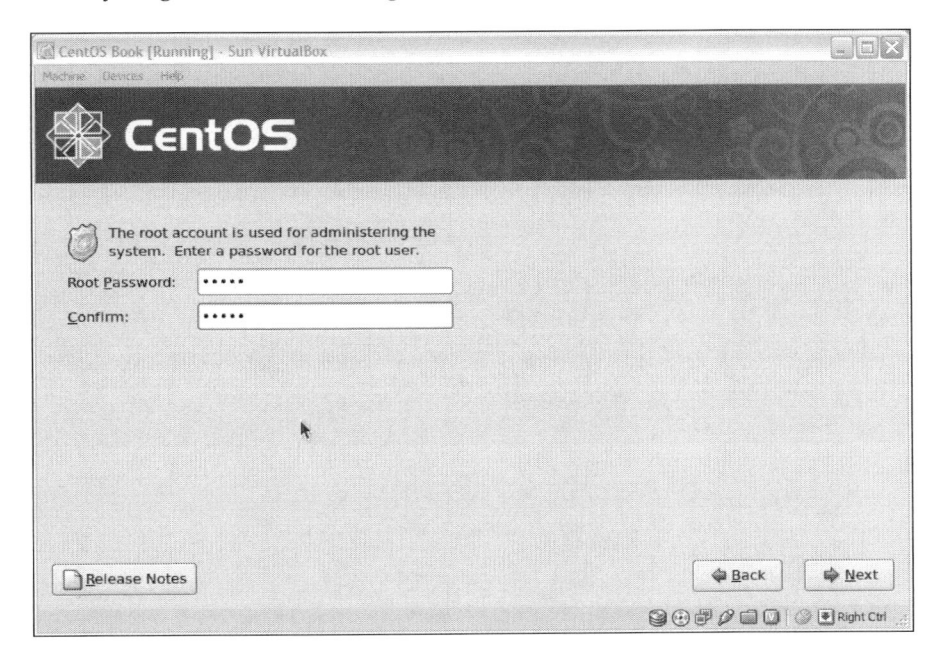

Installing SugarCRM on Linux

- When prompted, define a strong password for your *root* user and make sure to make a note of it in a safe place.
- Next, you will need to make some adjustments to the default selections on the software selection screen as shown in the following image:

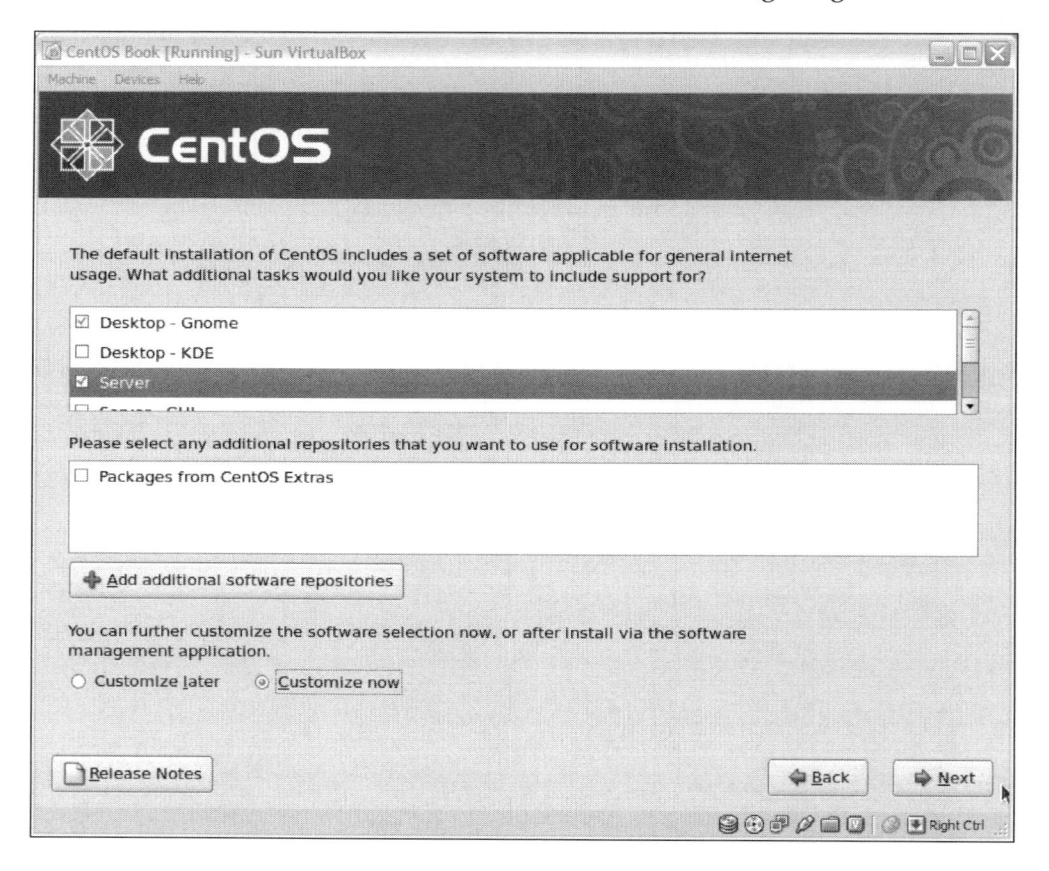

- Verify that **Server** and **Customize Now** are selected before proceeding. This will ensure that you install all the necessary components.
- On the screen that follows, select **Servers** and **MySQL Database**, as illustrated in the following image:

Appendix A

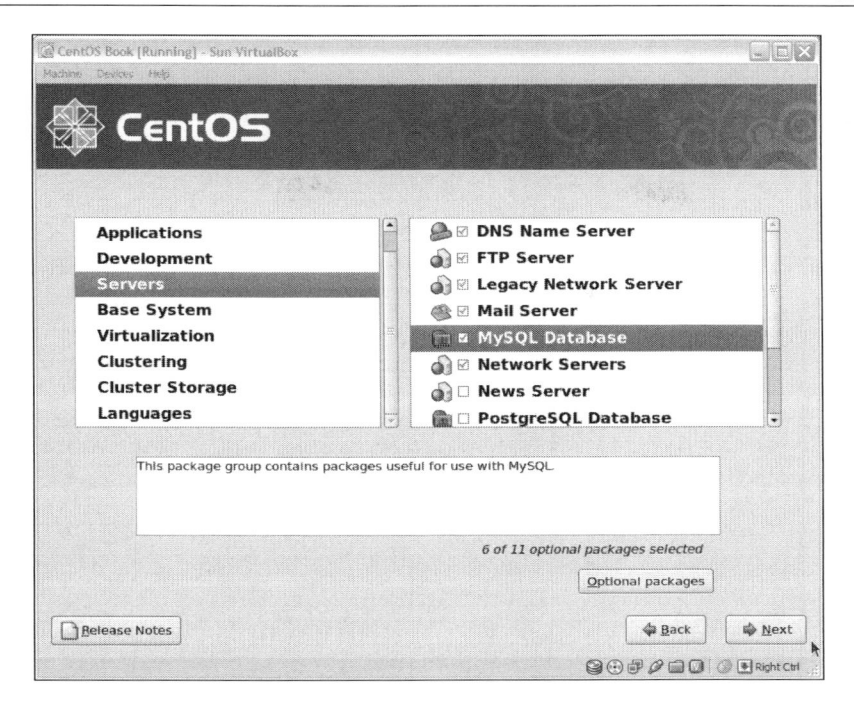

- Proceed with the remainder of the wizard and initiate the installation process as shown in the next image:

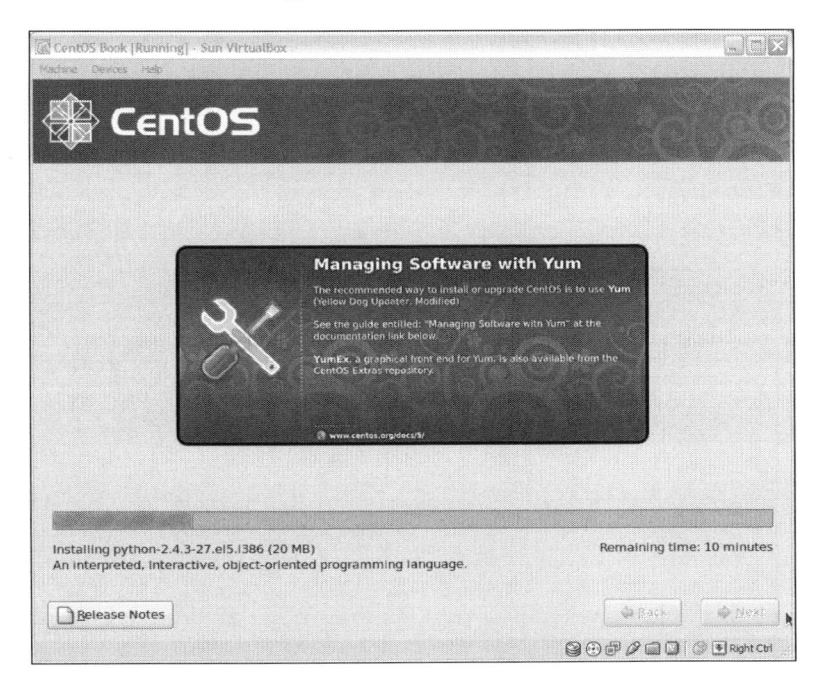

Installing SugarCRM on Linux

Once the installation process has been completed, we need to adjust some settings to ensure that our PHP environment is properly configured and at the right version level.

If you recall from earlier in this section, Version 5.4 of CentOS includes Version 5.1.6 of PHP, which should not be used with versions of SugarCRM newer than 5.2. There is no need to worry, however, as step-by-step instructions for installing an updated version of PHP are available at the following URL:

http://wiki.centos.org/HowTos/PHP_5.1_To_5.2

You may have noticed that the images were taken from an installation being performed on a **Sun VirtualBox** virtual machine. A virtual machine is precisely that, a digital representation of a physical server. VirtualBox is one of various software packages available today that provides this type of increasingly popular functionality.

The popularity of virtualization is primarily due to its ability to reduce costs. As a single physical server can be used to host multiple virtual machines, each performing different functions, hardware and other ancillary costs (such as electricity) are reduced. The danger, however, is that a major failure on the physical server has the potential to impact all the virtual machines it is hosting—this poses a bit of a risk.

If you are considering using virtualization technology for your SugarCRM deployment, either for the web or database server component, rest assured that it is a perfectly acceptable (and common) approach to deploying it, especially when using Linux.

Let us now proceed to configure our newly installed CentOS system to prepare it to host a SugarCRM installation.

Configure the CentOS Linux installation

Upon first booting up, CentOS will automatically prompt you to make some adjustments to its configuration to better tailor it to your needs. You can configure the firewall settings as shown in the following screenshot:

Appendix A

[Screenshot of CentOS 5 Firewall configuration screen in VirtualBox]

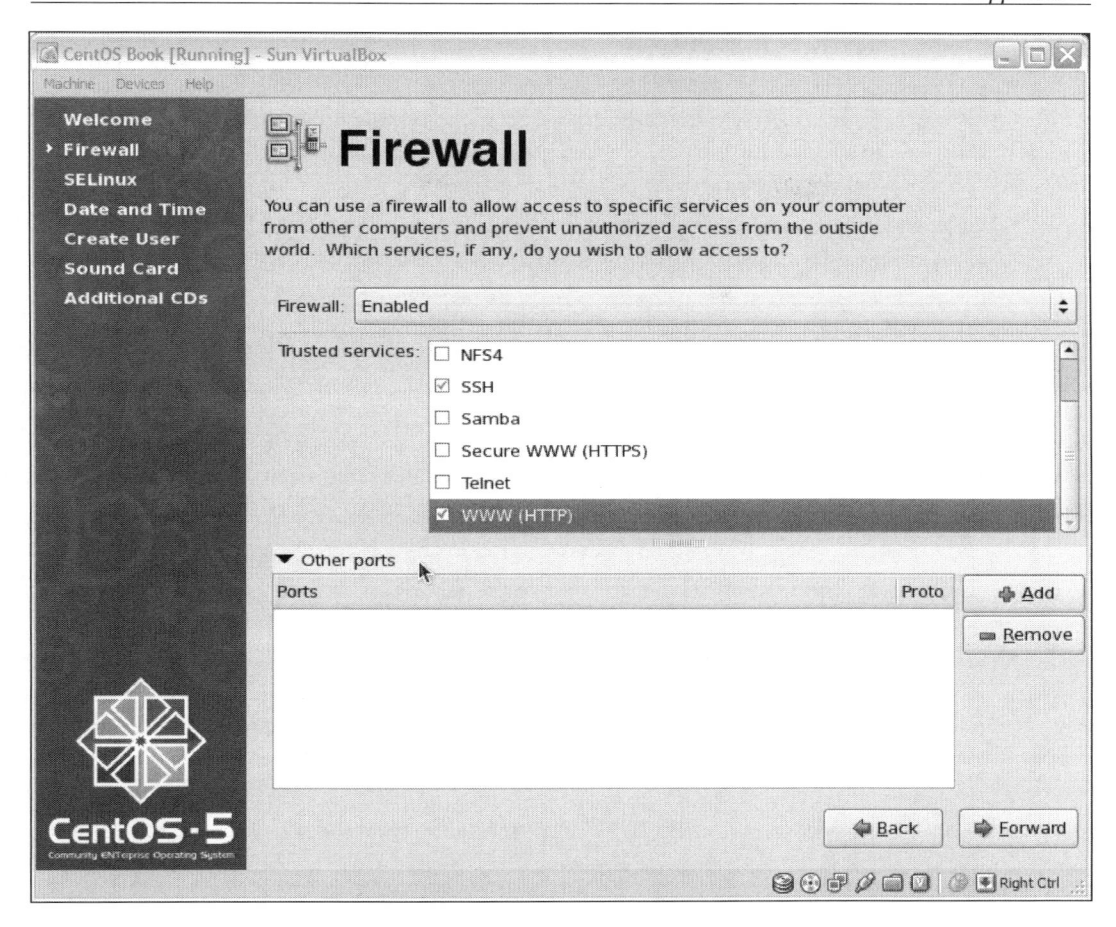

Carry out the following to configure the firewall settings:

- Adjust your firewall settings to enable **WWW (HTTP)** and **Secure WWW (HTTPS)** if you intend to use a secure connection to access your SugarCRM instance.
- If you intend to access your MySQL database from a system other than the server, you will need to add port **3306** within the **Other ports** section.

Installing SugarCRM on Linux

- Proceed through the remainder of the wizard, and when you reach the login screen (as shown in the following image), login as **root**, using the password that was defined at the time of installation.

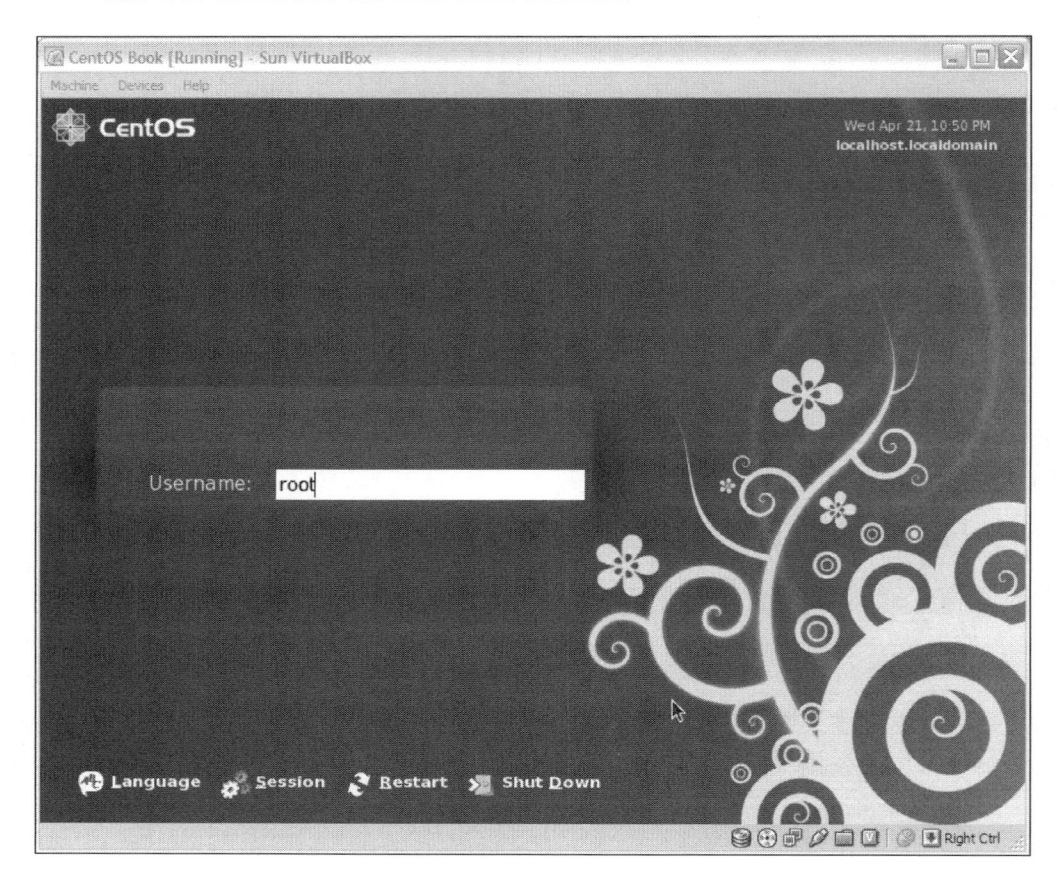

Now that you are logged into the system, we will need to verify our PHP settings and install some PHP extensions required by SugarCRM.

Updates to PHP should be installed at this time. If your intention is to install a version of SugarCRM that is newer than 5.2, do not proceed until you have already completed the upgrade. To check your version of PHP, select **Applications | Accessories | Terminal** and execute the command:

```
php -v
```

The remainder of this chapter assumes that you already have a supported version of PHP installed on the system. It also assumes that you are familiar with performing functions, such as browsing and editing text files within the Linux operating system.

[234]

Appendix A

Configuring PHP

Before you dive into adjusting PHP settings, you need to install a couple of important extensions. The first is `php-imap`, used for e-mail functionality and the other is `php-mbstring`, used for double-byte character support.

To install them, execute the following commands:

- `yum install php-imap`
- `yum install php-mbstring`

Once these extensions are successfully installed, proceed to modify your PHP configuration.

To modify your PHP configuration perform the following steps:

- Navigate to `/etc` and open the file `PHP.INI` using the text editor of your choice.
- Search for the **memory_limit** parameter and set its value to at least **64M** (**256M** would be preferred). If not adjusted, there is a tendency for blank screens and other odd behavior to occur while attempting to use SugarCRM.
- Search for **max_execution_time** and set it to **300**. Too low a value usually results in actions that starts, but remain incomplete. For example, exporting a large number of records may fail when exporting a smaller set of the same data succeeds.
- Set **max_input_time** to **300**. This allows a 5 minute window for large files to be uploaded. Inadequate values usually result in problems when using the **Upgrade Wizard**, uploading files/attachments, or using the **Module Loader**.
- Search for **display_errors**, and set it to **Off**. This will suppress the display of warning messages, which will otherwise disrupt the display.
- Search for **post_max_size**, and set it to **25M** to allow large documents to be uploaded. Then search for **upload_max_filesize**, and set it to **25M**. The effect of these two changes will be to allow a document file of 20 megabytes in size to be uploaded to the system.
- Search for **session.gc_maxlifetime**. Note that by default it is set to **1440** seconds, which is 24 minutes. This controls the length of time a SugarCRM session can be idle before the session is terminated. A session represents a unique connection to SugarCRM and is automatically initiated when a user accesses the system. If a user's session is terminated, the user will need to login again before they can interact with SugarCRM. A value of 3600, or 1 hour, is usually adequate, but feel free to increase or decrease its value.

- Make sure that when setting the aforementioned values in `php.ini`, the entire line is not preceded by a semicolon, as this indicates that the line is merely a comment and not to be processed.
- Lastly, we need to add the following lines to the Extensions section to enable the IMAP and MBString modules:

  ```
  extension=imap.so;
  extension=mbstring.so;
  ```

- Save your changes to the `PHP.INI` file, and restart your web server to apply the changes.

You may verify your PHP settings at any time by creating and viewing a PHP file with the following code in it:

```
<? php
phpinfo();
?>
```

Once verified, change the extension on the file to something other than `.php` to prevent unintended access to that information.

The environment should now be ready to host your SugarCRM installation. Let us proceed to walk through the process of installing SugarCRM on your CentOS server.

Installing SugarCRM Community Edition

Your first step after configuring the server will be to download the installation files for SugarCRM Community Edition. The files can be downloaded from the following URL:

`http://www.sugarcrm.com/crm/download/sugar-suite.html`

Clicking on the **Download now** button will deliver the most recent version of SugarCRM Community Edition. As of the time of writing this book, the most recent Version was 5.5.1. Before downloading, verify that the current version that is available for download does not contain the moniker **BETA**, **RC1**, **RC2** or the likes attached to its name, usually following the version number. Such iterations are *in-development* Versions of the product and should not be used in production. They should only be used for testing purposes.

Appendix A

You may also choose to download an older version available by using the **Previous Versions, Patches and Upgrades** link. Should you choose one of these older versions, make sure that you do not download an installation package whose name includes the label **Upgrade** or **Patch**.

A final note regarding the download page should draw your attention. Note that there are **stack installers** available for various operating systems. These installers simplify the process of deploying SugarCRM on various platforms. They do this by providing a package that installs the underlying foundation required by SugarCRM (web server, PHP, and MySQL/MS-SQL), as well as SugarCRM itself.

While useful for development, testing or training deployments, problems encountered in their usage can be difficult to troubleshoot. They can also be a challenge to modify, which is sometimes necessary, for example, when we need to update the included version of PHP.

The installation process that we will follow assumes that you have downloaded SugarCRM by clicking on the **Download now** button mentioned earlier in this chapter. The following image shows the download page for SugarCRM Community Edition:

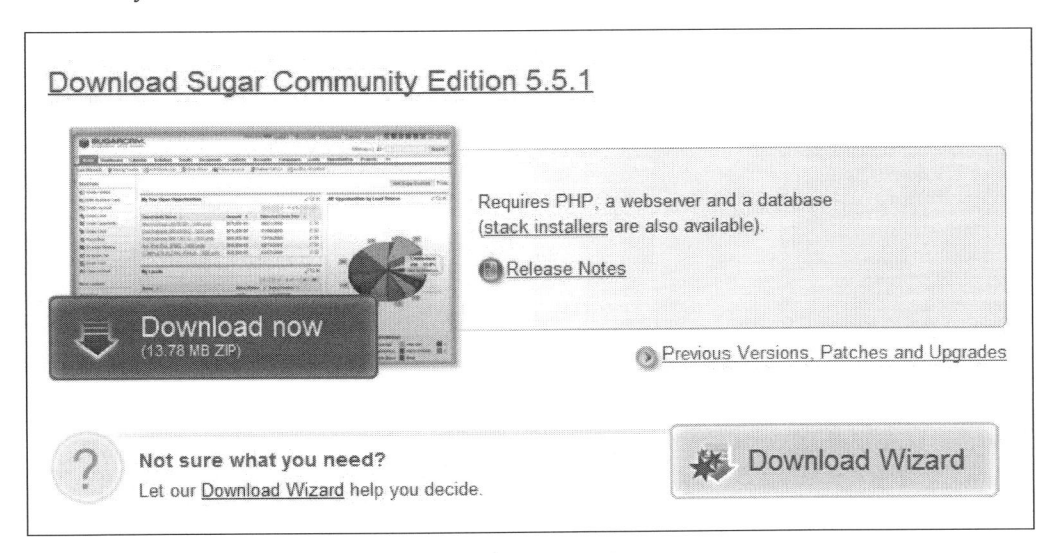

Carry out the following steps after clicking on the **Download now** button:

- Unzip the contents of the installation package to the /var/www/html directory.
- You should now have a folder, called /var/www/html/SugarCE-Full-5.5.1. Rename SugarCE-Full-5.5.1 as sugarcrm.

[237]

Perhaps the most often overlooked issue that causes installation problems on Linux servers, including CentOS, are permissions settings. Hence, it is important that you execute the following commands to ensure a successful installation.

- Change the ownership of the `sugarcrm` directory to the Apache user and group by executing the following command:

    `chown -R apache.apache sugarcrm`

- Modify file and directory permissions by executing the following command:

    `chmod -R 755 sugarcrm`

You should consult a security expert to verify that vulnerabilities are not introduced into the server's configuration as a result of any of these changes. The ultimate goal is to configure the security settings to allow the user under whom the web server is running to create, modify, and delete files from the `sugarcrm` directory. After the installation completes, you can tighten up security a bit more and restrict those changes to only the `cache` and `custom` subdirectories and its contents. In any case, if security is a concern, the advice of a qualified security expert should be sought, preferably someone who has experience with Linux systems.

The remainder of the installation process will be performed within your web browser. As such, it is important that we verify that the web server on your CentOS server is operational.

To test it, launch your web browser on your server and attempt to access `http://localhost`. If everything is working as expected, you should see an Apache test page.

If you encounter problems, verify that the required services are running. You can do so by executing the following commands:

- `service httpd restart`
- `service mysqld restart`

Should an error occur when starting, you will need to first resolve that problem before proceeding to the next section that takes you through the process of installing SugarCRM.

To begin the installation process, point your web browser to the following URL:

`http://<ip address of server>/sugarcrm`

Appendix A

If you intend to allow access to users from outside of your LAN or internal network, you should use the public or internet facing IP address that is associated with the server. If your intention is to restrict access to only those users who are on your LAN or internal network, you should use the IP address that all the intended users can utilize to connect to the server. Using `127.0.0.1` or `localhost` will result in access being limited to the server only.

You may use the `ifconfig` and `hostname` commands to determine the IP or server address respectively. Consult your network or DNS administrator if you require assistance for determining the public IP address.

Once you have entered the proper address into your web browser, it should automatically bring you to the installation wizard welcome page, as shown in the following screenshot:

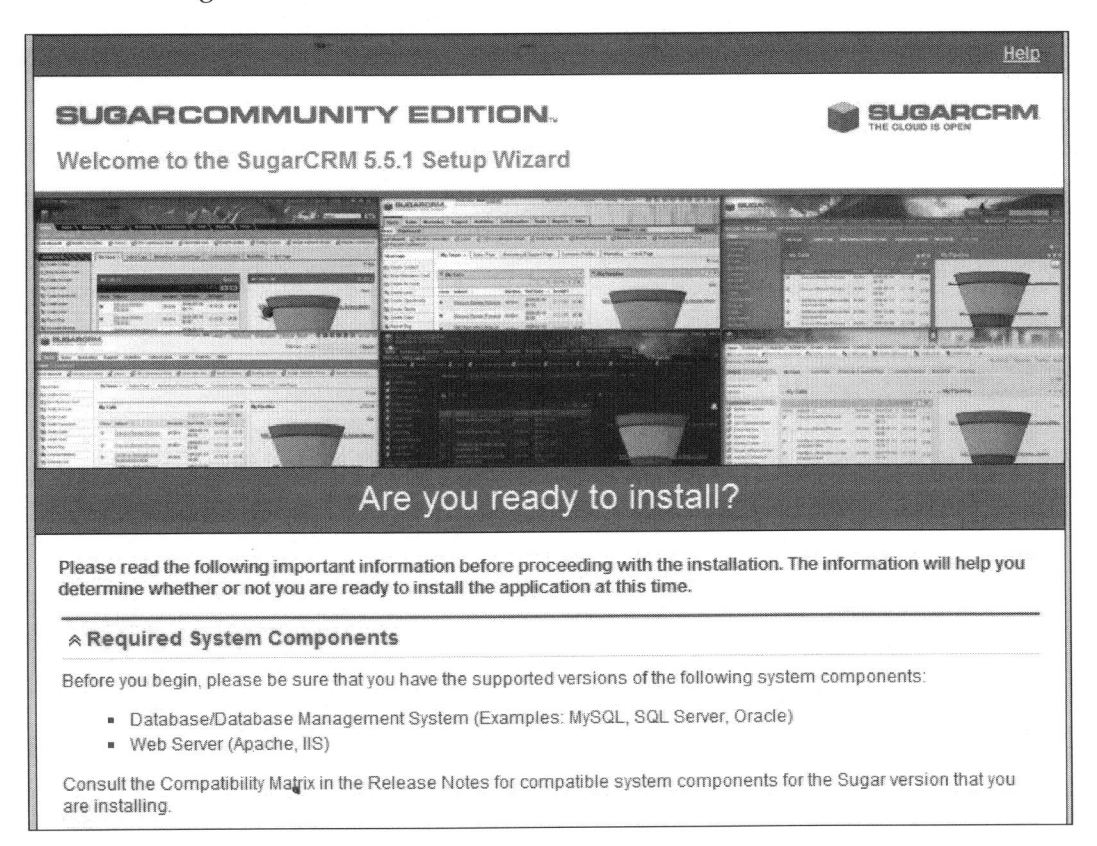

The installation procedure is as follows:

- **Welcome screen**: Click on the **Next** button to start the installation process.
- **License screen**: Review and accept if you agree to the terms as shown in the following screenshot:

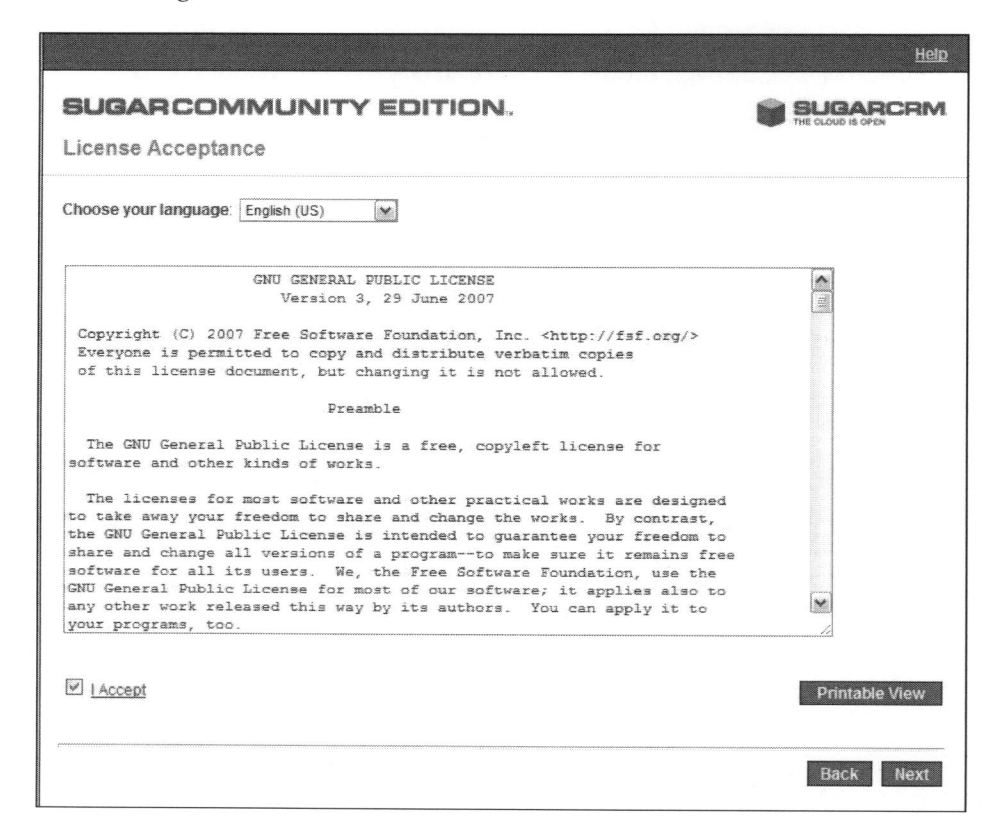

- **System check screen**: Next you see the **SugarCRM system check** screen. The SugarCRM installer checks several aspects of the installation environment, and reports their status to you on this screen. If something is not properly configured within your PHP installation, you will see a screen similar to the following image. Those errors need to be addressed before you can continue. Common issues include the following:
    - Missing or disabled PHP extensions
    - Incorrect file permissions
    - Improper PHP parameters

Appendix A

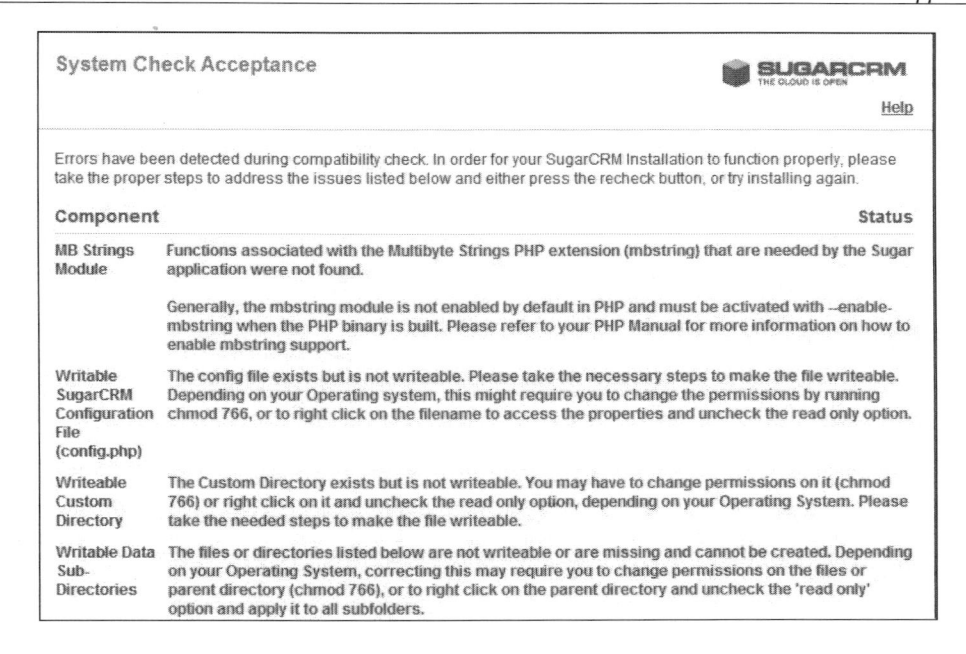

Component		Status
System Check Acceptance		

Errors have been detected during compatibility check. In order for your SugarCRM Installation to function properly, please take the proper steps to address the issues listed below and either press the recheck button, or try installing again.

Component		Status
MB Strings Module	Functions associated with the Multibyte Strings PHP extension (mbstring) that are needed by the Sugar application were not found.	
	Generally, the mbstring module is not enabled by default in PHP and must be activated with --enable-mbstring when the PHP binary is built. Please refer to your PHP Manual for more information on how to enable mbstring support.	
Writable SugarCRM Configuration File (config.php)	The config file exists but is not writeable. Please take the necessary steps to make the file writeable. Depending on your Operating system, this might require you to change the permissions by running chmod 766, or to right click on the filename to access the properties and uncheck the read only option.	
Writeable Custom Directory	The Custom Directory exists but is not writeable. You may have to change permissions on it (chmod 766) or right click on it and uncheck the read only option, depending on your Operating System. Please take the needed steps to make the file writeable.	
Writable Data Sub-Directories	The files or directories listed below are not writeable or are missing and cannot be created. Depending on your Operating System, correcting this may require you to change permissions on the files or parent directory (chmod 766), or to right click on the parent directory and uncheck the 'read only' option and apply it to all subfolders.	

- **Installation options**: Once the errors are corrected (or if none are identified), you will be prompted to select the installation method. Leave it set to the default of **Typical** and click on **Next** as shown in the following screenshot:

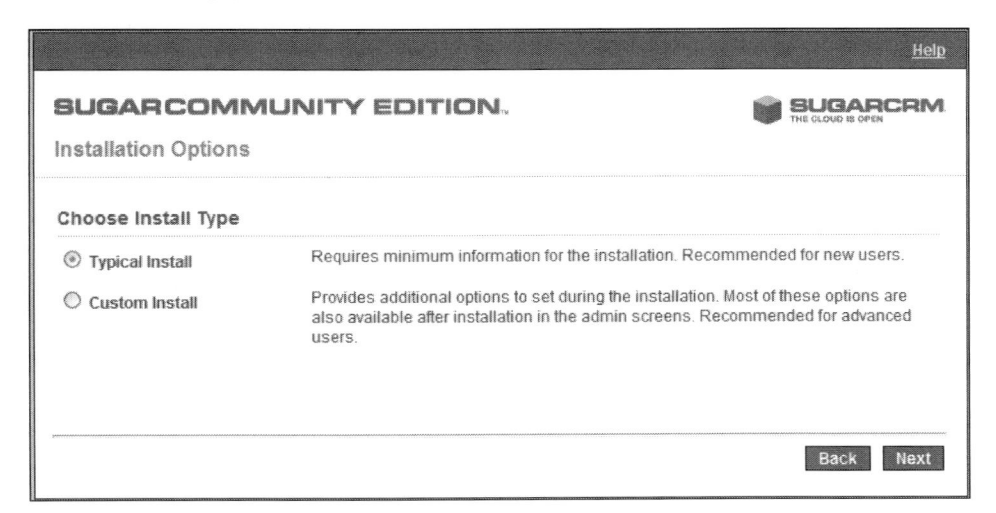

SUGAR COMMUNITY EDITION

Installation Options

Choose Install Type

- ◉ Typical Install — Requires minimum information for the installation. Recommended for new users.
- ○ Custom Install — Provides additional options to set during the installation. Most of these options are also available after installation in the admin screens. Recommended for advanced users.

[Back] [Next]

[241]

Installing SugarCRM on Linux

- **Database type**: Unless you added support for MS-SQL, your only choice should be **MySQL (MySQLi detected)** as shown in the following screenshot. Click on **Next** to proceed.

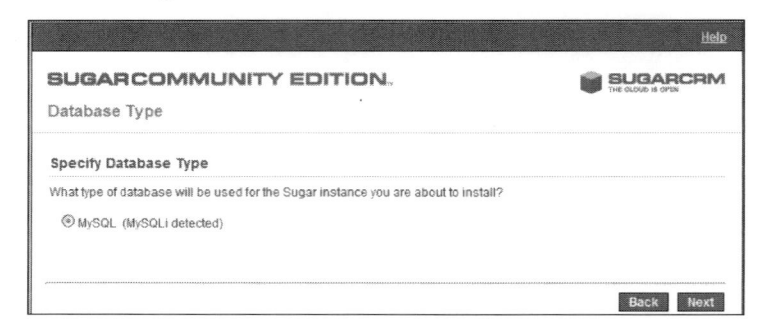

- **Database configuration screen**: Enter the parameters required to connect to your MySQL Server. Based on the work we did earlier to install CentOS, you should enter **sugarcrm** for the **Database Name**, **localhost** for the **Host Name**, **root** for the **Database Administrator Username**, and leave the **Database Admin Password** field blank. The only other setting that you may wish to change is the option of **Populate Database with Demo Data?** These are shown in the following image:

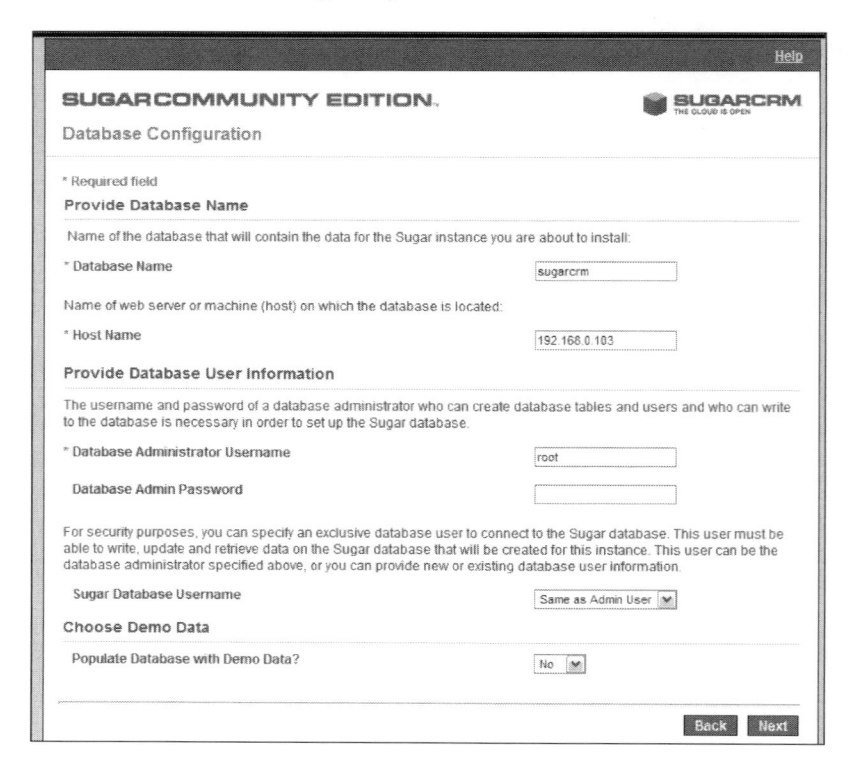

Appendix A

- **Site configuration screen**: Much like you provided a password for the **root** user for the CentOS installation, you must also provide a password for the default user **admin**. Make sure to store this password in a safe place. The site configuration screen is shown in the following image:

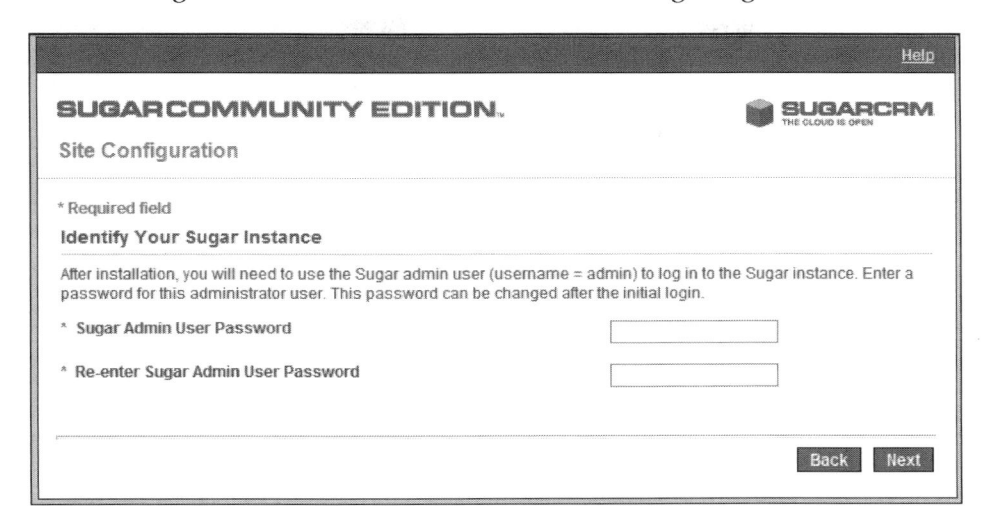

- **Locale settings screen**: You can also fine tune some default user preferences as a part of the installation process. These include date and time format and other settings as shown in the following image:

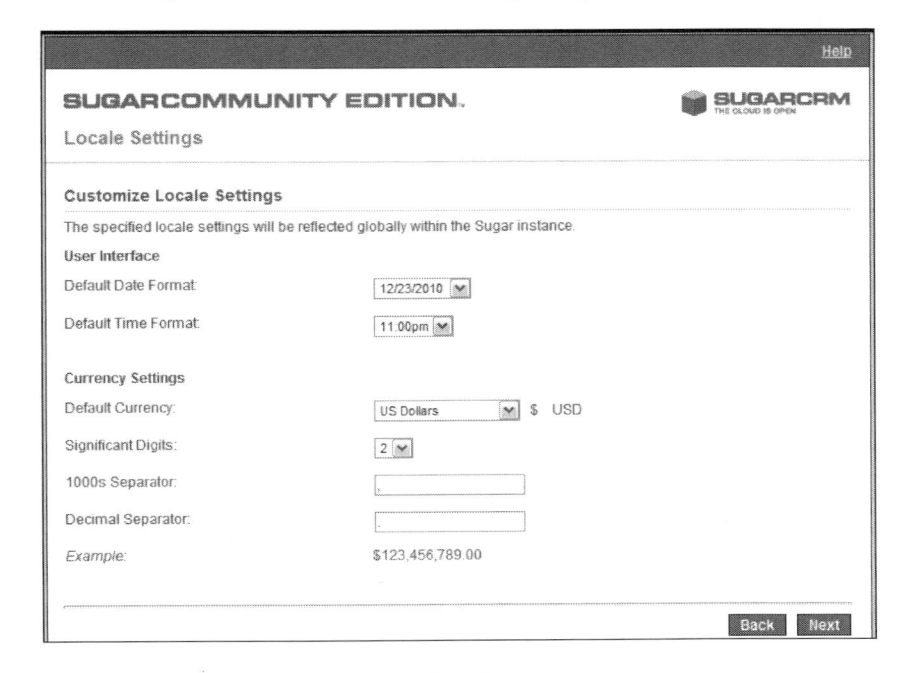

- **Confirmation screen**: Finally, the installer will present a summary screen including a number of the settings that were defined earlier in the wizard. If you need to make a change before installing, this is your last opportunity to do so. You may use the **Back** button to apply changes or click on **Install** to commit the installation. The confirmation screen should appear, which will be similar to the following image:

SUGAR COMMUNITY EDITION.

Confirm Settings

Database Configuration

Database Name	sugarcrm (will be created)
Database Administrator Username	root
Populate Database with Demo Data?	no
Drop Tables	No

Locale Settings

Default Date Format	12/23/2010
Default Time Format	11:00pm
Default Currency	US Dollars

The installation process will begin immediately after you click on the **Finish** button. The process normally takes less than a few minutes, but may take a bit longer if you chose to install the demo data.

Once completed, you should see a screen similar to the following:

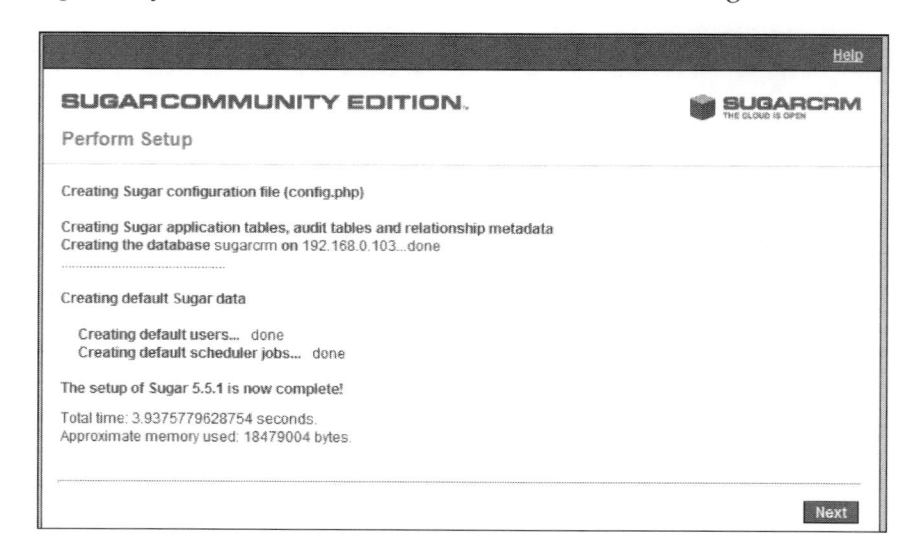

SUGAR COMMUNITY EDITION.

Perform Setup

Creating Sugar configuration file (config.php)

Creating Sugar application tables, audit tables and relationship metadata
Creating the database sugarcrm on 192.168.0.103...done

Creating default Sugar data

   Creating default users... done
   Creating default scheduler jobs... done

The setup of Sugar 5.5.1 is now complete!

Total time: 3.9375779628754 seconds.
Approximate memory used: 18479004 bytes.

Appendix A

Click on **Next** to continue and you will be prompted to register, as shown in the following image. It is not required, but it does help SugarCRM, so consider doing it.

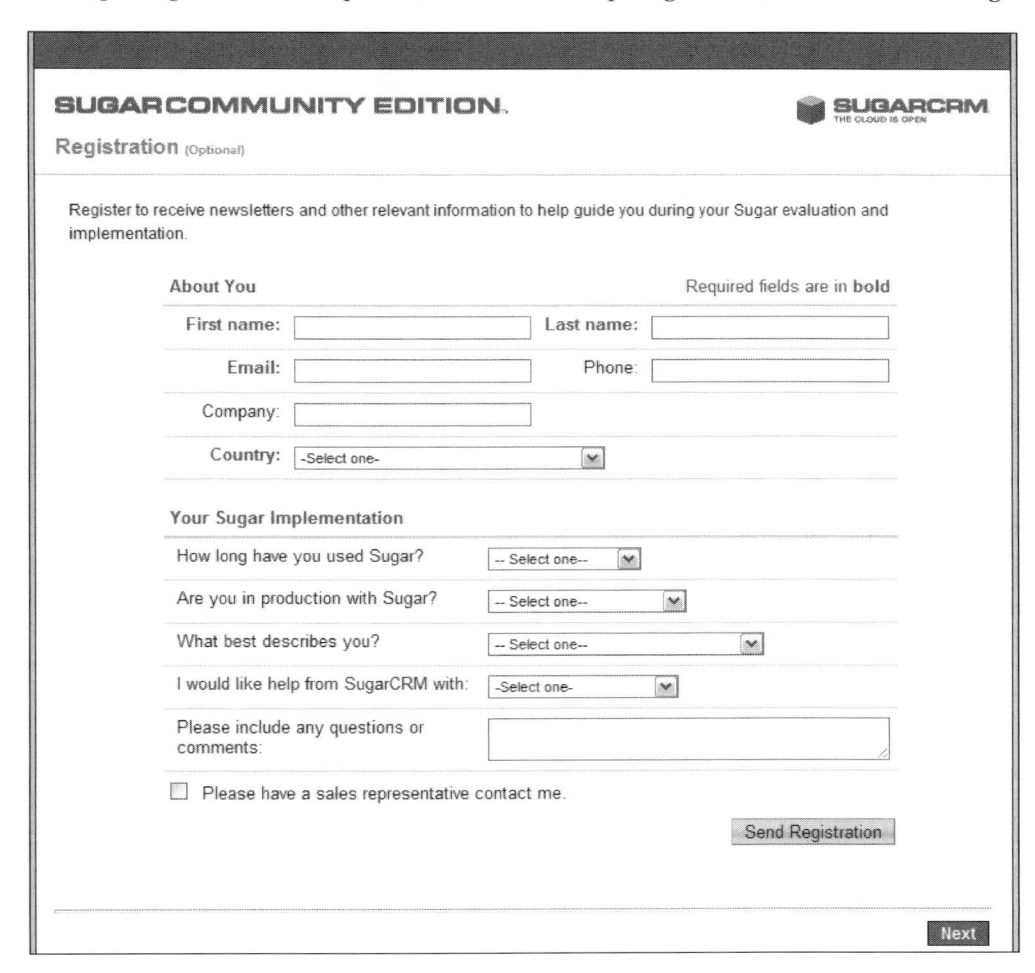

Click on the **Next** button once you are finished with the registration screen.

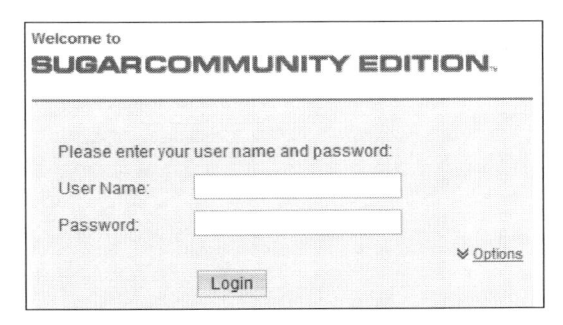

Congratulations! You have now successfully installed SugarCRM on your CentOS Linux server!

You should see a login screen as shown in the preceding image. You can log in (as a SugarCRM user) using the username *admin* and using the password that you defined during the installation process.

B
Installing SugarCRM on Windows Server

Copies of SugarCRM Community Edition are freely available for download at `http://www.sugarcrm.com/crm/download/sugar-suite.html`. Clicking on the **Download now** button will deliver the most recent version of SugarCRM Community Edition. As of the time of writing this book, the most recent version was 5.5.1. Before downloading, verify that the current version that is available for download does not contain the moniker **BETA**, **RC1**, **RC2** or the likes attached to its name, usually following the version number. Such iterations are *in-development* Versions of the product, and should not be used in production. They should only be used for testing purposes.

You may also choose to download an older version available by using the **Previous Versions, Patches and Upgrades** link. Should you choose one of these older versions, make sure that you do not download an installation package whose name includes the label **Upgrade** or **Patch**.

A final note regarding the download page should draw your attention. Note that there are **stack installers** available for various operating systems. These installers simplify the process of deploying SugarCRM on various platforms by providing a package that installs the underlying foundation required by SugarCRM (web server, PHP, and MySQL/MS-SQL), as well as SugarCRM itself.

While useful, problems encountered in their usage can be difficult to troubleshoot. They can also be a challenge to modify, which is sometimes necessary, for example, when we need to update the included version of PHP.

The installation process that we will follow assumes that you have downloaded SugarCRM by clicking on the **Download now** button mentioned previously in this chapter.

Before installing SugarCRM on a Windows based system, you must first make a couple of important decisions relating to the configuration of your system.

A word about our installation

Chapter 3 of this book discusses the manner in which SugarCRM leverages the LAMP stack as its foundation and the flexibility it affords. This latter point allows individuals with different preferences in technologies to easily leverage the technologies they are more comfortable with or prefer, while still being able to successfully use SugarCRM. A good example of this would be using Microsoft SQL Server instead of MySQL for the database server component.

Our example, however, assumes that the only variable that will change is the operating system. The following sections will guide you through the process of installing SugarCRM on a Windows based computer, using Apache and MySQL as the web and database servers respectively.

The final sections of this chapter discuss some important points regarding installations that utilize Microsoft's Internet Information Services (IIS) web server, or Microsoft SQL Server.

Selecting a version of Windows

You may have noticed that the previous discussion did not touch on the point of selecting a version of Windows. SugarCRM is quite neutral to this particular aspect, thus your decision should be based on other factors, such as expected load and hardware.

If your installation is for a single user, Windows XP is just as acceptable to SugarCRM as Vista or Windows 7. Of course, larger user loads should utilize more adequate versions, such as Windows Server Standard or other similar choices. Do not forget that licensing costs will vary depending on the version of Windows that you select.

Now, let us take a look at the installation process.

Installing SugarCRM using MySQL and Apache

Although the various editions of the Windows operating system include a built-in web server (IIS), some users prefer to use Apache web server. Apache is a widely used open source web server and can be downloaded from http://www.apache.org. Let us go through the process of installing it on a Windows system.

To simplify the process, it is recommended that you download the **MSI** installer package. Further to this, you should download the most recent stable version, usually identified by the moniker "*best available version.*" Further, you should consider downloading the version that includes SSL support, in case you have a need for it in the future.

In addition to Apache, we will also need to install PHP. Note that it will be necessary for you to install PHP even if you choose to instead use IIS, as PHP is not an embedded feature of your web server. You can download the necessary installation files for PHP from http://www.php.net.

Before you download PHP, verify that the version you have selected is supported for use by SugarCRM. A complete list of supported versions can be found on the official system requirements web page, on the SugarCRM website, located at the following URL:

http://www.sugarcrm.com/crm/products/supported-platforms.html

Likewise, you will need to download and install a supported version of MySQL. You can download a copy from http://dev.mysql.com.

The remainder of this section will assume that you have already downloaded the corresponding MSI installation packages for Apache, PHP, and MySQL.

Installing SugarCRM on Windows Server

Installing Apache web server

To install Apache, double-click on the corresponding MSI package that you previously downloaded. It should present the following screen:

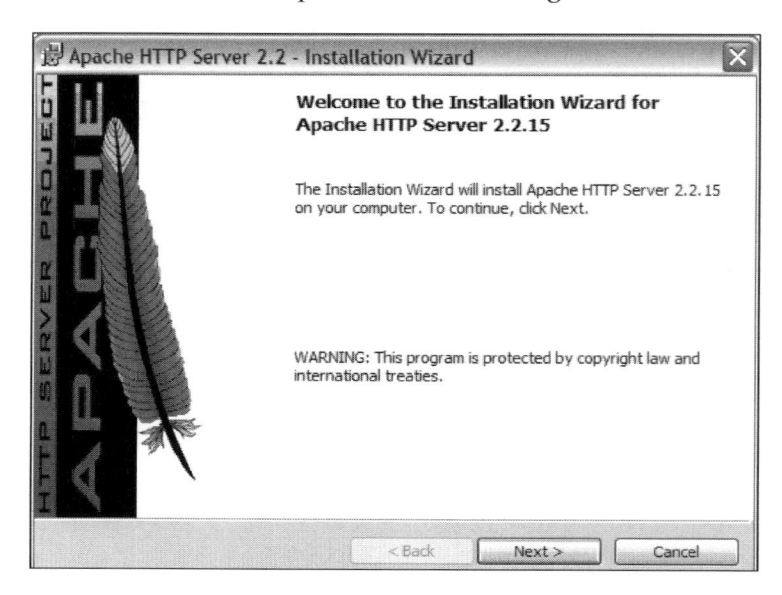

Proceed through the installation wizard normally, and enter your information into the screen that looks like the following:

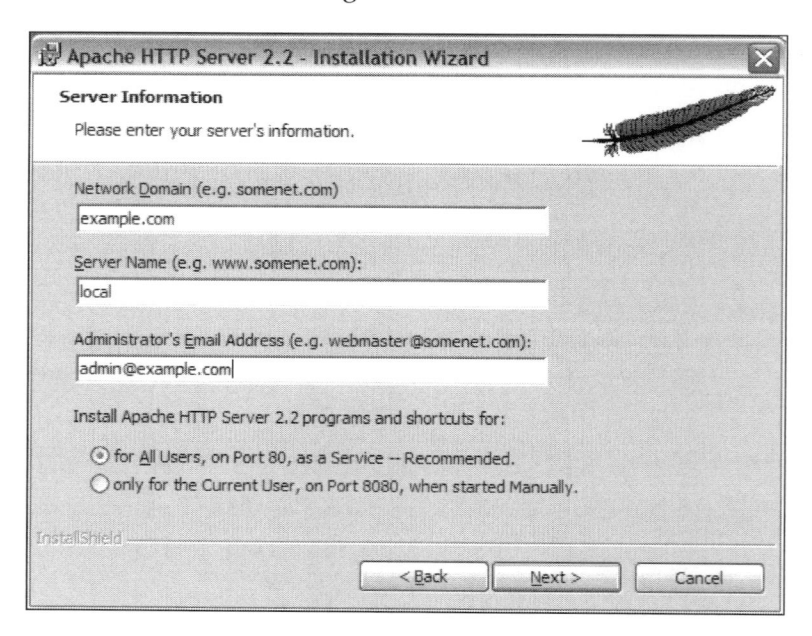

[250]

Appendix B

If you do not have a domain, you can use **example.com**. Furthermore, you should ensure that the **for All Users** option is selected in order to install it as a service. Click on **Next** to proceed. Continue through the remainder of the wizard, accepting the default options along the way.

Once the installation process completes, the installer will attempt to start Apache. If you have IIS installed and running on the same computer (or other applications, such as Skype), you may receive an error message that a port is already in use. To resolve this problem, you either need to shut down IIS, Skype, or other applications and then start Apache, or alternatively, you can change the port number to be used by Apache from the default number of 80, to another value that is not in use.

To change the port number to be used by Apache, select **Start | All Programs | Apache HTTP Server 2.2 | Configure Apache Server | Edit Apache httpd.conf configuration file**. Search for the line that reads **Listen 80**, and change **80** to a different value. Save your changes and then attempt to start Apache again by selecting **Start | All Programs | Apache HTTP Server 2.2 | Control Apache Server | Start**. Note that you may also need to adjust the SSL port (port 443 by default).

Installing PHP

After successfully installing Apache, proceed to install PHP. To install PHP, launch the corresponding MSI install package that you previously downloaded.

Click through the first few screens on the installation wizard until you reach the following screen:

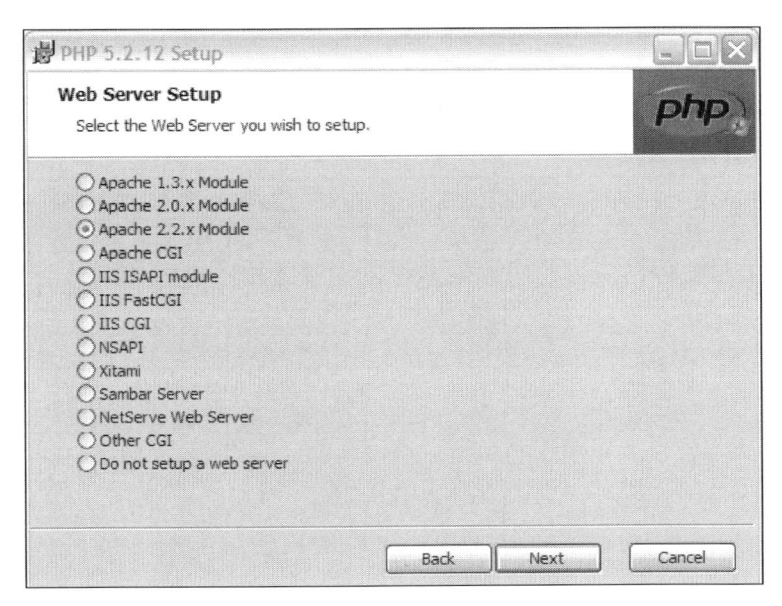

Installing SugarCRM on Windows Server

Verify that you have selected **Apache 2.2.x Module** on the preceding screen, and then click on **Next** to continue. You will then be presented with the following screen:

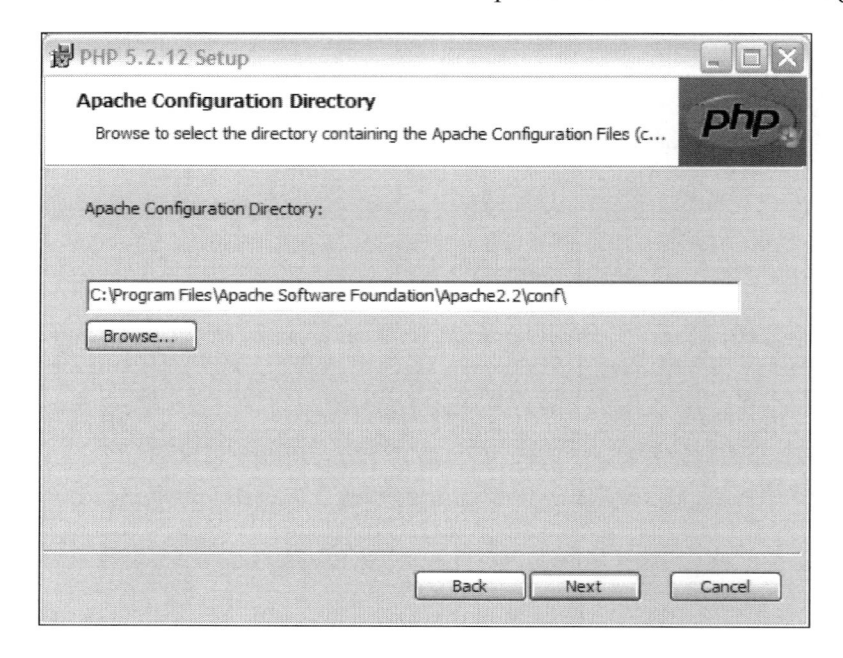

Enter the path to the Apache configuration files. By default, this path should be set to **C:\Program Files\Apache Software Foundation\Apache2.2\conf** as shown in the preceding screenshot. If you are unsure, search your system for the file named `httpd.conf`, and specify the path that contains said file.

SugarCRM requires several PHP extensions in order to function properly. The installation wizard allows you to define which extensions are to be installed. However, for the purposes of our example, we will simplify the process and simply choose to install all components by selecting **Entire feature will be installed on local hard drive** on the PHP node on the following image:

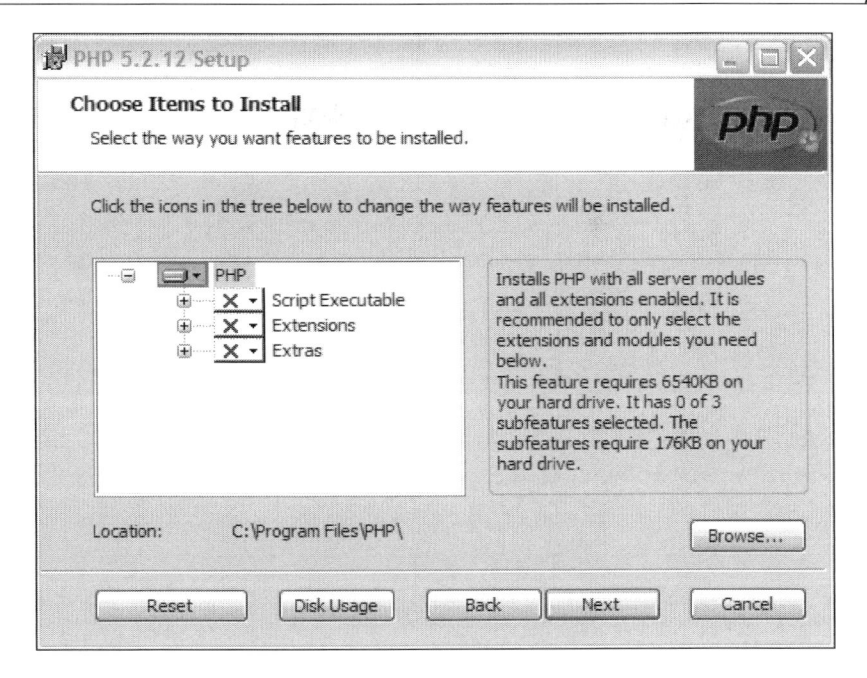

Proceed to complete the installation process and restart Apache. To verify that PHP is operational, create a file named `test.php` with the following content:

```
<?php
Phpinfo();
?>
```

Place the file at the following location:

`C:\Program Files\Apache Software Foundation\Apache2.2\htdocs` and attempt to open it through your web browser by navigating to `http://localhost/test.php` (you may need to adjust your URL to include a custom port number). If everything is working properly, you should see a screen with the PHP version number and other pertinent information.

Now that you have a working Apache and PHP installation, you need to install the database component.

Installing MySQL

As with the other components, initiate the installation process by launching the corresponding MSI package that you previously downloaded. The MySQL installation wizard will automatically appear as shown in the following screenshot:

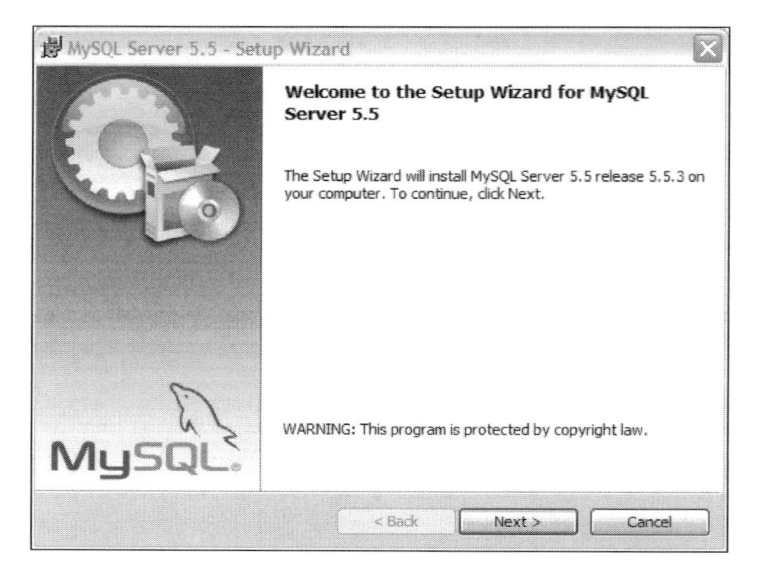

Proceed through the wizard, choosing the default options when prompted. Upon completion, you will have the option to configure your server, as illustrated in the next screenshot:

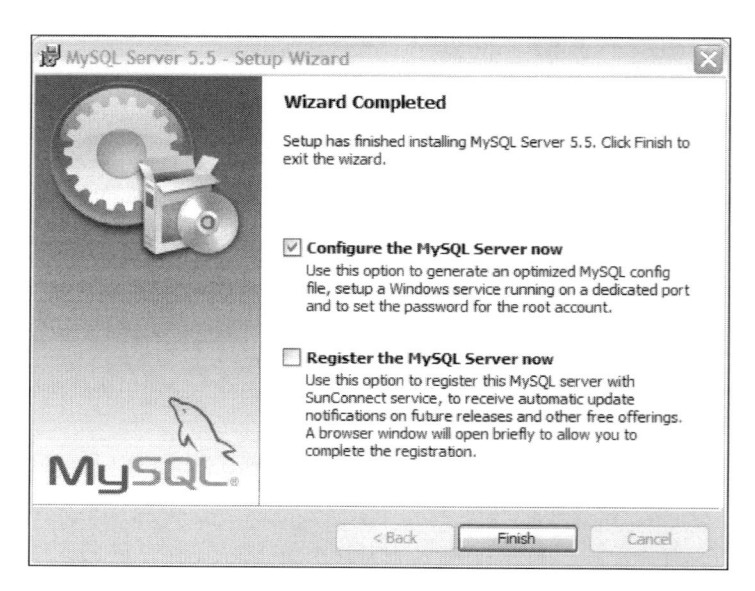

Appendix B

Verify that **Configure the MySQL Server now** is selected and click on **Finish**.

A series of screens will now be presented, allowing you to make modifications to the server configuration. The following screenshot shows the server instance configuration screen:

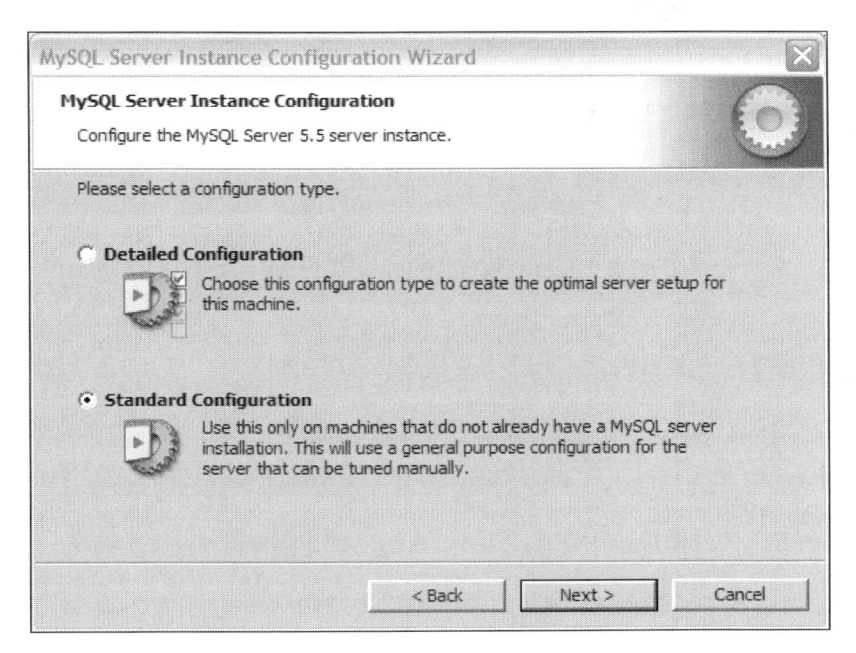

Select **Standard Configuration** at the **MySQL Server Instance Configuration** screen and click on **Next** to proceed.

On the screen that follows, accept the default option to install as a service and proceed. Provide a password for your **root** user (that is, default administrator level user) and continue through to the end.

All the components required for SugarCRM should now be installed and operational. Do not attempt to install SugarCRM if any of these items are malfunctioning as it is likely that this will cause problems within SugarCRM. Attempts at installing on misconfigured or malfunctioning stacks usually result in lost time and frustration.

Finally, you can now install SugarCRM.

Installing SugarCRM Community Edition

The installation process that we will follow assumes that you have downloaded SugarCRM by clicking on the **Download now** button mentioned at the beginning of this chapter. Once you have clicked on **Download now**, carry out the following steps:

- Unzip the contents of the installation package to the folder named `C:\Program Files\Apache Software Foundation\Apache2.2\htdocs`.
- You should now have a folder named `C:\Program Files\Apache Software Foundation\Apache2.2\htdocs\SugarCE-Full-5.5.1`. Rename `SugarCE-Full-5.5.1` to `sugarcrm`.

The remainder of the installation process will be performed within your web browser.

To begin the installation process, point your web browser to `http://<ipaddress of server>/sugarcrm`

If you intend to allow access to users from outside of your LAN or internal network, you should use the public or internet facing IP address that is associated with the server. If your intention is to restrict access to only those users who are on your LAN or internal network, you should use the IP address that all the intended users can utilize to connect to the server. Using `127.0.0.1` or `localhost` in place of either will result in access being limited to the server only.

You may use the `ipconfig` and `hostname` commands to determine the IP or server address respectively. To execute these commands, open a command window by selecting **Start** and then typing **cmd** and clicking on **OK**. Type the command into the window that appears. Consult your network or DNS administrator if you require assistance for determining the public IP address as it may require firewall or other network modifications.

Appendix B

Your web browser should automatically bring you to the installation wizard welcome page as shown in the following screenshot:

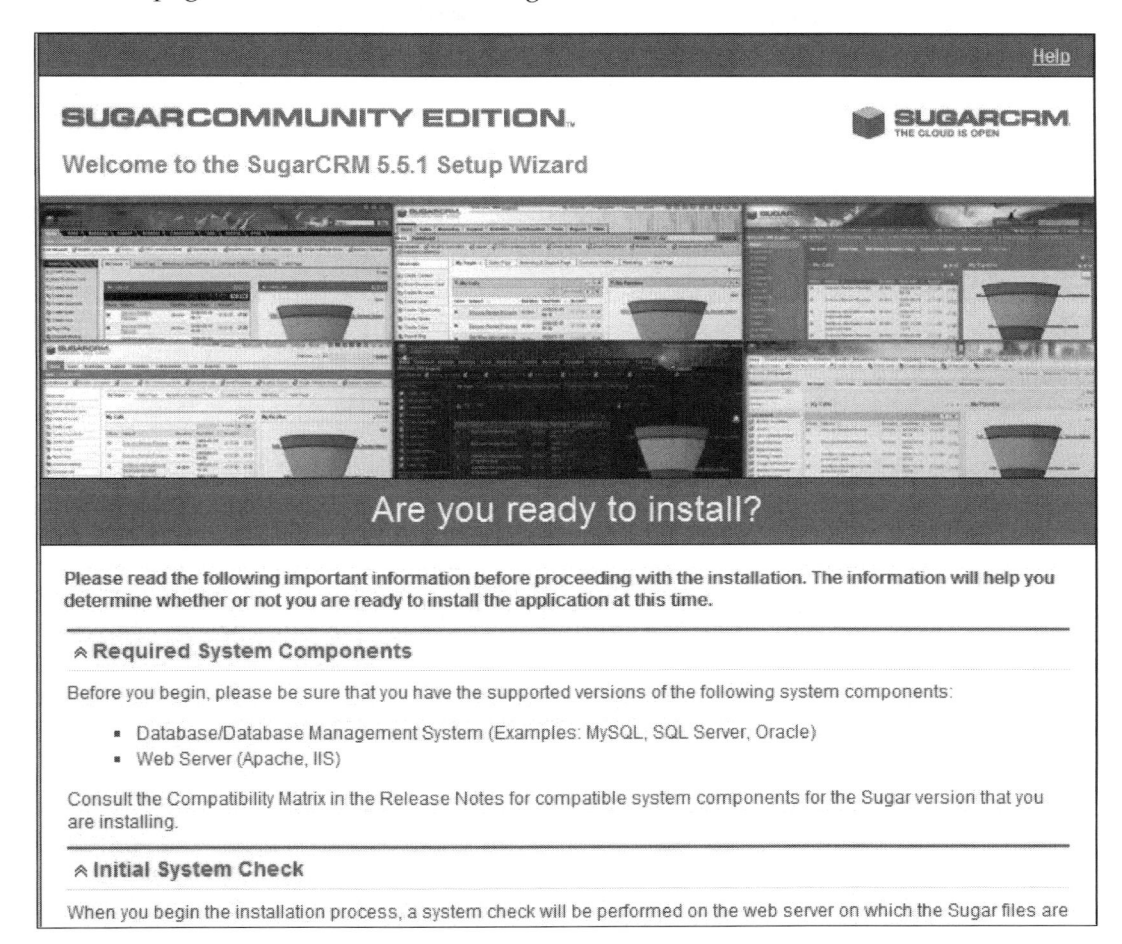

SUGARCOMMUNITY EDITION.

Welcome to the SugarCRM 5.5.1 Setup Wizard

Are you ready to install?

Please read the following important information before proceeding with the installation. The information will help you determine whether or not you are ready to install the application at this time.

Required System Components

Before you begin, please be sure that you have the supported versions of the following system components:

- Database/Database Management System (Examples: MySQL, SQL Server, Oracle)
- Web Server (Apache, IIS)

Consult the Compatibility Matrix in the Release Notes for compatible system components for the Sugar version that you are installing.

Initial System Check

When you begin the installation process, a system check will be performed on the web server on which the Sugar files are

Installing SugarCRM on Windows Server

The installation procedure is as follows:

- **Welcome screen**: Click on the **Next** button to continue to the license acceptance page, as depicted in the following screenshot:

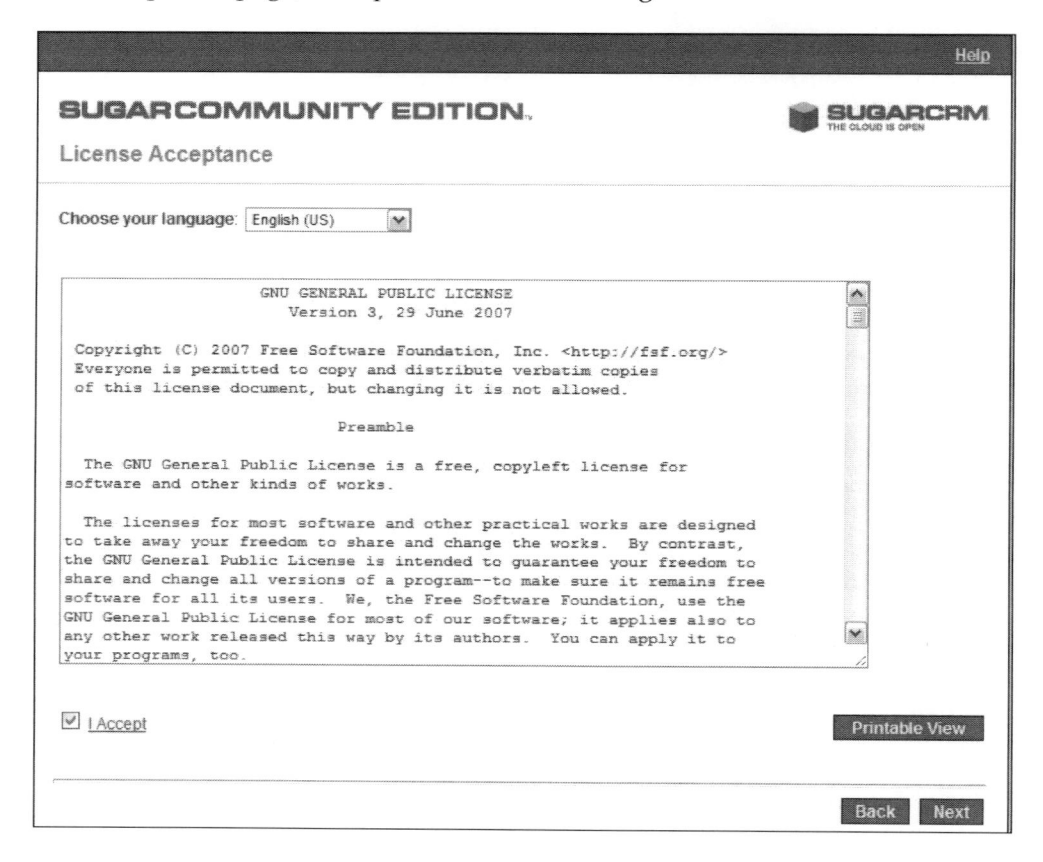

- **License screen**: Click on **I Accept** if you agree to the terms, then click on **Next** to proceed.

- **System check screen**: Next you see the **SugarCRM system check** screen. The SugarCRM installer checks several aspects of the installation environment, and reports their status to you on this screen. If something is not properly configured within your PHP installation, you will see a screen similar to the following image. Those errors need to be addressed before you can continue. Common issues include the following:
    - Missing or disabled PHP extensions
    - Incorrect file permissions
    - Improper PHP parameters

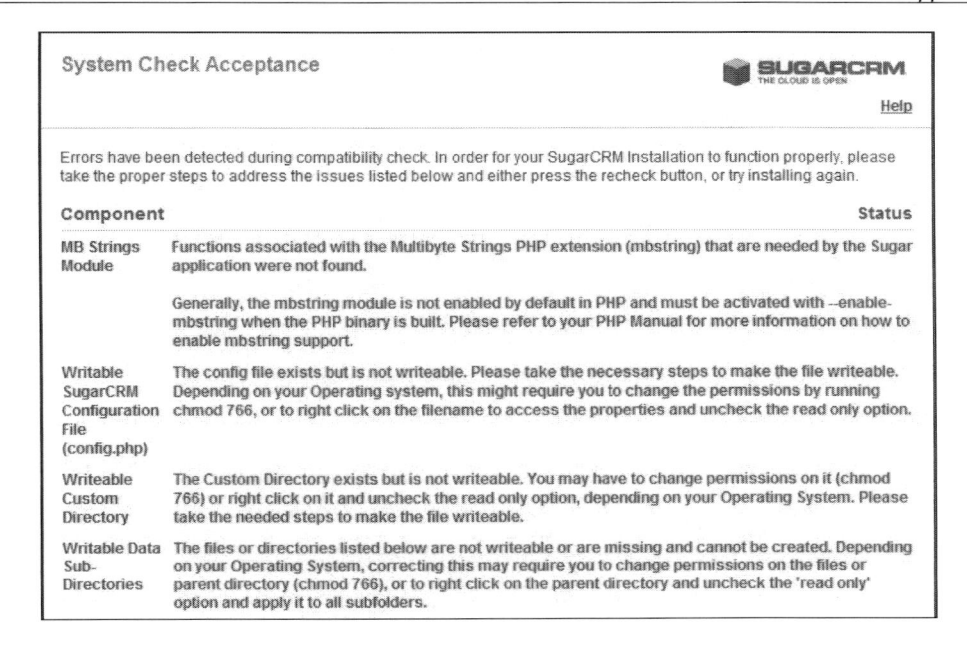

System Check Acceptance	
Errors have been detected during compatibility check. In order for your SugarCRM Installation to function properly, please take the proper steps to address the issues listed below and either press the recheck button, or try installing again.	
Component	**Status**
MB Strings Module	Functions associated with the Multibyte Strings PHP extension (mbstring) that are needed by the Sugar application were not found. Generally, the mbstring module is not enabled by default in PHP and must be activated with --enable-mbstring when the PHP binary is built. Please refer to your PHP Manual for more information on how to enable mbstring support.
Writable SugarCRM Configuration File (config.php)	The config file exists but is not writeable. Please take the necessary steps to make the file writeable. Depending on your Operating system, this might require you to change the permissions by running chmod 766, or to right click on the filename to access the properties and uncheck the read only option.
Writeable Custom Directory	The Custom Directory exists but is not writeable. You may have to change permissions on it (chmod 766) or right click on it and uncheck the read only option, depending on your Operating System. Please take the needed steps to make the file writeable.
Writable Data Sub-Directories	The files or directories listed below are not writeable or are missing and cannot be created. Depending on your Operating System, correcting this may require you to change permissions on the files or parent directory (chmod 766), or to right click on the parent directory and uncheck the 'read only' option and apply it to all subfolders.

- **Installation options**: Once the errors are corrected (or if none are identified), you will be prompted to select the installation method. Leave it set to the default of **Typical**, and click on **Next** to continue.

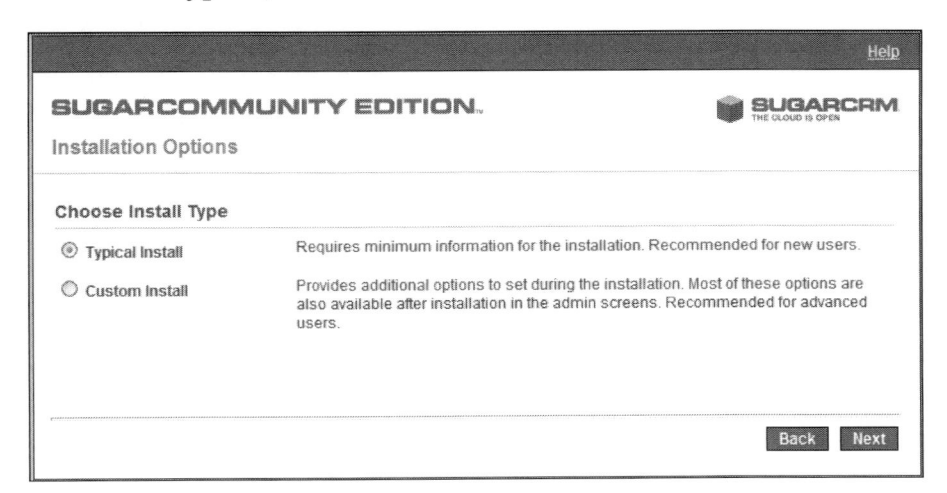

SUGARCOMMUNITY EDITION

Installation Options

Choose Install Type

- ⦿ Typical Install — Requires minimum information for the installation. Recommended for new users.
- ○ Custom Install — Provides additional options to set during the installation. Most of these options are also available after installation in the admin screens. Recommended for advanced users.

- **Database type**: Unless you added support for MS-SQL, your only choice should be **MySQL (MySQLi detected)** as shown in the following screenshot. Click on **Next** to proceed.

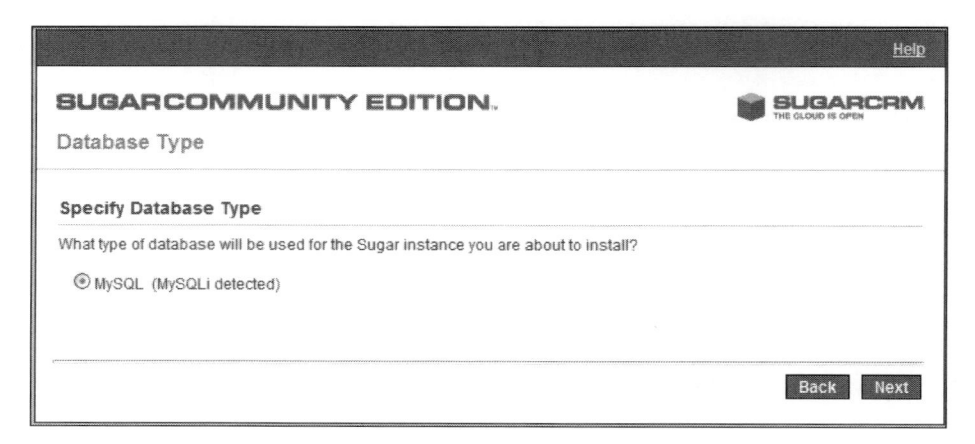

SUGARCOMMUNITY EDITION.
Database Type

Specify Database Type

What type of database will be used for the Sugar instance you are about to install?

◉ MySQL (MySQLi detected)

[Back] [Next]

- **Database configuration screen**: Enter the parameters required to connect to your MySQL Server. You should enter **sugarcrm** for the **Database Name**, **localhost** for the **Host Name**, **root** for the **Database Administrator Username**, and provide the **Database Admin Password** value. The only other setting you may wish to change is the option to **Populate Database with Demo Data?** These are shown in the following screenshot:

> IMPORTANT: The MySQL user root is the default MySQL administrator and has full access to all database operations. Its use is not generally recommended for production systems, as it poses a security risk. To strengthen security, it is recommended that you create a MySQL user for exclusive use by SugarCRM. Details on creating MySQL users and other MySQL administrative operations can be found at the following URL:
>
> http://dev.mysql.com/doc/refman/5.1/en/index.html

Appendix B

[Screenshot of SugarCRM Database Configuration screen showing fields for Database Name (sugarcrm), Host Name (192.168.0.103), Database Administrator Username (root), Database Admin Password, Sugar Database Username (Same as Admin User), and Populate Database with Demo Data? (No).]

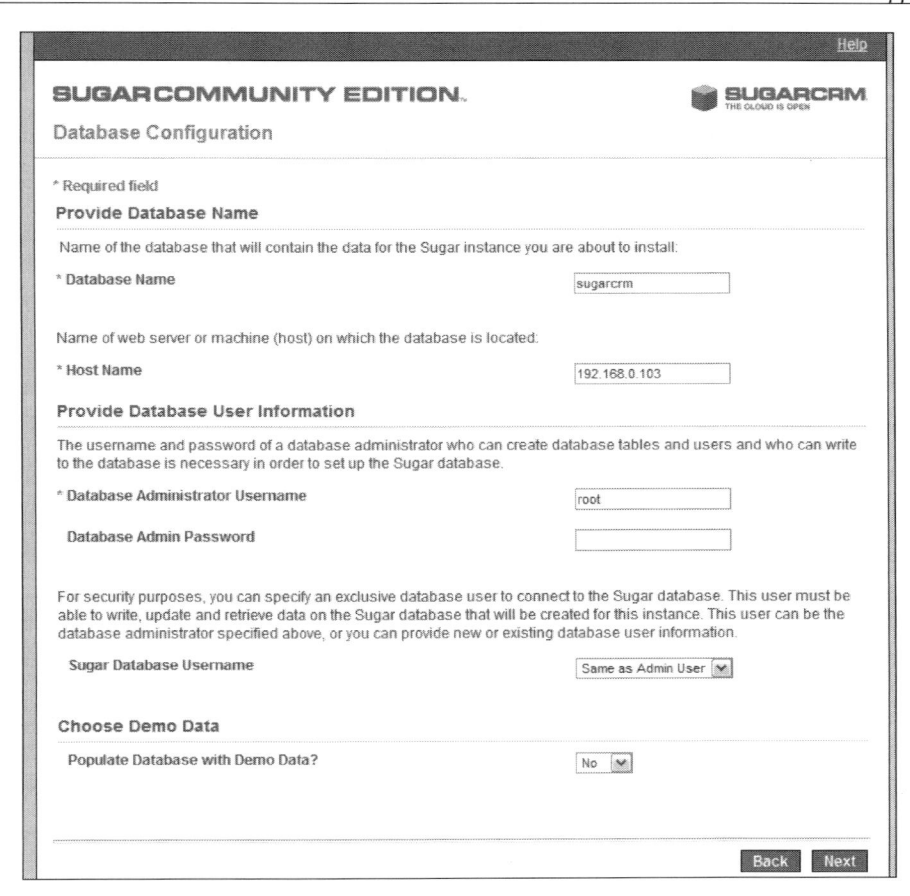

- **Site configuration screen**: You must provide a password for the default user **admin**, as shown in the following screenshot. Make sure to store this password in a safe place.

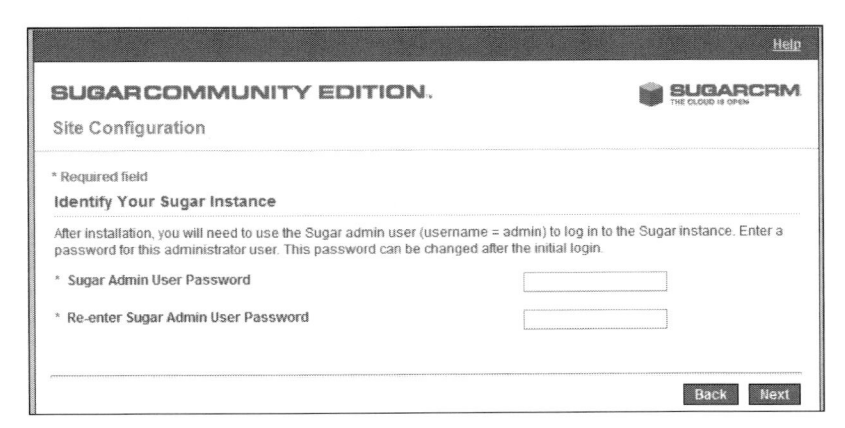

[Screenshot of SugarCRM Site Configuration screen showing fields for Sugar Admin User Password and Re-enter Sugar Admin User Password.]

[261]

Installing SugarCRM on Windows Server

- **Locale settings screen**: You can also fine tune some default user preferences as part of the installation process. These include date and time format and other settings as seen in the following image:

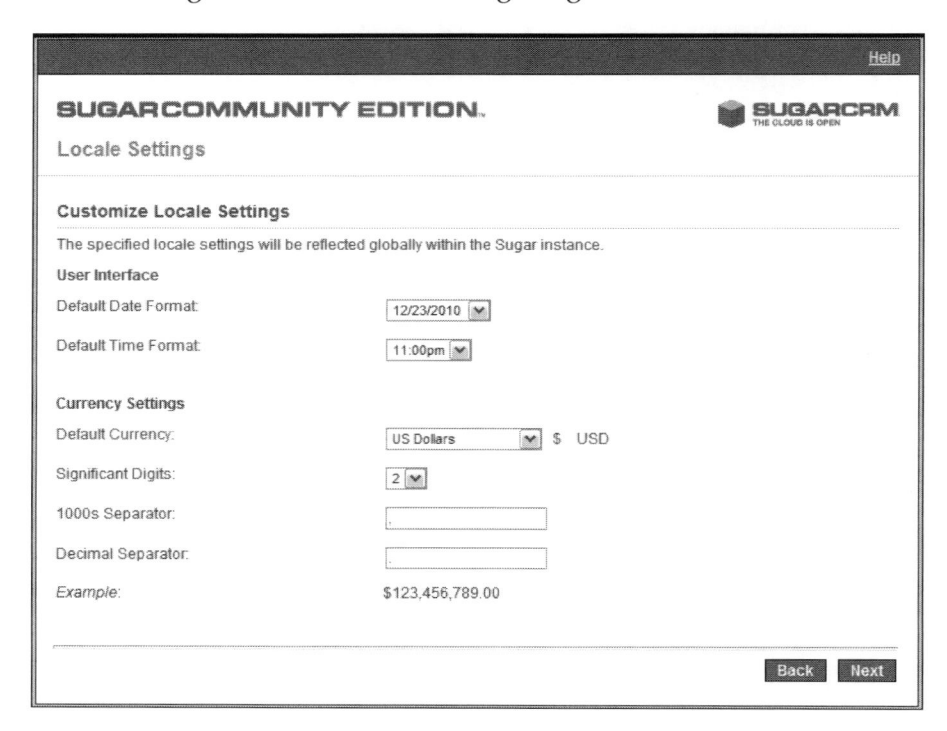

![Locale Settings screen showing Customize Locale Settings with User Interface options (Default Date Format: 12/23/2010, Default Time Format: 11:00pm) and Currency Settings (Default Currency: US Dollars $ USD, Significant Digits: 2, 1000s Separator, Decimal Separator, Example: $123,456,789.00)]

- **Confirmation screen**: Finally, the installer will present a summary screen including a number of the settings you defined earlier in the wizard. If you need to make a change before installing, this is your last opportunity to do so. You may use the **Back** button to apply changes or click on **Install** to commit the installation. The confirmation screen is shown in the following screenshot:

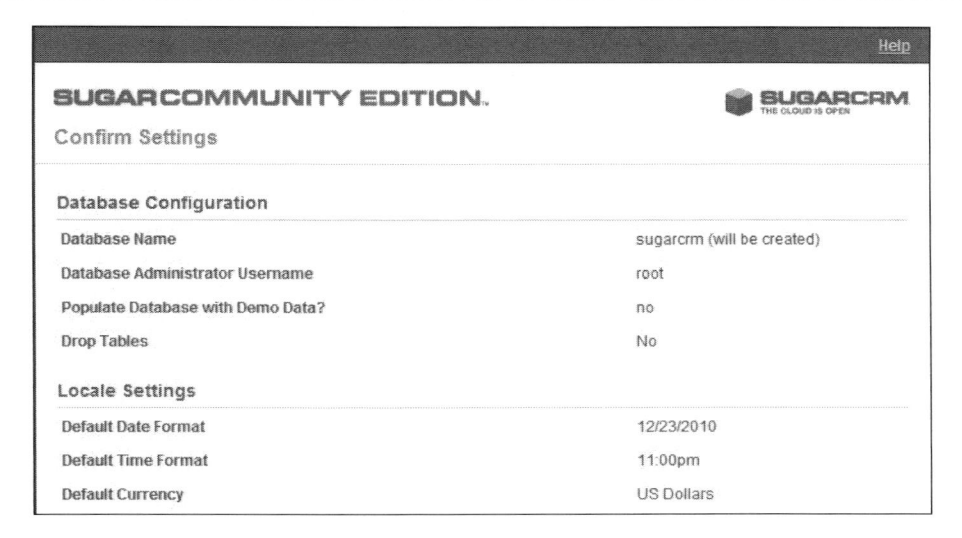

Confirm Settings

Database Configuration

Database Name	sugarcrm (will be created)
Database Administrator Username	root
Populate Database with Demo Data?	no
Drop Tables	No

Locale Settings

Default Date Format	12/23/2010
Default Time Format	11:00pm
Default Currency	US Dollars

The installation process will begin immediately after you click on the **Finish** button. The process normally takes just a few minutes, but may take a bit longer if you chose to install the demo data.

Once completed, you should see a screen similar to the following:

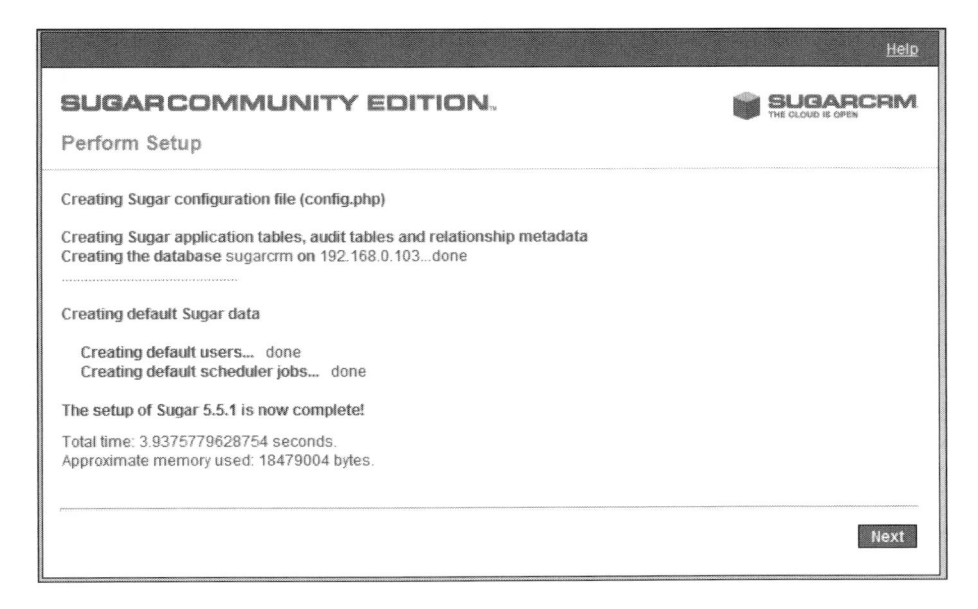

Perform Setup

Creating Sugar configuration file (config.php)

Creating Sugar application tables, audit tables and relationship metadata
Creating the database sugarcrm on 192.168.0.103...done

Creating default Sugar data

Creating default users... done
Creating default scheduler jobs... done

The setup of Sugar 5.5.1 is now complete!

Total time: 3.9375779628754 seconds.
Approximate memory used: 18479004 bytes.

Installing SugarCRM on Windows Server

Click on **Next** to continue, and you will be prompted to register. It is not required, but it does help SugarCRM, so consider doing it.

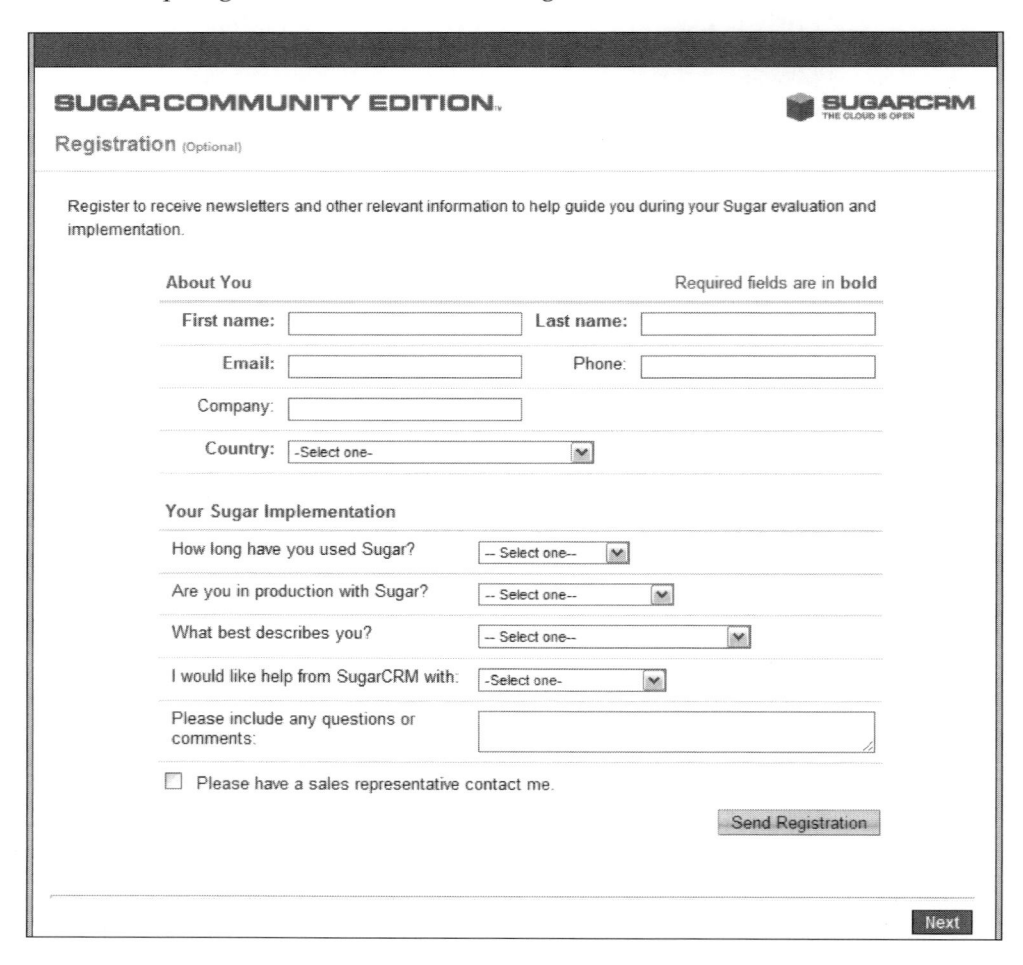

Click on **Next** once you are finished with the registration screen.

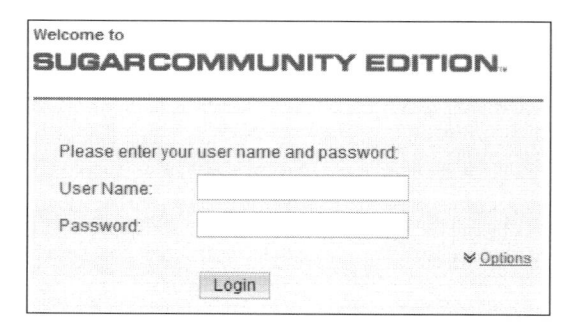

Congratulations! You have now successfully installed SugarCRM on your Windows server!

You should see a login screen, as shown in the preceding screenshot. You can log in (as a SugarCRM user) using the username *admin* and using the password that you defined during the installation process. To allow other users access to the system, simply provide them with the URL displayed in your web browser while at the SugarCRM login page. Of course, assuming that you have already created their usernames and passwords.

Installing SugarCRM with Microsoft SQL server

Using Microsoft SQL Server (MS-SQL) for your SugarCRM installation is no different than using MySQL. The main difference is that during the installation, you will need to choose **Microsoft SQL Server** for your database type, instead of the default **MySQLi**.

However, before you get to that point, you will want to make sure that you have a supported version of MS-SQL Server available, and that it is also functioning. If you require assistance for installing MS-SQL, you should check out the documentation on the Microsoft website, located at http://msdn.microsoft.com/en-us/library/ms143516(SQL.90).aspx

There are a couple of important notes to keep in mind regarding its use. Perhaps the most important note is to ensure that the MS-SQL server you wish to use is configured to support the use of **Mixed Mode** authentication. Failure to do will needlessly complicate the installation process, as you will not be able to utilize the default process of simply specifying a database administrator username and password when defining the database configuration parameters.

Secondly, your installation of PHP may not have the MS-SQL extension enabled. If the SugarCRM installation wizard does not allow you to choose MS-SQL as an option, chances are that the MS-SQL extension is not enabled or installed. If you encounter this scenario, check your PHP.INI, and verify that it contains the following line:

```
ext=php_mssql.dll
```

If it is missing, add it, save your changes, and then restart your web service and try again. If you encounter errors indicating that the extension cannot be found, it indicates that support for MS-SQL was not installed as part of your PHP installation. To resolve the problem, either reinstall PHP and make sure to install the MS-SQL extension, or locate the necessary DLL files and apply them to your PHP installation folder.

To restart your web service, select **Start | Run**. Type **services.msc** and click on **OK**. In the list that is displayed, right-click either on **Apache2.2** or on **World Wide Web Publishing** (depending on whether you are using Apache or IIS for your web server), and choose **Restart**.

Locating the DLLs can prove a little trickier. A good starting spot is the main PHP website located at http://www.php.net/, but it may also require some general searching of the internet.

Installing SugarCRM on Internet Information Services (IIS)

IIS may or may not already be installed on your target server. One quick way to check whether it is or is not installed is to select **Start | Control Panel | Administrative Tools**. If you see an option for administering Internet Information Services, you are all set. If you do not see anything relating to IIS, you will need to install it through the Add/Remove Programs tool.

To install IIS, select **Start | Control Panel | Add/Remove Programs** and click on **Add/Remove Windows Components**. Windows will present a catalog of components that can be added to your installation of Windows. Select **Internet Information Services** and proceed with the remainder of the wizard until it finishes installing IIS for you.

Perhaps the biggest challenge involved with installing SugarCRM on IIS is configuring PHP.

In general, installing PHP will involve following the same instructions as those outlined earlier in this chapter in the section titled *Installing PHP*. However, you will want to choose **IIS FastCGI** at the Web Server Setup screen of the installation wizard. You may have to use the **IIS ISAPI Module** or **IIS CGI** option if you are using a version of IIS older than 7.0. Additional help on this topic can be found at the IIS PHP website, located at the following URL: http://php.iis.net/

Appendix B

As with Apache, it is important to verify that PHP is operational and properly configured before attempting to install SugarCRM.

Once you have confirmed that PHP is operational, you are ready to start the installation process, but before you can do that, you must place the SugarCRM files in their proper location so that IIS is aware of them.

The section titled *Installing SugarCRM Community Edition* found earlier in this chapter, provides instructions on extraction and placement of the SugarCRM installation files as it relates to Apache web server. In it, you are asked to place your files in a folder named `C:\Program Files\Apache Software Foundation\Apache2.2\htdocs\sugarcrm`.

As IIS uses a different folder structure for its files, you will place the files in the following folder:

`C:\Inetpub\wwwroot\sugarcrm`.

After doing so, you will be able to follow the same installation instructions described earlier in this chapter.

Permissions

Permissions tend to be less of a problem on Windows than on other operating systems, such as Linux. However, it is important that you ensure that the corresponding SugarCRM folder is accessible to the user under whom your selected web server is running.

For IIS implementations, this is the Internet User account, which is easily identified by the fact that it always utilizes **IUSR_** at the start of its name. For Apache installations, you may need to use Windows Task Manager utility to check the user under whom it is running, and then set your permissions accordingly. To access the Windows Task Manager, right-click the Windows status bar and choose **Task Manager**. Click on the **Processes** tab and look for an entry entitled **apache.exe**. Check the value of the **User Name** column to determine the user under whom Apache is running. If the **User Name** column is not visible, select it under **View | Select Columns**.

C
Data Import and Export

One of the most important aspects of any CRM software is the ability to import and export data.

The former allows you to input data en masse using data sources, such as Comma Separated Values (CSV) files or other file formats. Through this functionality, the process of migrating data from other systems, such as an accounting solution, is simplified. It is also helpful for importing lead lists that you may obtain at a trade show, networking event, and so on.

Exporting capabilities are equally important. The export functionality allows you to easily extract valuable data from your CRM system, permitting you to process it in other systems, such as a data scrubbing service.

The ability to insert and extract data from the CRM system through import and export tools becomes increasingly important as the role of the CRM tool grows within an organization. This should be expected within your organization too, as your goal should be to create a culture where the CRM system becomes the hub or central storage point for all your business and pertinent customer data (except for accounting information).

SugarCRM supports the importing of various kinds of data from several different popular competitive systems, and from online data services or custom created data files.

Some of the highlights are as follows:

- Accounts may be imported from Salesforce.com, from ACT!, or from most other systems through a custom comma-delimited or tab-delimited file
- Contacts may be imported from Salesforce.com, from ACT!, Outlook, or from most other systems through a custom comma-delimited or tab-delimited file
- Leads may be imported from Salesforce.com, or from most other systems through a custom comma-delimited or tab-delimited file

Data Import and Export

Just like leads, opportunities, calls, meetings, and so on, various other data types can also be imported from Salesforce.com or through custom comma-delimited or tab-delimited files.

It is important to note that the options for Salesforce.com, Microsoft Outlook, and other competitive products merely provide a shortcut to field mappings which should save you some time in performing your import. The import tool, however, does not directly communicate with these other products to extract the data that is to be imported, and instead, still relies upon the use of a CSV file to perform the import.

The onus is on you to export the data from the other system into a properly formatted CSV file that in turn can be used within the import facility in SugarCRM.

Before we take a look at a few examples of the import tool in action, let us briefly mention an additional feature native to the import tool. In addition to allowing you to create new records in various modules, the import tool also allows you to update existing records. This is accomplished by using match keys, which we will discuss later in this chapter.

Let us take a look at the process of importing accounts and contacts.

Importing accounts and contacts

If you are importing account data from another CRM system, chances are that the system understands the distinction between an account and a contact. As a refresher, the former is usually an organization or company, the latter an individual. Moreover, one account can have multiple contacts, each with separate data.

Importing contacts into SugarCRM is fairly straightforward. First you use your old CRM application or a contact manager to export the data into a .csv file format. Then you use the import function within the **Contacts** module (accessible through the navigation shortcuts box) to import the data. If a contact record that is imported refers to an unknown account, then a new record is automatically created for an account of that name.

However, one thing to watch out for is that when account records are created automatically in this fashion, they are essentially empty—they have associated contacts, but no address or telephone information is recorded. As a result, you should typically import your account data first, creating the records complete with address and telephone information (plus perhaps account type and lots of other information, depending on your old CRM system). This avoids creating rather empty account records, and having to manually add the rest of their information later.

See the following sections for the exact steps for importing accounts, contacts, and leads.

Pre-import analysis

Your source csv file is likely to have data represented in a pattern that matches the following: "Value" followed by a comma.

For example:

`"Angel","Magaña","ACME CRM"`

`"John","Smith","Big Company"`

This pattern is *extremely important*, although it should be noted that the comma is not used after the last value. In this example, three columns are represented: first name, last name, and company name.

Furthermore, new records are separated by a new line marker. Thus, in the preceding example, the line with *Angel Magaña* as the name represents one record, and the line with *John Smith* represents a separate record.

If you are wondering about the possibility of using alternate delimiters besides double quotes, it is certainly possible. However, you must be consistent both across any given line as well as the entire file. You cannot use one delimiter for one column and another for a different column, nor one for one record and a separate one for a different record.

If the csv file that you are attempting to import does not have a consistent pattern, your import will *fail*. Some common problems that occur when the file is not properly formatted include the following:

- Available source field list is not complete
- Import fails after successfully importing one or more records
- Errors reading the source file
- Truncated data

Along with the list of common problems there is also a list of common sources of said issues. They include the following:

- Extraneous commas, double quotes or new line markers
- Mix of delimited and non-delimited data

Often, the aforementioned problems are the result of the export process that was used to create the csv file you are attempting to import.

Data Import and Export

For example, it is not uncommon for Microsoft applications to not delimit numeric values. This has the potential of causing problems because it disturbs the pattern as you end up with a line containing some columns with delimited values and other values that are not delimited.

Other issues are the result of the data itself. For example, if someone inputs a contact name with a comma (,) such as, *Magaña, Angel*, the resulting exported file may include a value that contains an extraneous comma. The extra comma throws off the file's pattern and causes read problems.

Another possibility is that your export file includes a multi-line text field. For example, a notes or comments area. Those fields are prime areas for extraneous new line markers, as users would have likely used a carriage return at some point while typing in the field in the other application. Given that a new line marker denotes a new record, the pattern of the file would again be skewed and the source file would not be read correctly.

All of these issues must be corrected through external tools. You should not attempt to import your data until you have performed a preliminary analysis of your source files to ensure that these issues are eliminated. Failing to do so only leads to frustration and loss of time.

This is also an opportune time to cleanse your data of duplicate records and other integrity issues. Performing this step before you import the data will help ensure that the end result in SugarCRM is of good quality and allows you to make immediate use of it.

We will assume that the file you exported is already in the proper state for importing.

Import accounts

Earlier in this section we touched on the point that other CRM systems from which you may be getting your source data might already recognize and compensate for the difference between accounts and contacts. However, if your data is being imported from a simpler contact manager—such as Microsoft Outlook, then the only data available is contact data, and you will need to be a bit creative if you wish to create an account-contact relationship for those records. See the section titled *Export contacts from your current contact manager* later in this chapter if you require assistance with exporting your data from Microsoft Outlook.

Appendix C

If you are importing account data from a system that distinguishes between accounts and contacts, proceed to step 6. If you only have exported contact data, and need to massage, or manually clean it to act as account data to be imported, perform steps 1 to 4 as follows (the example assumes the original data is in a file named `Contacts.csv`):

1. Copy your exported `Contacts.CSV` file, and name the copied file `Accounts.CSV`.

2. Edit the `Accounts.CSV` file using Excel. First, sort the file according to the company name.

3. Now the more complex part: As you scroll through your data sorted by company name, you will see successive records that have the same company name, because there is more than one contact from that account. To avoid multiple copies of the same account within SugarCRM, you may need to delete or merge these duplicates. Of course, you may have valid reasons for keeping multiple records with the same account name. For example, if you work with differing branches of the same organization.

4. Also look out for company names that are similar but not identical due to inconsistencies in the way the company name was entered—you should delete all duplicate records except the one with the company name spelled exactly as you wish to see it in SugarCRM.

5. Now that you have a nice clean set of account data, save the Excel file as a `.csv` file type, and let's proceed to import this account data.

6. Click on the **Import Accounts** function within the **Navigation Shortcuts** Box of the **Accounts** module.

7. Specify the **Data Source**. Select **Salesforce.com**, **ACT!**, **Comma Delimited**, or **Tab Delimited**. Choose the appropriate delimiter (if necessary) and then click on the **Next** button to continue. For massaged or manually cleansed Outlook files, where the field names no longer match exactly what is exported from Outlook, use the **Comma Delimited** data source.

8. Upload the export file. Use the **Browse** button to locate the `Accounts.CSV` data file, and then click on the **Next** button to continue.

Data Import and Export

9. **Confirm Fields and Import**. This screen (see the next figure) shows four columns of data. Column 2 (**Header Row**) is the key—this contains the names of the fields being exported from your old CRM or contact manager. Column 4 shows an example data from the first record you are about to import. Column 1 (**Database Field**) is where you come in—you need to use all of the drop-down box controls in this column to select the fields within SugarCRM into which each incoming **account** field is imported (or choose to skip it by selecting **Do not map this field**).

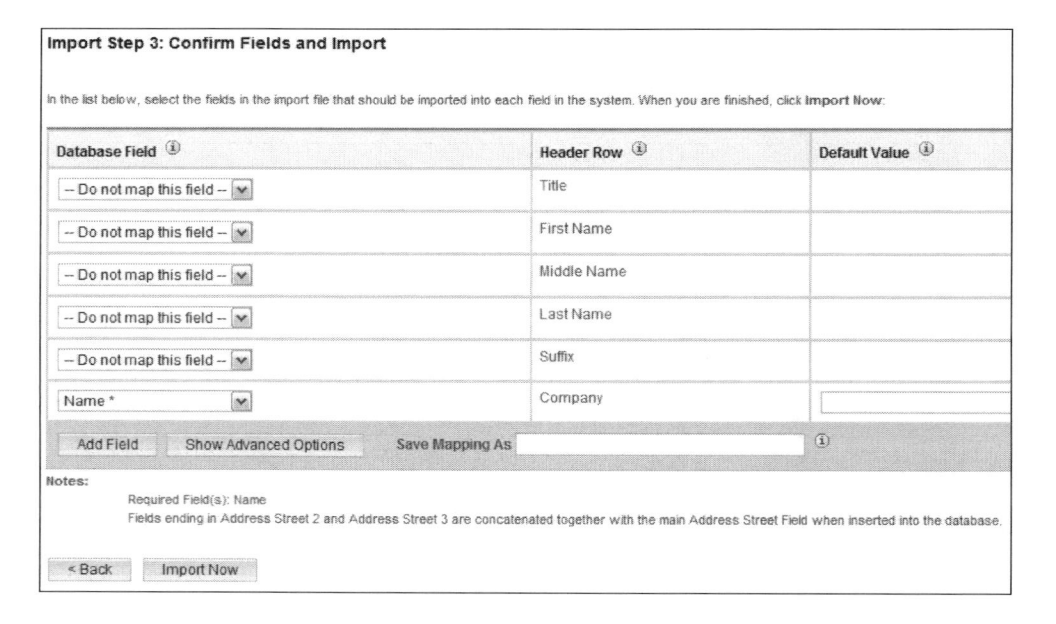

Import Step 3: Confirm Fields and Import

In the list below, select the fields in the import file that should be imported into each field in the system. When you are finished, click **Import Now**:

Database Field	Header Row	Default Value
-- Do not map this field --	Title	
-- Do not map this field --	First Name	
-- Do not map this field --	Middle Name	
-- Do not map this field --	Last Name	
-- Do not map this field --	Suffix	
Name *	Company	

[Add Field] [Show Advanced Options]   Save Mapping As [_____]

Notes:
Required Field(s): Name
Fields ending in Address Street 2 and Address Street 3 are concatenated together with the main Address Street Field when inserted into the database.

[< Back] [Import Now]

10. Spend some time with this, exploring the names of the incoming fields, and the names of the corresponding SugarCRM fields, until you are sure you have defined the optimum mapping between them. If you are importing from Outlook, a particularly important field mapping to get right is the mapping of the incoming **Company** field to the **Account Name** field within SugarCRM.

11. When you are satisfied you have the field mapping right, click on the **Import Now** button, at the bottom of the screen. Before you do this you may choose to click on the **Save As Custom Mapping** checkbox, and provide a name for this mapping so that it may be used again in the future.

12. The **Import Results** screen will be displayed. It will summarize the number of records imported and skipped, as well as provide information on the reasons for them being skipped. Below the summary there will be a complete list of all the data that was imported.
13. You can now choose to click on the **Undo Last Import**, **Import More**, or **Finished** buttons. Click on the **Finished** button if you are satisfied with the results of the data import, or **Undo Last Import** if you want to go back and try again—possibly the result of needing to adjust your field mappings.

Import contacts

Now that you have a set of account records with fully descriptive data, let's import your contact data as follows:

1. Click on the **Import Contacts** function within the **Navigation Shortcuts** Box of the **Contacts** module.
2. Specify the data source: Select **Salesforce.com**, **Microsoft Outlook**, **ACT!**, **Comma Delimited**, or **Tab Delimited** and then click on the **Next** button to continue.
3. Upload the export file: Use the **Browse** button to locate the data file exported by your contact manager, and then click on the **Next** button to continue.
4. **Confirm Fields and Import**: This screen (see the previous image) shows four columns of data. Column 2 (**Header Row**) is the key—this contains the names of the fields being exported from your old CRM or contact manager. Column 4 shows example data from the first record you are about to import. Column 1 (**Database Field**) is where you come in—you need to use every drop-down box control in this column to select the fields within SugarCRM, into which each incoming **Contact** field is imported.
5. Spend some time with this, exploring the names of the incoming fields, and the names of the corresponding SugarCRM fields, until you are sure you have defined the optimum mapping between them. A particularly important field mapping to get right is to map the incoming **Company** field to the **Account Name** field within SugarCRM, so that contacts are associated with the correct accounts. (Make sure that you have corrected inconsistent company names that you found in your data in step 4 of the *Import Accounts* section.)
6. When you are satisfied, and you have the field mapping right, click on the **Import Now** button, at the bottom right of the screen. Before you do so, you may choose to click on the **Save As Custom Mapping** checkbox, and provide a name for this mapping so that it may be used again in future.

7. The **Import Results** screen is displayed. It will summarize how many records were successfully imported, how many were skipped over, and the reasons why they were skipped over. Below the summary there will be complete lists of all the data that have been imported—both Contacts, and any Accounts that were automatically created.

8. You can now choose to click on the **Undo Last Import**, **Import More**, or **Finished** buttons. Click on the **Finished** button if you are satisfied with the results of the data import, or **Undo Last Import** if you want to go back and try again—usually to improve the field mapping.

Importing leads and opportunities

Leads and opportunities are typically only tracked by a full CRM system, not a simple contact manager. If your old system is Microsoft Outlook or a similar contact manager, then you may not have any data to import. If you are migrating from a full CRM system, such as Salesforce.com, then the lead and opportunity data may be exported from that system and imported into SugarCRM in a very similar fashion to importing contact data, as described earlier in the chapter.

Updating records

Earlier in this chapter it was mentioned that it is possible to update existing records through the import utility. To accomplish this, we must have a source file that contains a **match key** and a related **index**.

A match key is a unique value that exists both within the records in the target database and within the source data file being imported. It is used to link a record within the source file to a record that is already in the SugarCRM database. If the data in your source file was originally exported from SugarCRM, you can use the *ID* value as the key. If not, you will have to formulate a solution independently.

The key value itself can be a number, a character, or a mix thereof. In addition, its length does not matter. However, the value does need to meet two criteria. First, the value must be unique. Uniqueness ensures that only one record from the SugarCRM database would match any of the records in the source data file. Secondly, the SugarCRM database field containing the match key value must be indexed. Depending on which field within the SugarCRM database contains the match key value, it may be necessary for you to create a custom index.

The process of creating a custom index will vary slightly depending on your selected database platform. If you are unsure about the process, refer to the MySQL and Microsoft SQL server documentation, located at the following websites:

- `http://dev.mysql.com/doc/refman/5.0/en/index.html`
- `http://msdn.microsoft.com/en-us/library/ms130214(v=SQL.90).aspx`

Our example assumes that we are working with the **Accounts** module and are using a custom field named **custom_c** to store the match key value, for which we have created a custom index. As we have met the requirements, we can proceed to enable the update feature by clicking on **Create and Update Records** on the **Import Step 1** screen, as illustrated in the following image:

Data Import and Export

Proceed to select your file and advance to the import field mappings screen. There you will click on the **Show Advanced Options** button located at the bottom left. After clicking on it, you should see something similar to the following on the bottom right of the screen:

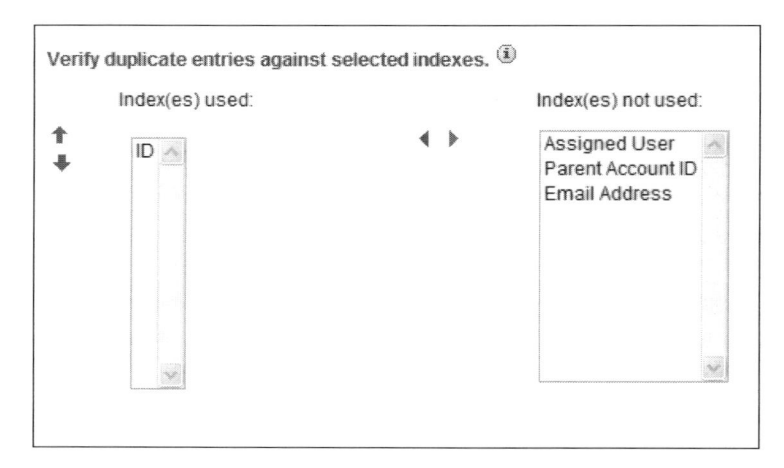

This area (as shown in the preceding image) permits us to select our match key by selecting its related index. Notice that the options are limited to only those indexes that are defined by SugarCRM, although it is possible to modify the list through a minor customization.

Assuming you have applied a custom index to your database (as we have for the **custom_c** field), you will need to make your SugarCRM system aware of the new index.

To add it to your system's configuration, you must first use Notepad, vi, or other text editor to create a file named `custom.php` with content similar to the following:

```
<?php
   $dictionary['Account']['indices'][] = array('name'
                   =>'idx_custom', 'type'=>'index',
                   'fields'=>array('custom_c'));
?>
```

Make a note of the **Account** reference as this specifies the module to be affected. Notice that it is specified in the singular form. Users will often make the mistake of specifying the module name in its plural form which will cause these types of customizations to fail. All module references must be in singular form.

The "name" section represents the descriptor that is displayed in the index list in the previous image. Feel free to use the value specified in this example or use a descriptor of your choice.

The "type" section should remain as illustrated in the preceding code snippet, but do take note of the "fields" section that immediately follows. This section is used to specify the column with the custom index. You will need to adjust it accordingly to reflect the name of the field that you have selected, in our case, **custom_c**.

Once finished, place the file in the following directory:

`custom/Extension/modules/Accounts/Ext/Vardefs`.

Access SugarCRM with an admin level account, and use the **Repair** option in the **Admin** control panel to perform a repair on the accounts module. The next time you use the import wizard in the accounts module, the new index will be available for selection as one of your match keys.

Exporting information

SugarCRM has flexible data exporting capabilities. Essentially, all of the SugarCRM modules have an export function, accessed by clicking on the **Export** link at the top left corner of the list portion of each list view screen, including all of **Activities**, **Accounts**, **Contacts**, **Documents**, **Leads**, **Opportunities**, **Bugs**, **Emails**, **Campaigns**, **Prospects**, **Projects**, and **Cases**.

In each case, a `.csv` file is produced that contains all the currently selected records from the module in use (not just those records that are currently displayed on the screen). The `csv` files can be opened for viewing by using Microsoft Excel, Notepad, WordPad, or other text editors and can easily be parsed as input files by most software.

	A	B	C	D	E	F
1	id	name	date_entered	date_modified	modified_user_id	created_by
2	86124f3a-c962-2bd4-0143-4ba17710c760	Kitty Kat Inc 452275	3/17/2010 17:43	3/17/2010 17:43	1	1
3	e459a962-7d0e-dacf-4bff-4ba177f74226	B.C. Investing International 504338	3/17/2010 17:43	3/17/2010 17:43	1	1
4	eeb87f4e-8b3c-a3b3-616b-4ba177ed79d1	MMM Mortuary Corp 527118	3/17/2010 17:43	3/17/2010 17:43	1	1
5	26de0e79-78d9-00a9-4ac1-4ba1772a6be6	BS Funding Coop 907660	3/17/2010 17:43	3/17/2010 17:43	1	1
6	36b5b707-49cb-48cd-a1fb-4ba177beae92	Grow-Fast Inc 662443	3/17/2010 17:43	3/17/2010 17:43	1	1
7	591c049a-4b31-4180-ef46-4ba1778acf5e	NW Bridge Construction 23984	3/17/2010 17:43	3/17/2010 17:43	1	1
8	8bafb5a6-b518-4c97-d2c0-4ba177060bbf	A B Hammer Group Inc 132186	3/17/2010 17:43	3/17/2010 17:43	1	1
9	ad1091d3-8ab7-0878-50d9-4ba177e3c340	CUMBERLAND TRAILS 626770	3/17/2010 17:43	3/17/2010 17:43	1	1
10	d98a82e1-b588-efdd-5c0d-4ba177702b731	2 Tall Stores 889459	3/17/2010 17:43	3/17/2010 17:43	1	1
11	e40666d3-cab3-5713-32fb-4ba177bbf3e1	A.G. Parr PLC 327537	3/17/2010 17:43	3/17/2010 17:43	1	1
12	123fa95f-cf50-be19-f13b-4ba177fb03ad	Powder Puff Suppliers 191582	3/17/2010 17:43	3/17/2010 17:43	1	1
13	29ecb239-b556-ea9c-37fe-4ba177aac83d	CONS TRUST (AZ) 817814	3/17/2010 17:43	3/17/2010 17:43	1	1
14	369a1400-d42c-c882-0539-4ba17753564e	X-SELL HOLDINGS 774114	3/17/2010 17:43	3/17/2010 17:43	1	1
15	5def414e-17a9-04e5-9ee0-4ba1774f7ace	K Kringle IncK.A. Tower & Co 389028	3/17/2010 17:43	3/17/2010 17:43	1	1
16	77ba8e47-391e-7c95-1576-4ba1775992a3	Itty-Bitty Conglomerate Inc 548773	3/17/2010 17:43	3/17/2010 17:43	1	1
17	9e3a5035-0b19-e6f9-75bd-4ba1770469cc	First National S/B 909917	3/17/2010 17:43	3/17/2010 17:43	1	1

Data Import and Export

A sample portion of a csv file, exported from the **Accounts** module and viewed in Microsoft Excel, is shown in the preceding screenshot. You can see that essentially the entire database table is exported in the csv file with column titles, including the **Record ID** (a long and largely incomprehensible string of letters and numbers used as a unique reference to each account record) and other fields that SugarCRM uses internally.

Export contacts from your current contact manager

We will use Outlook 2003 as an example of exporting contact manager data. Other systems tend to work in similar ways. To export the data from Outlook 2003 carry out the following steps:

- Under the **File** menu, select **Import and Export**. The **Import and Export Wizard** dialog box is then displayed.
- Select the action **Export to a file**, and click on the **Next** button.
- Choose to create a file of the type **Comma Separated Values (Windows)**, and click on the **Next** button.
- Select an Outlook folder from which to export—typically your contacts folder—and click on the **Next** button.
- Enter the filename and directory location for the exported file to be created, and click on the **Next** button.
- Confirm your intention to export this file by clicking on the **Finish** button.
- The desired .csv file is then created by Outlook 2003. You can view the file easily using Microsoft Excel or a simple text editor to confirm that the data you intended has been exported.

An excerpt of what the exported file might look like is as follows:

```
"Title","First Name","Middle Name","Last Name","Suffix","Company"

"","Angel","","Magaña","","ACME CRM"

"","John","","Smith","","Big Software Co."
```

Other options

While many users are well served by the built-in import and export features, others require more advanced solutions to migrate, export, or manipulate the data, perhaps for automated routines or data massaging/formatting. Fortunately, there are various tools that are quite capable of performing these tasks and are worth exploring. Some of those include the following:

- Talend Open Studio (`http://www.talend.com`)
- SnapLogic (`http://www.snaplogic.com`)
- Apatar (`http://www.apatar.com`)
- Jitterbit (`http://www.jitterbit.com`)

The best point concerning these tools is that they are also open source and based on proven open source technologies.

D
The System Administrator Role

This section is intended for system administrators of SugarCRM Community Edition. Administrators access an additional system administration control panel by clicking on the **Admin** link at the top right corner of the SugarCRM screen. Note that the **Admin** link is only displayed for users who have been given administrator access privileges.

Every shared business system needs a system administrator to perform system-wide housekeeping tasks. SugarCRM is no different in this regard.

Some of these duties occur around the time of initial system installation and set up. Others are general maintenance activities that are performed when new users join the system, or other users leave. In this appendix we will deal with topics such as the following:

- What are the system administration requirements during initial system setup?
- What are the ongoing responsibilities of the system administrator?
- Who should be the system administrator?
- Should more than one person have administrative access?

System administration duties

System administration duties fall into two categories. Those to be performed at the time of system installation and those that will need to be performed on a regular or ad hoc basis for the duration of the system's time in service.

During system installation, system administration duties include the following:

- Adding all the necessary users to the system, including their first and last names, username and password, and other user settings or preferences
- Sending users their respective username and password, and other login information
- Providing users with instructions for configuring their e-mail accounts and options
- Defining security roles and assigning users to them
- Using the configure tabs or configure tab groups feature to suppress and organize the navigation tabs
- Utilizing the rename tabs feature to change the name of any of the tabs as desired
- Using the system settings feature to change the system logo and define other system defaults
- Using Studio to apply module customizations, such as adding custom fields or changing field labels
- Defining system currencies and exchange rates
- Configuring system e-mail settings
- Using the Module loader tool to install system enhancements or additional modules
- Defining recurring system tasks (that is, crontab on Linux-based servers, or using the scheduler on Windows servers) in order to enable the system scheduler, which is used for e-mail marketing campaigns, running scheduled reports, and other scheduled system activities

After the system is installed and running, system administrators may periodically need to perform the following tasks:

- Add new users or deactivate the credentials of users who have left the organization
- Reset passwords for users who forget them
- Update currency rates

- Maintain role settings
- Check for SugarCRM updates
- Use the Upgrade Wizard to manage system upgrades when SugarCRM releases new versions of their software
- Create system backups of the SugarCRM program files and customizations
- Use MySQL administration tools, such as phpMyAdmin or SQLyog to back up the SugarCRM database
- Monitor disk space usage on the SugarCRM server

Who should be the system administrator?

As you can see from the preceding lists, the system administrator has a fair bit of work to do to help install and maintain the SugarCRM system.

This should tell you that whoever you choose as the system administrator needs to have some time available to complete these new responsibilities. Also, the administrator must be someone who can be trusted with all the user access information and with the company's most sensitive data, as the administrator can see all the data in the entire SugarCRM system.

Many businesses choose the same person who administers their PCs and their network as their system administrator. In smaller businesses, this person is frequently a part-time contractor, not an employee.

If an outside contractor is already administering all your network access information, it doesn't really make things any worse to hand them the keys to the CRM as well—so if that's your inclination—go ahead. However, make sure you have a good non-disclosure and non-competition agreement in place with that contractor.

The tasks themselves do not require serious technical skills in order to properly execute them. With a little technical advice, a senior manager in the business can fill the role of system administrator just fine—although it may not be a good use of their time to be resetting user passwords. However, they will have the knowledge of and the control over who is accessing the business's key data within the CRM.

Should more than one user be given system admin capability?

The system is designed so that if there is only one system administrator, that user cannot be disabled nor have its system administrator abilities removed. This prevents you from creating a situation where none of your users have administrator level privileges.

Normally, most businesses maintain two system administrators on the system. One is typically the real administrator, doing the bulk of the day-to-day work, while the other is typically a senior manager who keeps an eye on the system but does not regularly perform administrative tasks, except in the absence of the main administrator.

Administration duties at system installation time

The following screen shows the top-level administration screen. The administration capabilities referred to next can all be accessed from this screen.

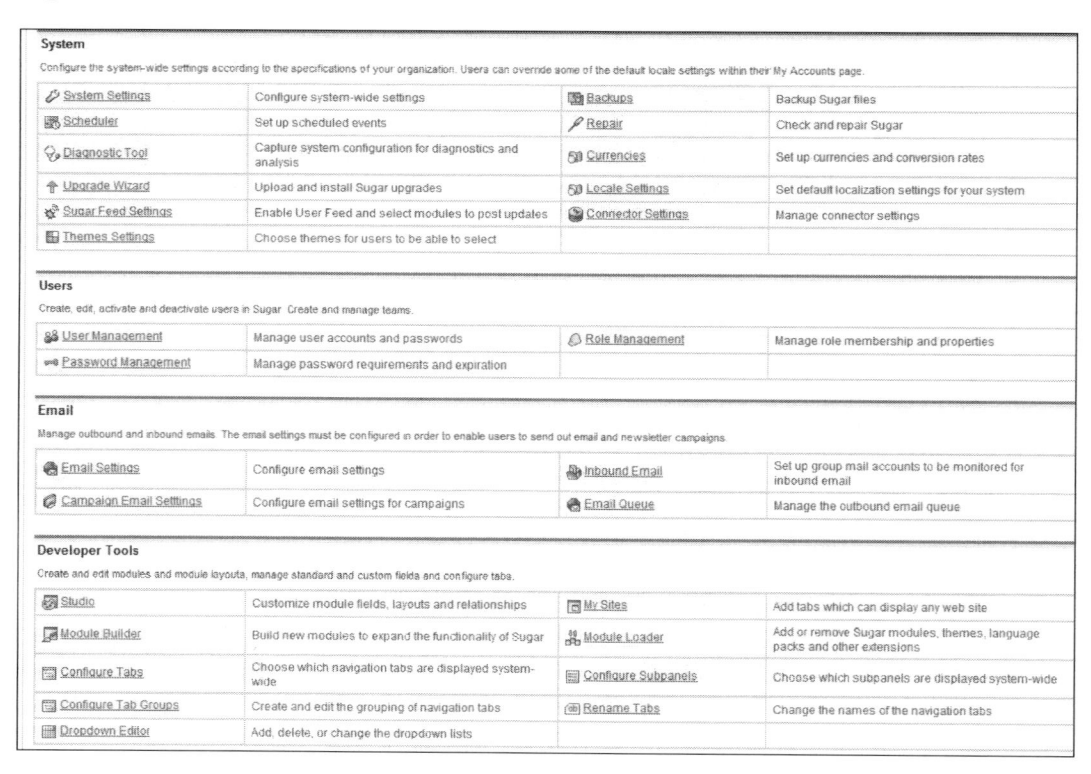

System

Configure the system-wide settings according to the specifications of your organization. Users can override some of the default locale settings within their My Accounts page.

System Settings	Configure system-wide settings	Backups	Backup Sugar files
Scheduler	Set up scheduled events	Repair	Check and repair Sugar
Diagnostic Tool	Capture system configuration for diagnostics and analysis	Currencies	Set up currencies and conversion rates
Upgrade Wizard	Upload and install Sugar upgrades	Locale Settings	Set default localization settings for your system
Sugar Feed Settings	Enable User Feed and select modules to post updates	Connector Settings	Manage connector settings
Themes Settings	Choose themes for users to be able to select		

Users

Create, edit, activate and deactivate users in Sugar. Create and manage teams.

User Management	Manage user accounts and passwords	Role Management	Manage role membership and properties
Password Management	Manage password requirements and expiration		

Email

Manage outbound and inbound emails. The email settings must be configured in order to enable users to send out email and newsletter campaigns.

Email Settings	Configure email settings	Inbound Email	Set up group mail accounts to be monitored for inbound email
Campaign Email Settings	Configure email settings for campaigns	Email Queue	Manage the outbound email queue

Developer Tools

Create and edit modules and module layouts, manage standard and custom fields and configure tabs.

Studio	Customize module fields, layouts and relationships	My Sites	Add tabs which can display any web site
Module Builder	Build new modules to expand the functionality of Sugar	Module Loader	Add or remove Sugar modules, themes, language packs and other extensions
Configure Tabs	Choose which navigation tabs are displayed system-wide	Configure Subpanels	Choose which subpanels are displayed system-wide
Configure Tab Groups	Create and edit the grouping of navigation tabs	Rename Tabs	Change the names of the navigation tabs
Dropdown Editor	Add, delete, or change the dropdown lists		

Configuring system settings

System settings has the following six sections:

- The first section is used to define the **User Interface** options. This section is used to control display features (such as the number of records displayed by default on a ListView screen, the ability to rearrange subpanels, the company logo used within SugarCRM, and other options).

- The second section is used to enable a proxy connection, (a connection that serves as a relay to the outside world or Internet) by which the SugarCRM server will access external information, such as information pertaining to SugarCRM updates. If it is enabled, you will need to define settings for the proxy host, port number, and other related options.

- The third section is used to enable or disable integration with **SkypeOut**. Enabling it allows users to click on phone numbers within the system to place outbound phone calls through Skype. Note that phone numbers must include their respective country code in order to leverage this feature.

- The fourth section is used to enable the SugarCRM **Mail Merge** feature. As the SugarCRM plugin for Microsoft Word is designed to only work with Professional and Enterprise Editions of SugarCRM and third-party solutions (such as GrinMark plugin for Microsoft Office) tend to not rely on the status of this option, the need to manipulate it is highly unlikely.

- The fifth section is for more **Advanced** settings. Among them are features for logging memory usage and slow executing queries. These features are helpful resources for optimizing your system. The **Developer Mode** option is helpful when customizing the system, as it causes SugarCRM to bypass its caching mechanism and apply customizations faster. This latter option should only be used while customizing the system and should be disabled at all other times.

- Lastly, the **Logger Settings** section at the bottom is a useful tool for monitoring and troubleshooting problems. For example, setting the **Log Level** to **Debug** would cause SugarCRM to log the SQL queries that it uses to perform functions, such as inserting or updating records. Later review of this information can help yield clues to the source of the problems, such as data not being saved or records not being displayed among other issues.

The System Administrator Role

The preceding six options are depicted in the following screenshot:

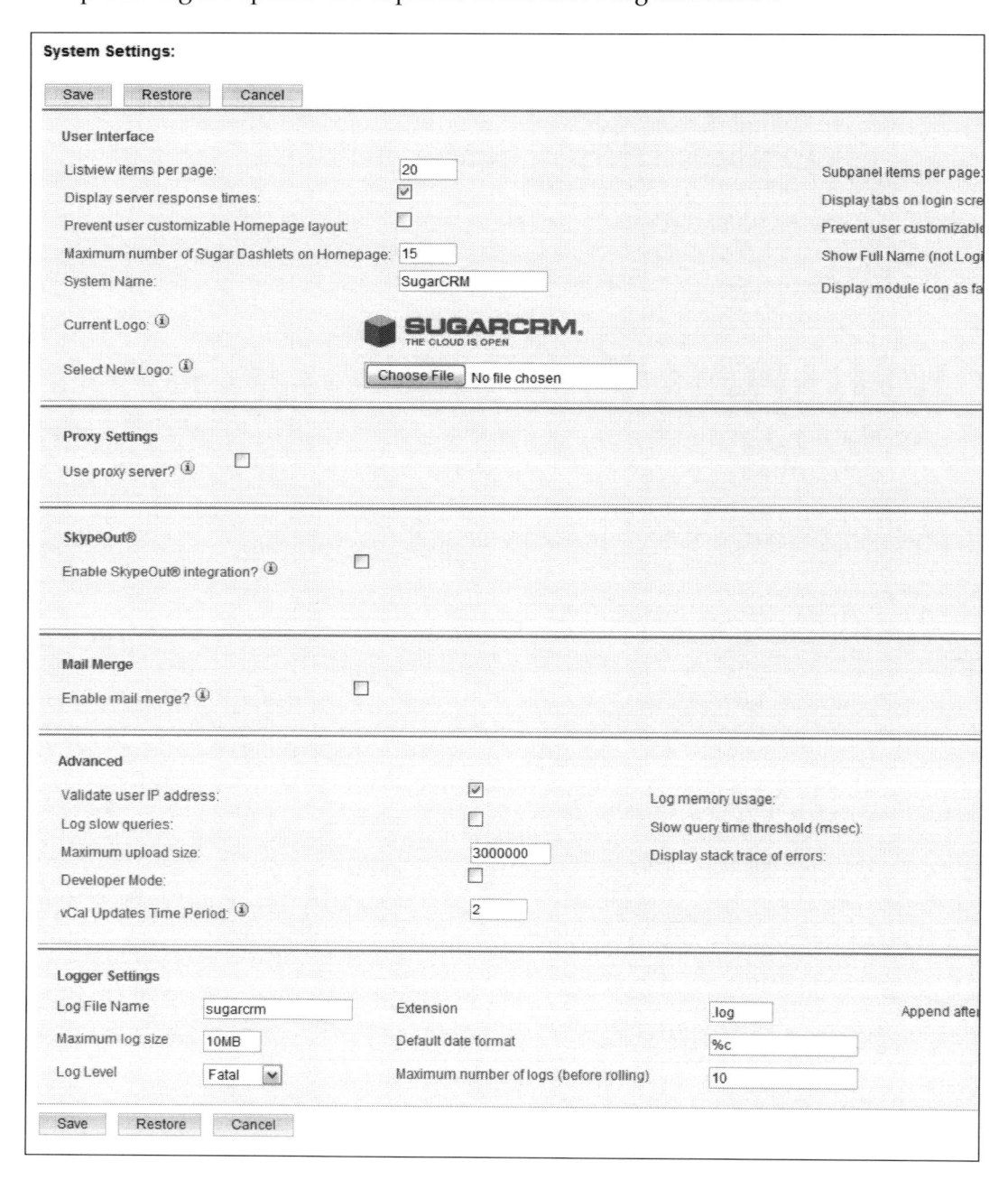

System Settings:

Save   Restore   Cancel

User Interface

Listview items per page:	20	Subpanel items per page:
Display server response times:	☑	Display tabs on login scre
Prevent user customizable Homepage layout:	☐	Prevent user customizable
Maximum number of Sugar Dashlets on Homepage:	15	Show Full Name (not Logi
System Name:	SugarCRM	Display module icon as fa
Current Logo: ⓘ	SUGARCRM. THE CLOUD IS OPEN	
Select New Logo: ⓘ	Choose File No file chosen	

Proxy Settings

Use proxy server? ⓘ   ☐

SkypeOut®

Enable SkypeOut® integration? ⓘ   ☐

Mail Merge

Enable mail merge? ⓘ   ☐

Advanced

Validate user IP address:	☑	Log memory usage:
Log slow queries:	☐	Slow query time threshold (msec):
Maximum upload size:	3000000	Display stack trace of errors:
Developer Mode:	☐	
vCal Updates Time Period: ⓘ	2	

Logger Settings

Log File Name	sugarcrm	Extension	.log	Append after
Maximum log size	10MB	Default date format	%c	
Log Level	Fatal ▾	Maximum number of logs (before rolling)	10	

Save   Restore   Cancel

[288]

Defining currencies and rates

The **Currencies** screen is used to define currencies other than the default US dollar. For each new currency defined, the name, the symbol (for example $), exchange rate to the US$, and ISO code (such as CAN for the Canadian dollar) must be entered (as shown in the following screenshot). Note that each user can select his or her default currency within their user preferences screen.

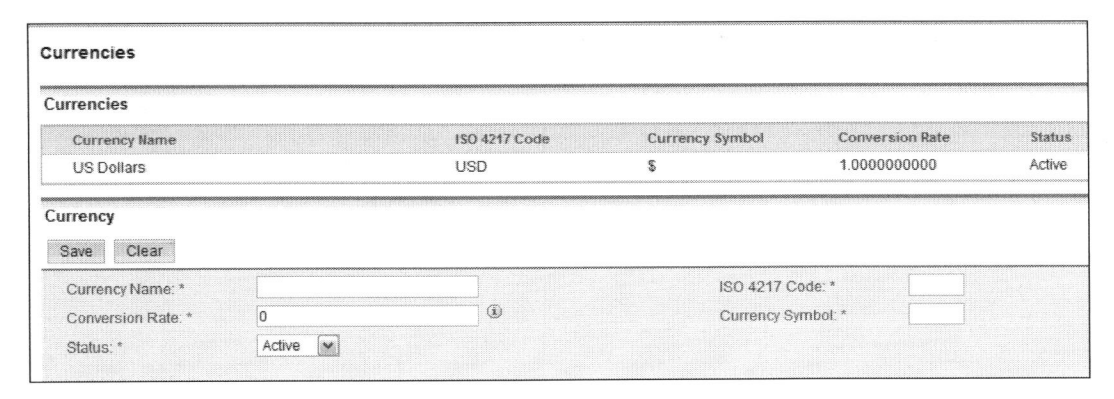

Currency Name	ISO 4217 Code	Currency Symbol	Conversion Rate	Status
US Dollars	USD	$	1.0000000000	Active

Currency

Save   Clear

Currency Name: *
Conversion Rate: * 0
Status: * Active
ISO 4217 Code: *
Currency Symbol: *

Defining security roles

Roles within SugarCRM serve the purpose of limiting the access of certain users within the system. Selecting the **Role Management** option from within the administration area will display the **Roles List** view screen. It lists the roles defined within the system and also offers shortcuts to create a new role, or list roles by user.

The System Administrator Role

You can define roles for groups of users and specify which modules those users should have access to. For example, sales staff will want access to the opportunities and dashboard modules, marketing staff will want access to the campaigns module, but not all staff will need access to these modules. As you can see in the following figure, each role defines the modules which will be visible to the users who are assigned the specific role, as well as the capabilities the user will have within each module.

	Access	Delete	Edit	Export	Import	List	View
Accounts	Not Set	Not Set	Not Set	Not Set	Not Set	Not Set	Not Set
Bug Tracker	Not Set	Not Set	Not Set	Not Set	Not Set	Not Set	Not Set
Calls	Not Set	Not Set	Not Set	Not Set	Not Set	Not Set	Not Set
Campaigns	Not Set	Not Set	Not Set	Not Set	Not Set	Not Set	Not Set
Cases	Not Set	Not Set	Not Set	Not Set	Not Set	Not Set	Not Set
Contacts	Not Set	Not Set	Not Set	Not Set	Not Set	Not Set	Not Set
Documents	Not Set	Not Set	Not Set	Not Set	Not Set	Not Set	Not Set
Email Marketing	Not Set	Not Set	Not Set	Not Set	Not Set	Not Set	Not Set
Emails	Not Set	Not Set	Not Set	Not Set	Not Set	Not Set	Not Set
Email Templates	Not Set	Not Set	Not Set	Not Set	Not Set	Not Set	Not Set

To create a role, click on the **Create Role** shortcut, type a name and a description for the role in the **Name** and **Description** fields respectively, and click on **Save**. Adjust the settings to control the modules that the role can access and the functions that may be performed within each module. Note that when a module is excluded from a role, access is also removed to the subpanels in other modules that relate to the excluded module. Click on **Save** to preserve those settings for your role.

To assign users to a role, use the detail view for that role. In the **Users** subpanel at the bottom of the screen, click on the **Select** button to display a list of users. You can check the usernames that you want to assign to this role. If a user belongs to multiple roles, their access in each module is defined by the most restrictive access any of their roles are assigned.

It is very important that you understand that by default, all users will have access to all the data and all the modules. The use of roles in conjunction with the use of the **Assigned To** field on individual records is the primary mechanism for controlling access to modules and their data. If you need to control the access of specific users to certain records, you should define your roles and assign them to the corresponding users before you allow users access to the system.

Appendix D

[💡 If you need to refresh your memory on the relevance or use of the "Assigned To" field, refer the section titled *SugarCRM basics: Security* in *Chapter 4* of this book.]

Configuring system tabs

The system administrators and users can easily configure which tabs appear at the top of the application. The **Configure Tabs** administration option allows administrators to define which menu tabs will be available for all users and which will be omitted. Administrators can also control whether or not individual users are allowed to change their respective tab settings, typically controlled through the **My Account** screen. Any tabs that an administrator excludes cannot be added back by a user.

Configuring tab groups

Selecting the **Configure Tab Groups** option on the administration page allows you to define tab groups similar to those provided by SugarCRM by default. This feature allows you to create groups that are more in line with your user's navigation requirements and usage of the system.

As an administrator, you can modify the existing tab groups or create new groups. Additionally, you may change the ordering of the groups. Users will not be able to manipulate the groups.

Adding system users

To add new users to the system or to edit user settings, select **User Management** from the main **Administration** screen. Note that users may not be deleted. They may be made **Inactive**, or be recycled into a new user record, but not deleted. SugarCRM is designed this way principally to avoid having data in the system that is associated to a user who does not exist.

The presence of data assigned to non-existent users is known to cause problems, sometimes seemingly completely disconnected with each other. In some rare cases, such records have been known to cause problems with upgrades. For this reason, it is recommended that you do not circumvent the system and forcibly delete users.

The user management screen is shown in the following screenshot:

Name	User Name	Title	Department	Email	Phone	Status	System Ad
Administrator	admin	Administrator				Active	✓
Jim Brennan	jim	VP Sales		jim@example.com		Active	
Sarah Smith	sarah	Sales Manager West		sarah@example.com		Active	
Sally Bronsen	sally	Senior Account Rep		sally@example.com		Active	
Max Jensen	max	Account Rep		tom@example.com		Active	
Will Westin	will	Sales Manager East		will@example.com		Active	
Chris Olliver	chris	Senior Account Rep		chris@example.com		Active	
Portal User	portal					Active	

Use the **Create User** shortcut to define a new user. You will need to provide not only the username, but also the password and the user's status. Once you have created the user, you can provide them with the URL to your SugarCRM install, plus their username and password so they may begin to use it.

Password management

As described in the previous section, the process of creating a new user involves the definition of a password, which is in turn provided to the intended user. Said user would then be able to change the password by accessing their **My Account** screen within SugarCRM.

This liberty creates a potential security problem. Given that the users are free to define a password of their liking, there exists the possibility that they may create one that is very easy to guess. Such a scenario may allow an unintended or a malicious user to have access to your SugarCRM system.

To counter this problem, administrators can define some restrictions on passwords. Restrictions are defined by clicking on the **Password Management** option on the administration screen. The following screenshot will be displayed after clicking on **Password Management**:

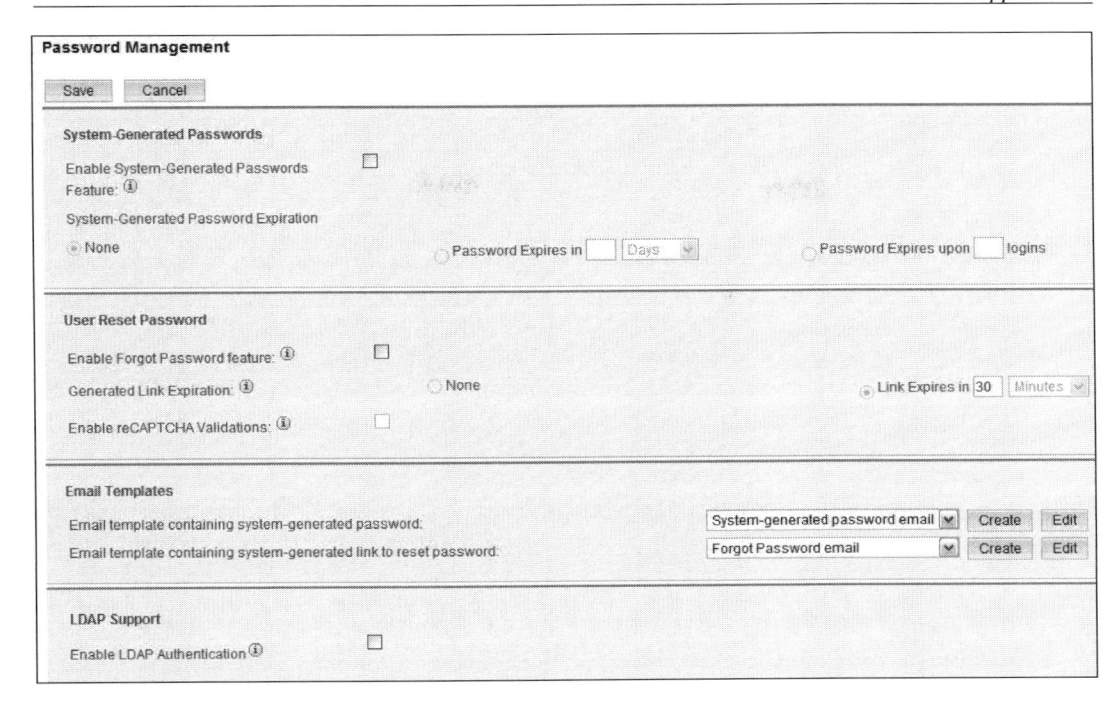

Using Studio

As an administrator, you will undoubtedly find yourself in a situation where you need to customize your SugarCRM installation. Fortunately, SugarCRM provides a number of tools that serve this purpose.

The Administration home page shows a number of tools grouped together as **Developer Tools**. They include the following:

- Studio
- Dropdown editor
- Module builder
- Module loader
- Rename tabs

These tools collectively enable administrative users to perform a broad range of customization tasks, reducing the need for custom software development. For more information on these tools, refer to *Appendix E*, which discusses these SugarCRM customization tools in detail.

Defining system e-mail

System e-mail settings serve a variety of purposes. The most basic use is to send e-mail notifications to users upon the assignment of records. It can also be used to monitor group e-mail inboxes, such as support@example.com or sales@example.com. Lastly, e-mail settings must be defined if you intend to send out mass e-mail through the built-in marketing campaign tool.

To configure e-mail settings, click on **Email Settings** on the administration screen. On this page, you will be able to define the mail transfer agent (sendmail or SMTP) for your installation, as well as enable the sending of notification e-mails to users by enabling the **Assignment Notifications** option. Note that your options will vary depending on the version of SugarCRM that you are using, as Version 5.5 and higher do not allow the use of **sendmail** by default.

Most Linux environments include **sendmail**, but SMTP is quite often an option as well. If you are unsure about which choice to make, consult your hosting provider (for hosted deployments) or review your server's e-mail services configuration.

If you would like to configure SugarCRM to monitor a group mailbox, click the **Inbound Email** option on the administration screen. Next, click on **Monitor New Mail Account** to enter the e-mail inbox settings, such as the server address, username, and password. Make sure to set a value for the **Assign To Group Folder** field. Once operational, SugarCRM will automatically retrieve e-mails for that account, and add them to the assigned folder. To access the e-mails, users can add the folder to their e-mail configuration and they will be automatically displayed.

Notice that the configuration screen also allows you to automatically create a support case every time an e-mail is retrieved from the specified e-mail inbox.

Perhaps one of the most common uses for the e-mail configuration is for the purposes of sending mass e-mails through the marketing campaign tool built into SugarCRM. If you are using SugarCRM within a hosted environment, you should check with your provider about any limitations or considerations that need to be observed with regard to the amount of e-mail you are allowed to send. In addition, you should investigate if any legislation in your area aims at controlling who you can send e-mail to or under which conditions.

To use e-mail campaigns within SugarCRM, the administrator must first enable the **System Scheduler** and configure the **Schedule list** within the **Scheduler** option within the System section of the administration home page.

The system scheduler is enabled in two different ways, one for a Linux server and another for a Windows server. For Microsoft Windows, you can use the task scheduler. For Linux, you can use cron.

For Linux, as a root user, type the following command at the shell prompt, replacing the `path-to-sugar` with your own path to the Sugar installation directory and replacing the `apache` with the proper username that the web server runs as (usually defaults to **apache** or **wwwrun**):

`/echo "0,10,20,30,40,50 * * * * cd /<path-to-sugar>; <path-to-php> ./scheduler.php" | crontab -u apache/`

This will setup a cron job to check every 10 minutes whether any e-mail needs to be sent out. If there are any, the mass e-mail queue manager will process the template and send an e-mail out immediately to the recipient. Further information on the **cron** utility can be found at http://en.wikipedia.org/wiki/Cron.

For Windows, you will first need to create a batch file that causes Windows to execute PHP and the script relevant to the SugarCRM scheduler functionality. Usually, it is a batch file with something similar to the following:

`cd C:\xampplite\htdocs\sugarce55\`

`php.exe -f cron.php`

Change `C:\xampplite\htdocs\sugarce55\` to reflect the appropriate directory that represents the location of your SugarCRM installation and paste into a text file named `SugarScheduler.bat`. Take note of where on your computer it is that you saved `SugarScheduler.bat` as we will need that information in the following step.

Next, select **Start | Settings | Control Panel | Scheduled Tasks**. Double-click on **Add Scheduled Task**. When the **Scheduled Task Wizard** asks you for the program you want Windows to run, browse for the `SugarScheduler.bat` file. Continue with the rest of the Wizard, making sure you click on the **Daily** option when asked when to perform this task. Note that you may need to login to Windows as admin level user in order to be able to complete this process.

Before you click on the **Finish** button for the Scheduled Task Wizard, check the box that says, **Open advanced properties for this task when I click Finish**. A new dialog box displays after you click on **Finish**. Click on the **Schedule** tab, and then on the **Advanced** button. Check the box for **Repeat task** and specify every 10 minutes within a duration of 24 hours.

Recurring administration duties

This section describes those administrative duties that need to be performed on a regular or ad hoc basis throughout the life of your SugarCRM Community Edition installation.

User management

New users will need to be created and existing users may need to be marked temporarily as **Inactive** if they take prolonged breaks, such as a maternity leave. You can see how to add a new user earlier in this section.

To mark a user as **Inactive**, go to the **Admin** main screen, select **User Management**. choose the user you wish to mark as **Inactive**, and click on the **Edit** button. Set the **Status** field to **Inactive** and then click on **Save**.

As mentioned previously, users may not be removed. Typically, the best solution is to mark a user as "Inactive" for a period of time (say six months) and then rename the user.

Resetting passwords

If you need to reset a user's password, go to the **Admin** main screen, select **User Management**, and then select the corresponding user. On their detail view screen, click on **Edit**, and then define the new password. Proceed to click on **Save** when finished.

You will then need to e-mail or telephone the user to inform them of their new temporary password. It is also helpful to provide them with instructions on changing their password once logged into SugarCRM.

Alternatively, you may choose to turn on the **Enable Forgot Password feature** in the **Password Management** panel. Doing so would allow users to reset their password without needing to bother the administrator with the task.

General maintenance

There are six topics that fall under general maintenance of the SugarCRM system. They are as follows:

- Updating currency rates
- Maintaining security roles
- Checking for and installing software updates
- System backups
- Data backups
- Monitoring

Some of these topics, such as the maintenance of currency rates and roles are explained sufficiently in the preceding section of this chapter, *Administration duties at system installation time*. However, let us explore the others.

Checking for updates to SugarCRM

You can check for updates automatically by using the SugarCRM administrative function, **Sugar Updates**, and then clicking on **Check Now** as shown in the following screenshot:

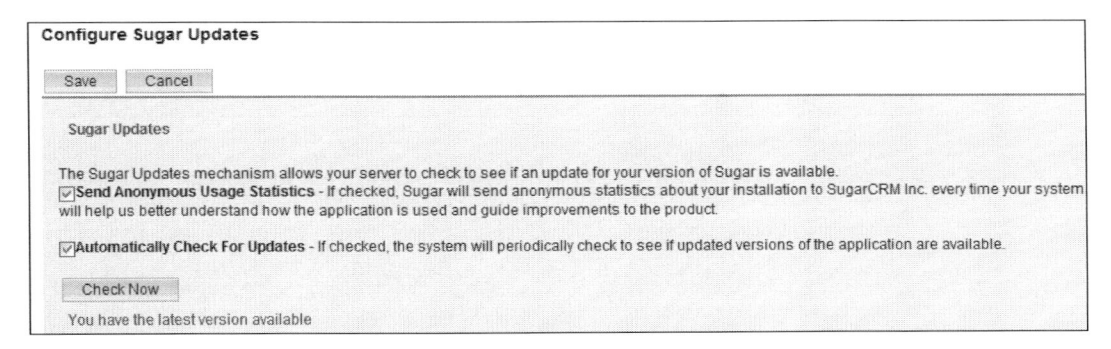

You can set the system to automatically check for updates, or you can do it manually. If you do it manually, the system will perform the update check, and will display the name of the most recent update just below the **Check Now** button.

You may also visit http://www.sugarcrm.com/crm/download/sugar-suite.html to check for software updates.

Either way, automatically or manually, if you find any updates for the SugarCRM software, you can download those upgrades or patch files and then use the Upgrade Wizard to install it. Further information on using the Upgrade Wizard is available later in this chapter.

System backups

There is no excuse for not having a solid backup routine in place. The value of your customer data contained within your SugarCRM system far outweighs the costs involved in implementing and maintaining a backup process.

To properly back up a SugarCRM installation, you must back up the SugarCRM system folder and SugarCRM database. The two should be considered inseparable, and also require different techniques. This section discusses the process for backing up the system folder *only*. The section that follows touches on the related topic of backing up the SugarCRM database.

Backing up the SugarCRM system folder, the folder containing the files composing your installation of SugarCRM (including customizations you may have installed into the software), is a fairly simple task. You can use the **Backups** function within administration screen to perform this backup.

To create a backup, enter the name of the folder in which the backup is to be stored and the filename for the backup file (in ZIP format) to be generated. It is recommended that you check the amount of available disk space in advance or the backup may fail. Note that the backup process will include e-mail attachments and other linked files, including those associated with documents and notes entries. If you make heavy use of these features, the size of your backup files will grow rapidly. Again, this backup process does not include the SugarCRM database and that must be backed up through different techniques, discussed in the section that immediately follows.

To restore the system software from the ZIP format file that was produced, a manual re-installation process must be performed, using this ZIP file instead of the distribution file you originally used. Much like the backup process that generated the ZIP file, restoring your SugarCRM installation through this ZIP file would not restore your SugarCRM database. The following screenshot displays a system backup screen:

Data backups

As mentioned in the preceding section of this chapter, there is no excuse for not having a backup of your database, especially given its volatility. It is strongly recommended that you also keep a copy of your backup media in a safe, offsite location, such as a bank deposit box. This will help safeguard against natural disasters, theft or other emergencies that might occur at the site where your original backups and/or server are located. At minimum, a backup of the database should be performed on a daily basis, and you should keep at least 2 weeks worth of backups in a rotation of backup sets. If you make heavy use of your SugarCRM system, you should also consider making incremental backups throughout the day.

To backup your system data from the MySQL server, use a MySQL administration tool, such as phpMyAdmin or SQLyog. Both provide access to all database administration functions, including the ability to create database backups. Alternatively, if you have shell access, you can simply perform a command-line dump in MySQL. To learn more about phpMyAdmin or SQLyog please visit the following websites:

- http://www.phpmyadmin.net
- http://www.webyog.com

Checking available storage

Other than completely losing the data on a hard drive, few things are quite as bad as having the drive run out of free space. You can check for free disk space on a Linux server by using the `df -h` command in a shell, while logged in as root.

You can check for free space on a Windows server by simply right-clicking on the hard drive used for data storage within **My Computer**. This will display a dialog box like the following:

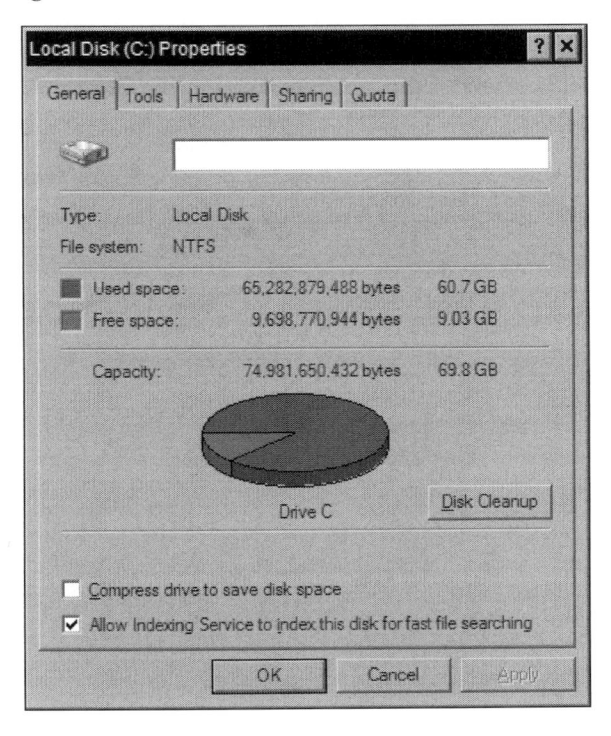

As long as there is at least 5 GB of free space on the hard drive, there is not that much to worry about. Anything equal or less is a cause for concern and should be considered the appropriate time to add a new hard drive, replace the existing one(s), or replace the server. Going through system e-mail (and attachments) and the document repository may also be a good idea, as that is where the bulk of disk space is used. For reference, those files are stored in the `cache/upload` folder within the SugarCRM folder structure.

The System Administrator Role

Deletions can be a bit tricky to handle as you should delete the record within the SugarCRM interface and then the related file should be deleted through the file system (for example, Windows Explorer, and so on). You can identify the related file by matching the name of the files in the `cache/upload` folder to the **ID** value of the deleted record in the SugarCRM database.

Using the Upgrade Wizard

The Upgrade Wizard is used to upgrade your system software from one revision to the next and is also accessed from the administration screen. It is a sophisticated piece of software that also executes SQL scripts that upgrade your database structure to apply changes needed for the revision being installed. The Upgrade Wizard screen is shown in the following screenshot:

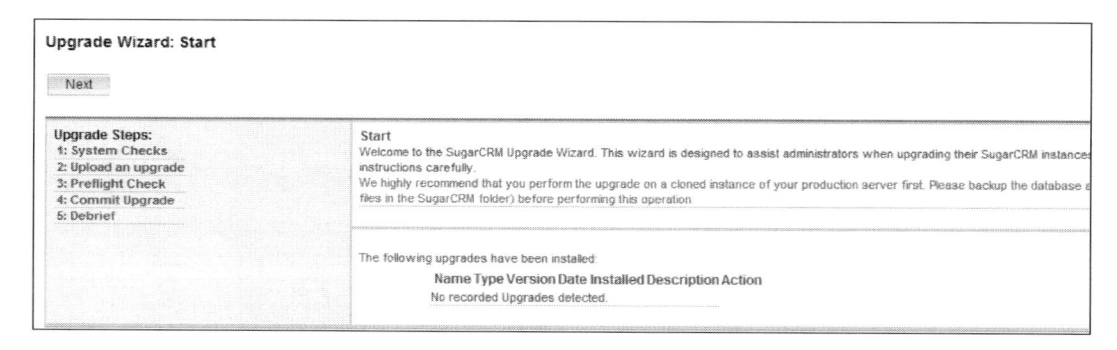

The Upgrade Wizard also provides a quick way to upload and install patches to existing versions.

Before installing, you should heed the warning in the Upgrade Wizard that recommends performing the upgrade on cloned instance. If you do not have a backup of the system and the database in its current state prior to attempting to upgrade, reverting to the older version from a failed upgrade may prove to be a difficult and time consuming challenge.

To install an update or patch, click on **Next** and then carry out the following steps:

- Make a note of any system issues the Upgrade Wizard highlights. You will need to correct them before you can proceed. Click on **Next** to continue once the environment is deemed acceptable.

- Browse to select the ZIP file for the upgrade and click on **Upload**. Uploading the file queues the upgrade files for installation. Next, whenever you like, you can click on **Install** to install the upgrade files.

[300]

Appendix D

- Proceed through the wizard and click on **Commit** to complete the installation.
- The Upgrade Wizard automatically unzips and installs the files. A history of all upgrades that have been queued and installed are displayed in a list on the **Upgrade Wizard** screen.

Note that you typically cannot uninstall upgrades, patches, or updates. The latter are smaller scale software updates that SugarCRM will regularly release and are primarily aimed at correcting issues that have been identified within the software.

In addition to making sure you perform your upgrade on a cloned instance and have a backup of your system, the second most important piece of advice to ensure success is to check your system requirements.

Many users encounter problems when attempting to upgrade installations of SugarCRM because they assume the version of SugarCRM they are currently using and the version to which they wish to upgrade, both have matching system requirements. Often that is not the case and this causes problems.

For example, Version 4.5.1 of SugarCRM supported Version 4.x of PHP, while Version 5.5 of SugarCRM did not. Attempting to upgrade without first upgrading PHP would result in numerous problems at the time of installation and afterwards.

Using the module loader

The module loader is a remarkably innovative feature that enables independent third-party software modules to be developed for the SugarCRM application framework, and then dynamically installed or uninstalled.

The module loader defines a standard packaging for a third-party module—a ZIP file that includes a manifest file. Some of the information that the manifest file contains includes the following:

- **Acceptable_sugar_versions**: The supported version(s) of SugarCRM that must be present to load this module.
- **Acceptable_sugar_flavors**: The supported editions of SugarCRM (Community, Professional, Enterprise). Currently Sugar supports Open Source, Professional, and Enterprise flavors.
- **Name**: The user-readable name for the module. This name will be displayed in the SugarCRM admin interface while loading and installing the module.
- **Description**: The description of the module that is displayed in the Sugar admin interface.

The System Administrator Role

- **Author**: The name of the person or company that authored the module.
- **Published Date**: The date the module was published or last revised.
- **Version**: The version of the module.
- **Type**: The type of package that is contained in the ZIP file.
- **Icon**: The relative path and name of the icon file in the ZIP file that the module loader should use to display in the SugarCRM Admin interface for this module.
- **Copy_files**: An array of file copy instructions that specify the **From & To** source and destination for folders and files. The installation process simply walks through this tree, moving the files as specified. Folders are copied recursively.

To use the module loader, simply select that option from the **Admin** main screen and the following screen will appear:

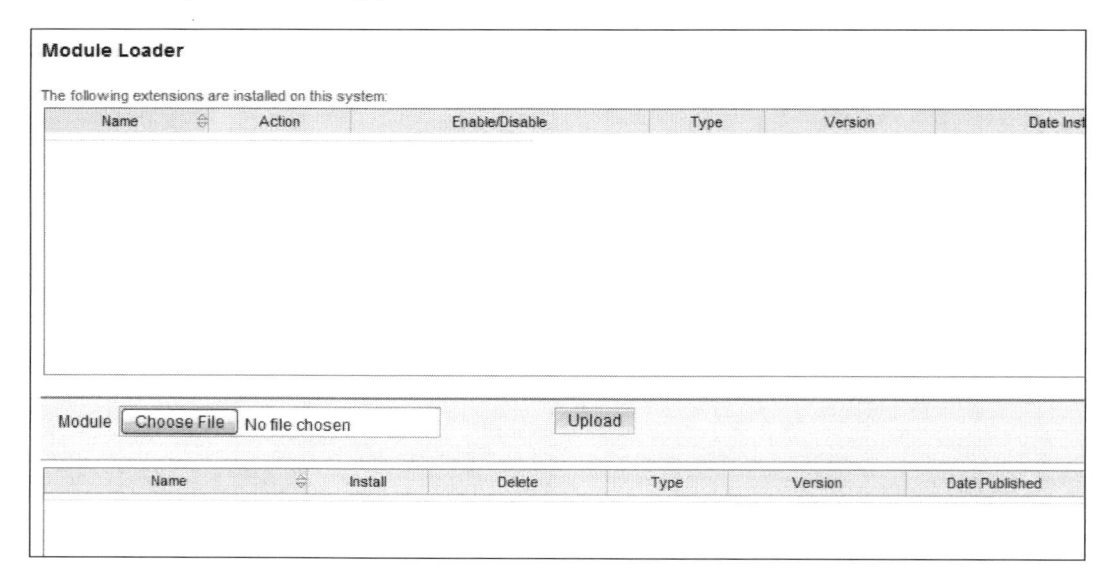

Name	Action	Enable/Disable	Type	Version	Date Inst

Module [Choose File] No file chosen   [Upload]

Name	Install	Delete	Type	Version	Date Published

The module loader screen is split into two panes. The upper half of the screen lists all the modules that are currently installed, while the bottom half lists those that have been uploaded, but not yet installed.

Assuming that you have already downloaded a ZIP file of a module that you wish to install, click on the **Choose File** button to browse for the ZIP file and then click on **Upload**. The module will then be queued for installation.

Once this step is complete, you may then click on **Install** to install the software, or **Delete Package** to remove the queued software. If you choose to install, you will be prompted to agree to a license and then commit the installation. The amount of time required to install a module will vary depending on the module being installed, but a progress bar will keep you abreast of the progress.

To uninstall a module, click on the **Uninstall** button next to its name on the upper half of the screen where the list of installed modules appear. You will then need to confirm your action before the module is actually uninstalled.

E

Customizing SugarCRM

You will undoubtedly have a need to customize your instance of SugarCRM in order to better adapt it to your business needs. As discussed in *Chapter 1* and *2* of this book, customizations generally fall into the following categories:

- **Cosmetics**: Changing color schemes, adding company logo.
- **User interface**: Suppressing certain features from being seen by all or specific users, rearranging screen layouts, adding and deleting fields from screens, changing field names, and editing the set of options presented on drop-down boxes.
- **Major application changes**: Adding entirely new modules to the application, or making major changes to the business logic and functionality of existing modules.
- **Application integration**: Linking the CRM application with other business applications and processes, to more thoroughly automate and integrate your business operations.

This appendix will discuss the techniques for applying such modifications and explore tools such as the following:

- **Studio**: Admin level tool for adding/removing fields, customizing the look and feel of modules, and other capabilities.
- **Module builder**: Admin level tool used to define custom entities within the SugarCRM system.
- **Logic hooks**: Programmatic tool that performs tasks based on user initiated events, such as saving a record.
- **Model-View-Controller (MVC)**: Allows you to extend the system in a variety of different ways and provides very rich and powerful capabilities.

Making changes to SugarCRM modules

Before you begin customizing your system, you should take a moment to identify the necessary changes and plan them accordingly.

For starters, you should methodically go through all the SugarCRM modules that you intend to use or are using, and then examine all the terminology (field labels, tab names, and drop-down values) used within the system by default.

The objective of the exercise is to identify all the areas within the application that require modification to match your organization's lexicon. Along the way you may also identify other types of changes that you would like to apply. For example, you might wish to change the behavior of a default field from a regular text field to a drop-down field. In other cases, you may find a need to add a new field to track additional attributes for a record.

Write down the full set of modifications that you identify and keep good track of them until they have all been addressed. Consult with your peers on the CRM implementation team to make sure everyone agrees on the necessary changes.

Once you have identified the changes that you need to make, you will want to start applying them to your system.

Non-upgrade safe and upgrade safe

Before we further discuss the process of customizing the system, it is important to comprehend a critical point regarding the flexibility and extensibility of SugarCRM.

Being an open source application means that all of the code is accessible and can be adjusted to suit your needs. However, making such changes presents a problem—upgrades to SugarCRM will not honor those modifications and you will need to re-apply them manually every time you need to upgrade the system. These types of modifications are termed as *non-upgrade safe*, and usually involve modifications to files found in the `include`, `cache`, or `modules` folders of your installation (among other folders).

You will find that often times, there are multiple ways of applying a specific modification to SugarCRM. Sometimes the non-upgrade safe approach seems the more appropriate or simpler solution. However, unless you intend to make fundamental changes to the internal workings of SugarCRM, it is unlikely that you actually need to make these types of modifications to obtain your goal. It is generally advised that you steer away from making non-upgrade safe modifications to avoid future problems and hassles.

Appendix E

SugarCRM offers a variety of tools and techniques that allow you to make a wide range of customizations in an *upgrade safe* manner. This latter term refers to the ability to make changes to the system in such a way that future upgrades do not cause harm or create situations where you need to re-apply them.

This section describes the various customization tools that allow you to make upgrade safe customizations. Through their use, you will be to accomplish goals such as adding new fields, change drop-down list values, perform actions based on user initiated events, and so on.

Let us begin by looking at the customization Studio. To access it, you need to go to the **Admin** area of your SugarCRM installation and click on **Studio** in the **Developer Tools** section.

Customization Studio

The customization Studio (shown in the following screenshot) allows you to apply a wide range of customizations. Some of the changes that you can make using this tool include the following:

- Layout modifications
- Label changes
- Adding/removing custom fields

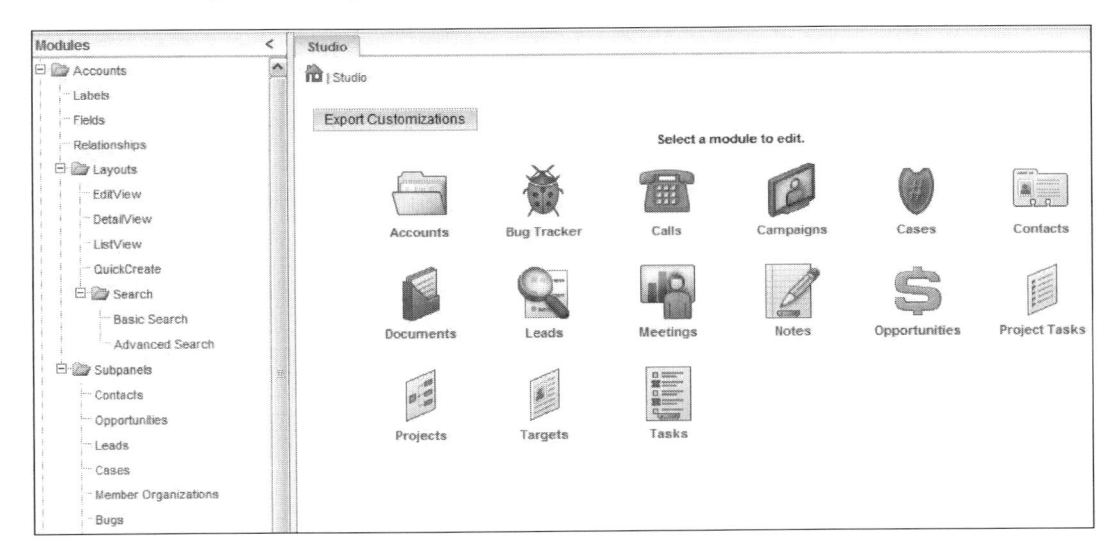

[307]

Customizing SugarCRM

The preceding image demonstrates the customization Studio. Notice the listing of modules on the left-hand side and the additional tools accessible at the bottom of the screen. If you expand one of the folders on the left panel, you will see a variety of additional choices. A description of these choices is as follows:

- **Labels**: Allows you to modify labels within the corresponding module. It can be used to make modifications to the labels for fields and subpanel titles.
- **Fields**: Tool for adding, removing, or modifying custom fields. Label changes are also permitted. Default fields cannot be modified through this tool, beyond field label changes.
- **Relationships**: Describes the established links between the current module and other modules within the system.
- **Layouts:** Modifications to the various views that make up a module can be made by selecting the appropriate view. For example, EditView to modify the edit view screen. You also have the ability to modify the search and quick create screens.
- **Subpanels:** Used to customize the subpanels displayed on the detail view screen of the current module. Notice that the activities and history subpanels are not accessible. This is due to the fact that the mechanics used to generate them are drastically different than those generating the other subpanels.

To use these tools, simply click on them and the Studio screen will be updated to reflect the selected option. For example, let us go through the process of adding a custom field to the Accounts module.

Assuming that you are already in Studio, expand the Accounts folder in the **Modules** section on the left-hand side of the screen. Next, click on **Fields** to view the list of currently defined fields. Had our goal been to modify an existing field, we would simply click on it from the list that is currently displayed. However, our goal is to create a new field, so we must now click on the **Add** button. The following screen should then appear:

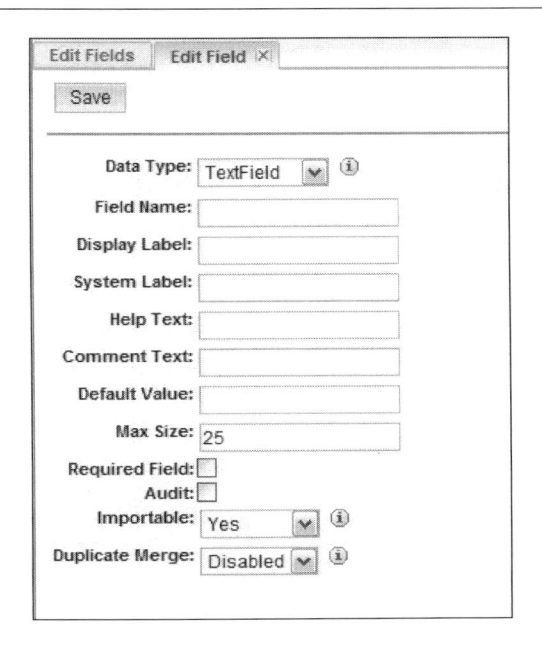

There are a few important items to note about this screen. First, SugarCRM allows you to select from a wide variety of field types, including text, integer, drop-down, checkbox, and so on. For our example, we will choose `TextField`. Fill in the remaining fields with the following parameters:

`Data Type: TextField`

`Field Name: test`

`Display Label: Test`

Click on the **Save** button after entering the aforementioned parameters to commit the field. It is important to understand that although the field is now part of the accounts module (and database structure); you will not be able to see the field within the module until you place it on one of the layouts. Thus the process of adding a field is actually twofold, involving the definition of the field, and secondly, the placing of the field on the necessary layouts to make it available for editing or visible to the user. To complete the process, let us place the field on the EditView layout for the Accounts module.

Begin by expanding the **Layouts** folder below the **Fields** option on the left-hand side of Studio. Click on **EditView** and you should see a screen similar to the following:

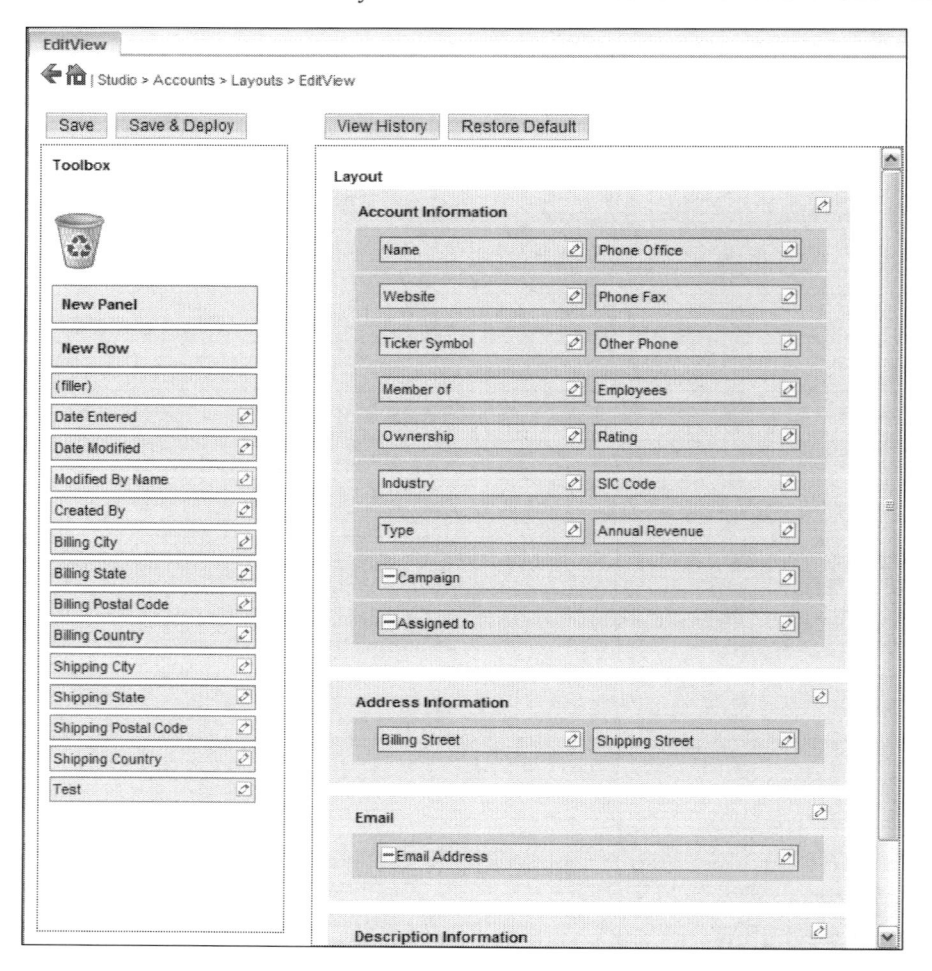

You must first find or create an empty **filler** area on the layout where you can place the field. To create a new **filler** area, you can simply drag the **New Row** component from the toolbox on the left to a desired area on one of the existing panels. The end result should resemble the following (the new row was inserted above the existing **Campaign** field):

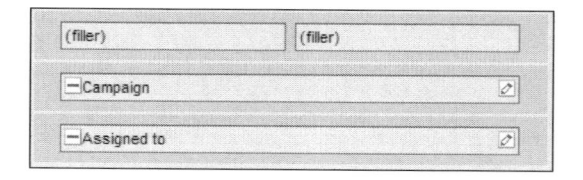

Appendix E

If you prefer to place the field on a new section or panel on the EditView, you will want to first use the **New Panel** component and place it on the EditView layout. Once you have created the new **filler** area, place the field on the view by dragging it from the toolbox and onto one of the empty **filler** areas.

You must now instruct SugarCRM to apply the changes to the system. To do so, click on the **Save & Deploy** button. You can verify that the changes were indeed applied by navigating to the edit view screen of an existing account or by creating a new account. In case you are wondering about the function of the **Save** button, it is used to save your modifications, but does not apply the changes to the system. This option is helpful for customizations that require a long time to complete and should not be deployed until fully completed.

If you take a look at the detail view screen of an account, you will notice that the new custom field is not visible. The reason for this is that you only added the custom field to the EditView layout. This example serves to highlight the point that the layouts work independent of each other. Adding or removing a field from the EditView does not affect the DetailView or the ListView and vice versa. To display the field on the DetailView, you must go back to Studio and modify the DetailView layout for the accounts module accordingly.

Other fields can be added using the same technique and if you would like to do so, you can also rearrange or remove already existing fields from the layout. To remove an item, access the appropriate layout in Studio, then drag the item from its current location over to the trash bin icon in the toolbox.

While working in Studio, you may have noticed a series of buttons at the bottom of the screen. They are used to access the additional customization tools, including **Module Builder** and **Dropdown Editor**. The Module Builder tool will be explored in detail later in this chapter. For now, let us examine the Dropdown Editor.

Dropdown Editor

The Dropdown Editor is a very valuable tool for the Administrator. It permits the values in all of the drop-down boxes in the system to be edited. The options presented to the user may be edited, deleted, rearranged, or new values may be defined. For example, if you enter a new Account record, you will notice there are various options to select from for the Industry field, including Apparel, Banking, Engineering, and a variety of other choices, but these may not be applicable to your business. By using the Dropdown Editor you can manipulate the order in which the values appear, as well as enter new values, or modify and remove existing values.

Customizing SugarCRM

To edit a drop-down list, click on the **Dropdown Editor** button in Studio and select a name of a drop-down list to edit. If you do not know which is the appropriate list that corresponds with the drop-down field you wish to edit, carry out the following steps to identify the drop-down list:

1. Click on the **Studio** button
2. Select the corresponding module containing the drop-down field in question
3. Expand the folder and click on **Fields**
4. Click on the entry corresponding to the field in question
5. Note the value for the **Drop Down List** parameter

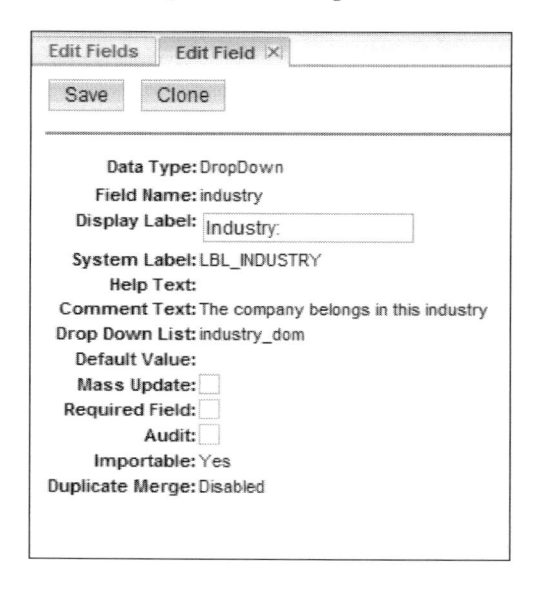

```
Edit Fields   Edit Field X
  Save     Clone

         Data Type: DropDown
        Field Name: industry
       Display Label: Industry:
       System Label: LBL_INDUSTRY
         Help Text:
      Comment Text: The company belongs in this industry
    Drop Down List: industry_dom
       Default Value:
        Mass Update: ☐
       Required Field: ☐
            Audit: ☐
         Importable: Yes
     Duplicate Merge: Disabled
```

Based on the preceding image, illustrating the settings for the industry field from the accounts module, the drop-down list to modify is named **industry_dom**. Thus you will want to click on the **industry_dom** list when you access the Dropdown Editor tool.

Appendix E

Doing so will present the following screen:

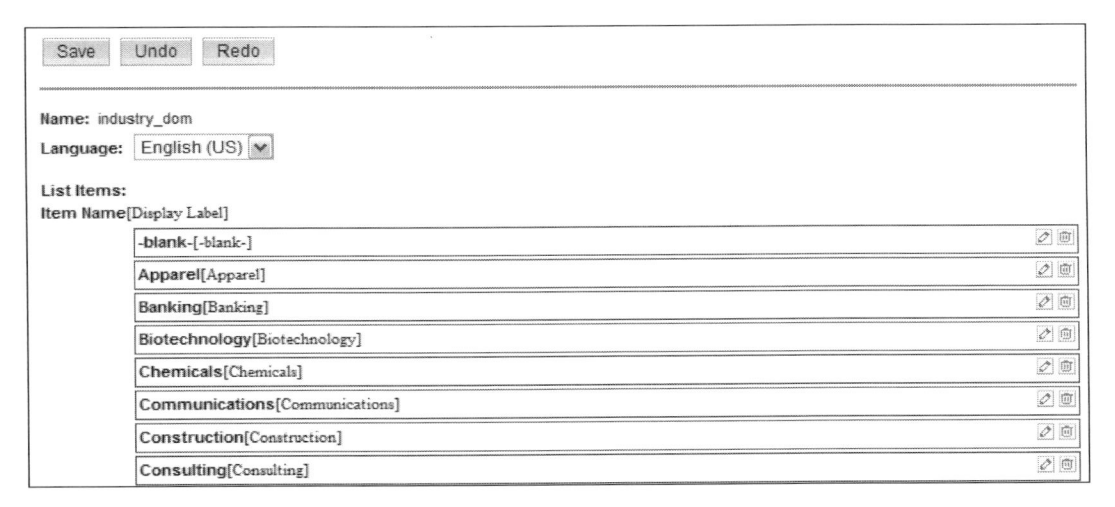

```
[Save] [Undo] [Redo]

Name: industry_dom
Language: English (US)

List Items:
Item Name[Display Label]
    -blank-[-blank-]
    Apparel[Apparel]
    Banking[Banking]
    Biotechnology[Biotechnology]
    Chemicals[Chemicals]
    Communications[Communications]
    Construction[Construction]
    Consulting[Consulting]
```

On the preceding screen, you can add, remove, or modify entries for the selected drop-down list. To add a value, scroll to the bottom of the page and type the value into the **Item Name** and **Display Label** fields, and then click on **Add**. You may be wondering why there are two fields if we are typing the same value into both. The reason for the dual field technique is that it allows you to define the value to store in the database and the value to display on the screen independently. A simple example of such usage would be a scenario where you might only want to store the letter **Y** or **N** in the database, depending on whether a user chooses **Yes** or **No**, instead of storing the entire value. In this example, **Y** would be the **Item Name** and **Yes** would be the **Display Label**. Modifications can be made by clicking on the pencil icon located on the far right of the entry, while clicking on the trash icon would delete the entry.

It is also possible to rearrange the order in which the items are displayed. To rearrange them, you can drag-and-drop them to a desired location or use the **Sort Ascending** or **Sort Descending** buttons at the bottom of the screen.

Once you have finished making your changes, click on the **Save** button at the top. Unlike modifications to the layouts, clicking on the **Save** button here not only preserves your changes, but also applies them to the system.

Logic hooks

All the techniques for customizing SugarCRM that we have examined up to this point have relied upon the use of built-in tools and do not require programming expertise to use them.

Logic hooks will be our first endeavor involving customization capabilities that can only be accomplished with some programming expertise. Access to the server's file system facilitates the process, but is not required.

First and foremost, let us describe a logic hook so that you have a clearer understanding of its capabilities. A logic hook is a bit of a custom PHP code that allows you to extend SugarCRM functionality. The code that makes up a logic hook is invoked upon certain activities occurring within SugarCRM. For example, a user saving a record (existing or new), deleting a record, and other actions. In turn, the custom PHP code that those actions trigger can be programmed to do just about anything that is possible through PHP. Your main limitation would be your PHP skills.

It is important to also understand that logic hooks are designed to interact with the data, not the user and they are intended to be upgrade safe.

To further clarify this latter point, a logic hook can be programmed to perform an action, such as automatically taking a value from a record upon it being saved in SugarCRM and then copying it to a data warehouse on another server. It, however, cannot be used to prompt the user with an on screen alert or pop-up, to notify them of a problem with the copy process, its success, or any other sort of interaction. Again, the logic hook can interact with the data, but not the user.

For our example, we will create a logic hook that ensures uniformity in entering contact names within this SugarCRM system. More specifically, it enforces the fact that whenever a contact is saved, the first and last name values are always saved in proper casing. For example, if a user enters the value JOHN and DOE for the first and last name fields respectively, the values are to be stored as John and Doe upon the data being saved.

To accomplish this goal, we need to create a logic hook that automatically changes the value of the first and last name fields to proper casing. We must first create a logic hook definition file that contains information used by SugarCRM to determine not only the actions that cause the custom code to run, but also the location of the file containing the custom code that is to be run. This is a standard PHP file and can be created using your text editor of choice (Notepad, vi, and so on), but its name must always be `logic_hooks.php`.

Appendix E

The `logic_hooks.php` file for our example will look like the following:

```php
<?php
  $hook_version = 1;
  $hook_array = Array();
  $hook_array['before_save'][] = Array(1, 'NameCasing',
                                 'custom/modules/Contacts/ProperCasing.php',
                                 'PC', 'convertToProper');
?>
```

All of the preceding code is standard, except for the last line. The last line is the most critical, as it tells SugarCRM when to execute the code (before_save), which file contains the relevant code (ProperCasing.php), the name of the class containing the relevant code, and finally, the function within the class that contains the code that should be executed.

If you are wondering about the first two parameters (1 and NameCasing), they are arbitrary values which you are free to define as you see fit. The number is used to order logic hooks, for situations where you have more than one, while the second value is merely a label for the current logic hook.

> Additional logic hooks of the same type are added by simply duplicating this last line, and updating the various parameters that it contains.

Next, we must create the file, namely, `ProperCasing.php` referenced above, which will contain the PHP code that ensures the data is entered in proper case. The file will look as follows:

```php
<?php
  class PC {
    function convertToProper(&$bean, $event, $arguments)
    {
      $bean->first_name = ucwords($bean->first_name);
      $bean->last_name = ucwords($bean->last_name);
    }
  }
?>
```

You will notice that there is actually very little code necessary. The $bean reference is a method for accessing the current record and database connection. This is what allows us to examine the data in any of the fields that make up the current record in the affected module and also permits us to change its value.

Customizing SugarCRM

The final step is to place the files in the proper location so as to instruct SugarCRM to invoke the code when a user is working with the contacts module. To do so, both the `logic_hooks.php` and `ProperCasing.php` files need to be placed in the `custom/modules/Contacts` folder of your installation. If the directory structure does not already exist, manually create it through Windows Explorer, FTP client, and so on. Make sure that the casing and spelling on the module names match with those found in the `sugar install directory/modules/` folder.

Once the files are in the proper folder, give it a try by entering a contact with all lower case values for the first and last name fields. Watch what happens to those two fields after the record is saved.

A number of other customizations can be applied to the system by means of various PHP files. This includes changing the behavior of default and custom fields, modifications to the various screens, and so on. The best part about it is that these changes are also upgrade-safe and the ability to perform these types of changes are central to the architecture of SugarCRM, which we will now examine.

Model-View-Controller (MVC)

SugarCRM's architecture utilizes the MVC design model which in turn makes it a highly customizable application. The goal of this model is to separate the various components of the system into functional areas, including the data (Model), user interface aspects (View), and database operations (Controller). It was first introduced in the 5.0 release of SugarCRM and has made the system significantly more customizable.

Some of the potential changes you could make include the following:

- Custom list, detail, and edit screens with special behaviors
- Addition or removal of buttons on the various views
- Creation of dependent drop-downs
- Insertion of custom JavaScript
- Suppression of specific subpanels
- Conditional styling of data

The possibilities are virtually endless and are only limited by your imagination and programming capabilities. Let us take a look at a couple of quick examples so you can get a taste of the ease and power of this architecture.

In our first example, we will change the default behavior of the name field within the cases module from text to drop-down. This will allow us to limit the values that are assigned to the field to only those defined within a list. This is a technique that helps enforce uniformity and improves metrics.

Note that creating a drop-down field requires the specification of a drop-down list containing the values from which a user can choose. We will assume that the drop-down list to be used for this exercise is one named `cases_names` which was previously created using the Dropdown Editor tool.

To modify the default behavior of the name field and convert it to a drop-down, create a PHP file with the following contents:

```php
<?php
    $dictionary['Case']['fields']['name']['type']='enum';
    $dictionary['Case']['fields']['name']['options']='cases_names';
?>
```

Save the file and name it `vardefs.ext.php`. Notice that the file is quite small, but rather powerful. The first line overrides the default type defined for the name field and changes it to enum, which is the value that SugarCRM uses for drop-down fields. The second line specifies the name of the drop-down list that the field should use. As mentioned earlier, the drop-down list containing the values we want to use is named cases_names.

Next, you will need to place the file in the directory named `sugar install directory/custom/Extension/modules/Cases/Ext/Vardefs`. Proceed to create the directory structure manually if it does not already exist, making sure to match the casing as illustrated earlier.

Lastly, the changes need to be applied to the SugarCRM system. This is accomplished by using the **Repair** option within the admin control panel. Login to SugarCRM as an admin level user, and then select **Admin | Repair | Quick Rebuild & Repair | Repair** to apply the modifications. *If you do not perform this step, your modifications will not appear*!

Once the repair process finishes, check your cases module and it should now reflect the name field as a drop-down field.

Let us extend this example a bit further and assume that we also want to highlight the **Assigned To** field by coloring its text in red when the detail view of a case is accessed. Doing so would help guide the user's eye to a critical piece of information and can be used for any other field you deem equally important.

The simplest way to accomplish this goal is to copy the default DetailView definition file (`detailviewdefs.php`), stored in `sugar install directory/modules/Cases/metadata` to `sugar install directory/custom/modules/Cases/metadata`. Again, if the directory structure does not already exist, create it manually.

Edit `detailviewdefs.php` using a text editor of your choice and locate the following:

```
array (
  array('name' => 'case_number', 'label' => 'LBL_CASE_NUMBER'),
  'assigned_user_name',
),
```

The preceding section corresponds with the definition of the display row containing the Assigned To value. To modify it so it displays this value in red, change the preceding code to reflect the following:

```
array('name' => 'case_number', 'label' => 'LBL_CASE_NUMBER'),
array('name' => 'assigned_user_name', 'customCode' => '
<span style="color: red">{$fields.assigned_user_name.value}</span>'),
```

The customCode section is the key to accomplishing our goal. This technique allows you to inject custom HTML/JavaScript/CSS into SugarCRM's default view configuration. Note that although we are specifically working with the DetailView, similar techniques can be used for the other views as well.

To finish the example and apply your change, make sure to once again use the **Repair** option within the **Admin** control panel.

Clearly, many things are possible by leveraging the MVC model, too many to cover within this book. Fortunately, the SugarCRM Wiki and Developer Blog contain more detailed information on this topic (as well as additional examples). You can access them at the following locations:

- `http://www.sugarcrm.com/wiki/index.php?title=Model-View-Controller_(MVC)`
- `http://developer.sugarcrm.com`

Module Builder

You may find that upon reviewing the SugarCRM system, it may not contain a module that is well-suited to store information that is critical to your business operations. For example, RayDoc may want to store information pertaining to the materials used for various jobs and link them to the corresponding customer entry. This would allow anyone at RayDoc to see a list of the materials used to execute a particular job.

Appendix E

By default, SugarCRM does not contain a natural location to store such information, but the Module Builder allows you to create a custom module to address such needs.

Using the Module Builder allows you to not only create and modify custom modules, but also allows you to link the data they contain to existing modules, or to establish relationships between them. They are especially helpful for tracking information where a *one-to-many* relationship exists between an existing module and the intended custom module.

The Module Builder can be accessed by opening Studio and then clicking on the **Studio Builder** button. If you choose to create a new module, you will notice that SugarCRM provides some templates that help cut down on the amount of work required to create it.

Custom modules can be used to track just about any type of data that your company needs. Some of those possibilities include the following:

- Products
- Membership information
- Personal details, such as hobbies

A great overview of the Module Builder's capabilities is available at the following URL:

`http://www.sugarcrm.com/crm/node/10024/task%3Dshow51modulebuilder/tmpl%3Dgw`

Integration using SOAP and REST API

SugarCRM includes a SOAP based API that allows you or others with programming expertise to programmatically interact with the data in SugarCRM.

This is helpful for integrating the system with other applications that are already in use at your company. For example, you can use it to exchange data with your accounting system, to integrate SugarCRM with your website, and to do numerous other things. You can use the API to add, modify, delete, or read data from SugarCRM.

With the release of SugarCRM Version 5.5, additional enhancements were introduced into the API that allowed it to support **Representational State Transfer (REST)** and custom methods.

Detailed information and examples are available at the following SugarCRM developer website:

`http://developer.sugarcrm.com`

F

A Word About SugarCRM 6.0

You may have noticed that although this book focuses on newer releases of SugarCRM, much of the content revolves around the 5.x iterations of the product. This is partly due to the fact that this project was initiated prior to SugarCRM 6.0 entering its testing phase, and thus, it was not accessible. It has since completed its release cycle and is worth briefly discussing.

What does SugarCRM 6.0 include?

The vast majority of the development work that went into the 6.0 release revolved around providing a new user interface, as illustrated in the following screenshot:

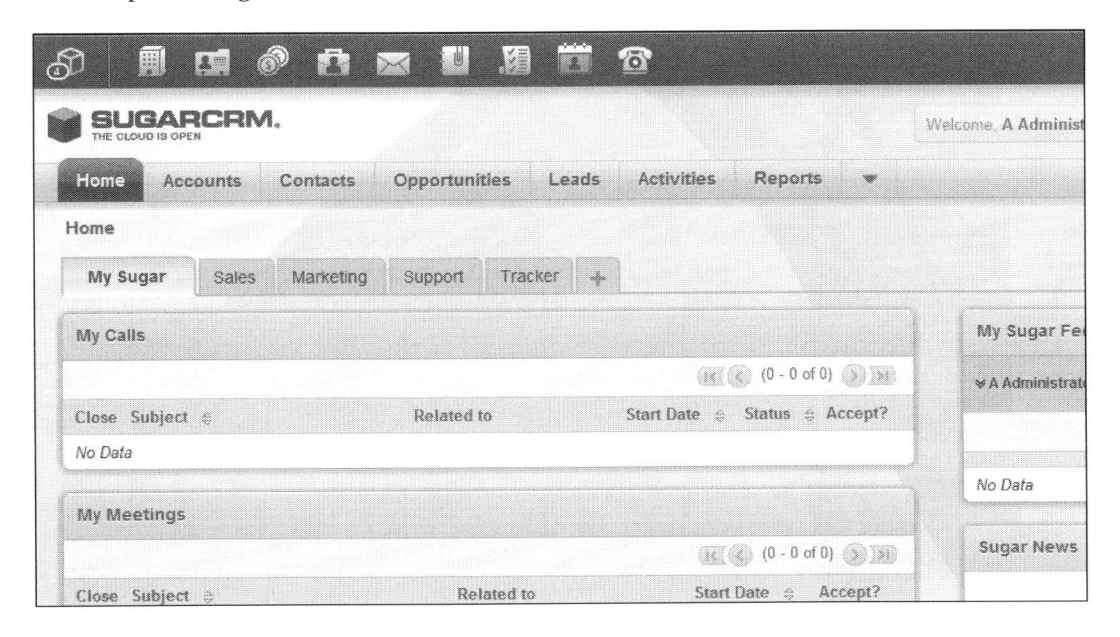

Vastly different from prior releases, the new interface greatly simplifies navigation and gives the system a slick new look.

In addition to the cosmetic changes, the **Studio** tool has been enhanced to allow for the customization of pop-up views used within the application when searching for related records.

Performance enhancements have also been incorporated into this release, along with the customary bug fixes that most other vendors tend to also include with new releases.

The most obvious change, of course, is the new interface. However, the new interface is a feature exclusive to Professional and Enterprise Edition users.

Community Edition users will notice some minor enhancements to the interface—mostly within the list, detail, and edit views. However, enhancements equivalent to the new interface of the Professional and Enterprise Editions should not be expected.

Should I use SugarCRM 6.0?

Normally, I would urge you to wait two to three months after release before upgrading any production systems or installing the new release of any software. It is a helpful, general rule of thumb that allows time for common issues and solutions to come to light through the experiences of the community at large and without the pain of hindering your production system. By the time this book goes to print, SugarCRM 6.0 will have been available for a few weeks and should be considered safe for use in production.

That, however, does not mean there are not any issues to consider.

The new user interface—exclusive to Professional and Enterprise Edition users, leverages a themes framework first introduced into SugarCRM upon the release of Version 5.5. Themes, as discussed in *Chapter 4* of this book, allow you to manipulate the look and feel of SugarCRM in a number of ways, including color scheme and placement of menu options.

Many SugarCRM users find this capability quite helpful. This is because it allows them to select a manner of working with SugarCRM that is more in line with their general preferences for an interface or for that matter, color selections that help users with visual impairments interact more easily with the system.

Appendix F

SugarCRM 6.0, however, only includes a limited number of themes when compared to prior versions. Community Edition in particular only includes a single theme. In addition, custom themes that were not developed using the 5.5 themes framework will not function upon upgrading, regardless of which edition of SugarCRM you are using.

The earlier discussion highlights important issues that should be considered before upgrading or installing Version 6.0.

In short, the major advantage of Version 6.0 is the new interface, but it is a feature that is exclusive to Professional and Enterprise Edition users. Furthermore, older themes are not compatible with Version 6.0 (regardless of edition), and will not be accessible after an upgrade. New users are unlikely to be impacted, unless, of course, the classic theme is not to their liking.

Index

A

acceptance testing 201
Access Control model, requisites 49
account-centric system 44
accounts, business activities
  about 33
  importing 270-274
ACT! 13
activity management, business activities 40, 41
agile programming 184
Amazon EC2
  URL 64
Amazon Elastic Compute Cloud. *See* Amazon EC2
analytics, business activities 43, 44
AND connector 148
Apache web server
  installing 250, 251
  SugarCRM, installing 249
  URL 249
Apatar
  about 190
  URL 281
Apple Safari support, SugarCRM 82
application changes, CRM customization 52
application integration 305
application server 71
asymmetric internet connections 78
average transaction value, requisites 46

B

B2B 33
B2B business model, requisites 44, 45
B2C 33
B2C business model, requisites 44
back-office applications 166
backup 74
bandwidth capacity, server requisites 76, 77
BETA 236, 247
BETWEEN operator 148
Bug Tracker module 212
Business-to-Business. *See* B2B
Business-to-Consumer. *See* B2C
business activities, CRM
  about 31, 32
  accounts 33
  activity management 40, 41
  analytics 43, 44
  contacts 33
  document management 43
  e-mail management 41
  employee directory 42
  interface consolidation 42, 43
  knowledge management 40
  leads 129
  marketing automation 41, 42
  reporting 43, 44
  sales force automation 36
  tracking leads 33-35
  tracking sales pipeline 37, 39
  tracking service cases 39
Business Intelligence (BI) software 37
business models, specific requisites 44
browser support, SugarCRM
  about 82
  Apple Safari 82
  Firefox 82
  Microsoft Internet Explorer 82

C

calendaring system, SugarCRM
  about 109
  calendar tab 110
  graphical calendar, accessing 110
  working 111-113
call
  scheduling 117, 118
calls activities, SugarCRM 114
campaign metrics 139
Cascading Style Sheets. *See* **CSS**
case management, business activities 39
Cases module 212
case study
  introduction 25
  requisites analysis 56-59
CentOS
  about 68, 226
  installing 228-232
  selecting, factors 227
  URL 227
CentOS, installing 228-232
CentOS Linux installation
  firewall settings, configuring 232, 233
  PHP extensions, installing 234
  PHP settings, verifying 234
Central Processing Unit (CPU), server hardware 70
chown -R apache.apache command 238
Client Access Licenses (CAL) 67
cloud computing
  about 64
  benefits 64
clustering 67
collocation model, CRM deployment 61-63
com_sugarbugs component
  about 214
  configuring 215
  installing 215
com_sugarcases component
  about 214
  configuring 215
  installing 215
Comma Separated Values. *See* **CSV files**
Community Edition (CE), SugarCRM versions 21
configuration management 144
contact-centric systems 45
contacts 130
contacts, business activities
  about 33
  exporting, from contact manager 280
  importing 270, 275
Content Management System (CMS) 212
contracts module
  about 143, 164
  capabilities 164
cookies support, SugarCRM 82
cosmetic changes, CRM customization 51, 305
Create from vCard shortcut, SugarCRM 124, 125
CRM
  about 12
  business activities 31, 32
  business benefits 17, 18
  capabilities 32
  data hub 54
  deployment models 61-64
  deployment options 20
  development partner, selecting 186-188
  features 14, 15
  history 19
  implementing 180-182
  issues, listing 31
  requirement analysis 30
CRM customization 15, 16
CRM implementation
  about 180
  factors 180
  groups, affected 180-182
  objectives 182
  pitfalls 183, 184
  planning 181, 182
  project goals, setting 186
  project goals, specifying 186
  system development 188
  team management, techniques 185
  team participation 184, 185
CRM solutions, smaller business
  Microsoft CRM 20
  NetSuite 19
  Salesforce.com 19

SalesLogix 20
CRM system
 data import 189
 defining 196
 enhancements 202
 feedback 202
 pilot testing 190
CRM technology
 about 12
 business benefits 12
CRM training
 goals 190
 prerequisites 195
 sessions 191-195
 slides 196-200
cron utility 295
Crystal Reports 142
CSS 51
CSV files
 about 122, 130, 269
 formatting, limitations 271
currencies
 defining 289
customer-centric business management 53
Customer Relationship Management system. *See* **CRM**
Customforce tool 16
custom index
 creating 277
customization, CRM
 drawbacks 55
customization, SugarCRM
 about 51, 52, 305
 non-upgrade safe 306
 upgrade safe 307
customization Studio 307-311

D

dashboard 37, 103
data backup strategy 74, 298
database
 resetting 127, 128
database server 71
data hub, CRM 54
data import 189
Decision Support software 37

Delete button, SugarCRM 123
deployment, CRM 61-64
deployment options, CRM
 about 20
 Hosted Application Pack 20
 On-Demand model 20
 On-Premise option 20
 Server Appliance option 20
detail views screen
 about 88, 89
 controls 91
development toolkit module
 about 142, 163
 benefits 163
 URL 163
df -h command 299
digital dashboard 37
distros 67
Doc Newhart 24
document management, business activities 43
drilldown 109
Dropdown Editor tool 311-313

E

e-mail activities, SugarCRM 114
e-mail management
 about 118, 119
 e-mail templates 120
e-mail management, business activities 41
e-mail marketing campaign
 about 129
 executing 134, 135
 targets, adding 136, 137
e-mail template
 about 120
 creating 134, 135
EDGE 47
edit view screen 92-94
EIS 37
employee directory, business activities 42
Enhanced Data rates for GSM Evolution (EDGE) 47
Enhanced search functionality
 about 141, 147
 AND connector 148

BETWEEN operator 148
EQUALS operator 148
IN operator 148
LIKE operator 148
OR connector 148
RLIKE operator 148
enhanced studio module
  about 142, 163
  benefits 163
  URL 163
Enter Business Card shortcut, SugarCRM 123, 124
Enterprise Edition (ENT), SugarCRM versions 21
Enterprise Linux Server 67
Enterprise Resource Planning (ERP) 166
EQUALS operator 148
Error Correction Codes (ECC) memory, server hardware 69
Executive Information Systems (EIS) 37
Export link, SugarCRM 122

F

features, CRM 14, 15
Fedora Core 68
fields 308
Firefox support, SugarCRM 82
firewall, security measures 75
forecasting module
  about 143, 170
  example 171, 172
form factor, server hardware 70
front office applications 166

G

general maintenance, SugarCRM
  about 296
  data backups 298
  storage availability, checking 299, 300
  system backups 297, 298
  updates, checking 297
Google connectors
  about 142, 149
  benefits 149
  configuring 149, 150

graphical chart
  Opportunities by lead source by outcome chart 106
  Pipeline by sales stage chart 105
  The all opportunities by lead source chart 108
  The outcome by month chart 107
GrinMark Microsoft Office Add-in
  about 151
  mail merge, performing 157, 158
  URL 151
Groupware 17

H

hard disk speed, server hardware 70
hard disk technology, server hardware 70
hardware, server requisites 68
Help icon, SugarCRM 122
Hosted Application Pack 20
hostname command 239, 256
HTML 51
Hyper Text Markup Language. *See* HTML

I

ifconfig command 239
inbound traffic, server bandwidth 77
information
  exporting 279
IN operator 148
installation, Apache web server 250, 251
installation, CentOS 228-232
installation, Joomla! 213
installation, MySQL 254, 255
installation, PHP 251-253
installation, SugarCRM Community Edition
  about 236, 256
  confirmation screen 244, 262
  database configuration screen 242, 260
  database type 242, 260
  license check screen 258
  license screen 240
  locale settings screen 243
  local settings screen 262
  login screen 246, 265

options 241, 259
registration screen 245, 264
site configuration screen 243, 261
system check screen 240, 258
welcome screen 240, 258
integration, CRM customization 52
interface consolidation, business activities 42, 43
international offices, requisites 49-51
Internet Information Services (IIS)
about 73
SugarCRM, installing 266, 267
ipconfig command 256
iReport 162
ISAPI Module 266

J

JasperReports 162
Javascript support, SugarCRM 82
Jitterbit
about 190
URL 281
Joomla!
about 212
installing 213
new Joomla! user, creating 218
SugarCRM cases, adding to 216, 217
SugarCRM portal, installing for 214
URL 213
Joomla!, components
com_sugarbugs 214
com_sugarcases 214
Joomla! user
creating 218

K

KINAMU Outlook Connector 151
knowledge management, business activities 40

L

labels 308
LAMP 72
LAMP stack
about 72

Apache web server 72
Linux operating system 72
MySQL database server 72
PHP server side scripting language 72
LAN interface, server hardware 70
Last viewed, SugarCRM 84
layouts 308
lead capture tool
about 206
web lead capture form, setting up 206-211
leads, business activities
about 33-35, 96-101, 129
importing 276
leads, capturing
about 206
lead capture tool, used 206
Leads module 206
LIKE operator 148
Linux
SugarCRM, installing 225
Linux-Apache-MySQL-PHP. *See* **LAMP**
list views screen 88, 89
location, requisites
about 46
multiple regional offices 47
outbound sales persons 47, 48
logic hooks 305, 314, 315

M

Main screen body, SugarCRM 85
manifest file, contents
Acceptable_sugar_flavors 301
Acceptable_sugar_versions 301
Author 302
Copy_files 302
Description 301
Name 301
Published Date 302
Type 302
Version 302
marketing automation, business activities 41, 42
marketing campaigns
about 128
creating 130-132
target 129-133

mass emailing queue 137, 138
match key 276
Maximizer 13
meeting
  scheduling 117, 118
memory size, server hardware 70
memory type, server hardware 70
Microsoft CRM
  about 20
  URL 20
Microsoft Internet Explorer support, SugarCRM 82
Microsoft office integration 142, 157
Microsoft Outlook 13
Microsoft outlook connector
  about 142, 151
  GrinMark Microsoft Office Add-in 151
Microsoft SQL Server (MS-SQL)
  SugarCRM, installing 265, 266
Microsoft Word 157
mixed mode authentication 265
Model-View-Controller (MVC) 305, 316-318
module builder 305, 318
module loader
  about 145, 301
  using 145, 146, 301-303
module loader tool
  about 146
  using 141
modules, SugarCRM
  about 87, 88
  modifying 306
MS-SQL Reporting Services 142
MSI installer package 249
MySQL
  about 72
  installing 254, 255
  SugarCRM, installing 249

N

navigation, SugarCRM
  about 87
  data relationships 94, 95
  detail view screen 88, 89
  edit view screens 92-94
  list views screen 88, 89
  main panel 90, 91
  searching 94, 95
  subpanel 90, 91
navigation shortcuts box, SugarCRM 85
navigation tabs, SugarCRM 84
NetSuite
  about 19
  URL 19
note
  creating 116

O

on-Demand model 20
on-Premise option 20
on demand model, CRM deployment 61-66, 227
on premise model, CRM deployment
  about 61, 63
  server issues 66
open quotes module
  about 143, 164
  capabilities 164
  URL 164
opportunities, business activities
  about 33-35, 96, 100-103
  importing 276
OR connector 148
outbound traffic, server bandwidth 77

P

Parallel Advanced Technology Attachment. *See* PATA disk drives
password management 292
passwords
  resetting 296
PATA disk drives, server hardware 69
permissions 267
Permissions Management Infrastructure (PMI), requisites 49
PHP
  configuring 235
  installing 251-253
PHP, configuring
  steps 235, 236
php-imap 235

php-mbstring 235
php -v command 234
phpMyAdmin
  URL 298
pilot testing
  about 190, 201
  example 190
Pipeline by sales stage chart 105
Portal Active checkbox 218
power supply, server hardware 70
pre-import analysis 271, 272
Print icon, SugarCRM 121
product based business model, requisites 45, 46
products catalog module
  about 143, 167
  functions 167
products module 143, 167, 168
Professional Edition (PRO), SugarCRM versions 21

Q

Quick New Item box, SugarCRM 85, 125
quotes module
  about 143, 168
  quote, creating 169
  quote list view screen 169

R

RayDoc
  about 26
  future 26
RayDoc Carpets, Doors, and Windows case study 25
RayDoc CRM requisites, case study 56-59
RC1 236, 247
RC2 236, 247
records
  updating 276, 278
recurring business model, requisites 46
Red Hat 67
Red Hat Enterprise Linux 226
redundancy, internet connections 78
Redundant Array of Inexpensive Disks (RAID), server hardware 69

relationships 308
reliability, server requisites 76, 77
reporting, business activities 43, 44
reporting module
  about 143, 172
  custom report, creating 173, 174
Representational State Transfer (REST) 319
requirement analysis 30
requisites, business models
  about 44
  average transaction value 46
  B2B 44, 45
  B2C 44, 45
  location 46
  products 45, 46
  recurring business model 46
  sales cycle 46
  services 45, 46
REST API
  SugarCRM, integrating 319
RLIKE operator 148
role management 175

S

sales activities, SugarCRM
  about 113
  call, scheduling 117, 118
  e-mail management 118, 119
  meeting, scheduling 117, 118
  note, creating 116
  task, creating 116, 117
sales cycle, requisites 46
Salesforce.com
  about 19
  URL 19
sales force automation, business activities 36
sales force automation, features 36
SalesLogix
  about 20
  URL 20
sales pipeline tracking, business activities 37, 39
sales teams module 143, 175
SATA disk drives, server hardware 69

screen layout, SugarCRM
  last viewed 84
  main screen body 85
  navigation shortcuts box 85
  navigation tabs 84
  quick new item box 85
  search box 84
  system links 84
Search box, SugarCRM 84
security 95
security, deployment server 75
security roles
  defining 289, 290
security suite
  about 143, 165
  URL 165
self-service portal
  about 211
  benefits 211
  capabilities 212
  configuring 212
  using 212, 219, 220, 222
Serial Advanced Technology Attachment.
  See **SATA disk drives**
Server Appliance option 20
server considerations, SugarCRM 74
server hardware, selecting
  hardware 68
Server Operating System
  about 64
  selecting 66-68
server requisites, SugarCRM
  about 65, 71
  backups 74
  bandwidth capacity 76, 77
  hardware 68
  security 75
  web-based application platforms 72
server security 75
service contract management, business activities 39
services based business model, requisites 45, 46
sessions, CRM training
  general user training 193, 194
  management training 191
  management training completion 192

product exposure 191
training completion 194, 195
shared server model, CRM deployment 61, 63
SierraCRM's Process Manager 211
Simple Object Access Protocol. *See* **SOAP**
size, requisites 48, 49
slides, CRM training
  accounts 197
  activities 198
  advanced interface features 199
  calendaring system 198
  contacts 197
  CRM, functional areas 196
  CRM implementations, goals 196
  CRM system, defining 196
  customer service management 200
  document management 200
  e-mail settings 198
  external sites 199
  home tab 198
  marketing campaign 199
  navigation 197
  opportunities 198
  project management 200
  remote access techniques 200
  RSS news feeds 199
  sales pipeline 198
  screen layout 197
  self service portal 201
  SugarCRM, defining 197
  system access 197
small and medium-size businesses
  Gartner Group, example 8
  requisites 10, 11
  small-to-medium size product/services based businesses 9
  small office/home office businesses 8
  small services based businesses 9
small or medium-size business. *See* **SMB**
SMB
  about 7
  administration 7
  CRM tools, using 7
  Information Technology group 7
  sales department 7
  senior management 7

[332]

SnapLogic
  about 190
  URL 281
SOAP API
  about 206
  SugarCRM, integrating 319
software bug tracking, business activities 39
speed, server requisites 77
stack installers 237, 247
Studio tool
  about 305, 322
  using 293
subpanels 308
SugarCRM
  about 11, 21, 38, 41
  benefits 22, 23
  calendaring system 109, 110
  calls activities 114
  Community Edition 144
  customization 23
  customizing 305
  database, resetting 127
  deployment options 23
  e-mail activities 114
  e-mail campaigns, using 294
  exporting capabilities 269, 270
  extensibility 23
  features 11, 13, 22, 23
  forums 176
  general maintenance 296
  hierarchy 86, 87
  importing capabilities 269, 270
  information, exporting 279
  installing, Apache used 249
  installing, MySQL used 249
  installing, on Internet Information Services (IIS) 266, 267
  installing, on Linux 225
  installing, with Microsoft SQL Server (MS-SQL) 265, 266
  integrating, REST API used 319
  integrating, SOAP API used 319
  internationalization 24
  leads, capturing 206-211
  marketing campaigns 128
  modules 87, 88
  modules, modifying 306
  online community 176
  open standards 22, 23
  partner directory, URL 187
  permissions 267
  RayDoc Carpets, Doors, and Windows case study 25
  relationship, among data entities 86
  sales activities 113-115
  screen layout 84, 85
  security 95
  server requisites 65, 71
  SugarCRM Professional/Enterprise Edition 165
  system administrator 283
  tasks activities 114
  template processing 158, 159
  themes 85
  URL 225
  versions 21
SugarCRM, accessing
  admin area, using 83
  browser support 82
  cookies support 82
  Javascript support 82
SugarCRM 6.0
  about 321
  advantages 323
  contents 321, 322
  using, conditions 322, 323
SugarCRM Community Edition
  about 144
  contracts module 143, 164
  development toolkit module 142, 163
  Enhanced Search functionality 141, 147
  enhanced studio module 142, 163
  Google connectors 142, 149
  installing 236-258
  Microsoft office integration 142, 157
  Microsoft outlook connector 142, 151
  module loader 145, 146
  open quotes module 143, 164
  security suite 143, 165
  SugarExchange 144
  SugarForge 144
  ZuckerReports 142, 159

SugarCRM developer
    URL 319
SugarCRM portal
    portal user, defining 214
SugarCRM Professional/Enterprise Edition
    about 165
    forecasting module 143, 170
    product catalog module 143, 167
    products module 143, 167, 168
    quotes module 143, 168
    reporting module 143, 172-174
    role management 175
    sales teams module 143, 175
SugarExchange
    about 141, 144
    URL 212
    versus SugarForge 145
SugarForge
    about 141, 144
    versus SugarExchange 145
Sun VirtualBox 232
support contracts, business activities 39
symmetric internet connections 78
system administrator
    about 283
    ad hoc duties 284
    installation duties 284
    selecting 285
system administrator, ad hoc duties
    general maintenance 296
    module loader, using 301-303
    password, resetting 296
    Upgrade Wizard, using 300, 301
    user management 296
system administrator, installation duties
    about 284
    currencies, defining 289
    password management 292
    security roles, defining 289, 290
    Studio, using 293
    system e-mail, defining 294, 295
    system settings, configuring 287
    system tabs, configuring 291
    system users, adding 291, 292
    tab groups, configuring 291
system backups 297, 298

system e-mail
    settings, enabling 294, 295
system links, SugarCRM 84
system settings
    configuring 287
system settings, configuring
    advanced settings section 287
    logger settings section 287
    mail merge feature, enabling 287
    proxy connection, enabling 287
    SkypeOut feature 287
    user interface section 287
system tabs
    configuring 291
system users
    adding 291, 292

T

tab groups
    configuring 291
Tab Separated Values files. *See* TSV files
Talend Open Studio
    about 190
    URL 281
targets, e-mail marketing campaign
    adding 136, 137
targets, marketing campaign 129-133
task
    creating 116, 117
tasks activities, SugarCRM 114
Team 96
team participation, CRM implementation 184, 185
telnet tool 138
The all opportunities by lead source chart 108
themes 85
The outcome by month chart 107
three-box configuration 69
Tracker URL 133
tracking leads, business activities 33-35
tracking sales pipeline, business activities 37, 39
TSV files 130

U

Ubuntu 68
undo last import option 275
Uninterruptible Power Supply. *See* **UPS**
Update button, SugarCRM 123
Upgrade Wizard
 using 300, 301
UPS, security measures 75
user-interface features, SugarCRM
 business card, inputting 123, 124
 contact, creating from vCard file 124, 125
 context-sensitive help 122
 information, exporting 122
 information, printing 121
 quick new item box 125
 records, deleting 123
 records, updating 123
user interface changes, CRM customization 51
user management 296
users, server hardware 70

V

vCard file
 contact, creating from 124, 125
VCR controls 91

versions, SugarCRM
 Community Edition (CE) 21
 Enterprise Edition (ENT) 21
 Professional Edition (PRO) 21
video, server hardware 70
VirtualBox 232
virtual machine 232
Virtual Private Network. *See* **VPN**
VPN, security measures 75

W

WAMP stack 73
web based application platforms, server requisites 72
WIMP stack 73
Windows
 version, selecting 248

Z

ZuckerReports
 about 142, 159
 capabilities 160
 report, creating 160, 161

[PACKT] open source*
PUBLISHING   community experience distilled

Thank you for buying
Implementing SugarCRM 5.x

About Packt Publishing

Packt, pronounced 'packed', published its first book "*Mastering phpMyAdmin for Effective MySQL Management*" in April 2004 and subsequently continued to specialize in publishing highly focused books on specific technologies and solutions.

Our books and publications share the experiences of your fellow IT professionals in adapting and customizing today's systems, applications, and frameworks. Our solution based books give you the knowledge and power to customize the software and technologies you're using to get the job done. Packt books are more specific and less general than the IT books you have seen in the past. Our unique business model allows us to bring you more focused information, giving you more of what you need to know, and less of what you don't.

Packt is a modern, yet unique publishing company, which focuses on producing quality, cutting-edge books for communities of developers, administrators, and newbies alike. For more information, please visit our website: www.packtpub.com.

About Packt Open Source

In 2010, Packt launched two new brands, Packt Open Source and Packt Enterprise, in order to continue its focus on specialization. This book is part of the Packt Open Source brand, home to books published on software built around Open Source licences, and offering information to anybody from advanced developers to budding web designers. The Open Source brand also runs Packt's Open Source Royalty Scheme, by which Packt gives a royalty to each Open Source project about whose software a book is sold.

Writing for Packt

We welcome all inquiries from people who are interested in authoring. Book proposals should be sent to author@packtpub.com. If your book idea is still at an early stage and you would like to discuss it first before writing a formal book proposal, contact us; one of our commissioning editors will get in touch with you.

We're not just looking for published authors; if you have strong technical skills but no writing experience, our experienced editors can help you develop a writing career, or simply get some additional reward for your expertise.

[PACKT] open source
community experience distilled

Liferay Portal 5.2 Systems Development

ISBN: 978-1-847194-70-1   Paperback: 552 pages

Liferay Portal 5.2 Systems Development

1. Learn to use Liferay tools to create your own applications as a Java developer, with hands-on examples
2. Customize Liferay portal using the JSR-286 portlet, extension environment, and Struts framework
3. Build your own Social Office with portlets, hooks, and themes and manage your own community
4. The only Liferay book aimed at Java developers

TrixBox Made Easy

ISBN: 978-1-904811-93-0   Paperback: 168 pages

A step-by-step guide to installing and running your home and office VoIP system

1. Plan and configure your own VoIP and telephony systems
2. Setup voicemail, conferencing, and call recording
3. Clear and practical tutorial with case study format

Please check www.PacktPub.com for information on our titles